Dr EMMA COWNIE gained her Ph.D. from the University of Wales at Cardiff; she currently holds a research fellowship at King's College, London.

ROYAL HISTORICAL SOCIETY

STUDIES IN HISTORY

New Series

RELIGIOUS PATRONAGE IN ANGLO-NORMAN ENGLAND 1066–1135

RELIGIOUS PATRONAGE
IN ANGLO-NORMAN ENGLAND
1066–1135

Emma Cownie

THE ROYAL HISTORICAL SOCIETY
THE BOYDELL PRESS

First published 1998

A Royal Historical Society publication
Published by The Boydell Press
an imprint of Boydell & Brewer Ltd
PO Box 9, Woodbridge, Suffolk IP12 3DF, UK
and of Boydell & Brewer Inc.
PO Box 41026, Rochester, NY 14604–4126, USA

ISBN 0 86193 232 3

ISSN 0269-2244

A catalogue record for this book is available
from the British Library

Library of Congress Cataloging-in-Publication Data
Cownie, Emma, 1967–
    Religious patronage in Anglo-Norman England, 1066–1135 / Emma
Cownie.
        p.   cm. – (Royal Historical Society studies in history. New
series, 0269-2244)
    Based on the author's doctoral thesis.
    Includes bibliographical references (p.   ) and index.
    ISBN 0–86193–232–3 (alk. paper)
    1. Monasticism and religious orders – England – History – Middle
Ages, 600–1500.   2. Aristocracy (Social class) – England – History.
3. England – Church history – 1066–1485.   4. Church history – 11th
century.   5. Church history – 12th century.   6. Great Britain –
History – Norman period, 1066–1154.   I. Title.   II. Series.
BX2592.C68   1999
271'.00942'09021 – DC21   98–9940

This book is printed on acid-free paper

Printed in Great Britain by
St Edmundsbury Press, Bury St Edmunds, Suffolk

Contents

List of Maps

List of Tables

Preface

The central theme of this book is the exploration of one particular aspect of the relationship between lay men and women and monks during the Norman Conquest of England, the giving of gifts to monasteries. One of the greatest frustrations and challenges for someone studying this subject nearly a millennium later lies in trying to understand the 'real' motives of the laity for pious generosity. What survives in charters and chronicles was composed and written by the monks themselves. Even charters written in the lay donors' names were preserved by the monks. The Church's role as record-maker and record-keeper was not a selfless act. Indeed, in almost all the lay wills that survive from the late Anglo-Saxon period the Church was a donee and an overwhelming proportion of the witnesses were ecclesiastics.[1] There is no fool-proof or definitive way of determining how much control over the contents of these charters the benefactor actually had. Were the words merely formulaic legal phrases, or coded terms full of meaning to contemporaries but obscure to those outside that society?

Monkish exhortations encouraging lay support for their endeavours towards salvation are relatively easy to come by. The charismatic Anselm of Le Bec, writing to the powerful lord of Tonbridge, Richard fitz Gilbert, remarked that as benefactors of Le Bec Richard and his wife would be included in the monks' daily prayers and their generosity would be rewarded in the heavenly kingdom.[2] Instances of the laity themselves verbalising their feelings on matters of salvation, however, are sadly very scarce. One rare gem that does survive is a letter to Henry I composed by one of his royal officials, Nigel d'Aubigny, when he believed himself to be dying. Nigel keenly felt that the conduct of his past life was a severe threat to his happiness in the next one. His letter begged the king to confirm the restoration of 'some small pieces of land' he had taken from various religious houses.[3] The tone of the letter is emotional: 'I fall at the feet of your majesty in spirit, with tears and lamentation, begging your pious majesty to concede and confirm those things which I have returned to these churches from my demesne for the redemption of my soul.' This was certainly not a formulaic pronouncement on Nigel's part.

---

[1] Eric Whiteside Hemming, 'Wills and inheritance in late Anglo-Saxon England, 871–1066', unpubl. Ph.D. diss. London 1991, 277, 291.
[2] *Sancti Anselmi Cantuariensis archiepiscopi opera omnia*, ed. F. S. Schmitt, Edinburgh 1946–51, iii. 220–1.
[3] R. W. Southern, *Medieval humanism, and other studies*, Oxford 1970, 220–1; *Charters of the honour of Mowbray, 1107–1091*, ed. D. E. Greenway, London 1972, 6–7. Nigel also wrote to his brother William, in more detail, requesting the same: ibid. 7–10.

It has to be understood that the motivation behind making a donation to a religious house was complex, particularly as spiritual concerns merged with temporal. Whereas modern eyes might see hypocrisy in Nigel d'Aubigny's eleventh-hour bid to secure salvation for himself, contemporaries would have viewed the situation with greater pragmatism. Indeed, in the late twelfth century the author of the Battle abbey chronicle advised his audience that 'the wise man is warned to insure himself eternal refuge while he may'.[4] This was what Nigel was attempting to achieve; salvation for his soul.

To even begin to appreciate the manifold significance of religious patronage the social and political framework in which benefactors existed needs to be taken into account. The control of land and the exercise of power were inseparable acts in medieval society. Concern over maintaining, and where possible extending, control over land was reflected in the way elite groups were organised: through the family and lordship. These were crucial factors in determining the political and social behaviour of these groups of people. It therefore follows that the giving of land as gifts to religious houses was a deed of profound political significance. This was never more true than in the context of the aftermath of the Norman Conquest of England. This is why the study of gift-giving in Conquest England is such a rich seam of information and insights into the socio-political life of the realm.

This book had its origins in a doctoral thesis, but has been rewritten, enlarged by the addition of an introduction and chapter 1, and reduced by the consolidation of two chapters into chapter 8. Parts of chapters 3, 4 and 11 have appeared in article form in D. Bates and A. Curry (eds), *England and Normandy in the Middle Ages*, London 1994, in *Anglo-Norman Studies* xviii (1996), and in the *Haskins Society Journal* vii (1997); parts of chapter 10 appear in K. S. B. Keats-Rohan (ed.), *Family trees: the prosopography of Britain and France from the tenth to the twelfth century*, Woodbridge 1997. I am grateful to the editors and publishers of these journals and books for permission to use extracts and figures from these articles. I would also like to thank the British Library for permission to reproduce the cover illustration which has been taken from the St Albans manuscript Cotton Nero D vii.

There are many other people whom I would like to thank for their time and help. I owe my biggest debt of gratitude to Professor David Bates for his patient and enthusiastic supervision of my Ph.D. research. Professor Jinty Nelson made invaluable comments on an early version of the introduction. I also would like to thank Professor David Crouch who made many helpful suggestions and observations on an earlier version of chapter 10 and for allowing me to see a chapter from his book *The image of aristocracy in Britain, 1000–1300* in advance of publication. I am also grateful to Dr Christopher Lewis who let me see a copy of a chapter from his forthcoming book *Welsh borders, 1042–1087: a regional history of the Norman Conquest*, John Crook

---

4 *The chronicle of Battle abbey*, ed. E. Searle, Oxford 1980, 91–3.

who kindly sent me a copy of his chapter on 'The architectural setting of the cult of St Edmund at Bury' from his Ph.D. thesis and Julia Crick and Pamela Taylor who sent me copies of their papers delivered at the Early Medieval Seminar at the Institute of Historical Research. Thanks also go to Dr Simon Walker whose comments and suggestions helped turned this ex-Ph.D. into, I hope, a more enjoyable read for the world. Publication of this volume was assisted by a generous grant from the Scouloudi Foundation.

Finally, I owe an enormous debt of gratitude to my friends and colleagues for their help and support over the years: Cathy Holt, Aman Singh, Ruth Lloyd, John S. Moore, Louise Tucker, Karen Pierce, Anne Jenkins, Sally Smitherman, Alasdair Richardson, Charles Insley, Rachel Fulton, Helen Nicholson, Susan Johns, Vince Moss, Peter Edbury and all my colleagues in the History departments at the University of Wales, Cardiff, and at King's College London. For invaluable technical support I am indebted to Richard Brown, my brother Matt, Geoff Boden and Caitlin Buck. I also want to thank my family for their love and support over the years. My father's timely donation of his computer – old, but more powerful than my own – certainly aided the completion of this book. Finally, I would like say a really big thank you to my partner Seamas Johnston for being there. Without his invaluable love and support, the completion of this book would have been a much lonelier and infinitely harder task. This book is dedicated to him.

Emma Cownie
October 1997

Abbreviations

Acta	*Regesta regum Anglo-Normannorum: the acta of William I, 1066–1087*, ed. D. Bates, Oxford forthcoming
ASC	*Anglo-Saxon chronicle*, ed. D. Whitelock, D. C. Douglas and S. I. Tucker, London 1961
BL	British Library
CDF	*Calendar of documents preserved in France illustrative of the history of Great Britain and Ireland*, ed. J. H. Round, London 1899
Cart.	Cartulary
Cha.	Charters
Chart.	Chartulary
Chron.	Chronicle
CUL	Cambridge University Library
DB	*Domesday Book*, ed. A. Farley, Record Commission, London 1783–1816
EYC	*Early Yorkshire charters*, ed. W. Farrer, i–iii, Edinburgh 1914–16; ed. C. T. Clay (Yorkshire Archaeological Society Record Series e.s. iv–xii, 1935–65) (e.s. iv, ed. C. T. Clay and E. M. Clay, publ. 1942, is the index to vols i–iii)
GEC	*Complete peerage* (by G. E. Cokayne), rev. edn, ed. V. Gibbs, H. A. Doubleday and G. H. White, London 1910–59
Mon.	*Monasticon Anglicanum*, ed. W. Dugdale, R. Dodsworth, B. Bandinel, J. Caley and H. Ellis, London 1817–30
OV	*The ecclesiastical history of Orderic Vitalis*, ed. M. Chibnall, Oxford 1969–80
PL	*Patrilogia Latina*, ed. J.-P. Migne, Paris 1844–64
Regesta	*Regesta regum Anglo-Normannorum, 1066–1155*, ed. H. W. C. Davis and others, Oxford 1913–69
S	*Anglo-Saxon charters: an annotated list and bibliography*, ed. P. H. Sawyer, London 1968
VCH	*The Victoria history of the counties of England*

Introduction

The Norman Conquest is one of the most controversial topics in British history. The problems of continuity and change and the nature of the Anglo-Norman realm have drawn the attention of legions of historians. Yet the history of the Church, although an integral part of the story, has often been treated by scholars in isolation from political and military events in post-Conquest England. Furthermore, the post-Conquest experiences of the Church have largely been characterised in terms of despoliation, so that the positive response that the Church received in certain quarters has never been thoroughly assessed or examined. Indeed, the century that followed 1066 was arguably a golden age for monasticism in England. Not only were hundreds of new monasteries and priories founded but many of the established Old English houses were able to consolidate their substantial estates, acquire new lands and privileges and expand their communities to levels hitherto unknown in England. Before the Conquest the most populous houses were probably Old and New Minster, Winchester, averaging together something between forty and fifty monks. By the mid twelfth century it was not uncommon for the wealthier houses, such as Gloucester, St Albans and Bury St Edmunds, to be home to nigh on a hundred monks each.[1]

The accounts of previous generations of scholars of the history of the Church in England omitted from their narratives of institutional growth any significant discussion of the cultural and social dimensions of religious life in the realm. For example, Frank Barlow's book on the Church in the early eleventh century made its focus explicit in the sub-title to the first edition: 'a constitutional history'.[2] Dom David Knowles's authoritative study, *The monastic order in England*, describes the establishment and growth of the Benedictines, Cluniacs, Cistercians and Augustinians in England primarily in terms of events and the individuals within the Church who influenced them – men such as Dunstan and Lanfranc.[3] His account made little mention of the people who had made the monks' and canons' endeavours possible by giving them land, money, vestments, legal and economic privileges; in other words, the lay benefactors. Furthermore, where general assessments of the political significance of patterns of gift-giving to monasteries by the Normans were

---

[1] For the growth in the numbers of monks in Benedictine houses see David Knowles, *The monastic order in England*, 943–1216, Cambridge 1966, 126, 160, 177, 181n., 182, 425–6, 679.
[2] Frank Barlow, *The English Church*, 1000–1066, London 1963.
[3] Knowles, *Monastic order*, 30–56, 425–6. Knowles does, however, acknowledge (p. 246) the importance of benefactors in the success of the Cistercians.

attempted, such as those by Professor Donald Matthew and the late John Le Patourel, the fate of the English houses was largely overlooked.[4]

During the last thirty years much work has been done by English scholars in exploring the political and social dimensions of gifts to monasteries in post-Conquest England.[5] The pious preferences of certain very wealthy Anglo-Norman families have been investigated.[6] Numerous local studies have also been undertaken, exploring the relationship of individual monasteries with their benefactors and their place within the local community.[7] The analysis of the socio-political, cultural and familial make-up of groups of religious benefactors has enhanced our understanding of the nature and workings of medieval society in a way that was impossible from the study of chronicle sources alone.[8] The names of a vast number of men and women survive in Donation charters, as donors, consenting kin and witnesses.

Individuals also appear in liturgical documents, such as obits and *libri vitae*, as well as landholding agreements as monastic tenants. These liturgical documents were essentially lists of the names of people to be commemorated in

---

[4] D. J. A. Matthew, *The Norman monasteries and their English possessions*, Oxford 1962, 28; John Le Patourel, *The Norman empire*, Oxford 1976, 38

[5] For example, see Pauline Stafford, *The east midlands in the early Middle Ages*, Leicester 1985, 128–34.

[6] For the patronage of the Clare Family see M. Chibnall, 'The history of the priory of St Neot', *Proceedings of the Cambridge Antiquarian Society* lix (1966), 67–74; J. C. Ward, 'Fashions in monastic endowment: the foundations of the Clare family, 1066–1314', *Journal of Ecclesiastical History* xxxii (1981), 427–51. For the Redvers family see S. F. Hockey, 'The house of Redvers and its monastic foundations', *Anglo-Norman Studies* v (1983), 146–52. For the Lacys see W. E. Wightman, *The Lacy family in England and Normandy, 1066–1194*, Oxford 1966. For the constables of Gloucester see David Walker, 'Miles of Gloucester, earl of Hereford', *Transactions of the Bristol and Gloucestershire Archaeological Society* lxxvii (1958), 66–84, and 'The "honours" of the earl of Hereford in the twelfth century', ibid. lxxix (1960), 174–211. For the Beaumont twins see David Crouch, *The Beaumont twins: the roots and branches of power in the twelfth century*, Cambridge 1986.

[7] For the post-Conquest experience of English abbeys see E. Miller, *The abbey and bishopric of Ely*, Cambridge 1951; Susan Wood, *English monasteries and their patrons in the thirteenth century*, Oxford 1955; Bennett D. Hill, *English Cistercian monasteries and their patrons in the twelfth century*, London 1968; E. King, *Peterborough abbey, 1086–1310: a study in the land market*, Cambridge 1973; H. B. Clarke, 'The early surveys of Evesham abbey: an investigation into the problem of continuity in Anglo-Norman England', unpubl. Ph.D. diss. Birmingham 1975; Emma Mason, 'The donors of Westminster abbey charters: c. 1066–1240', *Medieval Prosopography* viii (1987), 23–39, 'Westminster abbey and the monarchy between the reigns of William I and John (1066–1216)', *Journal of Ecclesiastical History* xxxxi (1990), 199–216, and ' "The site of king-making and consecration": Westminster abbey and the crown in the eleventh and twelfth centuries', in D. Wood (ed.), *The Church and sovereignty c. 590–1918: essays in honour of Michael Wilks*, Oxford 1991, 57–76; K. Cooke, 'Donors and daughters: Shaftesbury abbey's benefactors, endowments and nuns c. 1086–1130', *Anglo-Norman Studies* xii (1990), 29–45; H. Tsurushima, 'The fraternity of Rochester cathedral priory about 1100', *Anglo-Norman Studies* xiv (1992), 312–37; J. Wardrop, *Fountains abbey and its benefactors, 1132–1300*, Kalamazoo 1987; Janet Burton, *Monastic and religious orders in Britain, 1000–1300*, Cambridge 1994.

[8] For further discussion of this problem see ch. 1.

prayer by a monastery, or group of monasteries. By reconstructing familial, social and political linkages between monastic benefactors we can see a range of factors influencing their actions. For the motivation behind religious patronage was always mixed; primarily conditioned by locality, lordship and tenurial status it could also be influenced by ties of family and friendship, shifts in fashion and personal preferences and personalities.

The continental experience

It is evident that while English and continental monasteries may have fulfilled broadly similar social and religious functions, their political importance both locally and nationally was profoundly different. In England the regeneration of the monasteries in the tenth century had been inexorably bound up with the articulation of royal power and authority. Royal initiative was essential in the inception and continued achievements of monastic revival, for the geography of royal power essentially determined the extent of the spread of the newly reformed monasteries. Yet as royal power had grown it had increasingly trespassed on church property and ecclesiastical appointments.[9] This contrasts with circumstances to be found across the Channel in France. There the tenth to the eleventh centuries witnessed the transition from the Carolingian empire to the rise of the regional monarchies of the high Middle Ages. Royal power had declined both in the French principality and in the kingdom and, in effect, the Capetians' power was on the level of a not very powerful territorial prince.[10]

Furthermore, although Charlemagne and Louis the Pious had previously fostered monasticism, by the tenth and eleventh centuries it was characterised outside the royal demesne by claims to independence from lay control. The most notable example was the abbey of Cluny, in Burgundy, which had declared that it was exempt from all episcopal jurisdiction since 998. In 1024 the pope extended this privilege to all foundations affiliated to Cluny, further undermining episcopal authority.[11] Even when, in 1119, Cluny had turned to Louis VI for protection from local lords and placed its whole order in his guardianship, the king was only allowed to intervene when requested to do so.[12] Cluny's power and influence was further enhanced in the late eleventh century when the pope decided to place under Cluny's care a number of papal proprietary monasteries in France.[13] Thus the shifting of political power and

---

[9] The king could intervene in the choice of an abbot: *Regularis concordia*, ed. T. Symons, London 1953, 6.

[10] E. M. Hallam, *Capetian France, 987–1328*, London 1980, 64.

[11] G. Duby, *The three orders: feudal society imagined*, trans. Arthur Goldhammer, Chicago–London 1980, 140–1.

[12] Hallam, *Capetian France*, 117.

[13] H. E. J. Cowdrey, *The Cluniacs and the Gregorian reform*, Oxford 1970, at pp. 82–3, 85–7, 95–7.

authority from the centre to the regions and the Cluniacs' claim to freedom from lay control meant that the power and influence of the Cluniac monasteries in the locality were going to be fundamentally different from that of their English counterparts. On the other hand, elsewhere in the French kingdom, in Normandy especially, the monasteries founded by ducal families, sometimes to initiate or consolidate political control in disputed territory, maintained close relations with their founders and protectors.[14]

In the tenth century the reform movement in the empire bore more than a passing resemblance to that in England. Here too reform did not comprehensively cover the whole country, but was focused primarily on Lorraine.[15] The monasteries also relied heavily upon the support of the imperial house, as well as upon that of bishops and the aristocracy. Imperial foundations such as Quedlinburg and Gandersheim received large and numerous grants of property and financial privileges from the German kings.[16] This was a reciprocal relationship as in the tenth and eleventh centuries the Ottonian and Salian monarchs were reliant on royal monasteries in Saxony and in the 'transit zones' between imperial lands for political and economic support.[17] Furthermore, unlike the Cluniac foundations, the Lotharingian houses did not seek large-scale exemptions from episcopal jurisdiction. Even the south German semi-independent reformed monasteries, founded in the 1060s by bishops and the aristocracy and donated to the pope, were still subject to various degrees of lay and episcopal control, depending on the influence of their former founders.[18] Completely independent forms of monasticism in the empire were only to emerge with the later appearance of the 'new' orders.[19]

It is not only the differences in power structures that distinguished the continental monasteries from the English experience but also the different approaches continental and American scholars have adopted in their research. Cluny, in particular, has attracted the attention of historians, partly because of its historical importance as the nucleus of the tenth-century reform movement and partly because of its abundant extant documents.[20]

---

[14] The vassals of William of Normandy founded monasteries in the Vexin and Le Perche on the borders of the duchy. See D. Bates, *Normandy before 1066*, London 1982, 177; M. Chibnall, *The world of Orderic Vitalis*, Oxford 1984, 51–2.

[15] C. H. Lawrence, *Medieval monasticism*, 2nd edn, London 1989, 103–4. See also Karl Schmid, *Kloster Hirsau und seine stifter*, Freiberg 1959.

[16] John W. Bernhardt, *Itinerant kingship and royal monasteries in early medieval Germany, c. 936–1076*, Cambridge 1993, 293.

[17] The older Benedictine houses fulfilled an indispensable function as hostels for the itinerant royal household on its travels around the realm: ibid. 290–308. See also Timothy Reuter, *Germany in the early Middle Ages, c. 800–1056*, London 1991, 236–46.

[18] Gerd Tellenbach, *The Church in western Europe from the tenth to the early twelfth century*, Cambridge 1993, 301.

[19] Ibid.

[20] For a full discussion of the historiography of Cluny see B. Rosenwein, *Rhinoceros bound: Cluny in the tenth century*, Philadelphia 1982, 3–56. See also Maria Hillebrandt, 'Les cartulaires de l'abbaye de Cluny', *Mémoires de la société pour l'histoire du droit et des institutions des*

Influenced by the *Annales* approach to studying society and culture as well as political and military aspects of medieval life, continental and American scholars have recently used monastic charters and cartularies to reconstruct political, social and kinship structures.[21] Barbara Rosenwein and Stephen White are particularly notable for using prospographical and anthropological methodologies in their work. Combined with textual and statistical analysis of charters, this has yielded new insights into the nature of medieval property and social relations. Their work has emphasised that horizontal, rather than vertical, bonds in society were important and that kinship groups, not individuals, controlled land. Rosenwein has demonstrated how land acted as a bond between Cluny and its donors: land was not just given to Cluny but periodically taken back, re-donated, or exchanged, transactions sometimes taking place over several generations.[22] Similarly, monasteries in post-Conquest England were no strangers to renegotiating their control over land with donors' heirs and other relatives. However, although confirmation charters were commonly sought from heirs, disputes over donations, often protracted in their nature, only occurred in a minority of cases. White's study of donations received by Benedictine houses in western France explores in detail the practice whereby gifts of land were approved by the donor's relatives, the *laudatio parentum*. Although the consent and approval of heirs was recorded in English donation charters it was never in any sense a compulsory requirement.[23] Indeed, after 1100 the participation of heirs in laymen's charters became increasingly rare.[24]

Rosenwein also points out that gifts could in reality be disguised sales, and conversely, sales could conceal gifts. In England, determining the true nature

---

anciens pays bourguignons, comtois et romands l (1993), 7–18; Dietrich Poeck, 'Laien-begräbnisse in Cluny', *Frühmittelalterliche Studien* xv (1981), 68–179.
[21] For the religious patronage of continental houses see L. T. White, *Latin monasticism in Norman Sicily*, Cambridge, Mass. 1938; M. Morgan, *The English lands of the abbey of Bec*, Oxford 1946; M. Chibnall, 'Ecclesiastical patronage and the growth of feudal estates at the time of the Norman Conquest', *Annales de Normandie* viii (1958), 103–18; V. Chandler, 'Politics and piety: influences on charitable donations during the Anglo-Norman period', *Revue Bénédictine* xc (1980), 63–71; P. Johnson, *Prayer, patronage and power: the abbey of La Trinité, Vendôme, 1032–1187*, New York 1981; C. B. Bouchard, *Sword, miter and cloister: nobility and the Church in Burgundy, 980–1198*, Ithaca–New York 1987; S. D. White, *Custom, kinship and gifts to saints: the laudatio parentum in western France, 1050–1150*, Chapel Hill 1988; E. Z. Tabuteau, *Transfers of property in eleventh century Norman law*, Chapel Hill 1988; B. Rosenwein, *To be the neighbor of Saint Peter: the social meaning of Cluny's property, 909–1049*, Ithaca–New York 1989; Sharon Farmer, *Communities of Saint Martin: legends and ritual in medieval Tours*, Ithaca–New York 1991; M. C. Miller, 'Donors, their gifts and religious innovation in medieval Verona', *Speculum* lxvi (1991), 27–42, and *The formation of a medieval church: ecclesiastical change in Verona, 950–1150*, Ithaca–New York, 1993; A. J. Gurevich, *Categories of medieval culture*, trans. G. L. Campbell, London 1985, 221–39.
[22] Rosenwein, *To be the neighbor*, 4.
[23] See John Hudson, *Land, law, and lordship in Anglo-Norman England*, Oxford 1994, ch. vi, esp. p. 181.
[24] Ibid. 185–6.

of land transactions recorded in charters and cartularies as gifts is problematical. Extant charters and entries in English monastic cartularies are characterised by their succinct nature. Although the archives of the new foundations, such as Battle or Fountains abbey, record sales amongst their acquisitions such references are very rare as far as the Old English houses are concerned.[25] Occasionally, the proximity of a donated piece of land to existing monastery property raises the suspicion that it may well have been a concealed sale, but it is usually impossible to prove.[26] English monastic cartularies are also universally less forthcoming than their continental counterparts in recording the motivation behind religious patronage. Furthermore, the late date of many of the post-Conquest cartularies means that their entries have been subject to the harsh editing of later generations whose preoccupations and concerns rarely match those of the modern historian.

Until a generation ago, the historical value of liturgical documents such as libri vitae and libri memoriales was largely overlooked by scholars. However, the work of German scholars, such as Gerd Tellenbach, Karl Schmid, Karl Leyser and Joachim Wollasch, has changed all that.[27] They have demonstrated that the preservation of the memoria of dead patrons was a primary function of monastic communities.[28] Prosopographical techniques have also been adopted in their analysis of these liturgical texts, concentrating on studying the political, sociological and familial groupings that can be identified.[29] These texts have thus been used to analyse the changes in social structure in the period from the ninth to the eleventh century.[30]

Only a handful of these liturgical lists survive for English monasteries, namely for Durham, Hyde near Winchester, Lincoln cathedral, St Albans, Thorney abbey and Christ Church, Canterbury.[31] To date scholars have made

---

[25] Wardrop, Fountains abbey, 79–86; Chron. Battle, 118–20.

[26] For example William Guzienboded gave Abingdon one hide at Dumbleton, Gloucestershire, where the abbey already held land: see ch. 3.

[27] Joachim Wollasch, 'Eine adlige familie des frühen mittlealters: ihr selbstverständnis und ihre wirklichkeit', Archiv für Kulturgeschichte xxxix (1957), 150–88; Gerd Tellenbach, 'Liturgische gedenbücher als historische quellen', Mélanges Eugène Tisserant v (Studi e Testi, ccxxxv, 1964), 389–99; K. Leyser, 'The German aristocracy from the ninth to the twelfth century: a historical and cultural sketch', Past and Present xli (1968), 25–53; Karl Schmid, Euard Hlawitschka and Gerd Tellenbach (eds), Liber memorialis von Remiremont, Dublin–Zurich 1970; Karl Schmid, 'The structure of the nobility in the earlier Middle Ages', in Timothy Reuter (ed.), The medieval nobility, Oxford 1979, 37–59.

[28] For institutional memory in the early Middle Ages see P. Geary, Phantoms of remembrance: memory and oblivion at the end of the first millennium, Princeton 1994.

[29] See also Giles Constable, 'Review article: the liber memorialis of Remiremont', Speculum xlvii (1972), 261–77.

[30] Schmid, 'Structure of the nobility', 44.

[31] BL, MS Cotton Domitian A vii (printed in Liber vitae ecclesie Dunelmensis, ed. A. H. Thompson [Surtees Society cxxxvi, 1923]); BL, MS Stowe 944 (printed in Liber vitae: register and martyrology of New Minster and Hyde abbey, Winchester, ed. W. de Gray Birch [Hampshire Record Society v, 1892], and in The liber vitae of the New Minster and Hyde abbey, Winchester, ed. Simon Keynes [Early English Manuscripts in Facsimile xxvi, 1996]); BL, MS

surprisingly little use of them, with the notable exceptions of the late Cecily Clark, Jan Gerchow and, more recently, Hiro Tsurushima and John S. Moore.[32] In the course of writing this book I have studied the Thorney *liber vitae* and the St Albans fraternity list in detail and have made a cursory inspection of the names in the Hyde and Durham *libri vitae*. The problems in identifying the vast majority of the individuals listed in these liturgical registers are admittedly insurmountable. However, there are a significant number of names that can be safely equated with documented individuals. Their inclusion in liturgical lists reveals another dimension to their relations with a monastery, sometimes absent from other records. Furthermore, the make-up of groups of names in the list can also suggest something about their familial and political priorities. However, such observations usually remain provisional in their nature as it is frequently impossible to determine who was actually responsible for having the names of a family group inscribed in the leaves of a fraternity book.

Structure and aims

Although numerous studies of individual Anglo-Norman families and English monasteries have been undertaken there has been no comprehensive attempt to isolate and co-ordinate the experiences of the Anglo-Saxon monasteries in the post-Conquest period in England. It is the aim of this book to assess the impact of the Norman Conquest on the Old English Benedictine houses through an analysis of the distribution and timing of gifts given by the continental newcomers. At first sight, this might seem a narrow approach to understanding post-Conquest society. On the contrary, the gift is at the very foundation of social life and is never a simple exchange of goods. The actions of benefactors were always infused with social expression. Lordship and family were the ties that bound medieval society and they strongly influenced the nature and scale of religious patronage. In this context gift-giving involved the giving of wealth in the form of lands, money, rents, tithes, privileges and even individuals, as oblates, to religious communities. The concrete benefits

Cotton Nero D vii; BL, MS Add. 40000; BL, MS Arundel 68, fos 52v–3v. The Lincoln list, actually a twelfth-century obit list, is printed in *Giraldi Cambriensi opera*, ed. J. S. Brewer, J. F. Dimock and G. F. Warner (Rolls ser. xxi, 1861–91), vii. 153–64.
[32] For English *libri vitae* and necrologies see Jan Gerchow, *Die gedenküberlieferung der Angelsachsen*, Berlin 1988, 109–97; M. Blows, 'A Glastonbury obit-list', in L. Abrams and J. P. Carley (eds), *The archaeology and history of Glastonbury abbey*, Woodbridge 1991, 257–69; C. Clark, 'British Library Additional MS. 40,000 ff. 1v–12r', *Anglo-Norman Studies* vii (1985), 50–65, 'A witness to post-Conquest English cultural patterns: the *liber vitae* of Thorney abbey', in A. M. Simon-Vandenbergen (ed.), *Studies in honour of René Derolez*, Ghent 1987, 73–85, and 'The *liber vitae* of Thorney abbey and its 'catchment area', *Nomina* ix (1985), 53–72; Tsurushima, 'Fraternity of Rochester cathedral priory, 312–37; J. S. Moore, 'The Anglo-Norman family: size and structure', *Anglo-Norman Studies* xiv (1991), 153–96.

that donors anticipated in return for their generosity could include burial in the monastery cemetery, entrance into the community as a monk and prayers for their souls. However, benefits of a more intangible nature were equally important to donors: the prestige of being associated with an important monastery; helping to secure control over an insecure region or lordship; demonstrating political allegiance to a particular socio-political grouping through patronising the same abbey. Gift-giving was determined by many, sometimes seemingly contradictory, motives and the returns yielded were unquestionably valued by the donors.

The seventy-year period after 1066 has been chosen in order to focus specifically on the nature and structure of the Norman Conquest and the Anglo-Norman realm.[33] John Le Patourel's seminal work on the Anglo-Norman realm tried to view the history of England and Normandy as a unit, or union, rather than two countries that happened to be ruled by the same man. By studying which houses the Normans chose to patronise in England and on the continent, we can gain insight into the strength of links between the two countries. All too often the treatment England received at the hands of the Normans has been characterised as exploitation 'for the benefit of Normans and Normandy'.[34] It was not as straightforward as that. Aside from the well attested exploiters of England who were shipping the spoils of Conquest back to Normandy, there was another group of Normans who were more interested in their future in England. It is here that the decision to focus primarily on the religious patronage received by the Old English houses is particularly profitable. Through an examination of the distribution and timing of the patronage received by the Old English houses, the attitude of the Normans toward Anglo-Saxon institutions and their saints, and towards their adoptive country itself, can be established. The death of Henry I, in 1135, was decided upon as the terminal date for this study partly because of the succession dispute that ensued which resulted in national disorder and partly because the Cistercians only began to make a significant impact in the realm after Stephen's succession. The different patterns of patronage that emerged during the 'anarchy' deserve attention in their own right and certainly not as an appendage to 1066 and all that.

Part one of this book opens with an account of the relative experiences of the Benedictine monasteries and secular religious communities through the course of the tenth and early eleventh centuries (chapter 1). Both types of religious communities received substantial support, in the form of gifts of land, money, privileges and material goods, from the likes of the king, queen, the bishops and the social elite, but it was the minster tradition, healthy in 1066, that was adversely affected by the Conquest. The post-Conquest fate of the Old English monasteries after 1066 is then examined by means of case

---

[33] See Le Patourel, *Norman empire*.
[34] David Bates, 'Normandy and England after 1066', *English Historical Review* civ (1989), 851–76 at p. 870.

studies, a decision determined in part by the nature of the sources available and also by limitations of space. First five individual English abbeys are examined in depth: Abingdon (chapter 2), Gloucester (chapter 3), Bury St Edmunds (chapter 4), St Albans (chapter 5) and St Augustine's, Canterbury (chapter 6). These monasteries are in a sense unusual because in 1066, except for Gloucester, they were amongst the richest of the Old English houses. At the same time, their relative success has left a legacy in the form of a profuse amount of extant source material which makes them attractive propositions for the study of gift-giving. The collective experience of the Fenland houses (chapter 7) and the remaining Old English monasteries (chapter 8) is then dealt with in somewhat less detail. Many of these houses, such as Ely, Peterborough and Bath, have much less source material relating to religious patronage but their post-Conquest experiences are still vital for the construction of a convincing panoramic view of Anglo-Norman England. It is further argued in chapter 8 that the exceptional circumstances that existed in post-Conquest England meant that the abilities of particularly outstanding abbots had a profound impact on the volume of patronage their monasteries received.

The experience of the Old English houses is not, however, discussed in isolation from gift-giving to continental houses and to the numerous new foundations that were established after 1066. In part two of the book the experience of the Old English houses is located in the context of general trends in religious patronage, as well as in the social and political structure of the Anglo-Norman realm. The social significance of gift-giving in England is examined (chapter 9) as well as the practical reasons that determined where a benefactor made a gift (chapter 10), and it is argued that patterns of gift-giving to the 'new' religious foundations were inexorably linked to the needs of colonisation, the locality and the nature of lordship. The distribution and timing of gift-giving to religious houses on both sides of the English Channel is analysed (chapter 11), and the emergence, from before the death of the Conqueror, of a lower strata of the aristocracy whose predominantly English interests are reflected both in the patronage of the English abbeys and in the foundation of new religious houses, is discussed. Thus it will be demonstrated that the study of patterns of religious patronage provides considerable insight into the nature of social, political and familial linkages and the solidarity of political groupings, both locally and nationally.

1

Religious Life in 1066

Structure

The ecclesiastical structure that existed in England on the eve of the Norman Conquest was complex and diverse. In addition to the fifteen cathedrals, thirty-five Benedictine monasteries, their cells and nine nunneries, the kingdom was served by a elaborate patch-work of minster churches, proprietary churches, shrines, hermitages and oratories. In early Anglo-Saxon England the term 'minster' was used by contemporaries to describe a very wide diversity of religious houses.[1] Modern scholars, however, use the term 'minster churches' to mean houses served by priests who could staff the church and provide for the spiritual needs of the neighbourhood. In collegiate establishments the priests did not lead a communal life and were not required to renounce property or marriage. Monastic houses, on the other hand, were not necessarily part of a parochial system and were staffed by monks who had taken vows of enclosure, silence, stability and obedience.[2] The development of the ecclesiastical structure in England had been sporadic and irregular and this fact is reflected in the uneven geographical distribution and wealth of the Benedictine monasteries. Half of the total number of male monastic houses were located in the Wessex region, whereas there was no abbey west of the Severn, nor north of a line drawn from Worcester to Burton-on-Trent and thence to the Wash.[3] The minster churches were by no means homogenous in their nature, either, and they certainly underwent diverse experiences in different parts of the country both before and after 1066. In order fully to understand the nature and structure of religious life in England in

---

[1] For the discussion of terminology see Sarah Foot, 'Anglo-Saxon minsters: a review of terminology', in John Blair and Richard Sharpe (eds), *Pastoral care before the parish*, Leicester 1992, 212–25. The most important work on secular churches has been done by John Blair and many of my observations are based on his research: 'Secular minster churches in Domesday Book', in P. H. Sawyer (ed.), *Domesday Book: a reassessment*, London 1985, 104–42, and 'Minster churches in the landscape', in D. Hooke (ed.), *Anglo-Saxon settlements*, Oxford 1988, 35–58. For the recent debate on the development of the 'minster' church system in England see Eric Cambridge and David Rollason, 'Debate: the pastoral organization of the Anglo-Saxon Church: a review of the "minster hypothesis"', *Early Medieval Europe* iv (1995), 87–104, John Blair, 'Debate: ecclesiastical organization and pastoral care in Anglo-Saxon England', ibid. 193–212, and D. M. Pallister, 'Review article: the "minster hypothesis"', ibid. v (1996), 204–14.
[2] Knowles, *Monastic order*, 12.
[3] Ibid. 101.

1066 it is necessary to look in some detail at political developments and the changes in patterns of religious patronage that took place in the century before the Norman Conquest.

Monasteries and sources

Tenth-century England underwent a monastic revival which led to the foundation, or refoundation, of many of England's principal monasteries.[4] The great success of the monastic reform movement, however, was largely proclaimed by the Benedictine monks themselves: the movement's later champions, writing at the beginning of the eleventh century, made great claims on behalf of its earlier proponents. Yet not all the houses that came under the control of the reformers may have been reformed in this period. Dunstan, one of the leading reformers of the tenth century, certainly did not reform St Paul's, London, during his brief stint as bishop of London from 1057 to 1059,[5] and there is also some doubt whether Christ Church, Canterbury, and Glastonbury were ever reformed under him.[6] Although Glastonbury was hailed as the 'only true monastery in England' when Dunstan was made abbot, it is unlikely that he was able to 'impose real Benedictine discipline': Æthelwold wanted to leave because it was not strict enough for him.[7] However, the introduction of the square cloister at Glastonbury by Dunstan does suggest that some form of reform was introduced there.[8] There was also no explicit reference to monks at Canterbury until the 1020s.[9] It is interesting to note that another of the principal reformers, Oswald, refused point-blank to receive the monastic habit himself.[10]

Furthermore, the anti-clerical rhetoric of the early eleventh-century monastic reformers should be viewed with a great deal of circumspection. For instance, the claim made in the *Life of Æthelwold* that the Abingdon clerks gave

[4] D. H. Farmer, 'The progress of the monastic revival', in David Parsons (ed.), *Tenth century studies*, London 1975, 10–19, 209 at p. 10.

[5] P. J. Taylor, 'The estates of the bishopric of London from the seventh century to the early sixteenth century', unpubl. Ph.D. diss. London 1976, 39.

[6] S. E. Kelly, 'The pre-Conquest history and archive of St Augustine's abbey, Canterbury', unpubl. Ph.D. diss. Cambridge 1986, 48; Matthew Blows, 'Studies in the pre-Conquest history of Glastonbury abbey', unpubl. Ph.D. diss. London 1991, 346, 377.

[7] Eric John, *Reassessing Anglo-Saxon England*, Manchester 1996, 114.

[8] D. A. Hinton, *Archaeology, economy and society: England from the fifth to the fifteenth century*, London 1990, 99. For Dunstan and Canterbury see R. Gem, 'Reconstructions of St Augustine's abbey, Canterbury, in the Anglo-Saxon period', in Nigel Ramsay, Margaret Sparks and Tim Tatton-Brown (eds), *St Dunstan, his life, times and cult*, Woodbridge 1993, 57–73.

[9] N. P. Brooks, *The early history of the church of Canterbury: Christ Church from 597 to 1066*, Leicester 1984, 256.

[10] *The chronicle of John of Worcester*, ed. R. R. Darlington and Patrick McGurk, Oxford 1995, ii. 418.

the abbot a poisoned drink which failed to kill him is far from convincing.[11] The different versions of the *Anglo-Saxon chronicle* and John of Worcester's chronicle were monastic productions with an inherently anti-clerical bias running through them. This bias became more vociferous after the Conquest and particularly in the 1120s.[12] The only exception to the monastic control of sources is Domesday Book, which has its own peculiar difficulties being essentially incomplete and somewhat haphazard in its criteria for the collection of material.[13]

There is also a pronounced bias in the extant wills and charters in favour of the Benedictine monasteries. Whereas the beneficiaries in lay wills might include both monasteries and secular communities, or just reformed houses, there are few wills which benefit secular houses alone.[14] Even royal grants, a number of which survive for secular communities, tended to be preserved in monastic or cathedral archives.[15] The reason for this is two-fold; firstly a significant percentage of the material only survives in post-Conquest copies and, secondly, the evidence was usually written, and preserved, by the monasteries themselves. Indeed, this is why they survived at all.[16] Of the wills recorded in the revised edition of P. H. Sawyer's *Anglo-Saxon Charters* 90 per cent were originally preserved by the beneficiaries.[17] A small proportion of these were not monasteries, but they were almost invariably cathedral communities.[18]

This in itself is very telling. As a group the Benedictine monasteries triumphed after 1066, but by the end of Henry I's reign the secular foundations had failed to flourish in the same way as they had done under Edward the Confessor. Many of the greater minsters were either reduced in status, had been given to monasteries to become cells or were converted into Augustinian priories. As a result of this disruption and discontinuity the minsters did

---

11 Wulfstan of Worcester, *The life of St Æthelwold*, ed. Michael Lapidge and Michael Winterbottom, Oxford 1991, 34–5; Ælfric, *Life of Æthelwold*, in *English historical documents*, I: *c. 500–1042*, ed. Dorothy Whitelock, 2nd edn, London 1979, 903–11 at pp. 907–8. See also *Three lives of English saints*, ed. W. Winterbottom, Toronto 1972, 15–19, and N. P. Brooks and C. Cubitt (eds), *St Oswald of Worcester: his life and influence*, Leicester 1996.

12 D. L. Bethell, 'English black monks and episcopal elections in the 1120s', *English Historical Review* lxxxiv (1969), 673–98 at p. 690.

13 Blair, 'Secular minster churches', 106–14.

14 Bury St Edmunds is an exception to this but the fact that it was refounded in the reign of Cnut means it should be considered amongst the monasteries not the minsters.

15 S953, S992, S1036, S1067, S1101, S1104, S1162.

16 See also remarks made by P. Wormald, 'Charters and law and the settlement of disputes in Anglo-Saxon England', in W. Davies and P. Fouracre (eds), *The settlement of disputes in early medieval Europe*, Cambridge 1986, 149–68 at pp. 151, 153.

17 Fifty-five out of sixty-one wills were preserved by the beneficiaries: S1482–4, S1487–99, S1501–3a, S1504–5, S1508–14, S1516–25a, S1526–33, S1535–9. See also remarks made by Hemming, 'Wills and inheritance', 277, 291.

18 These were Christ Church, Canterbury, St Paul's, London, and Rochester cathedral priory.

not leave a legacy of literary or narrative texts comparable to that left by the Benedictine houses.[19] Furthermore, the disruption of the Norman Conquest had prompted the English monks to collect written evidence to support their title to land and to justify their practices and cults.[20] Thus, although bequests to secular communities are relatively common in Anglo-Saxon wills, there must have been many more for which written evidence does not survive.

Much of the material that contains evidence for the secular communities such as royal charters and lay wills, therefore, is generally preserved in monastic cartularies and monastic chronicles. This type of evidence was also susceptible to being harshly edited in later copies of monastic manuscripts; female beneficiaries, individual estates and special terms could all become casualties of editing.[21] Furthermore, many of the surviving Anglo-Saxon charters are spurious or interpolated. Charter information also varies significantly by region, so that, for example, Kent and Worcestershire are well represented in the charters whereas Durham, Lancashire, Cheshire and Bedfordshire are not.[22] Numbers of royal charters and writs vary from reign to reign. Thus only thirty-six charters and eight writs survive for the reign of Cnut, the least well represented of the English kings betweeen Æthelstan and Edward the Confessor.[23] This skewed picture therefore obscures other evidence that suggests that the 'triumph' of the Benedictines was less than absolute. It has to be remembered that the monasteries did not have a complete monopoly of religious life in late tenth- and early eleventh-century England. In fact, the monastic achievement was incomplete and occasionally went into reverse in certain areas.

Patterns of patronage

Royal initiative was essential in the inception and continued achievements of the Benedictine monastic revival in the tenth century. Bishop Æthelwold needed both royal and papal permission to expel the clerks from houses such as Abingdon and New Minster, Winchester.[24] The promoters of the monastic revival were at pains to create a special relationship between the monasteries

---

[19] For the loss of Anglo-Saxon writs and charters after the Conquest see M. T. Clanchy, *From memory to written record: England, 1066–1307*, 2nd edn, Oxford 1993, 29.
[20] Ibid.
[21] Julia Crick made this point in her research paper given at the Institute of Historical Research in March 1996 entitled 'Female bequests and family strategy in pre-Conquest England'.
[22] R. Fleming, *Kings and lords in conquest England*, Cambridge 1991, 18–19.
[23] M. K. Lawson, *Cnut: the Danes in England in the early eleventh century*, London 1993, 66.
[24] P. Wormald, 'Æthelwold and his continental counterparts: contact, comparison, contrast', in B. Yorke (ed.), *Bishop Æthelwold: his career and influence*, Woodbridge 1988, 13–42 at p. 34; Wulfstan of Worcester, *Life of Æthelwold*, 36–5; *English historical documents*, I: *c. 500–1042*, 908.

and the royal house. The monasteries were required to say prayers of intercession for 'the king and benefactors by whose bounty, under Christ, we are
maintained'.[25] The Benedictine monasteries looked to the king for endowment, land and protection and the king sought from the monasteries practical
help and service as well as theoretical support for the 'mystique of royalty'.[26]
Edgar's personal support was primarily focused on the communities most
closely associated with the main figures of the reform movement: Old Minster, Winchester, Abingdon and Glastonbury.[27] It is interesting that Glastonbury was probably not reformed at this time but this clearly did not diminish
the king's regard for the house as he chose to be buried there.[28] Edgar also
occasionally supported and endowed other secular foundations.[29] He granted
land in Cornwall to the minster of St Dawe and St Kew, and land in Hampshire to the church of St Andrew, Meon, while 'allowing' his father's widow,
Æthelflæd, to make a grant to St Paul's, London.[30]

Although the king and the bishops propelled the reform movement for-
ward, the spread of the reformed monasteries depended much on the aristocracy and local circumstances. The effects of the movement were restricted to
the south of the Humber: particularly north of the Thames, in Wessex and
the east midlands. The movement did not reach north of the Humber principally because before 1066 the king's estates in Northumbria were almost neg-
ligible. After the king, the most important champions of the monasteries
were the aristocracy. In different regions of England, depending on the king's
landed interests and influence there, the main proponents of reform could be
the local aristocracy and the bishops. This was the case in the east midlands
where the king had little land.[31] Bishops Æthelwold, Oswald and Thorketel
were collectively responsible for the refounding of Ely, Peterborough, Thorney and Crowland with the help and generosity of the king and local men
like Ealdorman Æthelwine of East Anglia.[32]

Aristocratic benefactors were influenced by a combination of motives:

---

25 *Regularis concordia*, 5.
26 Farmer, 'Monastic revival', 13. For royal patronage and land tenure see Eric John, 'The
church of Worcester and the tenth century reformation', *Bulletin of the John Rylands Library*
xlvii (1965), 404–29; Richard Allnatt,'The history of New Minster, Winchester, and its estates, 900–1200', unpubl. M.Litt. diss. Oxford 1991, 46–74.
27 For Abingdon see S673, S682, S688–701, S708, S724, S732–4, S756–60. For Glastonbury see S743, S764, S783, S791, S1173 S1768, S1769, S1770. For Old Minster see S699,
S804, S806, S807, S814–17, 819–24, S826, S827. No authentic charter of Edgar's survives
for Worcester but see S731, S751, S788.
28 ASC 'C', 1016.
29 See J. H. Denton, *English royal free chapels, 1000–1300*, Manchester 1970, 133–40.
30 S718, S810, S1795. See also Lynette Olson, *Early monasteries in Cornwall*, Woodbridge
1988.
31 Stafford, *East midlands*, 130.
32 Ibid. For the endowment of Crowland see S. Raban, *The estates of Thorney and Crowland:
a study in medieval monastic land tenure*, Cambridge 1977, and 'The property of Thorney and
Crowland abbeys: a study in monastic patronage', unpubl. Ph.D. diss. Cambridge 1971.

politics, locality, family and piety.[33] Ties of friendship with other dedicated champions of monastic reform were at play in the case of Ealdorman Æthelwine. Not only was he the foster brother of King Edgar but he also kept in close touch with Glastonbury where his father Athelstan 'Half King' had been buried, and it was whilst he was there that Bishop Oswald persuaded him to found Ramsey abbey on his Fenland estates in about 971.[34] Subsequently Ramsey had strong and enduring connections with the family of its founder: his mother, three successive wives, his brother Ælfwold and his wife were all benefactors of the abbey.[35] Æthelwine's close associate in East Anglia, Ealdorman Bryhtnoth, also made a grant of land to Ramsey abbey,[36] but his closest ties, and those of his successors, were with Ely,[37] to which he made very generous grants, some of which were confirmed and augmented by his widow.[38] This was an association which was to endure beyond the grave: the abbot and monks of Ely carried back Bryhtnoth's headless corpse from the Battle of Maldon in 991 for burial at the abbey.[39] Other family benefactors included Bryhtnoth's wife and his daughter, Ælfwine, the bishop of Elmham, said to be Bryhtnoth's son, his daughter's daughters, and the husband of one of them.[40] By 1066 over a 'score of more' of Ely's manors can be traced back to gifts of Brythnoth's family.[41]

It is also important to note that a family's support of one particular monastery did not necessarily translate into support for monasteries in general. During the succession dispute that followed the death of Edgar in 975 'the religious ealdorman' Bryhtnoth and Ealdormen Æthelwine, *Dei amicus*, 'assembled troops and defended the monasteries of the East Angles with great spirit'.[42] Despite this commendable action, Æthelwine was still capable of seizing an Ely estate which he claimed had been part of his patrimony.[43] Furthermore, Ælfhere, ealdorman of the rest of Mercia, who had gained

[33] See Janet M. Pope, 'Monks and nobles in the Anglo-Saxon monastic reform', *Anglo-Norman Studies* xvii (1995), 165–80.
[34] Barlow, *English Church, 1000–1066*, 55. For the early history and endowment of Ramsey abbey see J. A. Raftis, *The estates of Ramsey abbey: a study in economic growth and organization*, Toronto 1957, 5–21. For the endowment of Glastonbury abbey see Lesley Abrams, *Anglo-Saxon Glastonbury: church and endowment*, London 1993.
[35] Pope, 'Monks and nobles', 178; Fleming, *Kings and lords*, 27–8.
[36] S798.
[37] Miller, *Abbey and bishopric of Ely*, 22; Pauline Stafford, *Unification and conquest: a political and social history of England in the tenth and eleventh centuries*, London 1989, 191. Brythnoth also made a grant to Christ Church, Canterbury, in 991, and his wife later made a grant in 1002: S1637, S1639.
[38] *Anglo-Saxon wills*, ed. D. Whitelock, Cambridge 1930, no. xv.
[39] *Liber Eliensis*, ed. E. O. Blake (Camden Society, 3rd ser. xcii, 1962), 136.
[40] Miller, *Abbey and bishopric of Ely*, 22.
[41] Ibid.
[42] *Chron. John of Worcester*, ii. 426.
[43] A. Williams, '*Princeps Merciorum gentis*: the family, career and connections of Ælfhere, ealdorman of Mercia, 956–83', *Anglo-Saxon England* x (1982), 143–72 at p. 165.

prominence amongst Edgar's supporters after Æthelwine's father, Æthelstan, had retired, was opposed to Æthelwine and Oswald and he attacked the monasteries under their patronage.[44] This was not a sign of antipathy towards monasticism, as such, but rather a demonstration of favouritism, where one monastery might be supported at the material expense of another.

For many donors locality and past family association with a foundation were sometimes just as important, if not more so, than whether the foundation had been reformed. Sometime between 971 and c. 982, the southern noble Ealdorman Æthelmær made a bequest to New Minster, Winchester, where he wished to be buried, granting Tidworth 'for the souls of us both', i.e. himself and his wife.[45] Æthelmær also granted land to Old Minster and the nunnery at Winchester and gave sums of money to the communities at Old Minster, Winchester, Christ Church and St Augustine's, Canterbury, Rochester, Abingdon, Romsey, Wilton, Shaftesbury, Malmesbury, Bath, Cricklade and Bourne, as well as to his servants, lord and finally his wife. He made no overt distinction between the two minster churches, Cricklade and Bourne, and the Benedictine monasteries.

Edgar's successors all came to appreciate the importance of the association between the royal house and the reformed monasteries. However, the position of the monasteries deteriorated temporarily as a result of the actions of King Æthelred during the early years of his reign. He had come under the sway of a number of men who encouraged him to reduce the privileges and appropriate the property of certain churches to their benefit.[46] The king was prepared to be a party to the maltreatment of certain churches such as Old Minster, Winchester, where estates were appropriated, the diocese of Rochester which was ravaged in 986, and Glastonbury which was in dispute with a rich man, Ælfwold.[47] However, the situation was to improve for the Benedictine cause in the later years of the tenth and the early part of the eleventh century. After about 993, Æthelred, Cnut, and to a lesser degree Edward the Confessor, all chose to perpetuate the peculiarly close bond with Old Minster, Winchester, and Abingdon, but less so with Glastonbury.[48] Yet royal generosity towards the old established abbeys wavered and shifted emphasis through the years. These older monasteries often had to compete with newer religious projects for the monarch's attention. Æthelred granted a number of charters

44 Ibid. 157. For the revised view of Ælfhere's behaviour towards the monasteries see ibid. 146, 159, 166–7, and Stafford, East midlands, 126.

45 S1498; Anglo-Saxon wills, no. x.

46 Simon Keynes, The diplomas of King Æthelræd 'The Unready' (978–1016): a study in their use as historical evidence, Cambridge 1980, 177.

47 For Rochester see S864, S885, S893. For Old Minster, Winchester, see S891, S889, S891, S986.

48 For Old Minster, Winchester, see S835–7, S845, S889, S891, S972, S976, S1006, S1012, S1016, S1062, S1152–4. For Abingdon see S843, S896–7, S918, S937, S964, S967, S973, S993, S1020, S1023, S1025, S1065–6. For Glastonbury see S866, S966, S1774–8, S1780. See also Blows, 'Pre-Conquest history of Glastonbury', 346, 377.

to Glastonbury, but the abbey only received one confirmation charter from Cnut. Perhaps it was Glastonbury's unreformed status that inhibited Cnut's generosity. Likewise it has been suggested that the unreformed status of St Paul's, London, meant that 'it may have received fewer endowments during the late Anglo-Saxon period than it would otherwise have done'.[49] Old Minster and Abingdon, however, were favoured by all the English kings well into the mid eleventh century.

This munificence was not to the total exclusion of secular foundations. Æthelred founded, or possibly refounded, a minster at Cholsey, near Wallingford, in the early 990s supposedly for the soul of his murdered half-brother Edward.[50] He also patronised St Frideswide, Oxford, and St Paul's, London; Cnut granted privileges to St German's minster, Cornwall, and confirmed the rights of the priests of St Paul's, London; Edward the Confessor protected the rights of Bromfield minster and granted privileges to St Æthelbert's, Hereford, St Paul's, London, Waltham, Beverley and Hampton.[51] Æthelred rebuilt St Frideswide's minster after burning the Danes in 1002 and Edward the Confessor later restored St Frideswide's as a house of canons in 1049, after it had been briefly annexed in the time of Cnut.[52] Edward the Confessor was allegedly responsible for refounding Wimborne, Dorset, as a secular college.[53] It should be stressed, however, that these benefactions to minsters represented only a tiny proportion of the sum total of royal generosity. The bulk of the Confessor's energy, for instance, was concentrated on the Benedictine monasteries, primarily Westminster.[54]

The late tenth and early eleventh centuries witnessed many positive achievements for the monastic cause. Simon Keynes has argued that the reign of Æthelred after about 993 until 1006 'was one of the most prosperous for the advancement of the ecclesiastical cause before the Norman Conquest'.[55] During the 990s and early 1000s the king was surrounded by a number of men who were closely associated with the promotion of the monastic movement.[56] These included amongst the laymen Æthelwærd, Æthelmær, Ordulf and Wulfric Spot. During this period most of Æthelred's attention was focused on religious communities and he produced a substantial number of important diplomas for the Church. This was an important

---

[49] Taylor, 'Estates of the bishopric of London', 39.

[50] John Blair, Anglo-Saxon Oxfordshire, Stroud 1994, 114.

[51] S908–9, S945, S953, S992, S1036, S1056, S1067, S1101, S1104, S1155, S1162; Blair, 'Secular minster churches', 120–1.

[52] Idem, 'St Frideswide's monastery: problems and possibilities', in John Blair (ed.), Saint Frideswide's monastery at Oxford: archaeological and architectural studies, Gloucester 1990, 221–58 at pp. 226–7.

[53] Patricia H. Coulstock, The collegiate church of Wimborne Minster, Woodbridge 1993, 97.

[54] Edward the Confessor made thirty-seven grants and confirmations to Westminster a number of which survive in twelfth-century forged charters: S1011, S1031, S1039–41, S1043, S1117–23, S1126–30, S1132–50.

[55] Keynes, Diplomas of Æthelræd, 199.

[56] Ibid. 189.

period for the consolidation of monasticism in England, as privileges were confirmed, lands restored and houses founded and endowed. There was also extensive English missionary activity in Scandinavia, and notable advances in scholarship and material culture.[57] It was certainly an important achievement to have created a dynamic environment in which monastic ventures flourished at little financial cost to the king.

The early years of the eleventh century saw a move away from the royal and episcopal initiative of the 970s and away from East Anglia and Wessex. New enterprises were increasingly undertaken by the king's ealdormen. Monasteries were founded at Burton-on-Trent, Bruton, Cerne and Eynsham by Æthelred's ealdormen, Æthelmær and Wulfric Spot.[58] Wulfrun, the mother of Wulfric Spot, however, had chosen to found or refound the minster church of Wolverhampton in 994.[59] The reasons for the lessening interest in the old established monasteries in Wessex and East Anglia largely lay in changes in personnel at Æthelred's court.[60] The sheer length of Æthelred's reign had meant that many of his early supporters had simply died from old age, in battle or had been exiled; Ælfheah, ealdormen of Wessex, died in about 970/1, his brother Ælfhere of Mercia, died in 983 and Ealdorman Æthelwine of East Anglia died in 992.[61] The deaths of the heads of these families were setbacks from which many of them failed to recover. It opened the way for the king to promote other families to prominence, such as that of Leofwine of Mercia. See-sawing political fortunes also later affected the endowment of Wulfric Spot's foundation at Burton-on-Trent. After Wulfric's death, his brother Ealdorman Ælfhelm was murdered and his sons blinded.[62] Subsequently, at least five estates that Wulfric had granted to the abbey came into the hands of Cnut's earls.

With changes in personnel, new men emerged with their own local concerns, tastes and partialities. Thus, the already established houses at Abingdon, Ely, Glastonbury, Peterborough, Old Minster and New Minster, Winchester, and the cathedral priory of Worcester ceased to make any more

[57] Ibid. 199. See also Lesley Abrams, 'The Anglo-Saxons and the christianization of Scandinavia', Anglo-Saxon England xxv (1995), 213–49.

[58] Simon Keynes, 'Cnut's earls', in Alexander R. Rumble (ed.), The reign of Cnut: king of England, Denmark and Norway, London 1994, 43–88 at pp. 67–70; Blair, Anglo-Saxon Oxfordshire, 114; Keynes, Diplomas of Æthelræd, 192; Stafford, East midlands, 126; The charters of Burton abbey, ed. P. H. Sawyer, Oxford 1979, p. xliv. For the extent of Æthelmaer's endowment at Eynsham see Amin Hamid Zeinelabdin, 'Eynsham abbey, 1005–1538: a study in medieval Benedictine monasticism', unpubl. Ph.D. diss. Newcastle 1983, 1.

[59] S1380. See also Della Hooke, 'Wolverhampton: the foundation of the minster', in Medieval art and architecture at Lichfield (British Architectural Association Conference Transactions xiii, 1993), 11–16.

[60] Pauline Stafford, 'The reign of Æthelred II, a study in the limitations on royal policy and action', in David Hill (ed.), Ethelred the Unready: papers from the millenary conference (British Archaeological Records lix, 1978), 15–46 at pp. 27–33; Fleming, Kings and lords, 39–40.

[61] For the careers of these men see Blows, 'A Glastonbury obit-list', 257–69 at 263–7.

[62] Fleming, Kings and lords, 44.

substantial additions to their land holdings except through purchase and exchange.[63] Ramsey abbey had also acquired the bulk of its endowment in its first forty years, and subsequently changed tactics, concentrating on attracting grants from the lesser landholders in the locality.[64] In the mid years of Æthelred's reign royal action was characterised by the confirmation of the endowments of already established houses, such as Ely, Glastonbury and Old and New Minster, Winchester.[65] For Abingdon, Rochester and Old Minster, Winchester, however, this was the case only after Æthelred restored lands he had earlier alienated.[66]

The Danish invasions caused serious disruption in southern and eastern England, with monasteries and minsters alike being despoiled, sometimes by the local communities to pay for Danegeld.[67] However, Cnut's regime did feature a considerable degree of continuity for the Church in England.[68] On his accession the personnel of the bishoprics remained unchanged and the Benedictine monasteries flourished throughout his reign. Cnut's personal enthusiasm for religious patronage in England is well attested.[69] Like Edgar, Cnut's actions smacked of showmanship; he made lavish gifts to the poor of St-Omer on his way to Rome in 1027, according to Simeon of Durham he walked five miles barefoot to the church of St Cuthbert and he gave many magnificent gifts to English and continental monasteries.[70] It is interesting, then, that he largely ignored secular foundations, although Cnut's followers occasionally did not.[71] Possibly this was due to the influence of his wife, Emma, who was from Normandy where monastic reform was beginning to make some headway under William Volpiano.[72] Perhaps it was she who fostered a prejudice against the secular foundations. The list of English religious houses to which Emma and Cnut made gifts of works of art and relics is extensive: Abingdon, Christ Church and St Augustine's, Canterbury, Coventry, Crowland, Ely,

---

63 S1216, S1391, S1463, S1475, S1480; *Chronicon abbatiae Rameseiensis*, ed. W. Dunn Macray (Rolls series lxxxiii, 1886), 140, 143; *Gesta abbatum monasterii Sancti Albani*, ed. H. T. Riley (Rolls series xxviii, 1867–9), i. 32, 33; Stafford, *East midlands*, 133.

64 Raftis, *Ramsey abbey*, 7.

65 *The early history of Glastonbury: an edition, translation and study of William of Malmesbury's 'De antiquitate Glastonie ecclesie'*, ed. John Scott, Woodbridge 1981, 85, 86, 100, 101. Glastonbury received the bulk of its endowment during Edgar's reign: S1761–78. Ely received most of its property by 1035: Miller, *Abbey and bishopric of Ely*, 23; C. Hart, *The early charters of eastern England*, Leicester 1966, nos 168–309.

66 S864, S876, S885, S889, S891, S893, S896–7, S918, S937, S986.

67 See M. K. Lawson, 'The collection of danegeld and heregeld in the reigns of Æthelred II and Cnut', *English Historical Review* cix (1984), 721–38.

68 Idem, *Cnut*, 47.

69 See T. A. Heslop, 'The production of *de luxe* manuscripts and the patronage of King Cnut and Queen Emma', *Anglo-Saxon England* xix (1990), 151–95, and Lawson, *Cnut*, 117–60, but compare with Abrams, 'Christianization of Scandinavia', 226–9.

70 Lawson, *Cnut*, 134.

71 Cnut removed Southminster from the posession of St Paul's, London: Taylor, 'Estates of the bishopric of London', 47.

72 Heslop, '*De luxe* manuscripts', 180.

Evesham, Glastonbury, Westminster, Wilton and New and Old Minster, Winchester.[73]

During Cnut's reign royal initiative was the main force behind the foundation of new monasteries, mostly in eastern England. After 1016 new monastic communities were established at St Benet of Holme, Bury St Edmunds, Christ Church, Canterbury, Thetford, Minster in Thanet, Spalding, Stow, Coventry, Horton, Gloucester and Deerhurst.[74] It is hard to resist the conclusion that Cnut was all too aware that East Anglia and Kent were the areas that had suffered the most, both materially and financially, from the recent Danish invasions and wished to make amends, and thus neutralise resentment and potential opposition. It is evident that there was royal involvement in many of these projects. Cnut himself was responsible for refounding a handful of secular communities as Benedictine houses in eastern England. In 1019 he refounded St Benet of Holme, about a year later he refounded Bury St Edmunds and its first abbot Uvius subsequently founded a cell of monks at Thetford sometime between 1022 and 1044.[75] In 1027 Cnut gave Minster in Thanet, Kent, to the monks at St Augustine's, Canterbury.[76]

The handful of charters that survive for Harthacnut's brief reign suggest that he also intended to continue the royal tradition and perpetuate the advantageous link with Abingdon, Glastonbury, Ramsey and Winchester and also with his father's foundation of Bury St Edmunds.[77] Indeed, Bury is exceptional amongst the religious houses for receiving grants and bequests in any number at all during the period of Harold Harefoot and Harthacnut's rule. St Edmund was popularly believed to have successfully resisted Swein Forkbeard's demands for money and so it was a shrewd move to be seen to placate the saint and his guardians. A number of bequests to Bury may date from this period and grants were also made by Stigand and Thorketel.[78]

Relatively few of Cnut's followers were inspired to imitate his generosity and those who did so were usually closely associated with the king. They seem to have preferred Benedictine houses. Bovi, Cnut's thegn, founded Horton.[79] Wulfsige made a bequest to Cnut's refounded community at Bury St Edmunds.[80] In 1026 Scearpa, a hall-thegn, made a grant of land to Christ Church, Canterbury, and in 1032 Eadsige, one of Cnut's priests, chose to

---

[73] Ibid. 181.
[74] Antonia Grandsen, however, has argued that no Benedictine foundations can be reliably assigned to the reign of Cnut. In the light of Cnut's extensive patronage of almost exclusively Benedictine houses this conclusion seems questionable at best: 'The legends and traditions concerning the origins of the abbey of Bury St Edmunds', *English Historical Review* c (1985), 1–24.
[75] David Knowles and R. N. Hadcock, *Medieval religious houses: England and Wales*, 2nd edn, London 1971, 61, 75, 78.
[76] Kelly, 'Pre-Conquest history of St Augustine's abbey', 85, 144.
[77] S993–7; *Early history of Glastonbury*, 134.
[78] S1224–5, S1490, S1521, S1527, S1529.
[79] F. M. Stenton, *Anglo-Saxon England*, 2nd edn, Cambridge 1956, 408.
[80] S1537.

enter Christ Church as a monk.[81] Peterborough abbey received a small flurry of grants, two from men who were associated with the office of ealdorman of Mercia: Leofwine, father of Earl Leofric, Halfdene, son of Brenting, and Thorkell Hoche.[82] However, not everyone chose to patronise the Benedictines. The son-in-law of Osgod Clapa, Tofi the Proud, founded the first church at Waltham, Essex, which was probably a secular foundation.[83] Another of Cnut's thegns, Urk, founded or refounded the minster church of St Peter's, Abbotsbury, in about 1026, and his widow, Tole, subsequently bequeathed her lands and possessions to the church.[84]

Many of the great Benedictine monasteries received a respectable degree of attention from Edward the Confessor: on average six charters survive each for Ramsey, Old Minster, Winchester, Christ Church, Canterbury, and Abingdon.[85] None survive for Glastonbury abbey.[86] The only other exception to this treatment was Cnut's refoundation of Bury St Edmunds to which Edward the Confessor issued at least eighteen writs and charters.[87] Perhaps it was St Edmund's own reputation that attracted Edward's interest and generosity. It is more likely that the king appreciated the strategic advantage of creating a political force in Suffolk at the expense of his mother when, in 1043, Bury was initially granted control of eight and a half hundreds in western Suffolk.[88] Even after his mother, Emma, was restored to favour and her property, his concern for the abbey's rights and privileges was maintained consistently throughout the 1040s and 1050s. In his last years, he gave Bury to his favoured physician, Baldwin.

Edward the Confessor's pious energies, however, were well and truly focused on his own refoundation at Westminster, which was to become his mausoleum, making approximately thirty-seven grants and confirmations.[89] The abbey was also granted significant portions of land by its non-royal benefactors. Some of these people were officials such as Æthelric the chamberlain, Ulf the portreeve and the king's housecarl, Turstin, all of whom gave

---

81 S1221; Anglo-Saxon charters, ed. A. J. Robertson, 2nd edn, Cambridge 1956, no. lxxxvi.
82 Hart, Charters of eastern England, 328, 349, 350, 351.
83 Anglo-Saxon charters, 400.
84 S1064.
85 S1006, S1012, S1016, S1020, S1023, S1025, S1030, S1047, S1062, S1066, S1086–90, S1106–10, S1153–4. For comments on the structure of monastic estates during the reign of the Confessor see Peter A. Clarke, The English nobility under Edward the Confessor, Oxford 1994, 54–5.
86 See also N. E. Stacy, 'The estates of Glastonbury abbey c. 1050–1200', unpubl. D.Phil. diss. Oxford 1971, and Lesley Abrams, 'The pre-Conquest endowment of Glastonbury abbey: the growth of an Anglo-Saxon church', unpubl. Ph.D. diss. Toronto 1992.
87 S1045–6, S1068–75, S1077–80, S1082, S1084–5. For Cnut and Bury St Edmunds see Lawson, Cnut, 119, 140–3, 146; D. W. Rollason, Saints and relics in Anglo-Saxon England, Oxford 1989, 157. For William the Conqueror and Bury St Edmunds see Emma Cownie, 'Religious patronage at Post-Conquest Bury St Edmunds', Haskins Society Journal vii (1997), 1–9.
88 Frank Barlow, Edward the Confessor, London 1970, 77.
89 S1011, S1031, S1039–41, S1043, S1117–23, S1126–30, S1132–50.

grants with their wives.[90] Other benefactors were members of the royal court such as Earl Tostig, the king's foster-mother, Leofrun, Earl Sihtric and Edward's kinsman, Swein.[91] The pool from which the abbey was to draw its benefactors, i.e. officials associated with the royal court and their families, was to be virtually unchanged by the Norman Conquest.

During the Confessor's reign, however, the impetus for monastic expansion came chiefly from the aristocracy. Non-royal lay benefactors favoured monasteries in the eastern half of the country such as Ramsey, Peterborough, Christ Church, Canterbury, now served by a monastic community, and Bury St Edmunds, as well as patronising Westminster abbey.[92] Each of these monasteries secured grants from the king, archbishops and bishops, men and women of comital rank, and landholders of local significance. For the first time significant numbers of non-aristocratic laymen and women appear in the sources as benefactors of the monasteries. It is difficult to decide whether this is a new trend or rather the result of more documents surviving. It could be argued that if such donors had previously favoured secular communities evidence of their generosity would stand a poor chance of survival. However, the fact that these non-aristocratic donors can also be seen patronising secular foundations in this period would suggest that an increase in gift-giving was taking place rather than simply improved data survival. The peaceful domestic conditions that prevailed during the Confessor's reign must have encouraged this state of affairs.

In the reign of Edward the Confessor the upper echelons of English society all supported religious houses, both secular and monastic. Earl Leofric of Mercia and Countess Godgiva were the most active non-royal lay religious patrons. They founded and patronised both houses of canons and Benedictine monks. Around the year 1043 Leofric and Godgiva refounded an impressive Benedictine monastery at Coventry where the earl was to be buried in October 1057.[93] They also patronised Worcester and Evesham abbey, and built the church of Holy Trinity at Evesham.[94] Furthermore, they founded a house of secular canons at Stow St Mary and were patrons of secular communities at Leominster, Wenlock, St John's and St Werburgh's, Chester.[95]

---

[90] S1118–19, S1121.

[91] S1122, S1136–7.

[92] S997, S1106–7, S1109–10, S1229, S1231, S1234, S1490, S1499, S1516, S1519, S1521, S1529–31, S1535, S1608, S1645–7; Hart, *Charters of eastern England*, nos 322–6, 336–8, 343–4, 352–7, 359, 363–8; *The chronicle of Hugh Candidus, a monk of Peterborough*, ed. W. T. Mellows, London 1949, 69–73; *Chron. Ramsey*, 151, 153–4, 157–9, 160, 165, 169, 173, 175.

[93] John Hunt, 'Piety, prestige, or politics? The house of Leofric and the foundation and patronage of Coventry priory', in George Demidowicz (ed.), *Coventry's first cathedral*, Stamford 1994, 97–117 at p. 101.

[94] Ibid. 104. Hemming, at Worcester, severely criticised Leofric's family: A. Williams, '"Cockles amongst the wheat": Danes and English in the western midlands in the first half of the eleventh century', *Midland History* xi (1986), 1–22 at pp. 13–14.

[95] *Anglo-Saxon charters*, nos lxxviii, cxv.

Members of Leofric's family also had connections with the Fenland houses. They were patrons of Crowland and Peterborough, while his nephew and namesake was abbot at Peterborough (1052–66) and held in addition Burton, Coventry and Thorney.[96] In the middle years of the eleventh century, Odda of Deerhurst, possibly a descendant of Ealdorman Ælfhere, built a chapel dedicated to the Holy Trinity at Deerhurst in memory of his brother and also founded a monastery at Great Malvern.[97] Odda had at one time wielded considerable authority in the region as in 1051 he was temporarily granted some of Godwin's shires – Cornwall, Devon, Dorset and Somerset.[98] He died in 1056, taking the habit on his death-bed and was buried at Pershore where he was probably a benefactor.[99]

The powerful Godwin family, like the family of the earl of Mercia, did not ignore secular foundations: if anything they seemed to prefer them to monastic institutions.[100] The only known gifts of Earl Godwin of Wessex, father-in-law of Edward the Confessor, were to Old Minster, Winchester, in preparation for his burial.[101] Godwin may also have had a hand in the great minster of Bosham, located on his demesne manor in the heart of his holdings in Sussex.[102] His Danish wife, Gytha, had a reputation for religion. She refounded Hartland in Devonshire as a secular college, where twelve canons appear in 1086. Another of her minster churches was Nether Wallop, in Hampshire, and when widowed she patronised St Mary's, Exeter.[103] Earl Harold refounded the collegiate church at Waltham, in Essex, and his daughter, Gunnilda, became a nun at Wilton where her aunt, Queen Edith, was to join her after 1066.[104] Harold did not found Benedictine monasteries, but the *Peterborough chronicle* claimed that he patronised Peterborough abbey c. 1060. He was remembered in the Durham *liber vitae* and he was also known to have been good friends with St Wulfstan and to have visited Rome, and made

---

[96] Ibid. 467. For the patronage of Countess Godiva, her brother, Thorold of Buckenhale, Leofric's father, Leofwine, and Norman, the sheriff, possibly Leofric's brother see Knowles and Hadcock, *Medieval religious houses*, 58, 77; F. M. Page, *The estates of Crowland abbey*, Cambridge 1934, 7; *Chron. Hugh Candidus*, 68–72; Hart, *Charters of eastern England*, nos 348, 353; Williams, ' "Cockles amongst the wheat" ', 2, 7.

[97] Barlow, *English Church, 1000–1066*, 61.

[98] Idem, *Edward the Confessor*, 114–15.

[99] Williams, '*Princeps merciorum gentis*', 168.

[100] For Godwin's origins see David G. J. Raraty, 'Earl Godwine of Wessex: the origins of his power and his political loyalties', *History* lxxiv (1989) 3–19.

[101] *The life of King Edward who rests at Westminster*, ed. Frank Barlow, 2nd edn, Oxford 1992, 32.

[102] Barlow, *English Church, 1000–1066*, 190–1; *DB* i. fos 16b, 17b–c. For Bosham see Denton, *English royal free chapels*, 44.

[103] S1236; Barlow, *English Church, 1000–1066*, 58, 190. For Berkeley see B. R. Kemp, 'The churches of Berkeley Hernesse', *Transactions of the Bristol and Gloucestershire Archaeological Society* lxxxvii (1968), 96–110.

[104] For Gunnilda see Eleanor Searle, 'Women and the legitimisation of succession at the Norman Conquest', *Anglo-Norman Studies* iii (1981), 159–70, 226–29 at pp. 167–8, and Sharon K. Elkins, *Holy women of twelfth-century England*, Chapel Hill 1988, 2, 5.

'great gifts'.[105] His efforts to present himself as a benefactor and political player on the national and international stage were paralleled by the actions of his younger brother Tostig. As earl of Northumbria and Northampton he patronised, with his wife Judith of Flanders, the secular community that served Durham cathedral.[106] The couple had also visited the relics of the apostle in Rome.[107]

The number of new secular foundations appears to have equalled, and even exceeded, that of new Benedictine foundations in the reign of Edward the Confessor. Benedictine houses were founded at Coventry, Great Malvern, Spalding, Alkborough and Deerhurst, and secular foundations or refoundations were established at St Martin-le-Grand, St John at Clare, Wimborne, St Frideswide's, Oxford, Kirkdale in Yorkshire and Holy Trinity, Waltham. This was a significant change from Cnut's reign during which new secular foundations were very much in the minority.[108] When Siward, earl of Northumbria from about 1033 onwards, was buried it was in his own foundation, the church of St Olave's, York.[109] Ingelric, a priest, probably founded or refounded St Martin-le-Grand, as a royal college.[110] Orm, the son of Gamel, rebuilt St Gregory's minster, Kirkdale, in the years between 1055 and 1065.[111] Ælfric, son of Wisgar, an important landowner in the eastern counties in the reign of Edward the Confessor, founded the house of secular canons of St John the Baptist at Clare but was also a benefactor of Bury St Edmunds, giving land at Long Melford and half of the church of Stoke to the abbot of Bury.[112] Furthermore, the sum total of secular colleges in 1066 was augmented by a number of Benedictine monasteries, such as Bedford and Cholsey, which had been founded in the tenth century but had later become secular.[113] The impression that the reign of Edward the Confessor was a positive time for the secular foundations is reinforced by the fact that a number of

---

[105] Liber vitae ecclesie Dunelmensis (ed. Thompson); Life of King Edward, 52; Hart, Charters of eastern England, no. 357; Chron. Hugh Candidus, 69–73; Barlow, English Church, 1000–1066, 59. For the popularity of the Roman pilgrimage in Anglo-Saxon England see Veronica Ortenberg, 'Archbishop Sigeric's journey to Rome in 990', Anglo-Saxon England xix (1990), 197–246 at pp. 202–6.

[106] Simeon of Durham, Historia ecclesiae Dunelmensis, in Opera omnia, ed. T. Arnold (Rolls series lxxv, 1882–5), i. 94–5; Life of King Edward, 32. For Judith's career in England see Patrick McGurk and Jane Rosenthal, 'The Anglo-Saxon gospelbooks of Judith, countess of Flanders: their text, make-up and function', Anglo-Saxon England xxiv (1995), 251–308 at pp. 251–2.

[107] Life of King Edward, 52.

[108] Only the church of Waltham was a secular foundation whereas the Benedictines were established at Abbotsbury, Buckfast, Bury, Gloucester, Horton, Minster-in-Thanet, St Benet of Holme, Stow and Thetford.

[109] Knowles and Hadcock, Medieval religious houses, 82.

[110] Blair, 'Secular minster churches', 121.

[111] Ibid.

[112] C. Hart, The Danelaw, London 1992, 69; Stafford, Unification and conquest, 189, 190.

[113] Blair, 'Secular minster churches', 120.

secular cathedral priories were reformed along strict secular lines. Around the year 1051/2 ten of the fifteen sees were held by seculars, in 1057 twelve, but by 1066 only seven.[114] However, only four cathedrals were served by monastic communities. It seems clear that the reign of Edward the Confessor represented a renaissance in the fortunes of the secular communities and that this new phase was cut short by the Norman Conquest.

Monks and clerks in 1066

Monks and clerks fulfilled different but complimentary social and religious functions in pre-Conquest England. King Edgar had not only promoted the monastic cause but also took steps to ensure payment of tithes and, thus, strengthened the minster church system.[115] Æthelred's law codes, likewise, had showed concern that the status of the minster churches should be properly respected.[116] However, there is little indication of what the laity thought of the relative value of the monks and secular canons other than the evidence of their pious actions as benefactors. This evidence is, therefore, crucial. Investigation of these gifts proves that the new reformed monasteries of the tenth century did not have a monopoly of religious patronage, as already emphasised. There is plenty of evidence to show that the aristocracy did not choose to patronise the reformed houses to the complete exclusion of the minsters and nunneries. Old established centres such as Old Minster, Winchester, Christ Church, Canterbury, and non-reformed minsters and non-reformed monasteries 'remained favourites' with Anglo-Saxon patrons.[117] By the eleventh century patronage of the monasteries had ceased to be the sole preserve of royalty and the aristocracy, and the monasteries and colleges had both become firmly woven into the fabric of eleventh-century local society. But it is also hard to resist the conclusion that the Benedictines received many more grants of a substantial nature from the highest echelons of Anglo-Saxon society than the minsters south of the Humber ever did. The comparative evidence in lay wills and the difference in landholding patterns in 1066 also support this impression. As far as landholding was concerned, the overwhelming majority of the secular foundations were just not in the same league as the monasteries. Domesday records that, as a group, the Benedictines had control of approximately one-sixth of the land south of the Humber.[118] Furthermore, by 1066 the communities at Bury St Edmunds, Abingdon, Chertsey and Worcester had been granted control of large

114 Barlow, *English Church, 1000–1066*, 77.
115 Cambridge and Rollason, 'Debate: pastoral organisation', 101; *English historical documents*, I: c. 500–1042, 431–3.
116 Ibid. 448–9.
117 Stafford, *Unification and conquest*, 190.
118 Burton, *Monastic and religious orders*, 9.

Map 1. Pre-Conquest Benedictine monasteries (including cells)

BERKSHIRE
1. Abingdon

CAMBRIDGESHIRE
2. Ely
3. Thorney

CORNWALL
4. Bodmin

DEVON
5. Buckfast
6. Tavistock

DORSET
7. Cerne
8. Abbotsbury
9. Cranborne
10. Milton
11. Horton
12. Sherbourne Cathedral

GLOUCESTERSHIRE
13. Deerhurst
14. Tewkesbury
15. Gloucester, St Peter
16. Winchcombe

HAMPSHIRE
17. Winchester, New Minster
    Old Minster Cathedral

HERTFORDSHIRE
18. St Albans

HUNTINGDONSHIRE
19. Ramsey
20. St Ives
21. St Neots

KENT
22. Canterbury, St Augustine's
    Christ Church Cathedral
23. Minster in Thanet

LINCOLNSHIRE
24. Alkborough
25. Crowland
26. Spalding
27. Stow

MIDDLESEX
28. Westminster

NORFOLK
29. St Benet of Holme
30. Thetford

NORTHUMBRIA
31. Coquet Island

NORTHAMPTONSHIRE
32. Peterborough
33. Peakirk

OXFORDSHIRE
34. Eynsham

SOMERSET
35. Athelney
36. Bath
37. Bruton
38. Glastonbury
39. Mulchelney

STAFFORDSHIRE
40. Burton

SUFFOLK
41. Rumburgh
42. Bury St Edmunds

SURREY
43. Chertsey

WARWICKSHIRE
44. Coventry

WILTSHIRE
45. Malmesbury

WORCESTERSHIRE
46. Evesham
47. Pershore
48. Worcester Cathedral

NUNNERIES
49. Amesbury, Wilts
50. Barking, Essex
51. Chatteris, Cambs
52. Nunnaminster,
    Winchester, Hants
53. Polesworth, Warw
54. Romsey, Hants
55. Shaftesbury, Dorset
56. Wherwell, Hants
57. Wilton, Wilts

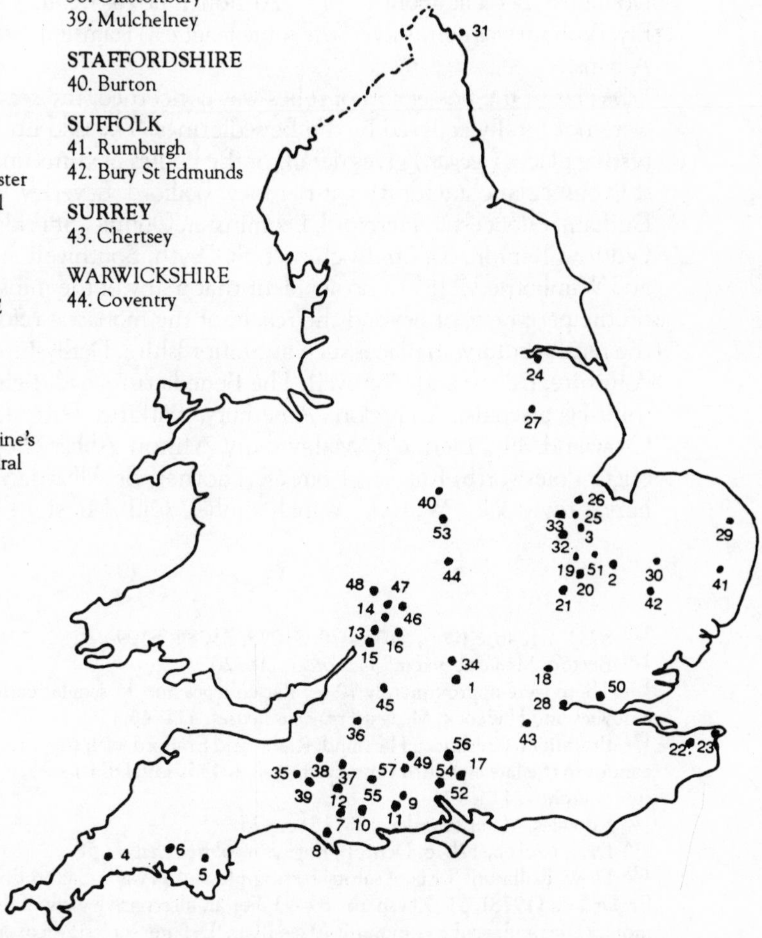

Source of information: D. Knowles and R. N. Hadcock, *Medieval religious houses: England and Wales*, 2nd edn, London 1971.

administrative districts in their respective regions.[119] These monasteries wielded considerable power in their localities, none greater than Bury St Edmunds with its eight and a half hundreds.

On the other hand, the secular communities had a monopoly of religious life in the kingdom north of the Humber, in Wales, along the borders with Wales and in Cornwall (see maps 1 and 2),[120] and secular colleges were more numerous than the monasteries, almost double the number.[121] The secular communities were admittedly of modest size, never supporting more than thirteen canons, but some of the Benedictine houses were even smaller.[122] Gloucester reportedly had only two monks and eight boys in 1072; Evesham and Worcester supported twelve monks each; St Benet of Holme supported twenty-six monks in the 1020s; Old and New Minster, Winchester, probably only averaged together between forty and fifty monks.[123] The seculars also included a few very wealthy institutions amongst their number. In 1066 the minster at Bosham had held lands in Sussex and Hampshire valued in Domesday Book at about £344.[124] Although not as wealthy as Glastonbury or Ely, Bosham was certainly in the same league as Ramsey, Peterborough and St Albans.

As far as the possession of relics was concerned, the secular communities were not totally eclipsed by the Benedictines. The Old English list of saints' resting places (secgan) gives details of the bodies of saints under the guardianship of secular communities at Bardney, Bedford, Beverley, Charlbury, Derby, Durham, Gloucester, Hereford, Leominster, Oundle, St Frideswide at Oxford, Padstow, Repton, Ripon, Rochester, St Osyth, Southwell, Stafford, Wenlock and Wimborne.[125] It was no accident that many of the minsters were located on the periphery, or beyond the reach, of the monastic reform movement of the tenth century, in places such as Staffordshire, Derbyshire, Yorkshire, Lincolnshire, Devon and Cornwall. The Benedictines had slightly more of these spiritual arsenals: Abingdon, Amesbury, Barking, Burton, Bury, Chertsey, Crowland, Ely, Lichfield, Malmesbury, Milton Abbas, Pershore, Peterborough, Polesworth, Ramsey, Romsey, Thorney, St Albans, St Neots, Shaftesbury, Tavistock, Wilton, Winchcombe, Old Minster, Winchester and

---

[119] S731, S1046, S1066, S1069–70, S1078, S1084, S1094.

[120] Burton, Monastic and religious orders, 18–20.

[121] There were approximately 70 secular colleges and 11 secular cathedral communities: Knowles and Hadcock, Medieval religious houses, 411–46.

[122] Bromfield, Credition, Hartland, Ripon and Stafford each supported twelve or thirteen canons in the late eleventh century: ibid. 424, 435, 439; DB i. fo. 252b; Blair, 'Secular minster churches', 114, 121.

[123] Knowles, Monastic order, 126, 181n, 425.

[124] DB i. fos 16b, 17b–c; Denton, English royal free chapels, 58.

[125] D. W. Rollason, 'Lists of saints' resting-places in Anglo-Saxon England', Anglo-Saxon England vii (1978), 61–93 esp. pp. 89–93. For an alternative view of the ratio between the monasteries and secular communities see Blair, 'Debate: ecclesiastical organisation', 202n.

Map 2. Pre-Conquest secular colleges

BEFORDSHIRE
1. Bedford

CHESHIRE
2. Chester, St John
   Chester, St Werburgh

CORNWALL
3. Crantock
4. Launceston
5. Probus
6. St Buryan
7. St Germans
8. Plympton

DERBYSHIRE
9. Derby, All Saints
   Derby, St Alkmund

DEVON
10. Axminster
11. Exeter Cathedral
12. Crediton
12. Cullompton
13. Hartland
14. South Molton

DORSET
15. Wimborne

ESSEX
16. Waltham

GLOUCESTERSHIRE
17. Berkeley
18. Bristol
19. Cirencester
20. Gloucester, St Oswald

HAMPSHIRE
21. Christchurch

HEREFORDSHIRE
22. Bromyard
23. Hereford, St Guthlac
   Hereford Cathedral

KENT
24. Dover
25. Rochester Cathedral

LEICESTERSHIRE
26. Leicester, St Martin

LONDON
27. London, St Martin-le-Grand
   London, St Paul's Cathedral

NORFOLK
28. Elmham Cathedral
29. Thetford, St Mary

NORTHUMBRIA
30. Durham Cathedral

NOTTINGHAMSHIRE
31. Southwell

OXFORDSHIRE
32. Dorchester Cathedral
33. Oxford, St Fridewide

SHROPSHIRE
34. Alberbury
35. Bromfield
36. Condover
37. Ellesmere
38. Morville
39. Much Wenlock
40. Oswestry
41. Pontesbury
42. Prees
43. Shrewsbury, St Alkmund
   Shrewsbury, St Chad
   Shrewsbury, St Julian
   Shrewsbury, St Mary
   Shrewsbury, St Michael
44. Shifnal
45. Wroxeter

SOMERSET
46. Taunton
47. Wells Cathedral

STAFFORDSHIRE
48. Great Ness
49. Lichfield
   Cathedral
50. Penkridge
51. Stafford
52. Tamworth
53. Tettenhall
54. Wolverhampton

SUFFOLK
55. Clare
56. Glemsford
57. Hoxne
58. Sudbury

SURREY
59. Southwark

SUSSEX
60. Arundel
61. Bosham
62. Boxgrove
63. South Malling
64. Selsey Cathedral
65. Steyning

WARWICKSHIRE
66. Warwick, All Saints

YORKSHIRE
67. Beverley
68. Ripon
69. York Cathedral

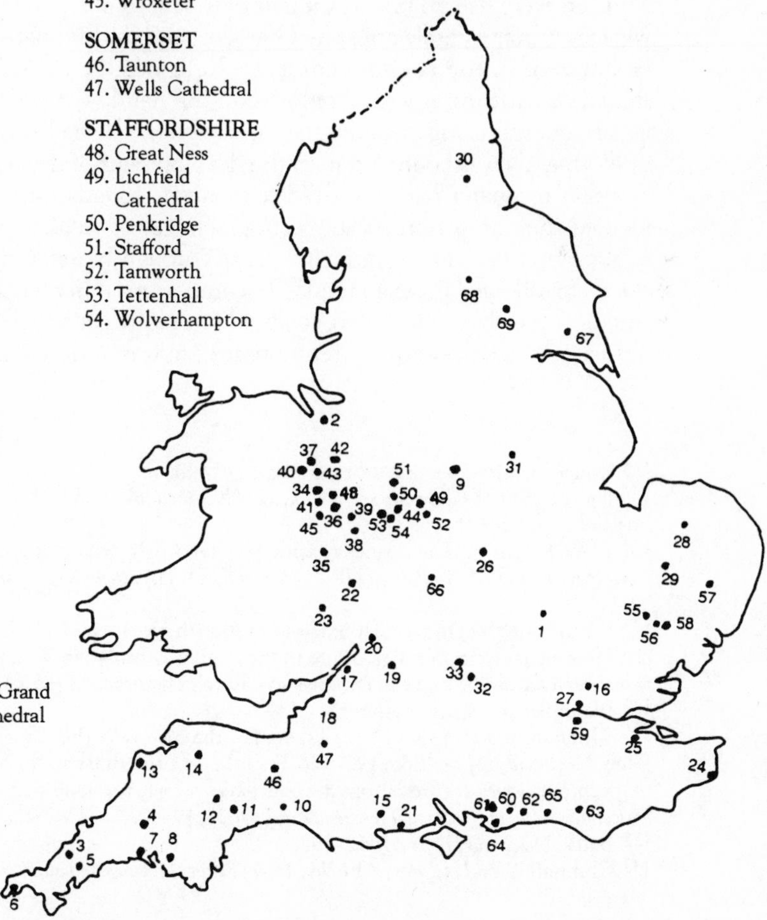

Source of information: D. Knowles and R. N. Hadcock, *Medieval religious houses: England and Wales*, 2nd edn, London 1971.

Worcester.[126] Furthermore, at Peterborough, Thorney and Old Minster, Winchester, the monks possessed the relics of a considerable number of saints. The possession of relics was not only prestigious for their community but could also be a potent spiritual and political tool. The communities that attended the incorrupt bodies of Edmund and Cuthbert knew this and used it to their advantage to create well-defined political, economic and spiritual zones around them.[127] Pilgrims and benefactors recognised the distinctive status relics conferred upon their guardians. The political importance of a town and the possession of a saint's relic often went hand in hand, as was the case at Bedford, Buckingham and Northampton.[128] The significance of the possession of relics by secular communities should not be underestimated. Relics were important assets and a new generation could easily choose to exploit them to their full.

1066 and after

Minsters were still an important part of the picture in 1066.[129] They were not wiped out immediately after the Conquest and minster parishes continued to be different in the twelfth century.[130] Religious life in Normandy, after all, shared many features with Anglo-Saxon England, with its own blend of collegiate churches and Benedictine monasteries.[131] The history of the Church in Normandy was bound up with the development of ducal authority.[132] The Norman magnates had initially left monastic foundations to the dukes and focused their attention on supporting colleges of secular canons, but by the 1030s monastic reform gradually spread through Normandy as the vassals of the duke followed his example.[133] The important difference from the English situation was that monastic revival did not really get under way in the duchy until almost a half century after monasticism was 'restored' in England. Thus,

---

126 Rollason, 'Lists of saints' resting-places', 87–93.
127 For the right of sanctuary see J. C. Cox, *The sanctuaries and sanctuary seekers of medieval England*, London 1911.
128 D. W. Rollason, 'The shrines of saints in later Anglo-Saxon England: distribution and significance', in L. A. Butler and R. K. Morris (eds), *The Anglo-Saxon Church*, London 1986, 32–50 at p. 40.
129 For the subject of the secular orders after 1066 in general see C. N. L. Brooke, 'Monk and canon: some patterns of religious life in the twelfth century', in W. J. Sheils (ed.), *Monks, hermits and the ascetic tradition* (Studies in Church History xii 1985), 109–29.
130 Blair, 'Secular minster churches', 139.
131 Chibnall, *World of Orderic Vitalis*, 46. For the history of the Church in Normandy see Bates, *Normandy before 1066*, 190–226. For other continental parallels see J. F. Lemarignier, 'Aspects politiques des fondations des collegiales dans le royaume de France au XIme siècle, *Miscellanea del centro di studi medievali* iii (1962), 19–40.
132 Bates, *Normandy before 1066*, 192.
133 Chibnall, *World of Orderic Vitalis*, 46–7; Bates, *Normandy before 1066*, 192.

1066 caught the monastic cause in Normandy at a more intense stage of development than in England.

The English minsters still had influence at the turn of the twelfth century as they remained popular with patrons for a more than a generation after 1066. Many were rebuilt, reorganised or newly founded. The Norman kings still maintained some of the greater minster churches, such as those at St Martin-le-Grand, Dover and Stafford, as usual sources of patronage for royal clerks.[134] Indeed, St Martin-le-Grand acquired the bulk of its endowment in the century after 1066.[135] In Cornwall and Devon, with little competition from Benedictine monasteries, it must be presumed that the minster church system was still thriving at least until 1068 when the arrival of the Bretons and Normans instituted 'considerable change' in the region.[136] William the Conqueror patronised St Probus, Bishop Leofric granted lands to St Germans and Earl Brian endowed a chapel at Launceston, Cornwall.[137] New colleges, non-parochial, were founded on some post-Conquest honors. For example, William de Braose founded a college at Bramber castle in 1073 and Robert d'Oilly built the church of St George in Oxford castle in 1074.[138] In Henry I's reign there were still many small collegiate bodies, 'some based on old minsters and others recent, which bore the stamp of Anglo-Norman patronage'.[139]

However, the coming of the Normans resulted in the impoverishment of many minsters as tithes were diverted to the new overlord's chosen monastery.[140] All Christians were meant to pay tithes to the church where they received the sacraments and, strictly speaking, that included monks who were forbidden to receive tithes.[141] One of the significant changes in the eleventh century was the church reform movement which discouraged laymen from holding tithes or proprietary churches.[142] This led to the accumulation of tithes and churches by monasteries. The tithes came to the monasteries by a number of different routes; through usurpation, by payment from their proprietary churches, by episcopal grants, or from lay men by gift, exchange,

---

134 Blair, 'Secular minster churches', 132–3.
135 Denton, *English royal free chapels*, 25.
136 D. F. Carley, 'Norman Conquest of Devon and Cornwall, 1067–1086', unpubl. M.Litt. diss. Oxford 1989, 162.
137 Ibid. 152, 162.
138 Blair, 'Secular minster churches', 135; Richard Morris, *Churches in the landscape*, London 1989, 171. For a discussion of Robert's patronage of the Augustinian priory at Oseney see R. W. Southern, *Western society and the Church in the Middle Ages*, London 1970, 245–6.
139 Blair, 'Secular minster churches', 137.
140 Ibid. 125.
141 Giles Constable, *Monastic tithes: from their origins to the twelfth century*, Cambridge 1964, 57.
142 For a brief summary of the movement see Karl F. Morrison, 'The Gregorian reform', in Bernard McGinn and John Meyendorff (eds), *Christian spirituality: origins to the twelfth century*, New York 1985.

restoration or sale.[143] Thus, by the twelfth century, 'most monks received tithes and many were freed from payment'.[144]

Many minsters lost their endowments, as did those in Cornwall to the likes of Robert of Mortain and Baldwin, sheriff of Devon, and were dissolved.[145] Some Benedictine foundations suffered similar hardships to the minsters; St Benet's of Holme also lost property, and others such as St Neots and Spalding were given as cells to Norman monasteries. However, unlike many of the Benedictine houses that suffered in the first generation after 1066, the minsters never recovered their pre-Conquest position. Lanfranc's reforms 'hastened the demise of the old minsters' and encouraged the trend towards smaller churches serving individual parishes with a permanent priest.[146] Furthermore, with the coming of the Augustinians in the early twelfth century, the minsters' position was hijacked and many were converted into Augustinian, and also sometimes Cluniac, houses.[147] By 1135 half of all Augustinian houses had been converted from existing secular colleges.[148] The secular chapters serving cathedrals were also not immune to the changes brought by the Norman Conquest. As Lanfranc was a monk himself, and he accepted using monasticism as a principal instrument of reform, he was inclined to replace secular chapters with monastic ones, as was rapidly done at Durham and Rochester. Indeed, within fifty years of the Conquest, the number of monastic cathedral chapters rose from four to nine.

The intractable problem of the nature and survival of the source material means that a full picture of the experience of the secular colleges can never be achieved. The sources do indicate that minster churches were being supported in the locality. Many members of the laity continued to make small grants and cash gifts and to found new secular communities in Devonshire, Dorset, Hampshire, Lincolnshire, Oxfordshire, Staffordshire, Suffolk and Yorkshire. With the Conquest, however, the ties of kinship, lordship and locality that these religious communities, both monastic and secular, had built up were swept away with the wholesale removal of the Anglo-Saxon aristocracy. It was not the Norman Conquest itself that brought about the demise of the minster churches; indeed they at first appeared just as likely to survive the storm as the monasteries. The Conquest, however, resulted in England being directly exposed to the wider institutional and cultural changes that were

---

[143] Ibid. 65–6. See also B. R. Kemp, 'Monastic possession of parish churches in the twelfth century', Journal of Ecclesiastical History xxxi (1980), 133–60.

[144] Constable, Monastic tithes, 1.

[145] Carley, 'Norman Conquest of Devon and Cornwall', 164.

[146] C. J. Bond, 'Church and parish in Norman Worcestershire', in John Blair, Minsters and parish churches: the local Church in transition 950–1200, Oxford 1988, 119–58 at p. 137.

[147] M. J. Franklin, 'The secular college as a focus for Anglo-Norman piety: St Augustine's, Daventry', ibid. 97–104 at p. 102. See also Southern, Western society, 240–50; J. C. Dickinson, The origins of the Austin canons and their introduction into England, London 1950, 108–29; Burton, Monastic and religious orders, 45–52.

[148] Blair, 'Secular minster churches', 138.

taking place in Latin Christendom.[149] The growth of institutional structures within the religious orders made the unreformed minster churches look increasing anomalous.[150] Thus it was the rise of the new religious orders in the late eleventh and twelfth centuries that dealt the fatal blow.

[149] See Robert Bartlett, *The making of medieval Europe: conquest, colonization and cultural change, 950–1350*, London 1993, 243–68.
[150] Ibid. 255–60.

PART ONE

THE CASE STUDIES

2

St Mary's, Abingdon

Abingdon has been chosen as the starting point for this part of the book because of the sheer range of experiences it underwent after the Conquest.
Taken individually these events illustrate many of the different features that
characterised the history of the English monasteries after the Norman Conquest. From 1066 to 1135 this moderately wealthy monastery suffered discrimination, both negative and positive, as well as the removal of its English
abbot, the spoliation of its lands, serious financial loss, the imposition of
knight service, as well as the beneficial effects of a particularly adept and
charismatic Italian abbot, Faritius. The wheel of fortune was to turn full circle
more than once for Abingdon.

The wealth of primary source material has also influenced the decision to
use Abingdon as a starting point. The post-Conquest history of the abbey is
well served by a lengthy and detailed chronicle, Domesday Book and a
number of related feudal and tenurial surveys.[1] The Abingdon chronicle survives in three thirteenth-century manuscripts: BL, MSS Cotton Claudius C
ix, Cotton Claudius B vi and Cotton Vitellius A xiii. Unfortunately, these
manuscripts are not without their problems, and these were compounded,
not elucidated, by the deficient edition of the chronicle printed in 1858.[2]
Although BL, MS Cotton Claudius C ix is the earliest of the three manuscripts, BL, MS Cotton Claudius B vi, written around fifty years later, has
been considered a 'revised and improved copy' of the first.[3] However, the
information recorded in each varies significantly in the degree of coverage
and reliability for the different periods of the abbey's history. BL, MS Cotton
Claudius B vi has been deemed of 'inferior authority' to C ix in matters relating to the foundation of the abbey.[4] BL, Cotton Claudius C ix appears to be
merely a transcript of a manuscript written sometime before 1170 by an
Abingdon monk, whereas the author of Claudius B vi continued to add new
entries down to the accession of Richard I.[5] Despite these difficulties, the
chronicle can be regarded as trustworthy for the post-Conquest era. Its author

---

[1] For Abingdon and its sources see F. M. Stenton, *The early history of the abbey of Abingdon*,
Reading 1913, 1–4; D. C. Douglas, 'Some early surveys from the abbey of Abingdon', *English
Historical Review* xliv (1929), 618–25; D. D. James, 'A translation and study of the *Chronicon
monasterii de Abingdon*', unpubl. Ph.D. diss. Rice 1986.
[2] For comments on the shortcomings of Stevenson's edition see Stenton, *Early history of
Abingdon*, 1–4.
[3] Ibid. 2.
[4] Ibid. 4.
[5] Ibid. 5.

was a member of the community from sometime before 1117, making him an eye-witness for the latter part of Henry I's reign and placing him in an excellent position to harvest the reminiscences and documents of his elders.[6] Indeed, the chronicle is not just useful as a record of the grants given to the abbey but also for establishing the social and political context within which these donations were made. The abbey's relations with the laity encompassed the local community, royal officials and the royal family. Indeed, without a wider discussion of Abingdon's post-Conquest fortunes the full significance of the religious patronage that it received cannot be fully appreciated.

Abingdon abbey had been at the heart, in both practical and intellectual terms, of the monastic reform movement that flourished during Edgar's reign in the tenth century.[7] It was the monastic rule that Æthelwold developed at Abingdon, the *Regularis concordia*, that was to become the liturgical manual for all the monasteries in pre-Conquest England.[8] King Edgar's personal support for Abingdon, fired by his long acquaintance with Æthelwold and Abingdon itself since childhood, was lavish and only outstripped by his enthusiasm for Old Minster, Winchester.[9] Besides restoring land at Bessels Leigh, Goosey, Longworth and West Ginge, all in Oxfordshire, he made numerous other grants of land, all within a fifteen-mile radius of the abbey: at Cumnor, Denchworth, Drayton, Fifield, Hanney, Hendred and Marcham, in Oxfordshire; and in Beedon and Oare, in Berkshire. Edgar made several grants further afield, but still in the south-west; land in Bedwyn and Burbage, in Wiltshire, a vineyard at Watchet, in Somerset, and royal dues at Southampton, as well as land at Hurstborne Tarrant and Ringwood, both in Hampshire.[10] The early years of Æthelred's reign witnessed a sharp, but ultimately temporary, decline in the abbey's fortunes as its wealth and privileges were trimmed to help fund the king's advancement of his supporters.[11] After c. 993 Æthelred reversed this policy and even chose to make good losses for which Edward the Martyr was responsible.[12] Cnut, Harthacnut and, to an even greater extent, Edward the Confessor all chose to uphold the close royal bond with Abingdon.[13] Cnut granted land twice, with a *monasteriolum* in Oxford on the first occasion, Harthacnut made one grant of land, and in the 1050s Edward the Confessor made three grants of land close to the abbey in

---

6 Ibid. 4–5.
7 Blair, *Anglo-Saxon Oxfordshire*, 113–14.
8 *Regularis concordia*.
9 Edgar's grants to the abbey were extensive: *Chronicon monasterii de Abingdon*, ed. J. Stevenson (Rolls series ii, 1858), i. 256–77, 279–83, 314–43; S673, S682, S688–90, S700–1, S708, S724, S732–4, S756–60. Edgar also made a grant to Bishop Æthelwold: S714; *Chron. Abingdon*, i. 337–9.
10 For the distribution of these estates see C. J. Bond, 'The reconstruction of a medieval landscape: the estates of Abingdon abbey', *Landscape History* i (1979), 59–75 at pp. 60–2.
11 S876, S918.
12 Burbage, Hurstbourne Tarrant and Bedwyn had been confiscated by Edward the Martyr, for which compensation was given by Æthelred: S688, S689, S756, S937.
13 S843, S896–7, S918, S937, S964, S967, S993, S1020, S1023, S1025, S1065–6.

Oxfordshire and Berkshire.[14] One of these grants was made in association with Queen Edith, and, importantly, Edward also granted the abbey control over the hundred of Hormer, in Berkshire.[15] Edward also used Abingdon to support his favoured servants and kinsmen; he appointed Spearhavoc, his goldsmith, abbot c. 1047, and on his brief promotion to the bishopric of London, in 1051, Edward appointed his aged and frail kinsman Rodulf (1051–2) as abbot.[16]

The English kings were not the only munificent patrons of Abingdon. A small but significant group of aristocratic men and women were generous benefactors in the second half of the tenth and the early eleventh centuries.[17] Between them these noble men and women, an archbishop, local landholders and a Dane gave land at more than eleven locations in Berkshire, Oxfordshire, and further afield in Buckinghamshire and Gloucestershire.[18] However, it was the abbey's relationship with one man in particular, Earl Harold, that was to have the most profound effect on its post-Conquest career. The Godwin family's involvement with the abbey was of course a mixed blessing. It was at Harold's suggestion that in 1054 Edward the Confessor granted four hides at Sandford on Thames, which Earl Godwin had previously held, to Abingdon abbey.[19] Harold also supported Abbot Ordric (1052–66) over the disputed manor of Leckhampstead and it was also on Harold's advice that the wealthy Thorkell had decided to commend himself to the abbot.[20] However, during the course of Edward's reign, Drayton, which had been granted to Abingdon by King Æthelred, had come into the possession of Earls Godwin and Harold.[21] Furthermore, in 1066 Blackman the priest held the three estates granted to Abingdon by Edward the Confessor, Sandford on Thames, Chilton and Leverton, not from the abbey, but from Harold himself.[22]

In October 1066 Abbot Ealdred (1066–71) had only recently been installed; he was one of Harold's few appointments.[23] Unsurprisingly, Abingdon's connections with the Godwin regime were to cause difficulties for the abbey and the Norman Conquest instigated a period of great insecurity. Ealdred initially submitted to William the Conqueror and it would appear that he was fairly successful in managing to steer his abbey through its early problems. He was fortunate in that he managed to secure the return of the three

[14] S876, S897, S918, S937, S964, S967, S993, S1020, S1023, S1025, S1066; Chron. Abingdon, i. 452–5, 464–74.
[15] For Edith's involvement in this grant, resulting from a visit to Abingdon, see ibid. i. 459–61, and Barlow, Edward the Confessor, 85.
[16] Chron. Abingdon, i. 462–4; Barlow, Edward the Confessor, 104–5.
[17] S1484; Chron. Abingdon, i. 416–17, 428–9; DB i, fo. 59b.
[18] Ælfric, archbishop, bequeathed part of Dumbleton, Gloucestershire, to Abingdon and part to Ælfnoth, for life, with reversion to Abingdon: S1488.
[19] S1022, S1025; Chron. Abingdon, i. 466–72.
[20] Ibid. i. 475, 484.
[21] DB i, fos 60b, 61d.
[22] Ibid. i, fo. 58d.
[23] Chron. Abingdon, i. 482.

abbey estates when their tenant, Blackman the priest, fled the country with Harold Godwin's mother, Gytha.[24] This led to the estates being taken into the king's hands, and Abbot Ealdred was only able 'with the greatest difficulty' to secure their return.[25] However, all this was jeopardised when Ealdred threw in his lot with the rebellion of some of the abbey's men against William in 1071. This turn of events effectively halted the return of other alienated estates. The chronicler makes this evident by saying that 'the abbot was successful in this case, and he might have proved his rights in other instances where lands had been alienated from the abbey if he had not incurred the enmity of the king'.[26] After the rebellion failed and Ealdred was imprisoned, the abbey was exposed to assault from the newcomers.[27] It was savagely plundered of the valuables deposited there by the English.[28] Some of the abbey's 'pilferers' were of very high rank indeed. Queen Matilda ordered the monks to send her their most precious ornament. The abbot and monks carefully made their selection and obediently sent it to the queen. Matilda, however, was not impressed by their choice, spurned it, and demanded another, much more impressive, specimen.[29] The seizure of the abbey's own gold, silver, vessels, books and vestments by royal officials was even more distressing for the monks.[30] Throughout its post-Conquest history Abingdon's relationship with royal officials was often precarious and troublesome. The chronicler bitterly declared that in the early years of the Conquest royal officials 'inflicted many injuries [. . .] upon the men occupying the remaining possessions of the abbey'.[31] Two officials, in particular, were singled out for criticism; Walter fitz Other, of whom the chronicler sardonically remarked that 'it profited no one to oppose him', and Sheriff Froger who was accused of being 'beset by stupidity as long as he lived'.[32] The upheaval and confusion that the Conquest brought to the region also resulted in the seizure of a number of abbey estates. Henry de Ferrers, for example, took control of two abbey estates after the former holders, Thorkell and Godric the sheriff, had been killed in battle.[33] Furthermore, the abbey failed to secure the return of South Cerney, in Gloucestershire, which Archbishop Stigand had allegedly obtained by force from the abbey in about 1056.[34] Similarly, the abbey had difficulties in

---

[24] Ibid. i. 484. For Edward's grants see S1020, S1023, S1025; DB i, fos 156d, 159b.
[25] In 1066 these three estates were worth over £11 and assessed at just over 21½ hides.
[26] Chron. Abingdon, i. 484, 486.
[27] ASC 'D' and 'E', 1071; Chron. Abingdon, i. 482; ii. 282–3, 493.
[28] Ibid. i. 493.
[29] Ibid. i. 485.
[30] Ibid. i. 495.
[31] Ibid. ii. 2.
[32] Ibid. i. 486, 494; ii, 7.
[33] Ibid. i. 485.
[34] S896, S897; DB i, fo. 169a; Chron. Abingdon, i. 373–7, 462–3.

regaining control over the manor of Leckhampstead which had been previously leased to Brihtmund and his family for the duration of three lives.[35]

The Thames valley region was of great strategic importance in the early days of the Conquest. The initial instability of the region, exacerbated by Ealdred's rebellion, meant the abbey was not to be considered for a favourably low quota of knight service. The abbey's assessment of thirty knights was fairly standard for a house of its wealth, but it was certainly not as advantageous as those settled upon some much richer houses: St Augustine's, Canterbury, for example, which was about £170 richer than Abingdon in 1086, owed only fifteen knights; Winchester, Old Minster, which was about £138 richer, did not owe any knights at all; and Ramsey abbey, which was only £104 poorer, owed only four men. Conversely, Abingdon had a lighter assessment than Peterborough abbey, which, although it was £139 poorer than Abingdon in 1086, owed sixty knights.[36]

The Abingdon chronicler held a generally unfavourable view of the new Norman abbot, Athelhelm (1071–83), a monk from Jumièges, as did the handful of Abingdon monks who temporarily deserted the abbey after his appointment.[37] It is not known why they left but the chronicler deplored the imposition of a large number of knights on the abbey estates, resulting in the loss of direct control over this land. The chronicler reported that the abbot assigned manors from the church's possessions to his kinsmen, in each case stating the terms of service.[38] However, some of this enfeoffment may well have also served the purpose of restoring control, even if it was indirect, over 'lost' estates.[39] Alfyard's sons, who were the pre-Conquest tenants at Lyford, in Berkshire, had chosen to commend themselves to Walter Giffard 'without the abbot's command'.[40] By 1086 the abbey had secured its title to Lyford, with Walter installed as the military tenant. The enfeoffment of the abbey's knights continued into the abbacies of Athelhelm's successors. These enfeoffments tended to be on an occasional basis and were usually used as a means of regaining rights over an appropriated estate.[41] The encroachment of the royal forest of Windsor on four hides of abbey land at Winkfield was another infringement on the abbey's rights which Athelhelm appears to have been powerless to rebuff.[42]

---

[35] Brithwin, Brithmund's youngest son, had the lease extended by Abbot Siward (1030–44) but was later compelled to restore it: *Chron. Abingdon*, i. 457, 475, 477–9.

[36] Knowles, *Monastic order*, 702–3.

[37] *The letters of Lanfranc archbishop of Canterbury*, ed. H. Clover and M. Gibson, Oxford 1979, no. 28.

[38] *Chron. Abingdon*, ii. 3–4, 283–4. For a discussion of this enfeoffment see John Gillingham, 'The introduction of knight service into England', *Anglo-Norman Studies* iv (1981), 53–64, 181–7 at p. 57.

[39] This was certainly the case at Ely: Miller, *Abbey and bishopric of Ely*, 68.

[40] *DB* i, fo. 59a.

[41] *Chron. Abingdon*, ii. 134–5. Herbert the chamberlain restored one hide in Farnborough and the service of one knight for the land of Leckhampstead, Berkshire.

[42] Ibid. i. 7; *DB* i, fo. 59b.

Continental abbots may have been considered by the Normans more acceptable and reliable than the Englishmen they replaced, but that alone did not automatically guarantee them royal favour. Royal intervention in the case of the unfortunate soldier, Hermer, who had been severely mutilated by pirates, resulted in the abbey's demesne lands being diminished.[43] Abbot Athelhelm was supposed to endow Hermer with abbey lands but decided not to on account of his injuries. However, Hermer successfully appealed to the king and was granted abbey land at Denchworth, Oxfordshire. The abbot was also caught out when the political wind changed direction in 1082. When Athelhelm purchased the manor of Nuneham Courtenay, in Oxfordshire, he had had the transaction confirmed by Odo of Bayeux in William the Conqueror's absence from England.[44] Odo's arrest in 1082 led the king to resolve that 'all those who had been helped by Odo's influence deserved his displeasure', and he revoked the abbey's confirmation and gave the property to another unnamed person. It is significant that Abbot Athelhelm was augmenting his abbey's possessions by purchasing new lands. He was one of the few abbots, of the Old English houses anyway, to be in a position to do this during the first twenty years after the Conquest. As well as buying Nuneham Courtenay, he also purchased land from an Englishman, Thorkell of Arden. This land comprised two hides in Hill and two hides in Chesterton, both in Warwickshire; one purchased and one held 'in pledge' by the abbot, together worth 150s. in 1086.[45]

The very fact that the abbey was able to afford to make these purchases suggests that despite the increase in enfeoffment and the handful of losses that were still outstanding in 1086, an efficient administration was in operation at Abingdon. This is borne out by Domesday Book: by 1086 the abbey's holdings had increased from approximately £458 18s. 3d. in value in 1066, to about £521 14s. 3d. in 1086.[46] Thus, the abbey's holdings value increased by £62 16s. 0d., in other words by 13 per cent over twenty years.[47] On a county-wide basis 70 per cent of Berkshire holdings fell in value after 1066 and 45 per cent failed to reach their pre-Conquest values by 1086.[48] The figures for Abingdon reflect trends similar to those found in Berkshire as a whole. By 1086 the value of Berkshire's manors had dropped by 17 per cent. Yet, out of forty-two of the abbey's holdings, for which values have been recorded for both 1066 and 1086, eighteen had declined in value, fourteen had risen and ten had maintained their value. In 1066 the abbey's lands were rated at

43 Chron. Abingdon, i. 6.
44 Ibid. ii. 9. On Odo's role in William the Conqueror's absence see D. Bates, 'The origins of the justiciarship', Anglo-Norman Studies iv (1982), 1–12, 167–71.
45 Chron. Abingdon, ii. 20–1.
46 This figure includes the rents from the abbey's houses in Wallingford and Oxford.
47 The figure for 1086 also includes the 'gifts' purchased from Thorkell of Arden after 1066: ibid. ii. 20–1.
48 R. W. Finn, The Norman Conquest and its effects on the economy: 1066–1086, London 1971, 78.

around 557 hides, whereas by 1086 this had fallen to approximately 374 hides. As the hidage assessment of land was the basis on which geld assessments were determined this fall was of great benefit to Abingdon. This reduction, by one third, of the abbey's hidage rating must be a significant part of the explanation for the 13 per cent rise in the value of the abbey's lands.[49] Indeed, the bulk of the abbey's increased yield was produced by just two manors. Between them Cumnor and Barton, in Berkshire, delivered an 80 per cent increase in their yield, from £50 to £90. It is no small coincidence that Cumnor and Barton had had their combined hidage values slashed by 40 hides, from 110 to 70 hides. This reduced assessment may well have been granted to help compensate for the additional burden of knight service and also suggests that the abbot was an able negotiator.

Evidently, despite the bitter complaints voiced by the chronicler, Athelhelm's abbacy was far from a barren period for the abbey. Considering the extremely dangerous nature of the crisis that embroiled the abbey in the early years after the Conquest, Abingdon was fortunate in having recovered so much property by 1086. Not all the Benedictine houses were so lucky; Ely and Glastonbury certainly were not. Furthermore, Abingdon was almost unique in making purchases of land so soon after 1066. Military demands had kept Athelhelm busy for most of his thirteen years as abbot, but more peaceful times saw the re-establishment of normal abbey life. Athelhelm embellished the church with ornaments and began saving for the renovation of the church but unfortunately his plans were cut short by his untimely death.[50] It seems, however, that the abbey was yet to make any significant impression on the Anglo-Norman baronage as a worthy recipient for their generosity. Athelhelm's abbacy yielded only one grant, in the form of Gilbert de Gant's gift of a house in London.[51] Gilbert may well have regarded this as a personal grant to Athelhelm himself, rather than to the abbey, as after the abbot's death he took the house back. Only Abbot Rainald's friendship with William Rufus, combined with the threat of anathema, eventually restored the house to Abingdon.

Under Abbot Rainald (1084–97), another Jumièges monk, some of the methods employed to produce greater yields from the abbey's lands are elaborated upon by the chronicler.[52] Procedures included the granting of deceased tenants' lands to 'strangers' on more advantageous terms and the tightening up of the collection of its harvest tithes.[53] Rainald's abbacy also witnessed an important shift in the attitude of the laity towards Abingdon. The first

---

[49] For the reassessment of hides in Berkshire during William's reign see S. P. J. Harvey, 'Domesday Book and its predecessors', *English Historical Review* cxxxvi (1971), 753–73 at p. 760.

[50] *Chron. Abingdon*, ii. 11.

[51] Ibid. ii. 15–16.

[52] For the administration of Abingdon see G. Lambrick, 'Abingdon abbey administration', *Journal of Ecclesiastical History* xvii (1966), 159–83.

[53] *Chron. Abingdon*, ii. 25.

change was in royal favour and the second was the growth of local support. The chronicler claims that Abbot Rainald, who had once been chaplain to William the Conqueror, was 'cherished [. . .] with honour' by William Rufus.[54] This partiality manifested itself in a favourable allotment by William Rufus of the treasures William the Conqueror had bequeathed on his death-bed for distribution to the Church and the poor. Unfortunately this promising relationship soured. The details of Rainald's fall from grace are not clear, but it appears to have been the result of the 'prompting of certain men hostile to the abbot'.[55] The conflict centred on the abbot's son-in-law, Rainbald, a tenant of several abbey estates, who was threatened with imprisonment by the king unless he paid him £500.[56] The abbot and several of the abbey's men, as his friends, between them put up the money.[57] However, unknown to them, Rainbald subsequently left England for the protection of the count of Flanders. This action resulted in the loss of the entire bond for the guarantors. Although Rainbald was later reinstated by the king this massive loss was not recovered and was still sorely felt by the abbey a generation later, when the author of the chronicle was writing.

Rainald's abbacy, however, did see the beginnings of a more promising and – importantly – stable relationship with Anglo-Norman landholders, both large and small. Abingdon's wealth and reputation were both valuable for attracting benefactions. In 1086 other locally established monastic houses were small in comparison with the wealthy Abingdon. In William Rufus' time the only other Berkshire house competing with Abingdon for grants was the tiny priory at Wallingford, which was been given to St Albans in the time of Abbot Paul (1077-93).[58] In Oxfordshire, where Abingdon's holdings were smaller in scale, there was local competition only from Eynsham which had been refounded by Bishop Remigius of Lincoln before the time of Domesday Book, but did not come into its own until the reign of Henry I.[59] Abingdon attracted the goodwill of a number of important individuals in this period. It has already been mentioned that William Rufus demonstrated his own initial approval with the generous distribution of his father's bequest.[60] Before 1086 Hugh, earl of Chester, had been aware of the abbey's claim, dating back to well to before the Conquest, to the manor of Shippon, in Berkshire.[61] Hugh dutifully returned the manor in return for £30 and

54 Ibid. ii. 41.
55 Ibid. ii. 42.
56 Ibid. ii. 37–8.
57 Ibid. ii. 38.
58 *Gesta abbatum*, i. 56; A. Binns, *Dedications of monastic houses in England and Wales, 1066–1216*, Woodbridge 1989, 88.
59 Ibid. 71. For Bishop Remigius and the foundation at Eynsham see D. Bates, *Bishop Remigius of Lincoln, 1067–1092*, Lincoln 1992, 29–33.
60 *Chron. Abingdon*, ii. 41.
61 Ibid. ii. 19.

confraternity for himself and his family.[62] This relationship with the earl of Chester and his family was again made to pay dividends around the year 1106 when Abbot Faritius secured from Earl Richard and his mother, Ermentrude, a confirmation of a grant made by Drogo de Andeleys, a tenant of the earl.[63]

The abbey's relationship with the castellan of Oxford, Robert d'Oilly, illustrates how the power of local lords could have a profound impact, both negative and positive, on a monastery's fortunes. In his early relations with the abbey, Robert was characterised as a 'molester of churches everywhere and especially Abingdon because of his greed [for money]'.[64] Abbot Athelhelm had granted Robert d'Oilly the manor of Tadmarton, in Berkshire, 'on account of his flattering speech'. This grant became subject to dispute between the abbot and Robert and resulted in an expensive compromise for the abbey.[65] Robert had also alienated the abbey's meadow outside Oxford, one hide at Dry Sandford, Berkshire, and two hides at Arncott, Oxfordshire.[66] It took a serious illness, which was literally the answer to the monks' prayers, and a particularly vivid and foul nightmare to make Robert penitent.[67] Robert dreamt that he was accused before the Virgin Mary by two Abingdon monks of having stolen the meadow situated outside Oxford from her monastery, i.e. Abingdon. The Virgin ordered him to be taken to the meadow where the two monks petrified Robert by setting light to his beard. After Robert related his frightful dream to his English wife, Ealdgyth, the daughter and heiress of Wigod of Wallingford, she encouraged him to make amends for his misdeeds. Robert subsequently returned the manor of Tadmarton to the abbey, bequeathed to the monks his moveable possessions and gave them £100 in silver in compensation for his past misdeeds and for rebuilding the church. Robert's repentance was welcomed wholeheartedly by the convent and he received burial for himself in the church.[68] The generous grants made by Robert can only be dated to within a seven-year period, but it is certain that they were granted in the earlier part of Rainald's abbacy.[69]

Like his predecessor Abbot Rainald wanted to take part in the 'great spate of building, in bishoprics and monasteries, that was happening everywhere'.[70] Abbot Athelhelm had supposedly collected the money for rebuilding the church but there is no mention of it in the time of Rainald. Instead, Rainald 'undertook to secure the help of the whole neighbourhood for this work'. Grants from men with local interests such as Hubert de Courson, Robert

---

62 Ibid. ii. 19–20. This agreement was formalised in 1090.
63 Ibid. ii. 69.
64 Ibid. ii. 12.
65 Ibid. ii. 7–8.
66 Ibid. ii. 25.
67 Ibid. ii. 12–15.
68 Ibid. ii. 284.
69 DB i, fo. 156d. For the history of Robert d'Oilly and Tadmarton, Oxfordshire, see Chron. Abingdon, ii. 7–8, 12–14.
70 Ibid. ii. 25.

Marmion, Robert d'Oilly and Sewallus may well have resulted from the abbot's drive for support from his neighbours.[71] Locality seems to have been a determining factor in the choice of gift as three grants of tithes are from lands neighbouring abbey property, or very close to them. The tithes were from ten hides at Lockinge, eleven hides at East and West Ilsey and four hides at Hendred, Berkshire.[72] Another local landholder, Ralph of Bagpuize, also made a grant of two *oras*, two doves, two pigs and two cheeses each year for the priest at the abbey's manor at Longworth, in Oxfordshire, during Rainald's abbacy.[73] It is not clear exactly when during Rainald's abbacy these four grants were made.[74] This means that it is impossible to tell whether Rainald's fall from favour with William Rufus had deterred potential donors from making gifts to Abingdon.

Abbot Rainald's death in 1097 did little to bring Abingdon abbey back into favour with William Rufus and the abbey remained without an abbot until after the king's death. Modbert, the prior who was appointed as the administrator of the abbey during this vacancy, was blamed by the chronicler for alienating abbey lands and failing to protect the monastery, choosing instead to advance the 'royal purse'.[75] These accusations are supported by a writ of Henry I dating from 1100 which orders Hugh of Buckland to reseise the abbey of the lands which Modbert had given or leased to Herbert the Chamberlain, Warin *calvus*, Turstin the Butler, Hugh of Buckland and others.[76] Most of these men were royal officials whose favour Modbert had clearly wanted to secure. When Modbert assigned the manor of Leckhampstead to Herbert the Chamberlain it was so that 'for as long as he was an public official, [so that . . .] the official duties of this house might be taken care of'.[77] Likewise Hugh of Buckland was given three hides at East Hanney, in Berkshire, by Modbert with 'the same purpose'.[78] As the sheriff of Berkshire and a local justice Hugh was a useful man to have on the abbey's side. Not all the losses attributed to Modbert's administration were the direct result of his grants and leases. Many tenants who had been installed under Abbot Athelhelm and Abbot Rainald took advantage of the confusion to cease performing service. It comes as no surprise then that the vacancy administered by Modbert which saw such losses did not see any new grants. There was little incentive to give grants to an abbey in crisis and without the effective leadership of an abbot. The true extent of the damage inflicted during this period can only be assessed accurately by gauging the number of possessions his successor Abbot Faritius (1100–17) eventually recovered. These included the lands or services due from no less than twenty-six holdings which accounted for well in excess of forty-seven hides.[79] The assertion in the chronicle that

---

71 *DB* i, fos 60c, 62a.
72 *Chron. Abingdon*, ii. 32–3.
73 Ibid. ii. 30.
74 Ibid. ii. 32, 33–4.
75 Ibid. ii. 42.

76 Ibid. ii. 86; *Regesta*, ii, no. 521.
77 *Chron. Abingdon*, ii. 43.
78 Ibid. ii. 43.
79 For Faritius' recoveries see ibid. ii. 65, 74, 126–35, 138, 288.

'sixty two plough-lands out of eighty' were lost by Modbert clearly has a basis in truth.[80] Besides depleting the abbey's lands Modbert has been credited with causing a decline in the number of monks at Abingdon by a third, falling from fifty monks to thirty-two.[81] No doubt a few monks did die in these years, but there must have been large-scale desertion to reduce the numbers by eighteen in less than three years. Although it is possible that the chronicler deliberately magnified the detrimental effects of Modbert's administration in order to emphasise Faritius' achievements, the loss of so many estates would have made it impossible to maintain a large number of monks.

In 1100 this inept administration was to end when the new king, Henry I, who had visited Abingdon as a young man in 1084, appointed as abbot his physician, an Italian monk called Faritius.[82] Henry appointed him apparently because he 'would be more useful to them than anyone else'.[83] Henry I clearly thought very highly of Faritius, raising this very capable monk of Malmesbury to be abbot of a wealthy monastery, which although it had recently fallen on hard times, was still very prestigious. Henry believed that Faritius' skills alone could heal him, and he later wanted him to succeed Anselm as the new archbishop of Canterbury.[84] It was the royal favour that Abbot Faritius was able to command which was instrumental in the restoration of Abingdon to its former glory.[85] Soon after his appointment Faritius procured writs from the king demanding the return of the abbey lands which Modbert had alienated.[86] He also succeeded in securing writs for the return of two of the abbey's properties in Berkshire, in 1105 the manor of Sparsholt and in 1110 two hides in Benham.[87] Henry's high regard for Faritius was exhibited in numerous other grants, confirmations and writs upholding the abbey's rights. The Abingdon chronicle contains some eighty-one writs and charters from Henry I and Queen Matilda which Abingdon received during the seventeen years of Faritius' abbacy. This figure compares very favourably with those preserved from previous and later abbacies: Athelhelm, three over thirteen years; Rainald, seven over thirteen years; Vincent, three over six years; Ingulf, during Henry I's reign, one in five years. However, such favours were not free. Faritius had to part with £60 of silver in order to secure the return of the manor of Fawler, in Berkshire.[88] Faritius also carefully worked on his relationship with the queen, as her physician, to gain practical help with the rebuilding of the abbey church. Indeed, he had so much confidence in his

---

80 Ibid. ii. 285.
81 Ibid.
82 Ibid. ii. 44–7.
83 Ibid. ii. 44.
84 Ibid. ii. 45.
85 See L. H. Jared, 'English ecclesiastical vacancies during the reigns of William II and Henry I', *Journal of Ecclesiastical History* xxxxii (1991), 362–93.
86 *Chron. Abingdon*, ii. 86; *Regesta*, ii, no. 521.
87 *Chron. Abingdon*, ii. 107, 126; *Regesta*, ii, nos 683, 956.
88 *Chron. Abingdon*, ii. 125.

relationship with her that he asked her to increase her original benefaction.[89] The recovery of the abbey's lost lands was just as impressive an accomplishment as the significant number of new grants he won for the abbey. Under Faritius the abbey experienced an explosion in the number of gifts it received. During these seventeen years it acquired more than thirteen grants of tithes, a fishery, the tithe of a fishery, three and a half mills, three houses, eight churches, ten hides of land and seven grants of unspecified amounts of land. This represented 71 per cent of all the grants Abingdon received under the Norman kings and averaged out at two grants *per annum*. This compares favourably with the averages from the abbacies of Rainald and Vincent, at just under half a grant a year each.

Faritius was deemed to have been blessed with 'secular prudence'.[90] Indeed, his design for the renewal of the abbey's wealth and status was achieved by a mixture of shrewd administration and the application of own personal charm. Besides entertaining many archbishops, bishops and nobles as his guests at the abbey, he also utilised his skills as a physician. Faritius' prompt measures soon proved effective as he 'industriously increased the crops on all the abbey's lands'.[91] Productive estate management, at least initially, rendered possible the means by which Faritius was able to play host to his many important guests at the abbey.[92] This socialising probably prompted gifts from the likes of William de Courcy, the royal *dapifer*, in 1105, William, bishop of Winchester, in 1115 and Henry d'Aubigny, the Bedfordshire landholder, in about 1107.[93] Faritius' medical skills also brought donations from grateful patients.[94] Adeliza d'Ivry, widow of Roger d'Ivry, who had been suffering from an incurable illness and gave a hide at Fencot, Oxfordshire 'for her eternal salvation', was probably his patient.[95] Besides this there are entries in the chronicle which specifically state that grants were given in return for medical treatment: by Robert fitz Haimo in 1107, Miles Crispin *c.* 1105 and Geoffrey de Vere whom the abbot had personally nursed for three months.[96] Geoffrey had the distinction of being thought of as having been more generous than his kin. This seems rather harsh on his father Aubrey I de Vere, probably a justiciar in Berkshire, who in 1111 founded and liberally endowed Earls Colne, in Essex, as a cell to Abingdon.[97] Another patient was

89 Ibid. ii. 50.
90 Ibid. ii. 44.
91 Ibid. ii. 48–9.
92 Ibid. ii. 44–6.
93 Ibid. ii. 52–3, 100, 111–12.
94 Ibid. ii. 44.
95 Ibid. ii. 72–3.
96 Ibid. ii. 55, 96–7.
97 Ibid. ii. 57–61; *Cartularium prioratus de Colne*, ed. J. L. Fisher (Essex Archaeological Society Occasional Publications i, 1946), 1–3. For the Vere family during the reign of Henry I see J. A. Green, *The government of England under Henry I*, Cambridge 1986, 276–7.

Robert fitz Haimo, the founder of Tewkesbury, who had suffered brain damage as a result of a blow to his head at Falaise in 1105.[98]

The donation of churches was more typical of the non-local royal official such as William de Courcy or Hubert de Montchesny.[99] These gifts of churches were not typical of the grants made to Abingdon. Grants of tithes of land and mills and small parcels of land were more common. The majority of benefactors who gave under Faritius were, as under Abbot Rainald, local men. Often grants of tithes and land were neighbouring or close to abbey holdings. This could apply to even more distant gifts such as the hide at Dumbleton, in Gloucestershire, given by William Guzienboded, which was close to the abbey's own holding of seven hides and two virgates at Dumbleton.[100] This is such a convenient gift of land, that it seems likely that it was in fact a purchase, or at the very least, the result of some convincing persuasion.

Many of Abingdon's benefactors were already connected with the abbey by geographical proximity or tenure. Not all can be traced through Domesday Book, but where their typonymics are English place-names this is probably the best guide to where their holdings were centred. Thus, the benefactor Ralph of Caversham most likely held land in Caversham, in Oxfordshire. This is substantiated by a writ of Henry I, issued in about 1111, which commanded Walter II Giffard and his mother Agnes to do justice to the church of Abingdon concerning land given to it by Ralph of Caversham.[101] In 1086 Water I Giffard held twenty hides and three houses in Caversham and was probably Ralph's overlord there.[102] Botley, which is located in North Hinksey, in Berkshire, is in the abbey's hundred of Hormer. The benefactors Ælfric and Ælwin of Botley were, therefore, likely to have been abbey tenants.[103] Ældred and Luured, 'men of the church of Wallingford', who gave a tithe of Welford, in Berkshire, were also most likely tenants of the abbey as Abingdon held the whole of Welford in 1086.[104] Other benefactors who were probably abbey tenants included William of Watchfield who gave his tithe of three hides in Watchfield and two hides in Boxford in about 1107, Turold of Hanney who gave the tithe of Hanney and William de Suleman who gave tithes in *Bulehea* and in Chilton c. 1104.[105] These are not the military tenants, but smaller fry.

Military tenants do appear as benefactors in the time of Faritius and after his death. The only military tenant to patronise the abbey in the previous

98 OV vi. 60; William of Malmesbury, *De gestis regum Anglorum libri quinque*, ed. W. Stubbs (Rolls series lii, 1887–9), ii. 475.
99 *Chron. Abingdon*, ii. 52–3, 61–3; *Regesta*, ii, nos 699, 1089.
100 *Chron. Abingdon*, ii. 35–6, 102; *Regesta*, ii, no. 893; DB i, fos 166a, 167b.
101 *Chron. Abingdon*, ii. 85; *Regesta*, ii, no. 979.
102 DB i, fos 56c, 157c.
103 *Chron. Abingdon*, ii. 152.
104 Ibid. ii. 144; DB i, fo. 58d.
105 *Chron. Abingdon*, ii. 141–2, 144; DB i, fos 58d, 59b, 59b, 60d, 61c.

thirty-four years had been Robert d'Oilly.[106] Robert's heir was his brother Nigel who later 'restored' land at Abbefield, Oxford, to the abbey c. 1106 for 'my brother's soul and for the remission of my sins'.[107] William of Seacourt, who gave the mill of Langford, was likewise a military tenant of Abingdon.[108] Roger Mauduit, who with his wife Odelina gave a house at Oxford for their burial in the abbey, was a kinsman, possibly the brother, of Robert Mauduit who held four hides at Weston, in Berkshire.[109] Ralph Basset's family had formed a relationship with Abingdon abbey when Ralph's kinsman, Gilbert Basset, had given his son, Robert, with accompanying gifts, to become a monk there in the time of Abbot Faritius.[110] This association proved advantageous to the abbey when Ralph was one of the judges of the *curia regis* in 1119 when Abingdon proved its exemption from geld on 120 hides held in demesne.[111] Ralph Basset had previously been involved in Abingdon's affairs as he witnesses several of Henry I's grants to the abbey.[112] This conjunction was to have further benefits for the abbey when Ralph became a generous benefactor of Abingdon himself. Gilbert and Ralph Basset had also been benefactors of the abbey of Eynsham, in Oxfordshire, before 1109, and Ralph again in 1120, but Ralph finally decided to be buried at the wealthier and more prestigious Abingdon and left the abbey a considerable legacy.[113]

After Faritius' death in 1117 the abbey was vacant until 1121. Prior Warengerius' administration during these years must have been relatively efficient since there was no repeat of the disasters of Modbert's time. Faritius' posthumous influence clearly remained strong for there was a benefaction from one of the abbey's military tenants, Hugh the Butler, in about 1119.[114] Royal interest, however, was weakened by his loss: although Henry I visited Abingdon in 1121,[115] his attention was diverted to his new foundations, Reading abbey in Berkshire, established between the years 1121 and 1123,

---

[106] *Chron. Abingdon*, ii. 4–6; *The red book of the exchequer*, ed. H. Hall (Rolls series lxxxxix, 1896), i. 305–6. For a discussion of Abingdon's knights' list see Douglas, 'Some early surveys', 618–25.

[107] *Chron. Abingdon*, ii. 74; *Regesta*, ii, no. 700.

[108] *Chron. Abingdon*, ii. 122–3.

[109] Ibid. ii. 139, 153. For the Mauduit family see Emma Mason, 'The Mauduits and their chamberlainship of the exchequer', *Bulletin of the Institute of Historical Research* xlix (1976), 1–23, and *The Beauchamp cartulary: charters 1100–1268*, ed. Emma Mason (Pipe Roll Society, n.s. xliii, 1980).

[110] *Chron. Abingdon*, ii. 145. The exact relationship between Ralph and Gilbert is unknown. For the Basset family see W. T. Reedy, 'The first two Bassets of Weldon: *novi barones* of the early and mid-twelfth century', *Northamptonshire Past and Present* iv (1966–72), 241–5, 295–8.

[111] *Chron. Abingdon*, ii. 160; *Regesta*, ii, no. 1211.

[112] *Chron. Abingdon*, ii. 52, 62, 64, 116, 160, 164; *Regesta*, ii, nos 550, 958, 970, 1000, 1089, 1211, 1477.

[113] *Eynsham cartulary*, ed. H. E. Salter (Oxford Historical Society xlix, li, 1907–8), i. 36–7, 91; *Chron. Abingdon*, ii. 170–1.

[114] Ibid. ii. 159.

[115] Ibid. ii. 78–9; *Regesta*, ii, no. 1258.

and the Augustinian house of Cirencester in Gloucestershire, founded in 1131.[116] Reading abbey was serious competition as local nobility passed over Abingdon and patronised the new house. Some Reading benefactors might otherwise have been patrons of Abingdon, for example Alice d'Ivry, the daughter of the Abingdon patroness in 1133, and Robert, earl of Leicester, who had been educated at Abingdon.[117] Thus Abingdon's near monopoly of religious patronage in Berkshire and Oxfordshire was finally broken in the 1120s. During Henry I's reign Eynsham abbey, in Oxfordshire, also attracted grants from men and women who had connections with Abingdon, such as Ralph Basset, his kinsman Gilbert, Reginald de St-Valéry, a military tenant of Abingdon in 1135, and his son Bernard.[118] Robert II d'Oilly's wife, Edith Forne, Helewisa and Dionisia, daughters of the abbey's tenant Walchelin son of Waard, with their husbands William Avenel and Hugh de Chesney were all Eynsham benefactors.[119] Abingdon's military tenants also began to found their own religious houses. This was a serious development as these new houses would act as a lasting focus for their founding families' patronage and support. Robert II d'Oilly and his wife Edith founded and endowed Oseney priory, in Oxfordshire, in 1129.[120] Robert of Sandford also endowed his own foundation, the priory of Littlemore, also in Oxfordshire, sometime before 1135.[121]

The loss of Faritius' personality and skills meant that even under their new abbot, Vincent (1121–30), the abbey's benefactors subsequently consisted of men and women with almost exclusively local interests. These comprised the military tenant, Rainbald of Tubney, whose son Athelhelm became a monk of the abbey, and who gave two virgates at Draycott Moor, in Berkshire; Joscelin 'the knight'; Norman 'the knight'; and Ralph Basset.[122] In the five years that Abbot Ingulf (1130–59) was installed at Abingdon before the death of Henry I, there are no recorded gifts. This does not necessarily mean that there were no grants in these years, for it is clear that cash donations were being made at the abbey shrine. Indeed, in Stephen's reign William of Ypres robbed the shrine of St Vincent at Abingdon of the money collected there.[123] Such donations to the abbey's shrine are essentially an unknown quantity in the overall picture of the benefaction received. Indeed there is very little written evidence about the vitality or profitability of any of the saints' cults at Abingdon. At least one grant was given specifically to the abbey 'on account

---

116 D. Knowles, C.N.L. Brooke and V.C.M. London, *Heads of religious houses, 940–1216*, Cambridge 1972, 63, 159. For Reading abbey see J. B. Hurry, *Reading abbey*, London 1901.

117 *Chron. Abingdon*, ii. 229; *Regesta*, ii, no. 1757; *Mon.*, iv. 29, 40–1.

118 *Cart. Eynsham*, i. 40; *Red book*, i. 305.

119 *Cart. Eynsham*, i. 45, 72–3, 81, 114.

120 *VCH, Oxfordshire*, ii. 90; *Cartulary of Oseney abbey*, ed. H. E. Salter (Oxford Historical Society lxxxix, xc, xci, xcvii, xcviii, ci, 1929–36), i. 1–2.

121 *VCH, Oxfordshire*, ii. 75–6.

122 *Chron. Abingdon*, ii. 169–70, 172.

123 Ibid. ii. 210.

of [. . .] love for the blessed Virgin Mary and the other saints who are venerated there'.[124] However, none of the other grants, as recorded in the chronicle, make any special association with the patron saint of Abingdon, the
Virgin Mary. Yet at least three gift-giving ceremonies were timed to coincide
with a feast of the Virgin Mary.[125] Relics were sufficiently important for Faritius to go to the trouble of obtaining the relics of the founder of the house,
Æthelwold, and translate them into a new reliquary amid great ceremony.
The shoulder blades of St Aldhelm and St Wilfrid and part of the arm of St
John Chrysostom were also acquired by Faritius.[126]

The abbots of Abingdon have so far only been examined in relation to
their skills in the administration of the abbey and its estates and in attracting
gifts from others. Yet they were often generous patrons themselves. Athelhelm, whose abbacy brought so many changes with it, 'embellished the
church with ornaments' and collected funds for the renovation of the building.[127] Abbot Rainald had the oratory of the church enlarged and started to
rebuild the tower that had fallen down in 1091.[128] The list of Faritius' gifts
and works for Abingdon is seemingly endless. Besides extensive rebuilding of
the monastery he donated an enormous number of ornaments and vestments
for use in the church.[129] He also purchased a house in Oxford for the infirm
and had a list of the abbey's relics compiled in 1116.[130] Abbot Vincent also
donated a purple chasuble and rebuilt more of the abbey buildings.[131] These
gifts from the abbots, in particular the rebuilding of the abbey, probably came
from funds given to the abbot himself. Thus the progress of the renovation of
the monastery fabric can be used as a roundabout guide to the abbey's prosperity under each abbot. All in all, the impressions gained in this manner are
reasonably well borne out by the more detailed analysis above.

The history of Abingdon abbey in these seventy years contains elements
which are both typical and atypical of the experiences of English religious
houses in post-Conquest England. All the English monasteries faced recur-
ring problems of some sort or another after 1066. Abingdon's experience was
typical in the uneven nature of its fortunes. Many of its problems was not
new; what was new was the scale of the difficulties produced by the upheaval
of the Norman Conquest. Its abbots' ability to deal with the perennial problems which they faced was directly influenced by the amount of royal favour
they could, or could not, command. The flip side to these problems was the
patronage the abbey received from the Anglo-Norman baronage. The pattern of patronage in this period paralleled the vacillating fortunes of the
house.

There was only a small handful of religious houses that possessed so
impressive a list of patrons as Abingdon in the early twelfth century. The

---

124 Ibid. ii. 34.
125 Ibid. ii. 141, 144–5.
126 Ibid. ii. 46–7.
127 Ibid. ii. 11.

128 Ibid. ii. 23–4.
129 Ibid. ii. 150–1.
130 Ibid. ii. 155–8.
131 Ibid. ii. 172.

number of benefactors associated with the royal court and the government of the realm is extremely impressive: Hugh, earl of Chester, Robert fitz Haimo, Aubrey de Vere, William de Courcy, Robert Gernon, Ralph Basset, Robert I d'Oilly, Nigel d'Oilly, Miles Crispin, Geoffrey de Vere, Hubert de Montchesney, Roger Mauduit, Robert Marmion, Walter son of Walter of Windsor, Hugh the Steward and not least of all, Henry I and his queen.[132] The catalogue of the Abingdon benefactors who were drawn from the locality is also extensive: Adeliza d'Ivry, Rainbald of Tubney, William of Seacourt, William of Watchfield, Hugh fitz Witgar, Sewallus of Ilsley, William de Suleman, Turold of Hanney, William fitz Aiulf, Roger fitz Alfred, Ældred and Luured, Ælfric and Ælwin of Botley, Athelhelm of Burgate, Henry d'Aubigny, Gilbert Basset, Hubert de Courson, Joscelin 'the knight', Norman 'the knight', Ralph 'the knight', Osbern, Richard fitz Reinfrid, Ralph the chamberlain of Abbot Faritius.[133] However, the national character of patronage which was largely attracted by the personality and efforts of Faritius' abbacy lasted only as long as he lived. The vacancy after his death, from 1117 to 1121, coincided with increasing competition from other local abbeys and priories. Abingdon's benefactors thereafter resumed their largely local, small scale nature.

---

[132] Ibid. ii. 12, 20, 33–4, 49, 52–7, 60–2, 64, 74–6, 96–8, 110, 112, 139, 159, 170, 284–5.
[133] Ibid. ii. 32, 60, 72–3, 100–1, 105–6, 108, 122, 141–2, 144–6, 152, 160, 169–70.

3

St Peter's, Gloucester

In 1066 the recently refounded St Peter's, Gloucester, was in an impoverished condition, its estates worth a paltry £29. But this was no indication of its future:[1] by 1104 the abbey's lands were easily worth more than £145 at Domesday values. Following the Conquest, the abbacies of Serlo (1072–1104), William (1107–13), Peter (1113–30) and Walter de Lacy (1130–9), witnessed the grant of more than 100 donations to the abbey from almost as many benefactors. These came from men and women of both local standing, such as Walter and Ermelina de Lacy, and of national importance, such as Arnulf de Hesdin, Roger Bigod and Gilbert fitz Richard.[2] This exceptional level of support for what had been an insignificant English monastery in 1066 was the consequence of a number of factors: the strategic location of Gloucester on the border with Wales; the abbey's past association with the Anglo-Saxon regime; active royal promotion; the intermittent presence of the royal court; and the outstanding personality and ability of Gloucester's first continental abbot, Serlo.

The sources for St Peter's in the post-Conquest period are relatively abundant. There is a shortish chronicle, known as the *Historia Sancti Petri Gloucestriae*, which was composed at the turn of the fourteenth and fifteenth centuries by Abbot Water Frocester (1382–1414) and is accompanied by an extensive index of the abbey's lands.[3] It has been demonstrated that, where they can be verified, the documents are reliable.[4] Unfortunately, many of the charters and notices of donations copied into the *Historia* have been edited

---

1 For the history of Gloucester abbey see C. N. L. Brooke, 'St Peter of Gloucester and St Cadoc of Llancarfan', in N. K. Chadwick (ed.), *Celt and Saxon: studies in the early British border*, Cambridge 1963, 258–332 (repr. in C. N. L. Brooke, *The Church and the Welsh border*, Woodbridge 1986, 50–94); D. Bates, 'The building of a great church: the abbey of St Peter's, Gloucester, and its early Norman benefactors', *Transactions of the Bristol and Gloucestershire Archaeological Society* cii (1984), 129–32. For Gloucestershire in the Norman period see David Walker, 'Gloucestershire castles', ibid. cix (1991), 5–23.
2 *Historia et chartularium monasterii Sancti Petri Gloucestriae*, ed. W. H. Hart (Rolls series xxxiii, 1863–7), i. 73, 85, 89, 92, 93, 106, 122, 123; *Regesta*, i, no. 379a (this is printed in *Regesta*, ii, p. 410).
3 This survives in three manuscripts: Gloucester Cathedral Library, MS 34, fos 1r–43v; BL, MS Cotton Domitian A viii, fos 145v–60v; Oxford, The Queen's College, MS 367, pp. 65–125. For the unpublished thirteenth-century version of the chronicle see Michael Hare, 'The chronicle of Gregory of Caerwent: a preliminary account', *Glevensis* xxvii (1993), 42–4.
4 Brooke, 'St Peter and St Cadoc', 54. Bates has suggested that the dates in the *Historia Sancti Petri Gloucestriae* may not be always be accurate but the conflicting dates of the

54

and condensed by the scribe and many names of witnesses and particular details of the grants have been omitted. However, there are also numerous charters, only a few of which are regarded as suspect, and even those that are dubious contain authentic information which can be used to supplement the picture which has already been drawn.[5]

St Peter's, Gloucester, was originally founded in the seventh century as a royal double monastery with an extensive parish,[6] and it seems that royal interest persevered well into the early tenth century.[7] However, the history of the house is obscure from then until the 1020s when it was reformed under the auspices of Bishop Wulfstan of Worcester, with the consent of King Cnut.[8] It is also clear that Gloucester became the 'focus of royal attention' during Edward the Confessor's reign, as the king paid more visits to it than to any other recorded location, except Westminster.[9] It was probably in response to the rising importance of Gloucester that Ealdred, bishop of Worcester and later archbishop of York, decided to rebuild its church from its foundations, consecrating it in 1058.[10] Yet, at the time of the Norman Conquest, Gloucester abbey was hardly a fit place for a royal ceremonial centre. It was, in fact, a very modest foundation, home in 1072 to only two adult monks and eight boys, which is hardly surprising given its valuation in 1066.[11] Gloucester's estates were all located in Gloucestershire; the most valuable group was closest to St Peter's at Barton, Barnwood and Tuffley, with another compact group just to the west of the Severn at Churcham, Morton, Higham and Morwent. The remaining estates were located in a circle at between twenty and twenty-eight miles distance from Gloucester itself: Aldsworth, Ampney St Peters, Boxwell, Buckland and Hinton-on-the-Green.[12] It seems that Bishop Ealdred had considered himself justified in reimbursing his expenditure on 'hospitality rather than necessity' by appropriating abbey estates at Northleach, Oddington, Standish and Barton, all in Gloucester-

---

examples quoted, as he indicates, conflict only with dates supplied by forged charters: 'Building of a great church', 129–32.

5 For example *Regesta*, i, no. 379a. For remarks on this charter see Brooke, 'St Peter and St Cadoc', 270. This *pancarta* appears to be based on one or two original charters, to which one grant from the reign of Henry I has been added.

6 Alan Thacker, 'Chester and Gloucester: early ecclesiastical organisation in two Mercian burhs', *Northern History* xviii (1982), 199–211 at p. 207.

7 Michael Hare, *The two Anglo-Saxon minsters of Gloucester* (Deerhurst Lecture), Gloucester 1992, 8. See also Carolyn Heighway and Richard Bryant, 'A reconstruction of the tenth century church of St Oswald, Gloucester', in L. A. S. Butler and R. K. Morris (eds), *The Anglo-Saxon Church*, London 1986, 188–95.

8 *Historia Sancti Petri Gloucestriae*, i. 8. For a different view on the date of the reform of Gloucester see Hare, *Two minsters*, 14.

9 Ibid. 22. There was a royal palace at Kingsholm.

10 *Historia Sancti Petri Gloucestriae*, i. 9; ASC 'D', 1058; Barlow, *English Church, 1000–1066*, 89–90; Hare, *Two minsters*, 17.

11 *Historia Sancti Petri Gloucestriae*, i. 10.

12 *DB* i, fos 165c–d.

shire.[13] The impetus for Gloucester's change in fortune came initially from William the Conqueror, who had shown an interest even before the court celebrated Christmas there in 1080.[14] The author of the *Historia Sancti Petri Gloucestriae* maintains that the Conqueror's influence was used to Gloucester's advantage over some of the lands disputed with the archbishop of York: when Abbot Serlo recovered the lost estates of Frocester and Coln St Aldwyns, in Gloucestershire, the *Historia* states that it was achieved 'with the help of King William'.[15] However, Domesday Book shows that in 1086 the archbishop of York was still in possession of three other Gloucester estates – at Oddington, Northleach and Standish, all in Gloucestershire.[16] William granted land at Nympsfield, in Gloucestershire, to Gloucester's English abbot, Wulfstan (1058–72), who subsequently died on pilgrimage to Jerusalem.[17] His death gave William the opportunity to appoint as abbot the talented and energetic Serlo, who had been a monk at Mont-St-Michel.[18] Other benefits were also forthcoming from the Conqueror: lands at Barnwood, in Gloucestershire, in Brampton Abbott's, in Herefordshire, and the church of St Peter, Norwich, were all gifts from William.[19] This last gift gave Gloucester one of its earliest interests outside Gloucestershire or Herefordshire. It also proved to be the precursor of numerous small grants in East Anglia given later in the time of William Rufus.

The revitalising of this Anglo-Saxon house had numerous practical advantages for William I and his sons. A thriving urban centre, Gloucester was located at a very important crossing point of the River Severn into Wales.[20] It was therefore an effective centre from which defensive or offensive action against the Welsh could be launched, as Harold had done in 1055.[21] The Normans found Gloucester invaluable for defence, communications and, not least of all, for hunting. Edward the Confessor had sometimes held his court at Gloucester and hunted in the Forest of Dean.[22] It was the city's political past, however, which was of greatest interest to William the Conqueror. He was always keen to emphasise the legitimacy of his claim to the English throne and it became important to stress the continuity in the government of the realm from Edward's reign to William's. (Harold's brief

---

[13] *Historia Sancti Petri Gloucestriae*, i. 9, 11–12.

[14] Martin Biddle, 'Seasonal festivals and residence: Winchester, Westminster and Gloucester in the tenth to twelfth centuries', *Anglo-Norman Studies* viii (1986), 51–72 at p. 65n.

[15] *Historia Sancti Petri Gloucestriae*, i. 11; Walker, 'Gloucestershire castles', 12.

[16] *DB* i, fo. 164c.

[17] *Historia Sancti Petri Gloucestriae*, i. 9, 101; *DB* i, fo. 163a.

[18] *Historia Sancti Petri Gloucestriae*, i. 10.

[19] Ibid. i. 65, 67, 102, 186; ii. 34.

[20] For the importance of the river and trade to Gloucester see Hinton, *Archaeology, economy and society*, 138.

[21] *ASC*, 'C', 1055.

[22] Barlow, *Edward the Confessor*, 207.

reign was thus consigned to legal oblivion.[23]) Martin Biddle has demon-strated that one of the forms that William's policy took was the crown-wearing ceremonies at Old English palaces at various seasonal festivals, at Westminster, Winchester and Gloucester.[24] Gloucester's wealth was, of course, meagre in comparison with that of the abbeys at the other crown-wearing locations. In 1086 their possessions were each worth six times those of Gloucester's.[25] Thus, patronage of St Peter's, encouraged by William's gen-erous example, was directed at emphasising his commitment to maintaining and advancing this tangible link with his Anglo-Saxon predecessors. Although its origins were English, Gloucester's wealth and subsequent influ-ence were very much a Norman creation.

The new lords in Gloucestershire and Herefordshire were imbued with a tradition of patronising Benedictine monasteries and Gloucester, safely under the rule of the Norman Serlo, was an acceptable recipient for their grants. Patronage of Gloucester was one means of not only anchoring, but also stabi-lising, the position of the new aristocracy and their followers in the locality. By 1086 Serlo had managed to secure the patronage of Gloucestershire's wealthiest lay magnates: the king, Walter de Lacy and his widow Ermelina and Arnulf de Hesdin.[26] Walter and Arnulf were strictly speaking great mag-nates with local interests; Arnulf held lands in thirteen Domesday counties worth over £270 and Walter's were worth £325 in all.[27] In 1080, with the consent of the king, Walter granted four hides in Upleaden, in Gloucester-shire.[28] In the following year Arnulf, again with the consent of the king, granted the manor of Linkenholt, in Hampshire, to Gloucester.[29] Within the first generation after the Conquest royal attention had served to promote Gloucester from obscurity to a position of relative significance within the locality. By 1086 Gloucester's modest wealth had already exceeded that of Winchcombe abbey, geographically Gloucester's closest monastic rival. Wealthier rivals with more splendid traditions and saints' relics, such as Eve-sham and Malmesbury, were sufficiently far away to enable Gloucester to take advantage of the generous inclinations of local lords like the Lacys.

The nature of the numerous grants that Gloucester abbey received in the reign of William Rufus indicates not only continuing royal concern with

---

23 For the evolution of this policy see George Garnett, 'Coronation and propaganda: some implications of the Norman claim to the throne of England in 1066', *Transactions of the Royal Historical Society* 5th ser. xxxvi (1986), 91–116.

24 Biddle, 'Seasonal festivals', 51–72.

25 David Knowles calculated that the Domesday lands of Westminster abbey were valued at £583 in 1086 and those of Winchester, Old Minster, at £600: *Monastic order*, 702–3.

26 *Historia Sancti Petri Gloucestriae*, i. 65, 67, 73, 85, 89, 92–3, 101–2, 374–5, 386–7.

27 For an assessment of the value of Arnulf de Hesdin's Domesday holdings see Cooke, 'Donors and daughters', 29–45 at p. 34. For the holdings of the Lacy family see C. P. Lewis, 'The Norman settlement of Herefordshire under William I', *Anglo-Norman Studies* vii (1985), 195–213 at pp. 203–5.

28 *Historia Sancti Petri Gloucestriae*, i. 92, 122, 374–5; DB i, fo. 165c.

29 *Historia Sancti Petri Gloucestriae*, i. 89, 93.

Gloucester, but also the extension of this interest to members of the royal court.[30] In 1093, when William Rufus was gravely ill at Gloucester, his belief that he was dying prompted, amongst other actions, his gift to Gloucester of the church of St Gwynllyn, in Newport.[31] Besides this he gave land at Chelworth and Rudford, both in Gloucestershire, and all the sturgeon caught in the royal fishery on the River Severn.[32] Like his father William Rufus appears to have sided with Serlo against the archbishop of York in the matter of the disputed estates. On Easter Sunday in 1095 Thomas, archbishop of York, formally returned these lands, but even so the dispute does not appear to have been satisfactorily settled until the abbacy of Hamelin (1148–79).[33]

Under William Rufus Norman penetration into Wales began to make significant headway.[34] Means of entrenchment were being sought in the newly conquered parts of that country, but as the Wales that the Normans invaded did not contain any foundations of a recognisable continental type, there was 'little hope that Norman generosity might be transferred to local monasteries'.[35] Gloucester's geographical position on the frontier therefore meant that it was one of the first in line for the fruits of the Norman conquest of south Wales. Bernard de Neufmarché and Robert fitz Haimo both gave generous grants of land, tithes and churches in Wales to Gloucester in Rufus' reign.[36] In 1088 Bernard de Neufmarché, with the consent of the king, gave to Gloucester Glasbury, the tithe of his demesne in Brecon, the church of Covern, the tithe of the parish and half a hide of land called *Bache*, in Herefordshire.[37] Robert fitz Haimo gave Gloucester the church of St Cadoc, Llancarfan, and fifteen hides in Penhow, in south Wales.[38]

In the course of Serlo's abbacy and the reign of William Rufus Gloucester attracted gifts from Anglo-Norman magnates, royal *curiales* and local land-

---

[30] See Frank Barlow, *William Rufus*, London 1983, 114–15.

[31] *Historia Sancti Petri Gloucestriae*, i. 84, 102.

[32] Ibid. i. 68, 109, 115, 239; *Regesta*, i, no. 445.

[33] *Historia Sancti Petri Gloucestriae*, i. 11, 19.

[34] For the Normans in Wales see J. E. Lloyd, *A history of Wales: from the earliest times to the Edwardian conquest*, London 1939; L. H. Nelson, *The Normans in south Wales, 1070–1171*, Austin, Texas 1966; A. J. Roderick, 'Marriage and politics in Wales 1066–1282', *Welsh History Review* iv (1968), 3–20; J. B. Smith, 'The Kingdom of Morgannwg and the Norman Conquest of Glamorgan', *Glamorgan County History* iii (1971), 1–44; David Walker, 'The Norman settlement of Wales', *Anglo-Norman Studies* i (1979), 131–43; I. W. Rowlands, 'The making of the Welsh March: aspects of Norman settlement in Dyfed', ibid. iii (1981), 143–57, 221–5; R. R. Davies, 'Henry I and Wales', in H. Mayr-Harting and R. I. Moore (eds), *Studies in medieval history presented to R. H. C. Davis*, London 1985, 132–47. For monasticism in Wales in this period see also F. G. Cowley, 'The Church in medieval Glamorgan', *Glamorgan County History* iii (1971), 87–166, and *The monastic order in south Wales, 1066–1349*, Cardiff 1977; H. Pryce, 'Ecclesiastical wealth in early medieval Wales', in N. Edwards and A. Lane (eds), *The early Church in Wales and the west*, Oxford 1992, 22–32.

[35] David Walker, *The Norman conquerors*, Swansea 1977, 85.

[36] *Historia Sancti Petri Gloucestriae*, i. 64–5, 80, 93, 122, 314–15; iii. 5; *Regesta*, i, no. 300.

[37] *Historia Sancti Petri Gloucestriae*, i. 64–5, 80, 122, 314, 315; iii. 5.

[38] Ibid. i. 93, 122.

holders. The monastery had gained a reputation for strict observance of the Benedictine Rule and the Anglo-Normans quickly came to regard it as a suitable place for themselves and their sons to enter as monks.[39] A large number of local landholders made grants of landed property to Gloucester. Robert *curtus* made a grant of a hide in Ashperton, Elias Giffard gave land and wood in *Bocholt*, Roger de Builli gave land in Clifford Chambers, Ermelina de Lacy gave five hides at Duntisboune Abbots, Gunnilda de Loges gave two hides at Guiting Power, Walter de Lacy gave Upleaden and Roger of Berkeley made a grant of land in *Clingre* and a grant of an unspecified amount of land at Scotts Quarry in Harescombe.[40] All these properties were in Gloucestershire, with the exception of the gift of Robert *curtus* which was in Herefordshire.

Furthermore, the royal court that sporadically visited Gloucester brought to St Peter's plenty of prestigious benefactors who otherwise had no connection with the locality. This was particularly evident under William Rufus when there were more than twenty such men, for example Hugh de Port, sheriff of Hampshire and Devonshire, Roger Bigod, sheriff of Norfolk and Suffolk, Odo fitz Gamelin, a Devonshire tenant-in-chief, Ranulf Peverel (of Hatfield Peverel in Essex), William d'Aubigny *Brito*, the royal justice, and Robert and Nigel d'Oilly, royal constables.[41] Some of their grants were very generous indeed, such as Hugh de Port's grant of Littleton, in Hampshire, William de Pomeroy's grant of Berry Pomeroy, in Devon, and Odo fitz Gamelin's grant of Plymtree, also in Devon.[42] Other grants were of a more modest nature such as the church granted by Roger Bigod, and the various grants of tithes made by Roger, William d'Aubigny *Brito*, Robert fitz Walter, William de Courson, Turstin fitz Guy and John fitz Richard.[43] Familiarity with a monastery was clearly not the only factor which prompted these grants. Visits by the court to Westminster and Winchester were more frequent than to Gloucester yet neither of those two abbeys received gifts on anything like the same scale.[44] Other forms of encouragement, either from the king, the abbot himself, or from the Lacy family, must have been major ingredients in the decision-making process.

Christopher Harper-Bill has pointed out that 'the support of a particular house was frequently the expression of corporate solidarity with a feudal

---

[39] *Letters of Lanfranc*, 168.
[40] *Historia Sancti Petri Gloucestriae*, i. 58, 63, 68, 72–3, 80–1, 92, 112. For the Berkeley family see H. Barkly, 'The earlier house of Berkeley', *Transactions of the Bristol and Gloucestershire Archaeological Society* viii (1882–4), 193–223.
[41] *Historia Sancti Petri Gloucestriae*, i. 70, 74, 93–4, 103, 123; *Regesta*, i, no. 379a.
[42] *Historia Sancti Petri Gloucestriae*, i. 65, 74, 93, 123.
[43] *Regesta*, i, no. 379a; *Historia Sancti Petri Gloucestriae*, i. 79, 92, 114.
[44] Hugh de Port spent his last days at Winchester as a monk and both he and his wife Orence appear in the Hyde abbey *liber vitae*: *Liber vitae: register and martyrology of New Minster and Hyde*, 73.

grouping'.[45] In William Rufus' reign the Lacy tenants copied their lords' generosity and patronised Gloucester. This pattern of behaviour was relatively common in England, but usually only on an honorial basis and then the house concerned would be a 'new' institution founded by the overlord's family, such as Lewes, Eye or Bridlington.[46] It was unknown in the patronage of existing English communities, apart from the monasteries of Gloucester and St Albans and the cathedral priory of Rochester.[47] The Herefordshire tenants of Walter de Lacy included Robert de Baskerville, Walter de Lyonshall and William Devereux who gave tithes and land in Gloucestershire and Herefordshire.[48] Just as Walter had not given to Gloucester exclusively, neither did his tenants. In 1100 Gilbert d'Eskecot gave land in Duntisbourne Abbots, in Gloucestershire, specifically 'for the soul of his lord Walter de Lacy'.[49] Locality and kinship influenced Gilbert too as he also gave a hide at Cuple, in Herefordshire, to the church of St Guthlac's, Hereford, where his nephew had become a monk.[50] The tenants of Roger Bigod joined their overlord in the harassment of St Benet of Holme in Norfolk and again in the endowment of his new Cluniac establishment at Thetford.[51] They also followed their overlord's example in patronising Gloucester although they are highly unusual in that they did not hold their lands locally, but rather in East Anglia. William de Courson, Turstin fitz Guy and John fitz Richard gave Gloucester abbey tithes from at least seven manors in Norfolk.[52] These numerous grants to a monastery on the other side of the country could not have served the 'usual' purpose of tying tenants to the lordship as those to Thetford did. These men probably travelled in Roger Bigod's entourage and had had personal contact with Serlo and his community.[53]

Henry I's attitude towards Gloucester and Abbot Serlo was initially favourable. In 1101 he granted Maisemore, in Gloucestershire, to Gloucester

---

45 C. Harper-Bill, 'The piety of the Anglo-Norman knightly class', *Anglo-Norman Studies* ii (1980), 63–77 at p. 67.

46 For tenants' patronage of honorial houses see ch. 11.

47 They were tenants of Odo bishop of Bayeux and William d'Aubigny *pincerna* and were also benefactors of Rochester. See also Tsurushima, 'Fraternity of Rochester cathedral priory, 312–37.

48 *Historia Sancti Petri Gloucestriae*, i. 81, 118; *Regesta*, i, no. 379a. For the Baskerville family see B. Coplestone-Crow, 'The Baskervilles of Herefordshire, 1086–1300', *Transactions of the Woolhope Naturalists Field Club* xliii (1979), 18–39.

49 *Historia Sancti Petri Gloucestriae*, i. 73.

50 Walker, ' "Honours" of the earls of Hereford', 174–211 at p. 186.

51 F. M. Stenton, 'St Benet of Holme and the Norman Conquest', *English Historical Review* xxxvii (1922), 225–35.

52 *Historia Sancti Petri Gloucestriae*, i. 79, 92, 114; *Regesta*, i, no. 379a; *DB* ii, fos 180b, 188b. Robert Courson, Ralph fitz Walter and Turstin fitz Guy were Domesday tenants of Roger Bigod in Norfolk and Suffolk: ibid. ii, fos 173b, 174a, 175a–b, 176a–b, 178b–9a, 181b, 183b–5a, 187a, 188b. John fitz Richard was a tenant-in-chief in Norfolk as well as tenant of Ely and St Benet of Holme in Norfolk: ibid. ii, fos 163b, 214a, 217a–b, 265b–6a.

53 Marjorie Chibnall has suggested that these grants of tithes were given in return for the grant of fraternity, as they were at Rochester cathedral priory (personal communication).

and before Serlo's death in 1104 he issued at least two, and possibly four, confirmation charters to the abbey.[54] For some reason Serlo's successor, Peter, failed to entice gifts from Henry and it was not until the abbacies of William Godeman and Walter de Lacy that royal grants resumed. These were grants of rights and tithes as well as land at Hartpury, in Gloucestershire, and Ruddle (or possibly Rodle) to pay for a light to be burned for the salvation of the soul of Robert Curthose, who had been incarcerated for so many years in Cardiff castle.[55] In 1134 Robert finally died and his body was brought for burial at Gloucester.

The multi-layered pattern of endowment that had been established in the time of William Rufus and Serlo continued in Henry I's time. Gloucester was still receiving grants of significant amounts of land, as well as increasing numbers of grants of churches and tithes. Donations from men with interests in Wales such as Winebald de Ballon, Hugh fitz Norman and Gilbert fitz Richard continued to be received.[56] The earliest of these came from Gilbert fitz Richard, who in 1111 gave land and the church of St Padarn, in Cardigan.[57] In 1126 Winebald de Ballon granted Gloucester a mill at Framilode, half a hide at Ampney, and Rudford, all in Gloucestershire.[58] In the 1130s Hugh fitz Norman granted the priory of Kilpec, the church of Taynton, in Gloucestershire, and a chapel as well as a virgate of land.[59] Royal officials were making fewer grants than previously, but there were some significant grants from Thomas de St-Jean who gave land at *Rugge* in Standish, in Gloucestershire, and Hugh Bigod who gave Forncett, in Norfolk.[60]

Walter de Lacy's family continued to patronise Gloucester after his burial there in 1085. Walter's son, Hugh de Lacy, confirmed and added to his father's gifts in the last years of Serlo's abbacy, but from the end of the first decade of the twelfth century his interest was diverted to his own foundation of Llanthony *Prima*.[61] Walter de Lacy's younger son, Walter, became Gloucester's abbot in 1130 and links between the abbey and his family were strengthened. Sybil de Lacy, Hugh's niece, to whom the bulk of his lands had descended c. 1121, granted lands to her uncle, the abbot.[62] Sibyl also made grants to another Lacy concern, the church of St Guthlac, in Hereford. This had been merged with the church of St Peter, Hereford, and both given to Gloucester in 1101 by Hugh de Lacy.[63] Sibyl's husband, Payn fitz John, the royal justice, was a benefactor of both Llanthony *Prima* and Gloucester abbey,

[54] *Historia Sancti Petri Gloucestriae*, i. 99, 100; *Regesta*, ii, nos 554, 673, 678, 1005, 1006.
[55] *Historia Sancti Petri Gloucestriae*, i. 72, 74, 78, 90, 110–11, 115; ii. 132, 134, 220.
[56] Ibid. i. 61, 77, 91, 106, 116, 124, 164, 285; ii. 73–6.
[57] Ibid. i. 106; ii. 73–4.
[58] Ibid. i. 61, 77, 123, 124, 164.
[59] Ibid. i. 91, 116.
[60] Ibid. i. 78, 109, 119.
[61] Ibid. i. 84–5, 100, 109, 123, 223, 326; ii. 92–3.
[62] Walker, ' "Honours" of the earls of Hereford', 188.
[63] Binns, *Dedications*, 75.

to which his father and brother had already given gifts, and where he was to be buried in 1137.[64] As royal involvement with Gloucester lessened, that of the Lacy family increased moderately, but although the Lacys and the sheriffs of Gloucester continued to make some donations, increasingly they chose to grant confirmation charters; gifts from their tenants were reduced to a trickle.

The appearance in the early twelfth century of new competition in the locality was a serious threat to Gloucester's continued growth and development. The wealthier and more influential of the locally important families were now choosing to establish their own foundations such as Llanthony *Prima* in Wales, Tewkesbury and, in 1136, Llanthony *Secunda*. Robert fitz Haimo's foundation at Tewkesbury attracted grants from at least two men who were also benefactors of Gloucester, Robert de Baskerville and Winebald de Ballon.[65] The sheriffs of Gloucester also made grants regularly, but not exclusively, to Gloucester throughout this period: Roger des Pîtres; his wife Adeliza; his son, Walter of Gloucester; his brother, Durand, and Durand's son, Roger of Gloucester, all in their time gave grants and confirmed each others gifts.[66] However, like the Lacy family, the sheriffs of Gloucester founded their own religious house in the twelfth century. Established on the outskirts of Gloucester in 1136 the Augustinian priory of Llanthony *Secunda* was somewhere else to which the grants of men who had previously given to Gloucester might be diverted.[67] In the eyes of the Gloucester monks this Augustinian house 'poached' grants from local families, many of whose representatives had previously given to St Peter's. Robert, earl of Gloucester, Hugh de Lacy, Payn fitz John, Ralph de Baskerville, Walter the constable and Miles of Gloucester, who had founded Llanthony *Secunda*, had all previously been connected with Gloucester. The tension over benefactors is illustrated by the long running row between Gloucester and Llanthony over where Miles's body was to be buried after his death in 1143.[68]

The author of the *Historia Sancti Petri Gloucestriae* cast Abbot Serlo as the hero responsible for the renewed wealth and influence of Gloucester.[69] By the time of his death in 1104 the community had supposedly grown from ten individuals to 100 souls. Other details about Serlo are hard to come by and his personal effect on Gloucester's fortunes is therefore difficult to ascertain, although it is clear that his successes were underpinned by the labours of a

64 *Historia Sancti Petri Gloucestriae*, i. 114; *Regesta*, i, no. 379a; GEC xii, pt ii. 270; Cowley, *Monastic order*, 30.

65 *Mon.*, ii. 65, 66.

66 *Historia Sancti Petri Gloucestriae*, i. 58, 69, 81, 112, 118, 235; *Regesta*, ii, no. 1041; *DB* i, fo. 181a.

67 *Mon.*, vi. 137; Walker, ' "Honours" of the earls of Hereford', 183.

68 For this dispute, which was only finally settled in the last decade of the twelfth century, see David Walker, 'A register of the churches of the monastery of St Peter's, Gloucester', in *An ecclesiastical miscellany* (Publications of Transactions of the Bristol and Gloucestershire Archaeological Society xi, 1976), 18–19.

69 *Historia Sancti Petri Gloucestriae*, i. 10.

very capable cellarer, Odo.[70] Serlo's impact on Gloucester was such that the author of the *Historia* praised 'his hard work and industry' which had allegedly increased Gloucester's 'lands and possessions many times over'.[71] The scale of the new abbey church begun under his direction certainly indicates that there was great confidence in the abbey's future revenue.[72] Analysis of the information recorded in Domesday Book demonstrates that Serlo's skills must have extended to estate management. The same lands that were worth only £29 in 1066 yielded £67 in 1086. This doubling in value was the 'exception rather than the rule' for Gloucestershire estate values in these years. Out of 300 of Gloucestershire's 363 estates just over a third remained at the same value, just under half dropped in value 'often [by] substantial proportions' and only a fifth rose.[73] Calculating the value of estates granted after the magic date of 1086 is very difficult. The value of all the lands Serlo acquired is uncertain and does not take account of lands in Wales or income from the numerous tithes and churches granted to Gloucester. Those estates for which a figure can be obtained from Domesday amount to £71 8s. 0d. The real figure must have been much higher. Thus by Serlo's death in 1104 Gloucester's estates had risen in value to over £138, in other words to over five times what they had been worth in 1066. On paper, then, Serlo's achievements look very impressive, and the frequency of grants does seem to have decreased somewhat after his death. Furthermore, the death of Odo the cellarer in 1123 could only have compounded the seriousness of the loss,[74] although the abbacies of William Godeman and Walter de Lacy did witness a resumption in the numbers of grants. Even by 1135, however, Gloucester was still nowhere near as wealthy as the most prosperous English houses such as Glastonbury, Ely or Bury St Edmunds, though its wealth must have compared well with the post-Conquest foundations such as Battle, Lewes and Reading.

By the end of Henry I's reign St Peter's abbey had been transformed from a tiny, poverty-stricken foundation with all its possession within a day's ride, to a prosperous and large community with possessions, temporal and spiritual, located all over southern England and Wales. In particular, the abbey had been able to increase its landed holdings close to the abbey both east and west of the Severn, as well as its spiritual possessions further afield in Herefordshire and Oxfordshire and lands in Hampshire and Devon. The endowment of Gloucester was not constant throughout this period nor was the status of its benefactors. There were just over 100 donations over seventy

[70] See Hare, 'Gregory of Caerwent', 43.

[71] *Historia Sancti Petri Gloucestriae*, i. 11.

[72] For the building of the church see C. Wilson, 'Abbot Serlo's church at Gloucester 1089–1100: its place in romanesque architecture', in *Medieval art and architecture at Gloucester and Tewkesbury* (British Architectural Association Conference Transactions vii, 1985), 52–83.

[73] David Walker, 'Gloucester and Gloucestershire in Domesday Book', *Transactions of the Bristol and Gloucestershire Archaeological Society* xciv (1976), 107–16 at p. 116.

[74] Hare, 'Gregory of Caerwent', 43.

years. Taking into account the different lengths of the three kings' reigns it is evident that under Rufus grants were being made at a tremendous rate. It was his reign, moreover, which witnessed a shift in the status of Gloucester's donors. Before 1087 endowments came largely from men with strong links with Gloucestershire like Walter de Lacy, Roger of Berkeley and Durand of Gloucester who augmented the abbey's holdings in the locality. The fact that a figure of such national standing as Arnulf de Hesdin, who had only a modest amount of property in the region, chose to make a donation in 1081, indicates that Gloucester was of more than just local importance.[75]

The next thirteen years witnessed gifts of both local lands and more distant property (principally in Devon, Hampshire and Wales) from both royal officials, their tenants and from local tenants. The list of benefactors is both extensive and impressive: William Rufus, Robert fitz Haimo, Hugh de Port, Nigel d'Oilly, Bernard de Neufmarché, Odo fitz Gamelin, Henry de Pomeroy, Roger Bigod, William de Courson, Ralph fitz Walter, John fitz Richard, Ralph Picot, Elias Giffard, Roger of Gloucester, Hugh de Lacy, William Devereux, Gilbert d'Eskecot, Gunnilda de Loges, Roger of Berkeley, Morgan fitz Morgan, Robert fitz Omer, Harold of Ewyas and Roger de Builli.[76] The varied status of Gloucester's benefactors was maintained throughout the thirty-five years of Henry's reign, although grants were being made less frequently. Grants came from Henry I, Robert, earl of Gloucester, William fitz Nigel, constable of Chester, Walter of Gloucester, Robert of Gloucester, Adeliza of Gloucester, Winebald de Ballon, Hugh de Lacy, Adeliza d'Ivry, William d'Aubigny *brito*, Hugh Bigod, Gilbert fitz Richard, Thomas de St-Jean, William de Pomeroy, Ermelina de Hesdin, Patrick de Chadworth (*Caorches*), Robert fitz Ercambald, Gilbert d'Eskecot, Robert de Baskerville, Robert of Beckford, Roger of Frampton, Richard fitz Nigel, Hugh son of William fitz Norman, Arnulf fitz Ralph, William Revel, Robert fitz Walter, Arnulf fitz Ralph, William de Builli and Wibert of Kingsholm.[77] The location of the donated lands was broadly comparable to the pattern of Rufus' reign, a mixture of local grants made by people with strong interests in the region, grants in Wales and a handful of distant donations from individuals who had inherited a concern for the monastery from their parents who had been patrons themselves; Hugh Bigod, Hugh de Lacy, Ermelina de Hesdin and William de Pomeroy were four such people.

Patronage of this nature and scale was remarkable in post-Conquest England. It can only be found on a comparable scale at Abingdon under Faritius (1100–17) and at St Albans during the abbacies of Paul of Caen (1077–93) and Richard d'Aubigny (1097–1119). There are similarities between circumstances at Gloucester, St Albans and Abingdon, not least the exceptional

---

[75] *Historia Sancti Petri Gloucestriae*, i. 92–3, 112; *DB* i, fos 169a–b, 181a.

[76] *Historia Sancti Petri Gloucestriae*, i. 62–3, 68–9, 73, 80, 91–3, 100, 102, 109, 112–14, 118.

[77] Ibid. i. 59–63, 65, 69, 73, 77–9, 81, 84, 88–90, 99, 100, 103, 105–6, 109–10, 112, 115–16, 118–19.

talents of their post-Conquest abbots, Serlo, Paul, Richard and Faritius. Although royal officials supported all these houses and royal involvement was also central to Abingdon's prosperity, it was the combination of the visiting royal court and the proximity of Wales that propelled Gloucester abbey into a position of distinction in post-Conquest England.

4

Bury St Edmunds

Bury St Edmunds is almost unique amongst the Old English Benedictine abbeys, with the exception, perhaps of Westminster, for thriving remarkably well in the first twenty years after the Norman Conquest.[1] Indeed, the amount and value of land granted to the abbey under Abbot Baldwin (1065–98) was only paralleled by that which Gloucester received under Abbot Serlo (1072–1104).[2] Yet despite all the special attention Gloucester received its total assets and spiritual prestige did not even come close to those possessed by Bury. Furthermore, that members of the Anglo-Norman baronage treated Bury St Edmunds so favourably so soon after the Conquest is in itself remarkable.

Sources for post-Conquest Bury St Edmunds are relatively abundant, consisting of the abbey's portion in Domesday Book, the Feudal Book, charters from three Bury cartularies which were printed by David Douglas in his 1932 collection of documents and two extant versions of a miracle collection entitled *De miraculis de Sancti Eadmundi*.[3] The Feudal Book survives in parts in two manuscripts, one in the twelfth-century Black Book of Bury St Edmunds now in CUL, MS Mm. 4. 19 and the other in the fourteenth-century register CUL, MS Ee. 3. 60.[4] The compiler of the Feudal Book stated that it was made

---

[1]   For the abbey's abbots see Antonia Gransden, 'Baldwin abbot of Bury St Edmunds, 1065–1097', *Anglo-Norman Studies* iv (1982), 65–76, 187–95; R. H. C. Davis, 'The monks of St Edmund, 1021–1148', *History* xl (1955), 227–39. For the literary traditions see Gransden, 'Legends and traditions', 1–24. For the cult of St Edmund see S. J. Ridyard, '*Condigna veneratio*: post-Conquest attitudes to the saints of the Anglo-Saxons', *Anglo-Norman Studies* ix (1987), 176–206 at pp. 187–9. On the abbey's privileges see H. W. C. Davis, 'The liberties of Bury St Edmunds', *English Historical Review* xxiv (1909), 417–31. For the library and abbey's buildings see R. M. Thomson, 'The library of Bury St Edmunds in the eleventh and twelfth centuries', *Speculum* xlvii (1972), 617–45; A. B. Whittingham, 'Bury St Edmunds abbey', *Archaeological Journal* cvii (1951), 168–89; R. Gem and L. Keen, 'Late Anglo-Saxon finds from the site of St Edmund's abbey', *Proceedings of the Suffolk Institute of Archaeology and History* xxxv (1984), 1–27.
[2]   For Gloucester under Serlo see ch. 3.
[3]   For the different versions of the *De miraculis*, two of which are printed in *The memorials of St Edmund's abbey*, ed. T. Arnold (Rolls series lxxxxix, 1890–6), see R. M. Thomson, 'Early romanesque book-illustration in England: the dates of the Pierpont Morgan "vitae sancti Edmundi" and Bury bible', *Viator* ii (1971), 211–25, 'Two versions of a saint's life from St Edmunds abbey: changing currents in a XIIth century monastic style', *Revue Bénédictine* lxxiv (1974), 383–408, and 'Twelfth-century documents from Bury St Edmunds abbey', *English Historical Review* lxxxxii (1977), 806–19.
[4]   For a discussion of the Feudal Book's relationship with Domesday Book see Harvey,

when William the Conqueror ordered the description of the whole of England, thus at much the same time as Domesday Book, although there is evidence for believing it was later revised by Abbot Albold (d. 1119).[5] There is also a list of benefactors inscribed in the *Registrum album*, BL, MS Add. 14847, fos 19v–20v, which includes both pre-1066, as well as post-Conquest, donors.[6] Collectively, these sources can be made to yield, sometimes-in an indirect fashion, valuable information about patronage, politics, pilgrims and the importance of the shrine of St Edmund.

Following its refoundation as a Benedictine house in the 1020s by Cnut, the fortunes of Bury St Edmunds rose very rapidly.[7] King Cnut and Edward the Confessor were both very generous supporters of the monastery, a generosity probably accentuated by the difficulties they both had with the neighbouring Fenland houses.[8] Besides royal patronage, Bury received a healthy number of grants and bequests from local men and women as well as from the bishop of Elmham, and from royal and monastic servants, Alnoth and Leofstan.[9] Furthermore, by the last decade of the Confessor's reign Bury had accumulated considerable political and economic power in the localities with its jurisdiction over eight and a half hundreds and its right to have a moneyer.[10] In his last year of life the Confessor made his favoured physician, Baldwin, abbot of Bury St Edmunds. Thus, at the time of the Norman Conquest, Bury was unique among English abbeys in possessing a continental abbot, one moreover who had been installed for less than a year and was well-equipped to steer the house through the coming crises. Baldwin had been born at Chartres and had been a monk of St-Denis and prior of Leberaw before coming to England to act as Edward's physician.[11] He was naturally better equipped both psychologically and linguistically to accept the new order.

Once the campaign of 1066 had defeated the Anglo-Saxon regime, Baldwin transferred his loyalty to his new masters: it was his steadfast loyalty towards the Conquerors rather than simply his continental origins that cushioned his abbey from many of the early difficulties that Ely, Peterborough and

---

'Domesday Book and its predecessors', 753–73 at p. 761, and R. V. Lennard, *Rural England, 1086–1135: a study of social and agrarian conditions*, Oxford 1959, 359.

5   The dating of the Feudal Book has been subject to some controversy with estimates ranging from 'just pre-Domesday' by Sally Harvey, to between 7 September 1087 and 4 January 1098 by David Douglas and to after Baldwin's death but before the death of Abbot Albold in 1119 by Lennard: Harvey, 'Domesday Book', 761; *Feudal documents from the abbey of Bury St Edmunds*, ed. D. C. Douglas, London 1932, pp. xlviii–xlix; Lennard, *Rural England*, 359.

6   There is a slightly different version of the list, in Latin, in the mid thirteenth-century manuscript of the *liber albus*: BL, MS Harley 1005, fo. 83r (printed in *Mon.*, iii. 138–9).

7   For a contrary view see Grandsen 'Legends and traditions', 1–24.

8   For Cnut and Bury St Edmunds see ch. 1.

9   Hart, *Charters of eastern England*, nos 363–8.

10   Barlow, *Edward the Confessor*, 77. Edward the Confessor had originally granted these hundreds to Bury after his mother's disgrace c. 1043 but must have returned them to her after her restoration to favour: Davis, 'Liberties', 420.

11   Knowles, Brooke and London, *Heads of religious houses*, 32.

Abingdon experienced. Yet Baldwin did not just keep his distance from potential insurrection; he managed to associate himself actively with the new regime by becoming physician to William the Conqueror and to William Rufus as well as to Archbishop Lanfranc.[12] Thus Bury St Edmunds was well placed amongst the English houses to attract royal favour and this it did with spectacular results. Baldwin's advantageous position was paralleled by that of William, bishop of London (1051–75). He too was unique; he was the only Norman bishop in England in 1066 and was also a confidant of Edward the Confessor and of William the Conqueror. It seems no coincidence that Bishop William was able to purchase a large number of estates and recover a number of 'lost' lands previously held by St Paul's.[13]

In 1086 Bury was among the five richest English houses in England with landed possessions stretching across seven counties.[14] Abbot Baldwin had a great deal to defend, and, despite his advantageous position, the post-Conquest years were not without their problems. William the Conqueror had all the abbey men who had fought against him in 1066 dispossessed, but by the time of Domesday Book many of these lands had been recovered by Baldwin.[15] Post-Conquest annexations of Bury St Edmunds's lands were comparatively light especially in Suffolk where the bulk of abbey lands were concentrated.[16] Domesday Book records Bury St Edmunds as having lost control over the manor of Mildenhall which had been a gift from Edward the Confessor.[17] Closer investigation reveals that this was not a post-Conquest alienation, but another pre-Conquest invasion by Archbishop Stigand.[18] William the Conqueror had probably chosen not to make good Stigand's appropriation as Mildenhall was a very valuable manor, assessed at £70 in 1086. The confusion caused by the Conquest was probably the reason for the loss of two carucates at Gislingham, in Suffolk. This manor had been leased out to Alsi and his wife for life by Abbot Leofstan (1044–65), but in 1086 it had become part of the lands of Gilbert the Crossbowman.[19] In Norfolk, further from the easy reach of the abbey, Bury's losses were heavier, but still far from serious. There were six cases of annexations or claims, but these tended to be smaller portions of land such as in Shimpling where the abbey claimed fourteen acres from the king.[20]

The question of how many estates had been invaded and subsequently recovered in the years between 1066 and 1086 is virtually impossible to

12 *Letters of Lanfranc*, 41.
13 Taylor, 'Estates of the bishopric of London', 52–3.
14 Knowles, *Monastic order*, 702–3.
15 *Feudal documents*, 47; *Regesta*, i, no. 40.
16 In 1086 Bury St Edmunds held land worth over £494 in Suffolk.
17 DB ii, fo. 288b.
18 See ch. 2.
19 DB ii, fo. 444b.
20 Ibid. ii, fo. 130a.

ascertain with accuracy.[21] Writs of the Conqueror show that the abbey's problems were more extensive than is indicated by the texts of the *De miraculis de Sancti Eadmundi*, the Feudal Book or Domesday Book. One writ, addressed to Richard fitz Gilbert and 'R' the sheriff, ordered that Abbot Baldwin should have the land of Brictwold, justice against Peter de Valognes and be repossessed of the men of Frodo at Buxhall, in Suffolk, which the men of Count Eustace had taken from him.[22] Domesday Book, however, enters Buxhall as a possession of Count Eustace without any mention of the abbey's claim of jurisdiction over certain men of Frodo there.[23] Another writ again addresses the problem of encroachments on abbey lands, especially that of Peter de Valognes who, probably as a compromise, was enfeoffed as a tenant of the abbey on the land he had taken.[24]

Information derived from Domesday Book reveals that despite these problems on the abbey's lands a very efficient and healthy administration produced impressive increases during the twenty years after the Norman Conquest. In 1086 Bury's lands stretched across seven of the eastern counties, in Bedfordshire, Northamptonshire, Oxfordshire, Cambridgeshire, Essex, Norfolk and Suffolk. The overwhelming majority of lands, in fact 90 per cent, were situated in Suffolk and Norfolk, and three-quarters of all Bury's lands, valued at £494 10s. in 1086, were located in Suffolk itself. The proximity of these estates to the abbey naturally made for easier and more efficient management. Excluding the lands which were acquired after 1066, which will be discussed below, the value of all the abbey's lands had increased by just under a third from £438 to £567.[25] In Suffolk values rose from approximately £345 by £106, in other words by 31 per cent, to £451.[26] Baldwin was well aware of the value of easy communications with the abbey's demesne estates. When William the Conqueror granted Baldwin the estates of Brictwulf fitz Leofmer to be granted out in return for knights service, Baldwin retained Chevington and Saxham in the church's demesne because they were close to the abbey.[27] The town of Bury St Edmunds itself had doubled in value from £10 to £20.[28] Such increases were not due to chance. Two mills and two ponds or fish ponds had been added as well as 342 houses which Abbot Baldwin had built

---

[21] Antonia Gransden has discussed three cases of Normans who caused disturbances on St Edmund's lands. With the help of St Edmund's intervention each ended happily for the abbey: 'Baldwin', 67.

[22] *Feudal documents*, 56; *Regesta*, ii, no. 243.

[23] *DB* ii, fo. 303b.

[24] *Feudal documents*, 56; *Regesta*, i, no. 258. It appears that as a compromise Peter was enfeoffed as a tenant on the abbey lands he had taken: *DB* ii, fos 365a, 366a, 366a–b, 367b.

[25] My own calculations.

[26] This excludes the manors of Chevington, Downham, Great Livermere, Preston, Santon, Saxham, Somerton and Tostock which were post-Conquest acquisitions. Great Livermere, however, was given to William the Conqueror by the abbot but was returned before 1070: *DB* ii, fo. 363b.

[27] *Feudal documents*, 4.

[28] *DB* ii, fo. 372a.

on land which had been arable before 1066, so that by 1086 the town had more than 500 dwellings. Baldwin also provided a new market-place which was 'crucial to the town's future prosperity'.[29] The impact of Baldwin's deliberate town planning is still in evidence today, manifest in the geometric design of Bury St Edmunds's streets.[30] Abbey lands were also made to yield an additional 35 per cent in Norfolk, from just over £60 to more than £80 in 1086.[31]

The Conquest produced comparatively less confusion on Bury St Edmunds's lands than on the lands of its neighbours Ely and Ramsey. Although like Bury St Edmunds, Ely and Ramsey were also among the five richest English houses in 1086 they both faced severe tenurial losses and became involved in extensive litigation in order to secure the return of these lands. Ely's involvement with the Fenland revolt of 1070–1, and subsequent disgrace, also gave Bury St Edmunds a crucially important strategic role to play in the defence of East Anglia.[32] This explains two things: first, why William the Conqueror gave the abbey a substantial quota of forty knights, and second, why he gave Abbot Baldwin five manors covering sixteen carucates of land, and valued at over £37, specifically to help the abbey fulfil its quota of knight service.[33]

This brings us to the subject of the post-Conquest acquisitions made by Bury St Edmunds. Usually Domesday Book is an unrewarding source for gifts to English abbeys simply because so few were made before 1086. In this respect the circumstances recorded by Domesday relating to Bury St Edmunds are truly exceptional. Whereas Abingdon and Gloucester had none or only one grant, respectively, recorded in Domesday Book, Bury St Edmunds had at least eight.[34] These gifts of land were located in five counties and amounted to at least fifteen hides, one virgate and ten carucates of land and were valued at well over £36. The Feudal Book also reveals that the abbey's possession of the five Suffolk estates mentioned above was the result of the grant of William the Conqueror. As with Westminster abbey, in this particular instance, William favoured granting lands which had recently come into his possession.[35] These holdings had been among the manors

---

[29] Jocelin of Brakelond, *The chronicle of the abbey of Bury St Edmunds*, ed. D. Greenway and J. Sayer, Oxford 1989, p. xix.

[30] C. Platt, *Medieval Britain from the air*, London 1984, 45.

[31] This figure excludes William the Conqueror's grant of the manor of Brooke, Norfolk.

[32] See Ridyard, 'Condigna veneratio', 187.

[33] *Feudal documents*, 4. The Conqueror was also quick to grant Abbot Baldwin confirmation of the abbey's control of the eight and a half hundreds and the right to have a moneyer: ibid. 50, 58–61; *Regesta*, i, nos 12, 42, 292–4, 392–4, 395.

[34] These were Brooke and Runcton in Norfolk, Preston and Great Livermere in Suffolk, Scaldwell and Warketon in Northants, Kinwick in Bedfordshire, and Little Waltham in Essex: *DB* i, fos 210c, 222b; ii, fos 20a, 210a, 275b, 359b, 363a.

[35] Emma Mason, 'Pro statu et incolumiate regni mei: royal monastic patronage 1066–1154', in S. Mews (ed.), *Religion and national identity* (Studies in Church History xviii, 1982), 99–117 at p. 102.

previously held by Brictwold fitz Leofmer and amounted to sixteen carucates of land. In the twenty years after the Conquest, Baldwin acquired land valued at over twenty-six carucates, fifteen hides and one virgate and in 1086 was assessed at over £73. This dramatic gain is even more impressive when added to the substantial rise in the value of the abbey estates over these years; from being worth approximately £446 in 1066 the abbey's landed assets had risen in value by £202 to £640 in 1086, an increase representing a remarkable rise of 46 per cent.

These were not the only grants and gifts Bury St Edmunds received in these two decades. Together, William the Conqueror and Queen Matilda were Bury St Edmunds's most generous post-Conquest benefactors. Between them they made grants of land to Bury in four counties amounting to twenty-three carucates, seven hides and one virgate and worth over £65 in 1086. The most valuable manor granted by William was Brooke, in Norfolk, 'when he first came to St Edmund'.[36] In the lists of benefactors and their gifts recorded in BL, MS Add. 14847 and MS Harley 1005, the grant of Warkton, in Northamptonshire, is credited to Queen Matilda, who made it 'of her own accord'.[37] This was no small gift as the estate was valued at £8 in 1086. It was also quite a *coup* for an English monastery as Matilda's religious interests lay largely in Normandy, and her generosity to English houses was otherwise limited to her grant of Garsdon, in Wiltshire, to Malmesbury abbey in 1081.[38] Matilda's attachment to Bury St Edmunds probably explains William the Conqueror's later grant of one hide and three virgates at Scaldwell, in Northamptonshire, after Matilda's death, specifically 'for the soul of Queen Matilda'.[39]

The other benefactors who made grants in the reign of William the Conqueror were diverse in their social standing. They ranged from the ill-fated Earl Waltheof and his wife Judith, a wealthy Englishwoman called Leofgifu, who was probably the same woman who was also benefactor of Bury with her second husband, Otto the goldsmith, and a 'knight', Werno of Poix. In his ten years after the Conquest, Earl Waltheof was an active benefactor of a number of English abbeys such as Crowland (whence he was brought for burial after his execution in 1076), Tynemouth, Jarrow and the see of Lincoln.[40] He was also in confraternity with Ely and Thorney abbeys.[41] By 1086 Judith had given part of her manor at Broughton, in Northamptonshire, 'by the king's leave' to St-Wandrille.[42] Their grant of three hides and three virgates at Kinwick, in Bedfordshire, to Bury St Edmunds in alms was valued at £4 in

---

36 *Feudal documents*, 13; DB ii, fo. 210a.

37 BL, MS Add. 47847, fo. 20r.

38 *CDF*, nos 93, 196; *Regesta*, i, no. 247.

39 DB i, fo. 222b.

40 For Earl Waltheof's career see F. S. Scott, 'Earl Waltheof of Northumbria', *Archaeologia Aeliana* xxx (1952), 149–213.

41 Ibid. 195.

42 DB i, fo. 229a.

1086, and must have been made sometime after their marriage c. 1070 or 1072 and before Waltheof's imprisonment in 1075.[43] On first examination the explanation for the connection between Waltheof, Judith and Bury St Edmunds is not an easy one to make. As earl of Northumberland Waltheof's interests lay in the north of England and the bulk of Judith's Domesday landed interests, which were to make up the honor of Huntingdon in the twelfth and thirteen centuries, did not obviously coincide with the bulk of those held by the abbey in Suffolk, Norfolk and Essex.[44] As Judith was William the Conqueror's niece his inclination for Bury St Edmunds and, just as important, the cult of St Edmund at Bury, may have influenced her to make a gift with her husband.[45]

Within four years of the Conquest Bury St Edmunds was perceived as an desirable place for Normans to spend their last years. Werno of Poix became a monk of Bury St Edmunds and gave two carucates in Great Livermere, Suffolk, to act as at least part of his entry gift whilst still supporting his daughter during her lifetime.[46] At least one other Norman, Ranulf, a courtier of William the Conqueror, also became a monk at Bury St Edmunds after having a vision of St Edmund.[47] Otto the goldsmith and his wife, Leofgifu, granted land at Hawstead, Suffolk.[48] Otto was the craftsman who was to bejewel the tomb of the Conqueror at Caen and Leofgifu was the surviving wife of a pre-Conquest citizen of London: through her Otto held extensive estates in Essex.[49] He was also probably the same Otto who held one carucate at Hawstead from the abbey. It is unclear whether the whole of Hawstead had been given or just the one carucate that Otto held according to Domesday Book in 1086.[50]

In the last years of the eleventh century Abbot Baldwin commissioned the archdeacon Herman to compose a new miracle collection, De miraculis Sancti Eadmundi. He also had Abbo of Fleury's Passio Sancti Eadmundi, composed in the mid tenth century, interpolated and disseminated.[51] Abbot Baldwin established a multi-media, and probably a multi-lingual, approach to the promotion of the cult of St Edmund. This strategy was probably adopted by the French abbot to circumvent the language barrier between the 'literate'

---

43 Ibid. i, fo. 210c. For the date of their marriage see Scott, 'Waltheof', 158, 185.

44 For Judith and the honor of Huntingdon see William Farrer, Honors and knights' fees, London–Manchester 1923–5, ii. 296.

45 Another point of contact between the abbey and Judith was Abbot Baldwin's tenancy of Judith's land in Blunham, Bedfordshire, in 1086. Bury St Edmunds also held four hides and a virgate at Blunham from the king in 1086.

46 Feudal documents, 47; DB ii, fo. 363b.

47 Memorials of St Edmund's, i. 75–7.

48 DB ii, fo. 358a.

49 OV iv. 110; VCH, Essex, i. 350–1; Feudal documents, pp. cxx, cxxxix.

50 Ibid. 61–2; Regesta, ii, no. 658. Otto arranged to retain a life interest in at least part of his gift.

51 It is significant that the three earliest extant manuscripts of Abbo's passio all date from the late eleventh century: S. J. Ridyard, Royal saints of Anglo-Saxon England: a study of west Saxon and East Anglian cults, Cambridge 1988, 65; Gransden, 'Legends and traditions', 3.

monks and the laity, the overwhelming majority of whom were, technically speaking, 'illiterate'. The abbot promoted visual and aural/oral means to communicate the character of his saint's cult directly to the pilgrims who visited the shrine. This was achieved through a formidable fusion of the visual and narrative through 'performances', which included preaching, public prayer and visual displays. An example of one great occasion on which the laity were preached to was the translation of St Edmund's body in 1095, accompanied by the translation of the relics of St Botulph and St Jurmin.[52] Baldwin also used visual means of communication by placing a board bearing the martyr's legend in the church and by publicly announcing one cure, if not more, to the 'assembling crowds in the church'.[53] Public displays of the abbey's relics were also a very influential means of involving the laity in the cult. In 1095, on the occasion of his translation into the new church, St Edmund's body was carried outside the church whilst prayers were said for the end of a long drought.[54] In the early twelfth century a crowd of pilgrims that had gathered at Bury St Edmunds one Pentecost 'was so impressed by the display of the relics of St Edmund that it forced the preacher to show them again'.[55]

The collection of miracles in Herman's late eleventh-century version of *De miraculis*, which covers the years of Baldwin's abbacy, portrays an energetic and widespread cult which appealed to the continental newcomers and the English alike.[56] Pilgrims travelled from places within England such as Essex, West Sussex, London, Northampton, Lincolnshire and Herefordshire and even from further afield, from Angers on the continent.[57] The cult of St Edmund had achieved such significance in the eyes of one of William Rufus' knights, called Ivo, that he named his son after the saint.[58] Pilgrims' offerings to the saint's shrine must have generated a healthy income for the abbey. Wulfmar, a man of the abbey, having fallen ill on return from Rome made an offering to the saint of 'four crystal stones which he had recently brought from Rome' in thanksgiving for his subsequent recovery.[59] The new abbey church, begun in about 1080, was almost certainly designed to allow pilgrims

---

52 *Memorials of St Edmund's*, i. 90–1, 158–60. This occasion is discussed by A. J. Gurevich, *Medieval popular culture: problems of belief and perceptions*, trans. J. M. Bak and P. A. Hollingsworth, Cambridge 1988, 4.

53 'Magno tabulatus opere': *Memorials of St Edmund's*, i. 83–4. For examples of miracles accounts being preserved on tables (at Glastonbury and York) and on a triptych (at Bamburgh, Norfolk) see R. M. Wilson, *The lost literature of medieval England*, London 1970, 87.

54 *Memorials of St Edmund's*, i. 90–1. See also A. Gransden, 'The alleged incorruption of the body of St Edmund, king and martyr', *Antiquaries Journal* lxxiv (1994), 135–68.

55 *Memorials of St Edmund's*, i. 173–4, cited by J. Sumption in *Pilgrimage: an image of medieval religion*, London 1975, 215.

56 For the strength of St Edmund's cult see Gransden, 'Baldwin', 75; Ridyard, 'Condigna veneratio', 189n.

57 *Memorials of St Edmund's*, i. 69–72, 74–5, 83, 89, 144, 160, 180.

58 Ibid. i. 77–8, 145–6.

59 Ibid. i. 160–2.

to circulate around the sanctuary shrines.[60] Abbot Baldwin's decision to start constructing the church on an exceptional scale and to have the transepts built to a plan not seen anywhere else in England was conceptually significant.[61] The total length of 500 feet meant that the church was to become one of the four largest churches in northern Europe.[62] Herman's De miraculis also refers to Abbot Baldwin's activities on the continent and St Edmund's miraculous powers in France and Italy.[63] It is thus evident that Baldwin's aspirations were not just limited to a national platform but stretched very much further across the English Channel.[64]

William Rufus did not show the same degree of interest in patronising Bury St Edmunds as had his father, but then the Conqueror had been very generous indeed. Rufus was willing enough to confirm the abbey's possessions and rights as they had been held under his father and gave permission for St Edmund's relics to be translated in 1095.[65] His grant of the whole of Hargrave, in Suffolk, was in itself fairly generous as in 1086 it was valued at £4.[66] Other benefactors to the abbey, besides those already mentioned in relation to the De miraculis, had local connections with Bury St Edmunds. The greatest of them all was Alan Rufus of Brittany whose centres of power lay in the north in Yorkshire and to the south in Brittany. Alan I Rufus, lord of Richmond and the son-in-law of William the Conqueror, was one of the ten richest lay tenants-in-chief in England in 1086.[67] He held lands in twelve Domesday counties worth £1,120 in 1086, was the chief landowner in

---

60 R. Gilyard-Beer, 'The eastern arm of the abbey church at Bury St Edmunds', Proceedings of the Suffolk Institute of Archaeology xxxi (1970), 256–62 at p. 260; B. Abou-El-Haj, 'Bury St Edmunds abbey between 1070 and 1124: a history of property, privilege, and monastic art production', Art History vi (1983), 1–29 at p. 3. For the effect of the cult of saints upon medieval church architecture in general see C. R. Cheney, 'Church-building in the Middle Ages', Bulletin of the John Rylands Library xxiv (1951–2), 20–36.

61 Gilyard-Beer, 'Eastern arm of the abbey', 260–2.

62 Abou-El-Haj, 'Bury St Edmunds', 2.

63 Memorials of St Edmund's, i. 56, 68–74.

64 Abbot Hugh (1157–80) had new shrines built for St Botulph and St Jurmin: I. G. Thomas, 'The cult of saints' relics in medieval England', unpubl. Ph.D. diss. London 1974, 161. Hugh also had an altar to St Thomas built in the church: Whittingham, 'Bury St Edmunds abbey', 172.

65 Feudal documents, 57–61; Regesta, ii, nos 291–4, 369, 392–4. For Bury's relationship with William Rufus and his court see A. Gransden, 'The question of the consecration of St Edmunds church', in I. Wood and G. A. Loud (eds), Church and chronicle in the Middle Ages, London 1991, 59–86 at pp. 60–1.

66 DB ii. fo. 435b.

67 C. W. Hollister, 'The greater Domesday tenants-in-chiefs', in J. C. Holt (ed.), Domesday Studies, Woodbridge 1987, 219–48 at p. 242. For the counts of Richmond see K. S. B. Keats-Rohan, 'William I and the Breton contingent in the non-Norman Conquest 1066–1087', Anglo-Norman Studies xiii (1991), 156–72 at pp. 159–60, and 'The Bretons and Normans of England 1066–1154: the family, the fief and the feudal monarchy', Nottingham Medieval Studies xxxvi (1992), 42–78 at pp. 77–8.

Norfolk and held considerable estates in Suffolk.[68] He is recorded as having given 'many great expenses' to the church of St Edmunds.[69] This would seem to imply that he had given cash. Alan's younger brothers, who were also his successors, Alan II Niger and Stephen, made separate grants to Bury St Edmunds 'for the soul of his father and brother earl A[lan]'. Alan had some interests in East Anglia, and had probably visited Bury St Edmunds on his way between his northern lands and the continent. His connection with Bury may have prompted the grant of Lidgate, in Suffolk, from another Breton, Reginald, also an abbey tenant. Reginald made this gift, valued at 60s. in 1086, 'for his salvation' before he set out on pilgrimage for Jerusalem.[70]

It was probably later in Baldwin's abbacy that Haimo Pecche's maternal grandmother, Ievita, the wife of the wealthy Suffolk Domesday tenant-in-chief, Hervey de Bourges, gave Bury St Edmunds the grant which her daughter, Isilia, and grandson, Haimo, confirmed in the time of Abbot Anselm (1121–48).[71] The generosity of the earls of Richmond towards Bury St Edmunds may have had an influence on Ievita, but it seems more likely that it was veneration for St Edmund himself that motivated her. In Herman's description of the saint's translation in 1095 in the presence of a vast multitude of men and women, he calls 'the female sex the special glory' of St Edmund.[72] Perhaps this was the occasion on which Isilia made her gift. The great magnate and important Suffolk landholder, Gilbert fitz Richard, made a grant of two men in Westley, Suffolk, to Bury St Edmunds some time between 1090 and Baldwin's death.[73] Although this grant was in reality a settlement of a dispute, Gilbert's charter uses the language of gift-giving for it employs the phrase, *pro salute mea*, and the concession was certainly of benefit to the abbey.[74] The Clare family's religious interests were centred around Gilbert fitz Richard's foundation of Clare, in Suffolk, as a cell of Le Bec which was later moved to Stoke by Clare.[75] This was not the end of Bury St Edmunds's dealing with the Clare family, however, as around 1145 Gilbert's grandson and namesake, the earl of Hereford, made another grant to the abbey.[76]

Under the guidance of Abbot Baldwin, Bury St Edmunds secured its position as one of the foremost pilgrimage centres and richest abbeys in England.

---

[68] For his great wealth see J. F. A. Mason, 'The honour of Richmond in 1086', *English Historical Review* lxxviii (1963), 703–4.

[69] *Memorials of St Edmund's*, i, 350.

[70] BL, MS Add. 14847, fo. 20v; *Feudal documents*, 22, 60; *Regesta*, i, no. 395. Reginald is called the brother of Hubert the Breton and held 1½ carucates at Great Livermere, Suffolk.

[71] *Feudal documents*, 159; DB ii, fo. 149b. For the descent of the Bourges lands in Suffolk see I. J. Sanders, *English baronies: a study of their origin and descent*, Oxford 1960, 48.

[72] *Memorials of St Edmund's*, i. 87.

[73] *Feudal documents*, 152–3.

[74] Ibid. p. xciv.

[75] For the patronage of the Clare family see Ward, 'Fashions in monastic endowments', 427–51.

[76] *Feudal documents*, 156.

Religious patronage received from the likes of the king and queen, magnates and people of local importance such as Otto the goldsmith augmented the abbey's possessions in Suffolk in particular, but also to a lesser degree in Essex, Bedfordshire and Northamptonshire.

Before 1100 the other Suffolk houses such as Felixstowe, Thetford and Eye appear poor rivals for religious patronage. But although these houses could never match Bury St Edmunds' wealth and prestige, the establishment of Felixstowe and Thetford by Roger Bigod did mean that these foundations, rather than Bury, attracted grants of tithes and churches from Roger Bigod's tenants, for example Hugh of Houdain and William de Bourneville.[77] The foundation of Eye priory by Robert Malet in about 1086/7 threatened a similar result. However, Robert Malet's fall from royal favour under William Rufus meant the priory's endowment not only ground to a halt, but actually went into reverse as Roger the Poitevin was given control of the honor of Eye and disendowed the priory in favour of Charroux and Lancaster.[78] Under Henry I Robert regained favour along with his honor and grants to the priory resumed. Other Suffolk houses were founded in the time of Henry I such as Ixworth priory and Redlingfield nunnery.[79] William Blunt, who founded Ixworth in c. 1100 as an Augustinian house, was tenant-in-chief in the area north of Bury St Edmunds. He was also a tenant of the abbot.[80] The grants that these foundations received were in effect missed opportunities for Bury St Edmunds, but the changing expectations and status of potential benefactors meant that it was impossible for Bury to maintain its pre-Conquest hegemony over patronage in Suffolk as it became more fashionable, even expected, that the lower ranks of the Anglo-Norman realm's tenants-in-chief would establish their own religious foundations.[81]

The death of Abbot Baldwin in 1098 brought disorder and trouble to the monks of Bury St Edmunds. Vacancies and depositions meant that until Albold of Jerusalem's appointment in 1114, Bury St Edmunds possessed a canonically consecrated abbot for no more than two years.[82] These troubled times certainly had a damaging impact on the output of the Bury *scriptorium*.[83] Henry I appears to have taken more than a passing interest in the abbey. He visited Bury during the 1102–7 vacancy, probably in 1106, when he issued three writs, one of which proclaimed that he had taken the abbey under his special protection.[84] One of the lists of abbey benefactors also

---

[77] Mon., v. 149.

[78] For the honor and priory of Eye see C. P. Lewis, 'The king and Eye: a study in Anglo-Norman politics', English Historical Review civ (1989), 569–87.

[79] VCH, Suffolk, i. 83, 105; Mon., iv. 26.

[80] DB ii, fos 367a–b, 370a.

[81] For further discussion the nature of cultural diffusion see ch. 9.

[82] For Baldwin's successors Robert I and Robert II and the disputes over the elections see Davis, 'Monks of St Edmund', 235–6.

[83] Thomson, 'Library of Bury St Edmunds', 629.

[84] Feudal documents, 65–6; Regesta, ii, nos 759–61. Henry I also granted numerous writs

credits him with giving Bury St Edmunds land in Canterbury.[85] This was possibly towards the end of his reign when Henry also gave Abbot Anselm a house in Rouen, one of the very rare grants in Normandy acquired by an English house in this period.[86] This was probably prompted by another visit to Bury St Edmunds by Henry in the last years of his reign, possibly in 1132.[87]

The ambitious building programme instigated by Baldwin in the 1080s was still under way during the vacancies that followed his death. Godfrey, the sacrist from c. 1096 to c. 1121, completed the refectory, the chapter house, the infirmary, the abbot's hall, the transepts, the central tower to roof level and two bays of the nave to full height.[88] The progress of the building work was not without its problems, but trouble over the quarrying and transport of the stone needed were not peculiar to this period of difficulties alone or indeed to Bury St Edmunds.[89] Building work cost a lot of money, but written evidence for donations to the abbey dries up almost completely in this period. This does not preclude the strong likelihood of cash donations being made at the saint's shrine. In the time of Abbot Robert II (1102–7) a confirmation by Archbishop Anselm for ten days' indulgence granted by John 'cardinal of the Roman Church' to pilgrims of the shrine of St Edmund was secured along with Archbishop Anselm's own addition of three days.[90] Perhaps such a grant was indicative of flagging pilgrim numbers which needed boosting. Despite Abbot Anselm's many absences from the abbey, his abbacy represented a much needed return to stability.[91] Henry I's concern for the welfare of the abbey is again in evidence in a letter to Anselm, possibly written in 1122, which begged him not to go abroad in search of a cure for his illness.[92] Apparently the objections of the abbey's monks and knights had reached the king's ears. Henry I also granted the abbot an annual fair at Bury St Edmunds, and although such grants were common and sometimes were merely confirmation of existing rights they were still worth having.[93]

Benefactions to Bury St Edmunds were generally rather thin on the ground throughout Henry I's reign, but they began to pick up again towards its end. Stephen, count of Brittany, granted land in Cambridge c. 1135 and sometime between 1121 and 1148 Haimo Pecche confirmed the grant made

confirming the abbey's liberties and its right to have a moneyer: *Feudal documents*, 62–8, 72, 74–9; *Regesta*, ii, nos 511, 644, 655–6, 672, 694, 759–61, 777, 861.
[85] *Mon.*, iii. 140.
[86] For other grants in Normandy made to English men and abbeys in England see Bates, 'Normandy and England after 1066', 851–76 at p. 869.
[87] *Feudal documents*, 76; *Regesta*, ii. no. 1733.
[88] Whittingham, 'Bury St Edmunds abbey', 170.
[89] *Feudal documents*, 57, 67; *Regesta*, i, no. 369; ii, no. 694. For the comparable difficulties suffered by the Fenland houses see ch. 7.
[90] *Feudal documents*, 153.
[91] For Abbot Anselm see Davis, 'Monks of St Edmund', 236–9.
[92] *Regesta*, ii, no. 1340.
[93] *Feudal documents*, 73; *Regesta*, ii. p. xxiv, no. 1599.

earlier by his grandmother.[94] Both these men had substantial landed interests in Suffolk and were from families that had previously patronised the abbey. Stephen continued in his brother's footsteps by trying to maintain an active role in his disparate interests in both the north and the south as well as in Brittany.[95] His son Alan III continued to link the family's interests in Suffolk together with those in the north by granting Rumburgh, in Suffolk, as a cell to St Mary's, York.[96] It seems that Alan I's foundation of St Mary, York, was finally exerting a more powerful pull on this lord of Richmond as Stephen chose to be buried there.[97] Haimo Pecche's gifts to religious houses mirrored his temporal interests as he was also a benefactor of the Le Bec cell of Clare and after its relocation in 1124 to Stoke by Clare.[98] In 1166 Haimo was a military tenant of Bury St Edmunds, Ely and the honor of Clare as well as being the constable of Clare in the time of Gilbert, earl of Hereford.[99] Haimo later became a benefactor in his own right and arranged to be buried at Bury St Edmunds with the consent of his sons Geoffrey and Gilbert.[100]

The benefactors of Bury St Edmunds differ from those of almost every other English house in that there are virtually no local officials amongst their number. As Bury St Edmunds had control of its 'miniature shire' of eight and a half hundreds, thus excluding the influence of royal officials from over a third of Suffolk the successive abbots may not have felt a great need to win their goodwill.[101] Anselm made the first perceptible move in this direction when he attempted to secure the favour of Robert fitz Walter, sheriff of Suffolk and Norfolk. Robert became a military tenant of the abbey in return for land at Long Melford, Suffolk, some time between Anselm's appointment in 1121 and Robert's death in about 1128.[102] Robert fitz Walter, like other local sheriffs such as Roger Bigod, Peter de Valognes and Robert Malet, had founded his own religious house dedicated to St Faith at Horsham, in Norfolk.[103] Robert's interests were not devoted exclusively to St Faith as he was also a benefactor of Castle Acre which was a cell of the Cluniac foundation at Lewes, in Sussex.[104] This was probably because his second wife, Aveline de Hesdin, had previously been a generous benefactor of Castle Acre with her first husband Alan fitz Flaad.[105] Roger Bigod and Peter de Valognes had been

94   *Feudal documents*, 155, 159.
95   For Stephen's foundations in Brittany see GEC x. 787.
96   Binns, *Dedications*, 83.
97   Brian Golding, 'Anglo-Norman knightly burials', in C. Harper-Bill and R. Harvey (eds), *The ideals and practice of medieval knighthood*, i, Woodbridge 1986, 35–48 at p. 44.
98   *Stoke by Clare cartulary*, ed. C. Harper-Bill and R. Mortimer (Suffolk Charters iv–vi, 1982–4), ii. 236.
99   *Red book*, i. 393, 363–4, 403; Ward, 'Fashions in monastic endowments', 193.
100 CUL, MS Mm. 4 19, fo. 147v.
101 Davis, 'Liberties', 419, 421.
102 *Feudal documents*, 123.
103 Binns, *Dedications*, 99.
104 *Mon.*, v. 50.
105 G. W. S. Barrow, *The Anglo-Norman era in Scottish history*, Oxford 1980, 14–15.

tenants of Bury St Edmunds at the time of Domesday Book, but this association does not appear to have yielded any gifts for the abbey. The fact that
many of these men's foundations had been established comparatively early, in
the reigns of William the Conqueror and William Rufus, must also have discouraged them from making gifts to such a powerful and wealthy house as its
patronage would do little to cement their tenants to their honors and to
themselves in the way that Eye, Thetford and Binham could. [106]

The extensive patronage Bury St Edmunds received in the first twenty
years after the Norman Conquest goes a long way towards proving that the
Anglo-Normans had no prejudice against English monasteries *per se*.
Although Abbot Baldwin himself was not English, his abbey was staffed by
officials and monks who were.[107] Together they were guardians of an English
royal saint whose reputation was not just local or even national, but international.[108] Baldwin's death brought a series of crises to the abbey which were
not resolved until towards the end of Henry I's reign. Only then did signs of
resuming patronage appear, exercised by men with strong local connections.

---

[106] For more on lordship and patronage see ch. 10.

[107] Benedict, Abbot Baldwin's prior, was English and had been chaplain to Edward the
Confessor and Queen Edith. Benedict was recruited from St John's, Beverley, by Baldwin:
Memorials of St Edmund's, i. 351. However, the promotion of Baldwin the prior to the abbacy
of Bury St Edmunds was supposedly opposed by Henry I because he was English: Davis, 'The
monks of St Edmund', 236.

[108] *Memorials of St Edmund's*, i. 69–72. Abbot Warner of Rebaix visited the shrine of St Edmund and was given a relic by Abbot Baldwin.

5

St Albans

By the time of Henry I's death the post-Conquest history of the abbey of St
Albans had been one of apparent success. As a representative of Old English
Benedictine monasteries, St Albans possessed an unparalleled number of
dependent cells and priories and its landed interests, together with those of
its dependants, stretched from Northumberland, through Yorkshire, Lincolnshire, Leicestershire, Northamptonshire, Norfolk, Buckinghamshire, Bedfordshire, Berkshire, Oxfordshire and Hertfordshire to Middlesex and Essex.
In contrast, in 1066 the majority of St Albans's lands had been located com-
pactly in Hertfordshire, with some outlying lands in Buckinghamshire, Bedfordshire and Berkshire, worth in total £280.[1] However, the prosperous
position of the abbey in the 1130s belies the fact that the early post-Conquest
years had been difficult ones. The later success of the abbey in recovering
many of the lands lost before 1077 and in attracting extensive patronage from
Anglo-Normans of both local and national importance was due mostly to the
series of accomplished men who were its abbots.

In the late eleventh and early twelfth centuries St Albans numbered some
of the greatest names in the Anglo-Norman realm among its benefactors.[2]
They included members of the Tosny family, the d'Aubignys, Roger Bigod,
Robert Malet and the counts of Mortain. An examination of the ties of lordship of the abbey's benefactors also reveals that there was a marked tendency
for tenants to follow their overlords' example. Much of this can be explained
by the unusually large number of priories that St Albans acquired after 1066
and the special circumstances that attended the endowment of priories in
post-Conquest England. Unlike other English monasteries which flourished
after 1066, such as Bury St Edmunds and Gloucester, the king's favour and
influence was slight. In the early years it was the archbishop of Canterbury,
Lanfranc, who had direct lordship over the abbey and whose actions promoted its wealth and standing.[3]

---

[1] My own calculations. See also E. Miller, 'The estates of the abbey of St Albans', *Transactions of the St Albans and Hertfordshire Architectural and Archaeological Society* v (1938),
285–300.
[2] See B. Golding, 'Wealth and artistic patronage at twelfth-century St Albans', in S.
Macready and F. H. Thompson (eds), *Art and patronage in the English romanesque*, London
1986, 107–17 at p. 112.
[3] For the archbishops of Canterbury's relationship with St Albans see remarks made by M.
Brett, *The English Church under Henry I*, Oxford 1975, 137.

St Albans was supposedly founded by Offa, king of Mercia, in 793.[4] Much of the early history of the abbey is obscure but it seems that the only other pre-Conquest king to patronise the abbey had been Æthelred.[5] A handful of lay wills also survive from the reigns of Æthelred and Edward the Confessor.[6] The sources for the post-Conquest history of St Albans need to be treated with caution too as, except for the abbey's entries in Domesday Book, all the sources are later copies of, or compilations from, earlier material; these include the thirteenth-century house chronicle, the Gesta abbatum monasterii Sancti Albani which Matthew Paris had copied from an earlier cartulary into his Liber additamentorum; a list of the abbey benefactors in a late fourteenth-century manuscript; entries in the various cartularies of the St Albans cells; and a fire-damaged late fourteenth-century manuscript.[7] Unfortunately, the Gesta abbatum is both vague and extremely unreliable for the history of the abbey before the advent of Abbot Paul of Caen (1077–93) and in particular concerning Ely's temporary, or otherwise, possession of the relics of St Alban.[8]

The years that followed the Conquest were traumatic for the abbey. The Gesta abbatum claims that during the vacancy that preceded Paul's appointment as abbot, the abbey lands were wasted by the king,[9] the abbey woods uprooted and its men impoverished. Evidence in Domesday Book also backs up the tale of the loss of abbey lands such as Flamstead and Aldenham, in Hertfordshire.[10] It also adds the loss of the valuable manor of Great Gaddesdon, two hides in Shephall, the loss of one hide, three virgates in Theobald Street, also in Hertfordshire, and one hide in Stotfold, in Bedfordshire.[11] Moreover, the turmoil of the Conquest prevented several pre-Conquest bequests from coming to fruition.[12] Around 1050 a rich local man, Eadwine of Caddington, had bequeathed land to the abbey at Watford, in Hertfordshire, after his death, and Barley, also in Hertfordshire, after that of his son, Leofwine. Neither ever came into the abbey's possession. At much the same time a certain Ulf decided that on his death land at Aston, in Hertfordshire,

---

4   S136, S138.
5   Simon Keynes, 'A lost cartulary of St Albans', Anglo-Saxon England xxii (1993), 253–79 at p. 259; S888, S912, S916. See also Taylor, 'The early St Albans endowment', 112–42.
6   S1235, S1488, S1497, S1517, S1532; Gesta abbatum, i. 39.
7   DB i, fos 56c, 59d, 135c–6b, 145d, 146. For criticism of Riley's edition and Matthew Paris's supposed contribution to the text of the Gesta abbatum see R. Vaughan, Matthew Paris, Cambridge 1958, 182–9, and now revised by Keynes, 'Lost cartulary', 260–2. The lists of benefactors are in BL, MS Cotton Nero D vii, fos 3v, 7r, 86r, 89r–115r, and there is also a fraternity list on fos 118r–27v. The fire-damaged manuscript is BL, MS Cotton Otho D iii.
8   For a discussion on the controversy between St Albans and Ely over the possession of the genuine relics of St Alban and the related texts see Vaughan, Matthew Paris, 198–204; Liber Eliensis, pp. xxxvii–xxxviii; Knowles, Brooke and London, Heads of religious houses, 65–6.
9   Gesta abbatum, i. 51.
10 For Flamstead and Aldenham see ibid. i. 40, 43; DB i, fos 135b, 138a–b.
11 Ibid. i, fos 139b, 133b, 134b, 213a.
12 S1517.

and Oxwick (in Codicote, Hertfordshire) should be given to St Albans.[13] Although Oxwick had come into the abbey's possession by 1086, Aston never did.[14] Finally, in the decade before Hastings, a local couple, Oswulf and Æthelgyth, granted Abbot Leofstan £1 and land at Studham, in Bedfordshire, retaining a life interest in return for admission into confraternity with the abbey.[15] Again, in 1086 this land was not held by St Albans. The values recorded in Domesday Book also show that in Hertfordshire the value of the abbey lands had fallen by almost one quarter after the Conquest.[16] By 1086 the abbey lands were worth about £244, having fallen from just under £280 in 1066. This decline occurred in the context of a county-wide decline in land values by 30 per cent in the early years after the Conquest.[17] By 1086 three-quarters of the county's holdings were still worth less than they had been in 1066, and as a whole the county's holdings had fallen by 20 per cent. These figures would therefore seem to bear out the account in the *Gesta abbatum* of the abbey's post-Conquest decline and then recovery under Abbot Paul.

The *Gesta abbatum* also claims that if the king had not been 'restrained by the chastisement of Lanfranc, he might have done irreparable damage, therefore Lanfranc himself effectively managed that Paul, his kinsman, whom he had brought into England with him, should be given command over the abbey'.[18] The central role played by Lanfranc in protecting St Albans is also borne out by other evidence. In the early twelfth century William of Malmesbury believed that it was Lanfranc who appointed Paul as abbot of St Albans.[19] The importance of Lanfranc's influence is demonstrated after his death when Abbot Paul secured a confirmation of the abbey's rights 'as on the day of Lanfranc's death'.[20] The list of benefactors in the fourteenth-century manuscript states that Lanfranc, 'pitying the disrepair of that church' gave 1,000 marks for the work of the church and restored the land at Redbourne, in Hertfordshire, which 'had been unjustly taken away'.[21] Redbourne and Langley, also in Hertfordshire, Grandborough, in Buckinghamshire, and *Thwangtune*, had been bequeathed to St Albans by Æthelwine *niger* in the 1040s.[22] By 1066 Archbishop Stigand was in possession of Redbourne, but his

---

[13] S1532.
[14] *DB* i, fo. 135d.
[15] S1235.
[16] Finn, *Norman Conquest*, 105.
[17] Ibid. 104.
[18] *Gesta abbatum*, i. 51.
[19] William of Malmesbury, *De gestis pontificum Anglorum libri quinque*, ed. N. E. S. A. Hamilton (Rolls series lxxxx, 1870), 72.
[20] *Regesta*, ii, no. 314c (printed in ibid. ii, p. 399); Matthew Paris, *Chronica majora*, ed. H. Richards Luard (Rolls series lvii, 1872–82), vi. 34.
[21] BL, MS Cotton Nero D vii, fo. 86r; *Mon.*, ii. 219.
[22] S1228.

successor, Lanfranc, subsequently returned it to the abbey before 1086.[23] Langley was never recovered.[24]

Lanfranc's other gifts reflect his concern for the resumption of normal religious life at St Albans. They included three great silver candlesticks, two silver candlesticks worth thirty marks, a gold chalice worth thirty marks, four caps, a tunic and a dalmatic. On his death he also left St Albans a bequest of £100, but it was claimed that only £50 was ever received. As well as being an extremely generous benefactor himself, Lanfranc also used his influence to secure for the abbey at least two, if not three, priories. An account of the acquisition of the priory of Belvoir, in Leicestershire, founded in 1076, relates that as Robert de Tosny, the founder, was having difficulty finishing his project he granted the incomplete buildings, 'consilio domini L[anfranci] archiepiscopi', to Abbot Paul to be a cell of St Albans.[25] The *Gesta abbatum* rather coyly states that Robert de Tosny was, 'spiritus devotione tactus'.[26] The founding of Wallingford priory, in Berkshire, came about in a rather different fashion.[27] Although the foundation was initiated by the grant of one and a half churches in Wallingford and half a hide of land outside the town, the impetus behind the establishment of a cell came from Abbot Paul himself rather than from the donor.[28] Lanfranc played a somewhat different role in affairs, again acting as advisor, 'de consilio Lanfranci archiepiscopi', but on this occasion he was guiding Abbot Paul.[29] It also appears that Lanfranc had been instrumental in persuading the earl of Northumbria, Robert de Mowbray, to grant Tynemouth priory to St Albans.[30] In the 1080s Tynemouth had been a dependency of Durham, but a quarrel broke out between Robert de Mowbray and the bishop of Durham, William de St-Calais. This culminated in Robert ejecting the handful of Durham monks from St Mary's, Tynemouth, and then 'acting with the good wishes of the king and archbishop Lanfranc', granting the priory to Abbot Paul.[31]

Although Lanfranc was evidently an important figure in the restoration of St Albans's fortunes, the deeds of his nephew Paul are given greater prominence in the text of the *Gesta abbatum*.[32] The text is full of examples of Abbot Paul's activities. He began to rebuild the abbey church on a magnificent

---

23 *DB* i, fo. 135d.

24 *Gesta abbatum*, i. 54. This manor is not recorded in Domesday Book.

25 *Mon.*, iii. 288; *VCH, Lincolnshire*, ii. 105.

26 *Gesta abbatum*, i. 57.

27 For an account of the foundation of Wallingford priory see *VCH, Berkshire*, ii. 77.

28 *Gesta abbatum*, i. 56.

29 Ibid.

30 For Tynemouth priory see H. H. E. Craster, 'The parish of Tynemouth', in E. Bateson and others (eds), *History of Northumberland*, Newcastle-upon-Tyne 1893–40, viii. 44–58.

31 Ibid. viii. 46; *Gesta abbatum*, i. 56.

32 For Paul's complimentary press by modern scholars see remarks in Knowles, *Monastic order*, 113; Barlow, *The English Church, 1066–1154*, 186; Golding, 'Wealth and artistic patronage', 108.

scale, reformed the rules of the house by introducing Lanfranc's *Consuetudines*, made regulations for the nuns in the almonry, donated a number of large silver candlesticks for use in services and fostered the abbey *scriptorium* as well as donating a large number of books himself.[33] Paul was also credited with having recovered the abbey properties of *Eiwoda*, Tewin, Napsbury, Redbourne and Kingsbury, in St Albans, Hertfordshire. These estates had been alienated from the abbey during the Confessor's reign and after the Conquest had come into the possession of three ecclesiastics, Odo of Bayeux, Remigius of Lincoln and Lanfranc.[34] Odo of Bayeux returned the three hides he held at Napsbury in exchange for £20, and he is remembered in the list of benefactors as having 'pardoned it for the sake of his soul'.[35] Remigius, the bishop of Lincoln, in whose diocese St Albans was located, had supposedly returned Kingsbury, but the dispute does not seem to have been finally settled until the time of his successor, Robert Bloet (1094–1123).[36] The manor of Childwick, in Hertfordshire, was also regained by Abbot Paul in the reign of William Rufus.[37] Paul was clearly an abbot of great abilities and energy and not without influence.

The acquisition of the priories of Tynemouth and Belvoir along with the establishment of Wallingford priory, has already been mentioned. The priories of Binham, in Norfolk, and Hertford, in Hertfordshire, were also founded as cells to St Albans during Paul's time, by Peter de Valognes and Ralph de Limésy, respectively.[38] The *Gesta abbatum* provides an impressively long list of the lands, churches and tithes which were granted to St Albans during this period.[39] Unfortunately, it only gives the names of two of the donors of these many grants.[40] The identity of some of them can be discovered by referring to the list of benefactors and, to a lesser extent, to Domesday Book, but unfortunately the location of several of the place-names of the grants cannot be identified with any great certainty. Accurate identification of a place-name does not indicate whether the donor was the holder of that place or his/her tenant. For example, the donor of the three virgates in Potton, Bedfordshire, which had been held by 'R' the Fleming, is not named in the *Gesta abbatum*.[41] Domesday book records that Countess Judith was the overlord of Potton and the list of abbey benefactors includes an entry stating that it was she who gave

---

[33] *Gesta abbatum*, i. 52–3, 58–60; BL, MS Cotton Nero D vii, fos 13v–14r. Abbot Paul gave twenty-eight books, eight psalters, choral books, a letter collection and two decorated texts.
[34] *Gesta abbatum*, i. 53–4. According to Domesday Book the abbey held Redbourne and Napsbury in 1086 but Tewin was held by the abbot of Westminster and Peter de Valognes: *DB* i, fos 135b, 135d, 141c. For the manor of Aldenham disputed with Westminster abbey see remarks made by Bates, *Acta*, no. 293.
[35] BL, MS Cotton Nero D vii, fo. 86r; *Mon.*, ii. 219; *DB* i, fo. 135d.
[36] Robert Bloet may have seized this land after his succession.
[37] *Gesta abbatum*, i. 54.
[38] Ibid. i. 57; *Mon.*, iii. 299; *Regesta*, ii, nos 828, 1150.
[39] *Gesta abbatum*, i. 55–6.
[40] The named benefactors were the abbot of Westminster and Ivo de Tigerville.
[41] *Gesta abbatum*, i. 55.

the three hides in Potton.[42] The main problem with this list of benefactors is that as a compilation which includes grants from the late twelfth century, it is often difficult to assign a date to the grants with accuracy. In this example, however, the conjunction of all three sources, the *Gesta abbatum*, Domesday Book and the benefactor's list, means that Countess Judith's grant can be dated to sometime time between 1086 and Abbot Paul's death in 1093.

Identifying the donor of West Hendred, in Berkshire, is a relatively simple matter as Domesday Book states that this valuable manor, worth £10 in 1086, had been given to St Albans by the Bedfordshire noble, Nigel d'Aubigny.[43] Edward of Cambridge is listed in the list of benefactors as having given the church of St Benedict in Cambridge, with his mother.[44] The grant of land in Tallington, Lincolnshire, mentioned in this section of the *Gesta abbatum* is credited to William Bos-le-Hard and his wife Adeliza, in the benefactor's list.[45] William Bos-le-Hard and his brother were Domesday tenants of the founder of Belvoir priory, Robert de Tosny, holding four hides in Clifton Reynes, in Buckinghamshire.[46] As the tithe of *Cliftona* was also granted to St Albans in the time of Abbot Paul, it seems quite possible that William was the donor of this grant as well.[47] However, William de Cairon, whose name is entered in the St Albans fraternity list, held at Clifton, in Bedfordshire, as a tenant of Nigel d'Aubigny and was just as likely to have been the donor.[48]

Another benefactor who was contemporary with William was Ivo de Tigerville, also a tenant of Robert de Tosny.[49] William Bos-le-Hard and Ivo de Tigerville and his son Berengar were all attestors to Robert de Tosny's charter granting Belvoir as a priory to St Albans.[50] According to the *Gesta abbatum* Ivo de Tigerville gave St Albans three *manses* with all of their gardens and one carucate of land, all of which were in Long Clawston, Leicestershire.[51] The list of benefactors recorded Ivo's grant of the church and one carucate in Long Clawston, made in conjunction with his wife and his son, Berengar.[52] The grant of two parts of the tithe of Setterington, in Yorkshire, where Abbot Paul died on his return from Tynemouth in 1093, was made by

---

[42] *DB* i, fo. 217c; BL, MS Cotton Nero D vii, fo. 92r; *Mon.*, ii. 220.

[43] *DB* i, fo. 59d. For Nigel d'Aubigny and the honor of Mowbray see *Cha. Mowbray*; Wardrop, *Fountains abbey*, 136–7.

[44] *Gesta abbatum*, i. 55; BL, MS Cotton Nero D vii, fo. 92r; *Mon.*, ii. 220.

[45] *Gesta abbatum*, i. 55; BL, MS Cotton Nero D vii, fo. 92r; *Mon.*, ii. 220.

[46] *DB* i, fo. 149b.

[47] *Gesta abbatum*, i. 56.

[48] BL, MS Cotton Nero D vii, fo. 118r; *DB*, i, fo. 212c.

[49] In 1086 Ivo de Tigerville held from Robert de Tosny of Belvoir in Ringstone, Ropsley and North Kyme in Lincolnshire, and in Long Clawson in Leicestershire: *DB* i, fos 233d, 353a–c.

[50] *Mon.*, iii. 288–9.

[51] *Gesta abbatum*, i. 55.

[52] BL, MS Cotton Nero D vii, fo. 92r; *Mon.*, ii. 221.

Robert de Tosny's brother, Berengar.[53] The benefactors' list attributes to Berengar and his wife Albreda the grant of the church of *Thorp* and the tithe of Setterington and in Domesday Book Berengar is recorded as holding nine carucates in Setterington.[54]

Other donors of tithes included Hardwin de Scalers, the Hertfordshire and Cambridgeshire tenant-in-chief, who probably gave a quarter of the tithe of Bramfield, in Hertfordshire, as he was the Domesday tenant-in-chief of that place.[55] The list of benefactors also records him as the donor of the vill and church of Bramfield, in Hertfordshire.[56] Nigel de le Vast, Domesday tenant of Nigel d'Aubigny in Bedfordshire and Buckinghamshire, gave the tithe of *Ringeton*, as the list of benefactors assigns the grant of *Ceccinge* and *Ringeton* with 100s. to Nigel as well as the later grant of the church of Millbrook, one carucate of land and the church of Ampthill, in Bedfordshire.[57] Humphrey d'Anneville, styled Humphrey of Knebworth in the benefactors' list, who was the Domesday tenant of Eudo *dapifer*, was probably the donor who gave two parts of the tithe of Essendon, in Hertfordshire, as the lists states that Humphrey granted his tithe of *Efresduna* for the sustenance of the monks.[58] Humphrey of Knebworth's name is also entered in the St Albans fraternity list.[59]

The evidence for the identity of the remaining donors of tithes is much less certain. Hardwin de Scalers may have given the tithe of Wakeley, in Hertfordshire, as he held forty acres there in 1086, but Count Eustace of Boulogne and Count Alan of Brittany each held forty acres there as well.[60] Ralph Baynard, sheriff of Essex, held Hertingfordbury, in Hertfordshire, in 1086, but there is no other evidence to suggest that it was he who gave two parts of the tithe of that place to St Albans.[61] Identifying the donor of the tithe of *Bretheham* is impossible.[62] There is the added complication of there being two places called Brettenham, one in Norfolk and one in Suffolk, and out of the seven Domesday entries for these two places at least three men, Roger Bigod, John the nephew of Waleran and Robert, count of Mortain, were all benefac-

---

53 *Gesta abbatum*, i. 56; Simeon of Durham, *Historia ecclesiae Dunhelmensis*, ii. 221, 261, 346.

54 BL, MS Cotton Nero D vii, fo. 92r; *Mon.*, ii. 220; *DB* i, fos 282a, 314c.

55 *Gesta abbatum*, i. 56; *DB* i, fo. 142a.

56 BL, MS Cotton Nero D vii, fo. 92r; *Mon.*, ii. 220.

57 Ibid.

58 *Gesta abbatum*, i. 56; BL, MS Cotton Nero D vii, fo. 92r; *Mon.*, ii. 220. Essendon, Hertfordshire, is not in Domesday Book.

59 BL, MS Cotton Nero D vii, fo. 118r.

60 *DB* i, fos 137a, 137c, 141d.

61 Ibid. i, fo. 138c; *Gesta abbatum*, i. 56. For the Baynard family see L. Landon, 'The Bainard family of Norfolk', *Norfolk Archaeology* xxii (1929), 209–20; R. Mortimer, 'The Baynards of Baynards Castle', in C. Harper-Bill and others (eds), *Studies in medieval history presented to R. Allen Brown*, Woodbridge 1989, 241–54.

62 *Gesta abbatum*, i. 56.

tors of St Albans.[63] The identification of *Herlaga* is also uncertain, although Geoffrey de Mandeville's manor of Hurley (*Herlai*), in Berkshire, seems a strong possibility.[64] Thus, out of seventeen grants of tithes only five donors can be identified with any certainty.

The list of benefactors contains at least one other grant which took place in Abbot Paul's abbacy although it is not mentioned in the *Gesta abbatum*. Robert, count of Mortain, and his wife Almodis granted one virgate in Codicote and half a hide in Redbourne, worth 40s. in 1086, both in Hertfordshire.[65] The grant of land at Codicote was actually a quitclaim as Domesday Book records that in 1086 the hundred had testified that the count of Mortain's men had annexed fifteen acres of land in Codicote.[66] As Robert of Mortain died in 1095 this gift must have been made sometime between 1086 and then.[67] It also seems likely that Robert's butler, Alvred *pincerna*, made his grant to St Albans at much the same time or shortly after the death of Robert.[68] With his wife and son, Alvred gave seven carucates in Norton, which was supposedly located in Warwickshire. Arnulf de Hesdin's grant of one carucate in Warwickshire and the church of Appleton, in Yorkshire, with £10 also probably belongs to Paul's abbacy.[69] In 1086 Arnulf held extensive lands in England and was a generous benefactor of many religious houses both in England and on the continent. As Arnulf was involved in the 1094/5 conspiracy against William Rufus and subsequently left England for the First Crusade, never to return, his gift to St Albans probably took place before Abbot Paul's death in 1093.

The *Gesta abbatum* and the list of benefactors both record the gift in the time of Abbot Paul of two 'great and loud' bells from an Englishman called Lyolf and his wife.[70] This survivor from the pre-Conquest English landholding class apparently sold many of his goats and sheep in order to purchase one of the two bells, while his wife bought the other. A certain 'Robert d'Oilly' is also recorded in the list of benefactors as having given £10 and a drinking horn.[71] This might have been Robert I d'Oilly, who died in about 1090, the royal constable who became a generous benefactor of Abingdon abbey, or Robert II who died in 1142. As overlord of Wallingford, Robert I d'Oilly would have had to have given his consent to the gift of one and a half

---

63 *DB* ii, fos 183b, 213b, 239b, 266a, 291b, 369a, 397b.

64 *Gesta abbatum*, 56; *DB* i, fo. 62a.

65 BL, MS Cotton Nero D vii, fo. 92r; *Mon.*, ii. 220; *DB* i, fo. 136d.

66 Ibid. i, fos 135c–d.

67 For the date of Robert of Mortain's death see J.-M. Bouvris, 'Aux origins du prieuré de Vains', *Revue de l'Avranchin et du Pays de Granville* lxiv (1987), 67–81 at p. 74.

68 BL, MS Cotton Nero D vii, fo. 92r; *Mon.*, ii. 220.

69 A confirmation charter of Henry II describes *Apeltona* as being in Yorkshire: ibid. ii. 228; *EYC* ii. 282–3.

70 *Gesta abbatum*, i. 60–1; BL, MS Cotton Nero D vii, fo. 92r; *Mon.*, ii. 220.

71 Ibid. ii. 221.

churches in Wallingford which was made in the time of Abbot Paul.[72] The entry in the St Albans fraternity list of the names of Miles Crispin, Robert's sworn brother, and his wife, Robert I's daughter, suggests that Robert I rather than Robert II was probably the donor in this instance.[73]

The St Albans fraternity list includes the names of a number of people who can be shown to have been living and holding lands in 1086. Although Humphrey d'Anneville's inclusion in the list can be attributed to the fact that he was a benefactor of the abbey, these other men could have been included for other reasons. Thorkell of Digswell, in Hertfordshire, was a survivor from pre-Conquest days who had become a tenant of Geoffrey de Mandeville by 1086.[74] Thorkell may have been a benefactor, but he could just as easily have been involved in some legal matter which had earned St Albans's gratitude. The *Inquisitio Eliensis* reveals that Thorkell had been one of the jurors who had sworn in Broadwater hundred where ten St Albans manors lay. Another Domesday tenant of Geoffrey de Mandeville in Hertfordshire, Thorold of Bushey, is also entered in the fraternity list.[75]

Several important trends can be identified in the patronage St Albans received during the abbacy of Abbot Paul. Aside from the foundation and acquisition of five priories, in Hertfordshire, Berkshire, Norfolk, Lincolnshire and Northumberland, the majority of the grants that St Albans received were tithes or parts of tithes. Churches and gifts of small parcels of land were also common, whereas grants of significant portions of land such as the five hides at West Hendred were exceptional. St Albans succeeded in attracting some extremely wealthy and influential people as benefactors such as Robert, count of Mortain and his wife Almodis, Countess Judith, who had been a benefactor of Bury St Edmunds with her husband Earl Waltheof, as well as other people of national importance who had local interests such as Nigel d'Aubigny, Robert and Berengar de Tosny and Hardwin de Scalers. The exercise of identifying donors has illustrated another trend, which is that the kin of donors often made additional gifts to St Albans.

The text of the *Gesta abbatum* is not all praise for Abbot Paul. He is disparaged over his treatment of the tombs of the former abbots of St Albans and his failure to move the remains of King Offa into the new church.[76] Another unpopular aspect of his abbacy was the granting out of abbey lands but compared with Abingdon's quota of thirty knights, St Albans appears to have got off lightly with only six knights as its *servitium debitum*.[77] Perhaps 'the chastisement of Lanfranc' had also led William the Conqueror to curb his

---

[72] VCH, *Berkshire*, ii. 77n. For the honor of Wallingford see K. S. B. Keats-Rohan, 'The devolution of the honor of Wallingford 1066–1148', *Oxoniesa* liv (1989), 311–18.

[73] BL, MS Cotton Nero D vii, fo. 119v.

[74] Ibid. fo. 118r; *DB* i, fo. 139c.

[75] BL, MS Cotton Nero D vii, fo. 118v; *DB* i, fo. 139c.

[76] *Gesta abbatum*, i. 62. For the discussion on the attitude of the post-Conquest abbots towards Anglo-Saxon saints see Ridyard, '*Condigna veneratio*', 179–206.

[77] Knowles, *Monastic order*, 702–3.

demands for knight service.[78] William Rufus forced Paul to enfeoff Hugh de *Envermeu* with a vill in return for homage and service, but it was Paul's own nepotism, his alienation of lands to his nameless and 'illiterate' relatives, which was particularly disliked.[79] Peter de Valognes, the sheriff of Essex and Hertfordshire who founded Binham priory, was enfeoffed with the woods of Northaw, in Hertfordshire, by Paul.[80] The terms of this grant were the subject of some dispute, but the grant was renewed by Abbot Geoffrey (1119–46) and in the same way Paul's grant of land at Sarratt, also in Hertfordshire, to Robert the Mason was renewed by Abbot Richard d'Aubigny (1097–1119).[81]

After Paul's death in 1093, St Albans, like the abbeys of Ely, Bury St Edmunds and Christ Church, Canterbury, was forced to endure a four-year vacancy.[82] Unlike the vacancies at other abbeys, that at St Albans came to an end within William Rufus' lifetime. The *Gesta abbatum* complains that his officials cut down the abbey's woods and taxed its tenants.[83] It seems however, that no long-lasting damage was done to the abbey and in 1097 Richard d'Aubigny, a monk of Lessay, was appointed as abbot.[84] The Bedfordshire d'Aubigny family had been benefactors of St Albans at least eleven years before Richard's appointment. If, as Loyd convincingly argues, Nigel d'Aubigny was the brother of Richard then his appointment may well have been secured, at least partly, by Nigel. As Nigel had headed a successful expedition force to Scotland against King Malcolm Canmore in the early or mid 1090s, if he had petitioned the king in favour of his brother's appointment to St Albans he would probably have stood a good chance of success.[85] Richard's effective management of St Albans quickly proved he was well-qualified for the position.

The *Gesta abbatum* claims a good number of important and influential friends for Abbot Richard d'Aubigny, including William Rufus, Henry I, Pope Urban II and Archbishop Anselm.[86] Yet the writs and charters of William Rufus and Henry I show little special warmth in their supposed

[78] *Gesta abbatum*, i. 51.
[79] Ibid. i. 64.
[80] Ibid. i. 63.
[81] Ibid. i. 63, 72, 95.
[82] The vacancy at Ely was by far the longest, lasting from 1093 to 1100. At Abingdon the three years under the administration of the monk Modbert (1097–1100) were ruinous for the abbey and at Bury St Edmunds the vacancy lasted two years (1098–1100). For remarks on Rufus' treatment of abbeys during vacancies see Barlow, *William Rufus*, 234–5.
[83] *Gesta abbatum*, i. 65. For William Rufus' writs confirming to the abbey various rights and tithes see *Regesta*, i, nos 400a, 400b; ii, no. 404; Matthew Paris, *Chron. majora*, vi. 35.
[84] *Regesta*, i, no. 199; ii, no. 395. Roger d'Aubigny and his son Rualoc were benefactors of Lessay abbey in 1084; Richard and Nigel d'Aubigny were most likely younger sons of Rualoc. For the d'Aubigny family tree see L. C. Loyd, 'The origin of the family of Aubigny of Cainhoe', *Bedfordshire Record Society* xix (1937), 101–12.
[85] For this expedition see Barlow, *William Rufus*, 291.
[86] *Gesta abbatum*, i. 66.

friendship: William Rufus made only a few grants to Richard,[87] while Henry I granted numerous charters confirming various rights and grants that the abbey had received, but only gave one grant, of an eight-day fair and the manor of Biscot, in Bedfordshire.[88] This stands in stark contrast to the kind of wealth Henry I's friendship brought Faritius, abbot of Abingdon. Archbishop Anselm had supposedly become a benefactor of St Albans after Abbot Paul had helped him when he was impoverished by William Rufus, but what he gave, or when, is unrecorded.[89] Abbot Richard was said to have extracted St Albans from its obedience to Canterbury and subjected it to the bishop of Lincoln by his profession.[90] The consecration of the new abbey church in 1116 was presided over by Robert Bloet, bishop of Lincoln, without the presence of Ralph d'Escures, the archbishop of Canterbury.[91] It does seem, therefore, that the special relationship with Canterbury ended, but this did not adversely affect St Albans's fortunes.

Under Abbot Richard St Albans began to prosper once more as in the time of Lanfranc and Paul.[92] The abbey received a wealth of religious patronage and also acquired two additional priories, Wymondham, in Norfolk, and Hatfield Peverel, in Essex.[93] Wymondham was founded as a cell to St Albans before 1107 by Henry I's butler and Norfolk landholder, William d'Aubigny.[94] William was probably the nephew of Abbot Richard and of Nigel d'Aubigny, the benefactor of St Albans, as well as being the husband of Robert de Tosny's grand-daughter, Matilda Bigod. Hatfield Peverel had been founded in the time of William Rufus as a college of secular canons by Ingelrica, the wife of Ranulf Peverel.[95] In Henry I's reign her son, William Peverel, converted the establishment into a Benedictine priory and granted it to St Albans, whilst adding to the endowment.[96] Norman de Montfaltpel, who was also a benefactor of Lenton priory before 1108, was a tenant of William Peverel as he granted St Albans two parts of his tithe at Harpole and Paulerspury, in Northamptonshire, both of which places William held as tenant-in-chief in 1086.[97] The small cell at Millbrook, which was later merged with a new priory at Beaulieu, in Bedfordshire, was also founded during Richard's abbacy.[98]

St Albans's priories of Binham and Tynemouth flourished under Abbot

---

87 *Regesta*, i, nos 199, 314b, 314c, 368; ii, nos 395, 399.
88 Ibid. ii, nos 690, 1102.
89 *Gesta abbatum*, i. 61.
90 Ibid. i. 71–2, 92, 106.
91 Ibid. i. 70–1; Matthew Paris, *Chron. majora*, vi. 36–8; *Regesta*, ii, no. 1102.
92 For a different interpretation of St Albans under Richard d'Aubigny see Golding, 'Wealth and artistic patronage', 109.
93 *Gesta abbatum*, i. 67.
94 For the career of William d'Aubigny *pincerna* during the reign of Henry I see Green, *Government of England*, 229–30.
95 *VCH, Essex*, ii. 105.
96 *Mon.*, iii. 295.
97 BL, MS Cotton Nero D vii, fo. 92r; *Mon.*, ii. 220; v. 108; *DB* i, fos 226a–b.
98 *VCH, Bedfordshire*, i. 351; *Mon.*, iii. 276.

Richard. Tynemouth, in particular, received substantial grants of land.[99] It was given Monkseaton, Whitley Bay and Seghill, in Northumberland, and a toft in Newcastle, by Henry I; Bewick and its church, Lilburn, Harehope and Wooperton by Queen Matilda; Eglingham and its church by Wihenoc the hunter; the churches of Woodham and Bywell St Peter's and the tithes of Bothal, Ovington and Wylam by Guy de Baillol; the tithes of Seaton Delaval, Dissington, in Cumbria, and Black Callerton, in Northumberland, by Hubert de la Val; and *Stantona*, East and Middle Chirton, Earsdon and Coquet island, in Northumberland, by a number of unidentified donors.[100] In 1110 the relics of St Oswin were translated into the new church at Tynemouth which was dedicated to SS Oswin, Alban and Mary in the same year.[101] Binham priory received the grant of the whole manor of Binham and other possessions.[102]

The *Gesta abbatum* provides a list of the acquisitions made in the time of Abbot Richard. Like the passage concerning Abbot Paul, these grants are again recorded without naming the donors. These, who can be identified from the list of benefactors, are dominated by members of the various branches of the d'Aubigny family. William d'Aubigny *pincerna*, the founder of Wymondham priory, gave the tithes of Burnham Thorpe and Fring with one carucate of land, in Norfolk.[103] His brother, Nigel, gave Eastwell, in Kent, 'ad eandem ecclesiam me sepeliendum deposui'.[104] In the early years of Henry I's reign Nigel had received the honor of Mowbray with Robert de Mowbray's wife as well as part of the Stuteville estates. His benefaction of the mother-house of Tynemouth, which Robert de Mowbray had patronised, was part of the wide net of patronage he cast across northern religious foundations. The Bedfordshire baron, Henry d'Aubigny, son of Nigel and nephew of Abbot Richard, gave, with his brothers William and Nigel, the church of Clophill, in Bedfordshire, with its tithe and half an acre of land, and the tithes of Coton, in Northamptonshire, and of Cainhoe, in Bedfordshire.[105] Henry also confirmed his father's gifts of the church of Holy Trinity and half of the church of St Mary, Wallingford, and the manor of West Hendred, Berkshire.

Other early twelfth-century benefactors included Henry I, who gave Biscot, in Bedfordshire, and Nigel de le Vast, who gave the church of Millbrook, both mentioned above, and Adeliza, wife of Theodoric de For, who gave one hide of land in Greensted, Essex.[106] The identity of the donor who gave the

---

99 *Gesta abbatum*, i. 68.
100 Craster, *History of Northumberland*, viii. 48–50; *Regesta*, ii, nos 624, 631, 640–1, 822, 955, 1170, 1172, 1177.
101 Craster, *History of Northumberland*, viii. 56–7.
102 *Gesta abbatum*, i. 68.
103 By the reign of Henry I William d'Aubigny had acquired the Norfolk Domesday lands of William de Warenne to which Fring and Burnham Thorpe belonged: *DB* ii, fos 163b, 169a.
104 *Regesta*, ii, no. 1161; *Cha. Mowbray*, 6–7.
105 BL, MS Cotton Nero D vii, fo. 92r; *Mon.*, ii. 220.
106 *Regesta*, ii, no. 1102; Matthew Paris, *Chron. majora*, vi. 36; BL, MS Cotton Nero D vii, fo. 92r; *Mon.*, ii. 220.

tithes of Hugh de Verly, the Domesday tenant of Geoffrey de Mandeville in Essex, is uncertain.[107] The grant of the manor of Wyboston, in Bedfordshire, was probably made by the Domesday tenant Pirot, or his son Alan.[108] In 1086 Pirot was the tenant of Nigel d'Aubigny in Bedfordshire and Eudo *dapifer* in Bedfordshire and Essex, of whose foundation of Colchester he was a benefactor.[109] By 1166 Alan had become a tenant of William d'Aubigny *pincerna* and had given his chapel and tithe of Knowlton, in Kent, to St Albans and had his father's and his wife's names entered in the abbey's fraternity list as well as his own.[110] The *Gesta abbatum* also records that St Albans received one virgate in Codicote, and half a hide in Redbourne, both in Hertfordshire, and the vill of Stanmore, in Middlesex.[111] The first two places were originally granted to St Albans by Robert, count of Mortain, in the time of Abbot Paul.[112] The manor of Stanmore was granted to St Albans by Robert's son, William, some time between 1100 and 1106, for the soul of his sister Mable who was buried at St Albans.[113] St Albans was the only English house that received Robert of Mortain's patronage, but if Mable had predeceased her father this would explain his uncharacteristic patronage.[114]

The list of benefactors also records the gifts of Roger Bigod, John, nephew of Waleran, and Robert Malet of specified amounts of eels to be given annually.[115] Roger, who died in 1107, was the sheriff of Norfolk and the son-in-law of the founder of Belvoir, Robert de Tosny. Robert Malet held extensive lands in Suffolk centred around Eye and died in 1106.[116] The grants of eels are similar to the one Roger Bigod made to Belvoir priory and probably arose from that occasion.[117] Roger's son-in-law, William d'Aubigny *brito*, was also a benefactor of Belvoir and chose to be buried there.[118] Roger Bigod also attested the foundation charter of his other son-in-law, William d'Aubigny *pincerna*, to Wymondham priory. Nigel of Stafford, probably a kinsman of Robert de Tosny, made the grant of the church of Norton, in Warwickshire, and one carucate and the tithe of that vill, which was confirmed by Richard earl of Chester.[119] This gift nicely complimented Alvred *pincerna's* earlier grant of seven carucates in the same place. Great men of the realm were

---

107 *Gesta abbatum*, i. 68; *DB*, i, fo. 63a.

108 Ibid. i, fo. 214c.

109 Ibid.; Farrer, *Honors and knights' fees*, iii. 217.

110 BL, MS Cotton Nero D vii, fos 118r, 120r; *Red book*, i. 398; *Mon.*, ii. 221.

111 *Gesta abbatum*, i. 68.

112 BL, MS Cotton Nero D vii, fo. 92r; *Mon.*, ii. 220.

113 BL, MS Cotton Otho D iii, fo. 73r.

114 For Robert of Mortain see I. N. Soulsby, 'The fiefs in England of the counts of Mortain: 1066–1106', unpubl. M.A. diss. Cardiff 1974; B. Golding, 'Robert of Mortain', *Anglo-Norman Studies* xiii (1991), 119–44.

115 BL, MS Cotton Nero D vii, fo. 92r; *Mon.*, ii. 220.

116 For Robert Malet see Lewis, 'The king and Eye, 569–87'.

117 *Mon.*, iii. 290.

118 Ibid.

119 BL, MS Cotton Nero D vii, fo. 92r; *Mon.*, ii. 220; Farrer, *Honors and knights' fees*, ii. 57.

lining up to patronise St Albans, even if their grants were of a distinctly modest nature.

The entries in the list of benefactors are often difficult to date as none of
them, bar one, makes any reference to the abbacy in which the grant was
made. As many of the grants in the benefactors', list are not mentioned in the
Gesta abbatum, dating them can become a matter of guess work. There are a
number of such donors who appear holding lands in Domesday Book and so
must belong to the abbacies of Paul and of Richard rather than of Geoffrey.
So grants made by men who were alive in 1086 such as Nigel de Bereville,
William Lovet, Turstin, brother of William de la Mare, and William of Letch-
worth could have been made in the abbacies of either Paul or Richard.[120]
However, gifts given by Roger de Valognes and his cousin Walter, Matilda de
Hesdin, Adam fitz William of Hatfield, Roger and Walter de Mandeville,
Ansgod of Lindsey, William de la Val and Manasser Arsic cannot be dated
with any certainty to either Richard's or Geoffrey's abbacy.[121]

Whereas Robert de Tosny and his tenants dominated the picture of religious patronage under Abbot Paul, it was the members of the d'Aubigny family
and their tenants who dominated the picture in the time of Abbot Richard
d'Aubigny. Men from families with interests similar to those of the
d'Aubignys were commonly supporters of English monasteries. These were
the men Sir Richard Southern referred to as 'of modest means but with the
instincts of great landlords'.[122] They also commonly established their own
foundations, increasingly Augustinian priories. The establishment of priories
as cells to English Benedictine monasteries, however, was rare, especially
before the reign of Henry I, and the large number of dependent priories St
Albans possessed must therefore have brought prestige to its abbots. The
range and number of the abbey's benefactors were actually more impressive
than the gifts given. As in Paul's abbacy grants of tithes, churches and small
parcels of land constituted the bulk of the gifts given.

The author of the *Gesta abbatum* complained of alienations made by Richard in the same way as he disapproved of Paul's abbacy.[123] Richard's alienations appear to have been either counter-gifts or payment for service to the
abbey. Grants of land were made to men who were, or were to become, benefactors of St Albans and its priories. Richard granted lands in Northumberland to Gospatric son of Gospatric, a benefactor of Tynemouth priory, and
Waltheof his son, in the same way that Paul had granted lands to the founder
of Binham, Peter de Valognes. Richard also granted the payment of 10s.
annually to William, the chaplain of another Tynemouth benefactor, Guy de

---

[120] BL, MS Cotton Nero D vii, fo. 92r; *Mon.*, ii. 220; *DB* i, fos 56b, 61b, 71d, 138a, 138d,
151c, 216b.
[121] BL, MS Cotton Nero D vii, fo. 92r; *Mon.*, ii. 220.
[122] Southern, *Western society*, 245.
[123] *Gesta abbatum*, i. 72.

Baillol.[124] Peter, the butler of William, count of Mortain, was granted land in Sarratt, Hertfordshire, with his nephew, but this was done against the wishes of the convent. Abbot Richard's magnificent dedication of the new abbey church in 1116 did much to publicise St Albans' position as one of the more prestigious houses in the country. The dedication was attended by Henry I and Queen Matilda, who had been benefactors of Tynemouth priory, and many of the great men of the realm, including the founder of Wymondham priory, William d'Aubigny *pincerna*.[125] The occasion was marked by the granting of an indulgence to pilgrims to encourage greater numbers. Richard's abbacy was rightly remembered by the author of the *Gesta abbatum* as one of prosperity for St Albans.[126]

The abbacy of Richard's successor, Geoffrey de Gorham (1119–45), a native of Maine, appears to have been largely concerned with the internal organisation of the abbey's administration, the consolidation of the abbey's assets and local initiatives.[127] The number of grants made to the abbey during this period may well have lessened but Geoffrey was none the less an energetic abbot.[128] He continued his predecessors' work by having a new shrine built for the relics of St Alban and the relics translated in 1129.[129] He also founded the hospital of St Julian in St Albans, on the road to London, and built the priory of Sopwell for the nuns of St Albans *c.* 1140. He acquired the hermitage of Modry from Robert d'Aubigny, the son of Henry d'Aubigny of Cainhoe, which was merged with the small cell at Millbrook to create a small priory called Bealieu, in Bedfordshire.[130] Despite this apparent achievement it should be pointed out that all these projects were locally based. St Julian's hospital was funded by small grants, mostly of tithes from manors in Hertfordshire and Bedfordshire from local men like Peter of Sarratt and William fitz Asketil of Codicote who were almost certainly abbey tenants.[131]

Abbot Geoffrey secured two small grants of two parts of tithes at Stanford and Silsoe, in Bedfordshire, from Simon de Beauchamp and Roger de Candos, respectively. Simon de Beauchamp was a Bedfordshire baron, whereas Roger de Candos was lord of Caerleon and a tenant-in-chief in Herefordshire.[132] The church and one carucate in Stanford had already been granted to St Albans in the time of Abbot Paul and Silsoe had been held by Nigel

---

124 Guy de Baillol's name was also entered in the St Albans fraternity list: BL, MS Cotton Nero D vii, fo. 119v.
125 *Gesta abbatum*, i. 71; *Regesta*, ii, no. 1102; Matthew Paris, *Chron. majora*, vi. 36–7.
126 *Gesta abbatum*, i. 69.
127 Ibid. i. 73–8.
128 For an assessment of Geoffrey's abbacy see Golding, 'Wealth and artistic patronage', 109–10.
129 *Gesta abbatum*, i. 82–7.
130 Ibid. i. 77–8, 80–2.
131 Ibid. i. 77. Sarrat and Codicote in Hertfordshire were St Alban's manors.
132 Sanders, *English baronies*, 10, 79; W. Levison, 'St Alban and St Albans', *Antiquity* xv (1941), 337–59. Levison discusses the apparently anomalous existence of a church in or near Caerleon, south Wales, which received an additional dedication to St Alban sometime

d'Aubigny of Cainhoe in 1086.[133] The foundation of Sopwell nunnery attracted the patronage of the local baron, Robert d'Aubigny, whose sister Amice entered the nunnery.[134] The *Gesta abbatum*'s list of property acquired under Geoffrey is relatively modest. Except for the above-mentioned hermitage of Modry, Geoffrey was given a saltworks at Westwick, in Hertfordshire, by Hugh fitz Osbern and one hide in *Meindeltona* with the tithe of its church,[135] and himself purchased twenty solidates of land at Biscot, in Bedfordshire, from Henry I. The volume of grants had evidently dropped quite dramatically from the heady heights of the abbacies of Paul and Richard. In the 1120s it also looked as if St Albans was going to lose Tynemouth when the bishop of Durham made a formal complaint about St Albans' retention of it. This resulted in the priory being taken into the king's hands in 1122.[136] Henry I's writ of 1122 gave the monks of Tynemouth leave to elect their own abbot who would have full authority to receive new members into the congregation.[137] This writ was soon disregarded and Abbot Geoffrey regained his hold over the priory.

The apparent decline in the volume of religious patronage is perhaps only due to the nature of the sources. Many other donors may have given during Geoffrey's abbacy, but the *Gesta abbatum* does not list them. As would be expected, the dependent priories rather than the mother-house attracted grants from the descendants of their founders. The care of Belvoir had passed from its founder, Robert de Tosny, to his son-in-law, Roger Bigod and then to William d'Aubigny *brito*, husband of his daughter, Cecilia. William chose to be buried next to Robert de Tosny in the priory church at Belvoir as did his son William II and his wives, Adeliza and Cecilia.[138] On occasion St Albans still received grants from the descendants of the founders of these priories. Roger de Valognes, son of the founder of Binham, and his cousin, Walter, were both benefactors of St Albans.[139] As Roger lived until 1141–2 his grant could have been made in Geoffrey's abbacy. However, the general tendency was for the patronage that St Albans received in the time of Abbot Geoffrey to be almost exclusively local. However, the significance of Geoffrey's projects should not be under-estimated; after all it was Geoffrey who helped Christina of Markyate in her struggle to follow her vocation and eventually found a priory at Markyate, Hertfordshire, which was dedicated *c.* 1145.[140] Nevertheless it seems that whereas Abbot Richard could count on his influ-

between 1113 and 1142. Roger de Candos's patronage of the hospital in part explains this dedication.

133 *DB* i, fo. 214b.
134 *Mon.*, iii. 365.
135 *Gesta abbatum*, i. 78.
136 Craster, *History of Northumberland*, viii. 58.
137 *Regesta*, ii, no. 1331.
138 *Mon.*, ii. 289.
139 BL, MS Cotton Nero D vii, fo. 92r; *Mon.*, ii. 220.
140 See S. Thompson, *Women religious*, Oxford 1991, 3–4, 16–24.

and friends Geoffrey could only really count on local men. Thus the picture of a prosperous abbey in the 1130s, drawn at the beginning of this chapter, not only conceals St Albans's early post-Conquest difficulties, but also the recent shift in the abbey's focus and a decline in patronage from men of national importance.

6

St Augustine's, Canterbury

The Post-Conquest history of St Augustine's, Canterbury, is unusual on two counts; first in that the religious patronage that St Augustine's received in this period was almost exclusively, directly or indirectly, associated with one man, Odo bishop of Bayeux. Secondly in that, like Glastonbury and Ely, traumatic events led to a serious disruption of the daily life of the abbey and the dispersal of the abbey's monks.[1] The abbots of St Augustine's were subsequently forced to resort to extensive litigation in an attempt to recover abbey lands, tithes and customs. It is also evident that such disputes were partly the result of Bishop Odo's removal from local and national politics. Furthermore, St Augustine's faced serious competition from three other Kent religious institutions: Christ Church, Canterbury, Rochester and the priory of St George, Canterbury. It is no coincidence that evidence for grants of religious patronage to St Augustine's after the 1080s dries up almost completely.

St Augustine's rejoiced in being one of England's most ancient monastic houses, founded by St Augustine himself and King Æthelbert in the very early seventh century.[2] Dunstan had reformed and rebuilt the ancient church in the mid tenth century and St Augustine's steadily increased in affluence into the mid eleventh century.[3] Particularly noteworthy was the acquisition of 'the body of St Mildred with all her land [on Thanet] and with all the customs belonging to her church' during the reign of Cnut, worth £100 in 1086.[4] Edward the Confessor granted the abbey his share in the borough of Fordwich and confirmed the abbey's lands on Thanet and its rights on its own lands.[5]

The extant source material for St Augustine's is at once abundant and diverse in nature, and of variable reliability. First, there are a number of

---

[1] The main sources for the post-Conquest history of St Augustine's are *The Domesday monachorum of Christ Church, Canterbury*, ed. D. C. Douglas, London 1944; the inquisition known as the *Excerpta*, printed in *An eleventh century inquisition of St Augustine's, Canterbury*, ed. A. Ballard (British Academy Records of Social and Economic History of England and Wales iv, 1920); *The register of St Augustine's, Canterbury*, ed. G. J. Turner and H. E. Salter, London 1915–24. For Canterbury see also *The charters of St Augustine's abbey, Canterbury*, ed. S. E. Kelly (Anglo-Saxon Charters iv, 1994); S. E. Kelly, 'Some forgeries in the archive of St Augustine's abbey, Canterbury', *Falschungen im Mittelalter*, Monumenta Germaniae Historica Schriften xxxiii (1988), 347–69, and 'Pre-Conquest history of St Augustine's abbey'.
[2] Bede, *Historia Ecclesiasticam gentis Anglorum*, ed. C. Plummer, Oxford 1896, i. 33; Kelly, 'Pre-Conquest history of St Augustine's abbey', 47–8.
[3] S989–90, S1048, S1091, S1400–1, S1472, S1467, S1502.
[4] S990; *DB* i, fo. 12b; Kelly, 'Pre-Conquest history of St Augustine's abbey', 149–51.
[5] S1091, S1092.

related eleventh-century surveys which contain information about the abbey's lands. These are Domesday Book, the *Domesday monachorum* and the St Augustine's inquisition, commonly referred to as the *Excerpta*. Then there are the royal writs and charters of the Norman kings, most of which are preserved in two cartularies dating from the thirteenth and fourteenth centuries,[6] and also a late thirteenth-century register, known as the Black Book, which was edited by G. J. Turner and H. E. Salter in 1915 and 1924.[7] These records are supplemented by the account of the translation of the relics of St Augustine in 1091 and the life, miracles and translation of St Mildreth written for the abbey in the late eleventh century by Goscelin of St-Bertin.[8] Finally, the abbey features in Eadmer's *Historia novorum* and in the *Acta Lanfranci*, and there are a number of other chronicle accounts of its history.[9] These are the chronicles of William Thorne, and of Thomas of Elmham and William Sprott's *Vitae abbatum*.[10] This last was the earliest of three, written in the thirteenth century and used by Thorne as the basis of the post-Conquest section of his late fourteenth-century chronicle. A certain amount of the information in Sprott's chronicle coincides with the charters in the cartularies but it appears that he also had access to charters and notices now lost as his work contains much information which is not recorded elsewhere.[11] Thomas of Elmham's fifteenth-century chronicle is actually unfinished, ending in 806. After a few particulars for the year 1087 the work becomes no more than a collection of charters, the latest of which has been dated to the last decade of the twelfth century. Elmham's work also includes a chronological table

6   BL, MS Cotton Julius D ii; BL, MS Cotton Claudius D x. The latter is known as the Red Book and contains some copies of late eleventh- and early twelfth-century charters given by private individuals and of agreements made by St Augustine's abbots.
7   *Register of St Augustine's*, ii. 462–3, 385. Much of the information recorded in the Black Book which relates to religious benefactions belongs to the late twelfth and thirteenth centuries.
8   The text of Goscelin's *Historia translationis S. Augustini episcopi* is printed in *PL* clv. 13–46. The *Vita Deo dilectae virginis Mildrethae* is printed in D. W. Rollason, *The Mildreth legend*, Leicester 1982, 108–43. For an assessment of the work of Goscelin of St-Bertin at St Augustine's, Canterbury see R. Sharpe, 'Goscelin's St Augustine and St Mildreth: hagiography and liturgy in context', *Journal of Theological Studies* xxxxi (1990), 502–16.
9   Eadmer, *Historia novorum in Anglia*, ed. M. Rule (Rolls series lxxxi, 1884); *Acta Lanfranci*, printed in *Two of the Saxon chronicles parallel*, ed. J. Earle and C. Plummer, Oxford 1892–8, i. 287–92, and translated in *English historical documents*, II: *1042–1189*, ed. D. C. Douglas and G. W. Greenaway, 2nd edn, London 1981, 676–81.
10   *William Thorne's chronicle of St Augustine's abbey, Canterbury*, ed. A. H. Davis, Oxford 1934; Thomas of Elmham, *Historia monasterii S. Augustini Cantuariensis*, ed. C. Hardwick, (Rolls series viii, 1858); A copy of Sprott's chronicle is preserved in a fourteenth-century manuscript of St Augustine's under the title of *Vitae abbatum* in BL, MS Cotton Tiberius A ix, fos 107r–80r. See also M. Hunter, 'The facsimiles in Thomas Elmham's *History of St Augustine's, Canterbury*', *The Library* 5th ser. xxviii (1973), 215–20.
11   One such example is the account of the leasing of land at Sibertswold, Kent, to Hugh fitz Fulbert and his subsequent bequest of his property in return for burial in the abbey's cemetery: *William Thorne's chronicle*, 53.

which consists of concise notices of events concerning the abbey. However, some of the dates given in these chronicles can be shown to be inaccurate, while, more seriously, certain passages which deal with the consecration of Abbots Wido (1087–93) and Hugh I (d. 1126) look very much like later fabrications, constructed to both obscure embarrassing events in the abbey's history and bolster claims to particular rights and privileges. The chronicle accounts therefore need to be treated with great caution, although when employed in conjunction with the thirteenth- and fourteenth-century cartularies they can produce a largely credible picture of St Augustine's post-Conquest years.

In the reign of the Conqueror St Augustine's, Canterbury, outshone the other religious houses in Kent and the abbey's possessions remained relatively intact. This went against the experience of the other Kentish foundations, for which the post-Conquest era was one of many difficulties, exacerbated by the chaos of the Conquest itself. Although extremely wealthy, since 1038 Christ Church, Canterbury, had endured the episcopate of two archbishops who were less than ideal. Under the first, the ailing Archbishop Eadsige, lands were lost to Earl Godwin and his sons and this was compounded by the rule of the second, the pluralist Stigand, who was deposed in 1070.[12] Christ Church's circumstances were not helped by the fact that on 6 December 1067 the cathedral was partially ruined by fire.[13] The other Kent religious houses held much less land than the two great Canterbury houses. In 1066 the lands of the bishop of Rochester, Siward, who was by now an old man, were worth just under £110.[14] These were swiftly seized by William the Conqueror and given to Odo, bishop of Bayeux.[15] Although much of the land was subsequently recovered by Lanfranc at the trial held on Penenden Heath, Rochester underwent fundamental and disrupting change, as it not only changed hands twice between 1075 and 1077, but at Lanfranc's behest had its canons replaced by monks.

St Augustine's also had its fair share of problems after 1066. In the confused political situation of the early years after the Conquest, Abbot Ælfsige (1061–?67) apparently attempted to win backing from the newly-arrived

[12] D. Bates, 'The character and career of Odo, bishop of Bayeux (1049/50–1097)', *Speculum* l (1975), 1–20 at p. 9.
[13] ASC, 'D', 1067. For Christ Church, Canterbury see Brooks, *Christ Church from 597–1066*, and for the community's pre-Conquest losses see Fleming, *Kings and lords*, 80–2. For Norman Canterbury and Kent in this period see W. Urry, 'The Normans in Canterbury', *Annales de Normandie* viii (1958), 119–38; F. R. H. Du Boulay, *The lordship of Canterbury: an essay on medieval society*, London 1966; C. Clark, 'People and language in post-Conquest Canterbury', *Journal of Medieval History* ii (1976), 1–33; T. Tatton-Brown, 'The churches of Canterbury diocese in the eleventh century', in Blair, *Minster and parish churches*, 105–18; N. Ramsay and M. Sparks, 'The cult of St Dunstan at Christ Church, Canterbury', in Ramsay, Sparks and Tatton-Brown, *St Dunstan*, 311–23.
[14] My own calculations.
[15] A. M. Oakley, 'The cathedral priory of St Andrews, Rochester', *Archaelogia Cantiana* xci (1976), 47–60 at p. 47.

Normans by granting them abbey lands 'against the will of his brethren'.[16]
One such grant, which was to be the subject of a long dispute, was that of
Fordwich, in Kent, which had been granted to Sheriff Haimo.[17] According to
Canterbury tradition Ælfsige fled to Denmark, 'thinking of his own safety
rather than that of the flock entrusted to him', and was never seen again.[18] It
seems, however, that Ælfsige was in fact sent there by William the Conqueror on a peace-making mission.[19] Ælfsige's departure was swiftly followed,
in April 1070, by the council of Winchester at which his patron, Stigand, was
deposed. Yet this was not the end of Ælfsige's career in England as he subsequently made his peace with the king, returned to England and from 1080
until his death in 1087 was abbot of Ramsey. Scotland (1070–97), a monk of
Mont-St-Michel whom Orderic described as being 'famed for his learning
and virtue', was subsequently appointed as abbot of St Augustine's.[20] Orderic
also observed that 'in other monasteries too, a change of master speedily took
place [. . .] but in some places fraught with dangers, for the abbots no less than
the monks'. This may well have been a veiled reference to conditions at St
Augustine's where, for example, violent sentiments were certainly felt
towards Scotland's successor, Wido (1087–93), culminating in a plot against
his life. There was evidently some earlier ill-feeling about the appointment of
Scotland, as the monks were described as putting up with his appointment for
the time being, 'though not without bitterness of the soul'.[21]

The chroniclers of St Augustine's clearly had mixed feelings about Abbot
Scotland as he was on the other hand reputed to have been responsible for
the recovery of many abbey properties which had been stolen and for the
acquisition of new properties. Indeed, it is significant that whereas many
other pre-Conquest bequests were disrupted by the events of the Conquest
and settlement, at St Augustine's the abbey managed to realise the promises
made in the will of a Kentish landowner called Æthelric Bigga who had left
land at Bodsham and Wilderton, in Kent.[22] However, during the twenty years
before the making of Domesday Book a sizeable number of abbey lands were
lost. Only Scotland's determination, use of his contacts in high places, and
litigation meant these losses did not become permanent. The abbey's estates
at Badlesmere, Milton Regis, Newington, Pumstead and Forwich, all in Kent,
as well as the lands held by Bruman, were all restored through the courts, two

16 *William Thorne's chronicle*, 49.
17 Ibid. 50.
18 Ibid. 49.
19 For Ælfsige see R. W. Southern, 'The English origins of the miracles of the Virgin',
Medieval and Renaissance Studies iv (1958), 176–216 at pp. 194–8; Knowles, Brooke and
London, *Heads of religious houses*, 62.
20 OV ii. 248.
21 *William Thorne's chronicle*, 50.
22 S1502; DB i, fos 12b, 12d.

with royal backing.[23] Litigation was to remain a recurrent feature of St Augustine's history, especially during the reign of Henry I.

In 1086 St Augustine's was one of the six richest monasteries in England,[24] but as well as encroachments on its lands and rights, it faced another serious threat to its financial well-being. The abbey's estates were geographically compact, all situated, except for Plumstead, in the eastern half of Kent. Such an arrangement facilitated administration of the estates, but in October 1066 meant they were in the path of the Conqueror's invading forces.[25] After the victory at Hastings William's army travelled east along the line of the coast from east Sussex to Dover, in Kent. The abbey's holding at Burmarsh was close to, or on, the route, and according to Domesday Book, the holding's value fell accordingly from £20 in 1066, to £10, 'later'.[26] Far-reaching damage was done in the neighbourhood of Dover, Sandwich and Faversham.[27] The abbey's manor of Minster, on the Isle of Thanet, just over a mile to the north of Sandwich, fell in value from £80 in 1066 to £40 'when the abbot acquired it', conceivably meaning when Scotland became abbot in 1070.[28] The abbey's manors of Northbourne and Great and Little Mongeham were no more than a few miles from Sandwich and their values also plummeted from £80 and £22 respectively in 1066, to £20 and £10 'later'.[29]

St Augustine's estates are recorded in Domesday as having been 'later' worth about 25 per cent less than they were in early 1066, falling from £434 in King Edward's lifetime to £322. However, by 1086 they had more than doubled this intermediate value and were worth approximately £640. Thus, over twenty years the abbey's lands had recovered from the disruption of the Conquest and grown in value by 46 per cent. Very effective estate management had evidently been undertaken to produce so impressive a recovery. Astute, or maybe simply pragmatic, land management was also evident in the enfeoffment of tenants on the abbey lands. In common with many of the first post-Conquest continental abbots appointed to the English monasteries, Scotland was accused of granting abbey lands to the continental newcomers

[23] Ibid. i, fos 2a, 10b; *Excerpta*, 3–5; *Historia Cant.*, 50, 349, 350; *Regesta*, i, nos 66, 88, 98; *William Thorne's chronicle*, 50, 52. For the losses of Christ Church, Canterbury see D. Bates, 'The land pleas of William I's reign: Penenden Heath revisited', *Bulletin of Historical Research* li (1978), 14–17; W. Levison, 'A report on the Penenden trial', *English Historical Review* xxvii (1912), 717–20; D. C. Douglas, 'Odo, Lanfranc, and the Domesday survey', in J. G. Edwards, V. H. Galbraith and E. F. Jacob (eds), *Historical essays in honour of James Tait*, Manchester 1933, 47–57; J. Le Patourel, 'The date of the trial on Penenden Heath', *English Historical Review* lxi (1946), 378–88, and 'The reports of the trials on Penenden Heath', in R. W. Hunt, W. A. Pantin and R. W. Southern (eds), *Studies in medieval history presented to Frederick Maurice Powicke*, Oxford 1948, 15–26.
[24] Knowles, *Monastic order*, 702.
[25] *Florentii Wigorniensis monachi chronicon ex chronici*, ed. B. Thorpe, London 1848–9, i. 228.
[26] DB i, fo. 12d.
[27] Finn, *Norman Conquest*, 45; DB i, fo. 1a.
[28] Ibid. i, fos 12a–b.
[29] Ibid. i, fo. 12c.

without the consent of the convent.[30] Yet Scotland was not unmindful of his actions as he had written agreements drawn up with Ansfrid Male the clerk, Wadard and Hugh fitz Fulbert.[31] Unfortunately the *Carta baronum* only discloses that the abbot owed fifteen knights as his *servitium debitum*. The names of the abbey's military tenants are not revealed, let alone how much each tenant owed.[32]

It is evident that behind Scotland's efforts for the recovery of the abbey's properties and the acquisition of religious patronage, there lurks the figure of Odo, bishop of Bayeux. Many of St Augustine's named tenants were also Odo's men.[33] The community of St Augustine's turned to him for advice on the translation of a set of the abbey's relics.[34] Furthermore the bishop continued to enjoy a good reputation at St Augustine's despite his fall from grace with William the Conqueror and imprisonment during the years 1082–7. Having inherited Plumstead as one of the Godwin family's encroachments, Odo returned this manor and, in addition, made other benefactions to the abbey.[35] These included his houses in Fordwich, a third of the borough of Fordwich, land adjacent to Plumstead called *Smedetune*, the tithes which Æthelwold the Chamberlain had held of Odo at Knowlton, *Tickenhurst* and *Ringleton*, at that date held by Turstin Tinel, the tithe of his tenant Osbern fitz Letard's land at Buckland and Betteshanger and the tithe of Osbern Paisforiere's land at Buckland.[36]

Within a decade of Scotland's appointment, at least two Normans had become monks at St Augustine's. In 1079 Herbert fitz Ivo chose to enter St Augustine's, granting the abbey the tithes of five of his holdings in Kent.[37] Herbert was evidently an adult convert, with no children of his own, who was to live at least another seven years as he appeared as a tenant of Odo of Bayeux in Domesday Book.[38] Ranulf Flambard's father, Turstin, also became a monk at St Augustine's, but the date of his admission is difficult to

---

30 *William Thorne's chronicle*, 50.

31 BL, MS Cotton Julius D ii, fos 107v–8r; *William Thorne's chronicle*, 52–3. For Wadard, who was one of Odo of Bayeux's knights depicted in the Bayeux Tapestry, see *The Bayeux Tapestry: a comprehensive survey*, ed. F. Stenton, London 1957, plate 47.

32 *Red book*, i. 194.

33 Bates, 'Penenden Heath', 17. For Odo see also N. P. Brooks and H. E. Walker, 'The authority and interpretation of the Bayeux Tapestry', *Anglo-Norman Studies* i (1979), 1–34.

34 Bates, 'Character and career of Odo', 10.

35 *Historia Cant.*, 350; *Regesta*, i, no. 88. The editor judged this charter as spurious or inflated but in 1086 St Augustine's was in possession of this manor and a copy of Odo's grant of the moiety of Plumstead does survive: *Historia Cant.*, i, 353.

36 *Regesta*, i, nos 99, 100; *Historia Cant.*, 351, 352. These holdings were valued at just over £27 in 1086.

37 BL, MS Cotton Julius D ii, fo. 108r. This transaction was witnessed by Reginald and Wadard: *William Thorne's chronicle*, 52.

38 DB i, fos 135d, 209d. Herbert is recorded in Domesday Book as holding land from Odo of Bayeux in four locations in Bedfordshire and as having appropriated one hide of scrub from the abbey of St Albans at Abbot's Langley in Hertfordshire.

establish.[39] Ranulf's father had been a village priest in the diocese of Bayeux and the association with St Augustine's had probably arisen through his diocesan bishop and probable patron, Odo, or through his son's connection with the region as head of the college of canons at St Martin, Dover.[40] As Ranulf had been approaching seventy at the time of his death in 1128, and his father could have been anything from twenty to thirty years his senior, it seems plausible that he entered the abbey under Abbot Wido, who was also remembered at Durham.[41]

Shortly after his appointment of Scotland to St Augustine's, William the Conqueror made several grants to the abbey. Aside from restoring the manors of Plumstead and Fordwich, in Kent, William granted Scotland the churches of Faversham and Milton Regis and eight prebends with land in Newington and confirmed various rights and customs of the abbey.[42] A list of churches and their annual renders survives in the White Book of St Augustine's. This catalogue provides an valuable inventory of the churches subordinate to Milton Regis and Newington.[43] The only other post-Conquest acquisition by the abbey was that of Elmstone, in Kent, which had previously been held in freehold by a certain Englishwoman, Godesa.[44]

Abbot Scotland's seventeen-year abbacy was plainly a dynamic period of growth: he had travelled to the court of Alexander II to obtain advice and blessing for his plans to rebuild the abbey church;[45] 'famed for his learning and virtue', he had nourished the Anglo-Saxon artistic and literary traditions at St Augustine's; and his monastery most likely provided the designer of Odo's tapestry sometime before 1082.[46] However, after Scotland's death in September 1087 the wheel of fortune turned sharply downwards for St Augustine's.[47] Although his successor, Wido, completed the translation of the abbey's relics and the rebuilding of the church, and commissioned various works by Goscelin of St-Bertin, actions which were normally associated with encouraging benefactions, there is little sign that any gifts were in fact granted. The subsequent history of the abbey was more concerned with litigation than with anything else.

In the last years of the eleventh century the monks of St Augustine's faced two disastrous crises. The first centred around Lanfranc's imposition of Wido,

---

[39] 'Turstinus monachus Sancti Augustini, pater Rannulfi episcopi': *Liber vitae ecclesiae Dunhelmensis* (ed. Stevenson), 140.

[40] Southern, *Medieval humanism*, 196.

[41] This was suggested by Barlow, *William Rufus*, 193.

[42] *William Thorne's chronicle*, 50–1; *Historia Cant.*, 348–50; *DB* i, fo. 2d; *Regesta*, i, nos 66, 88, 98.

[43] G. Ward, 'The list of Saxon churches in the Domesday monachorum and the White Book of St Augustine's', *Archaeologia Cantiana* xxxxv (1933), 60–89.

[44] *Excerpta*, 21; *DB* i, fo. 12d. Godesa had also held the manor of Betteshanger, Kent, from Edward the Confessor.

[45] *William Thorne's chronicle*, 53.

[46] *OV* ii. 209; Clark, 'People and languages', 7; Brooks and Walker, 'Bayeux Tapestry', 18.

[47] *Historia Cant.*, 344.

a Christ Church monk, as abbot of St Augustine's sometime between September 1087 and March 1088.[48] Abbot Ælfsige, however, had previously obtained from Alexander II the right to wear the mitre and the sandals of primatial abbot, and probably had forgeries drawn up over a number of years to reinforce the abbey's claims. Lanfranc had Wido consecrated and then brought into St Augustine's, in the company of Odo of Bayeux, recently released from imprisonment at Rouen, although it is not clear in what capacity Odo was acting. The monks refused to accept Wido as their abbot, but Lanfranc enthroned him none the less, and subsequently persuaded or coerced most of the monks into obedience and had the ringleaders of the revolt imprisoned. The alternative version of events that was concocted at St Augustine's in later centuries and preserved in Sprott's manuscript and in Thorne's printed chronicle is unconvincing. According to this, Wido was in fact a monk of St Augustine's and the community's choice in opposition to Lanfranc's candidate, a monk of Christ Church.[49] Lanfranc, however, was eventually compelled to consecrate Wido, this being done on the feast of St Thomas the apostle (21 December).[50] There is a problem with the dates here as this section in the chronicle is followed by the notice that Lanfranc died in the following year. As Lanfranc died in May 1089 that would place these events in December 1088 which is in direct opposition to the date suggested by the version of events in the Acta Lanfranci. The St Augustine tradition also makes no mention of the second major crisis at St Augustine's in which a plot against's Wido's life was hatched by the monk Columbanus.[51] Lanfranc had Columbanus publicly flogged in front of the abbey church and thence driven from the city. More was to follow. After Lanfranc's death in May 1089, the monks rebelled against Wido and the citizens of Canterbury rose up in their support and attempted to kill the beleaguered Wido in his house. Fortunately for the abbot, members of his household protected him, some at the cost of their own lives, and he was able to escape unharmed.[52] After the riot was subdued, Bishop Gundulf of Rochester and Bishop Walchelin of Winchester expelled the monks involved and created a new community at St Augustine's, introducing monks from Christ Church and elsewhere.

Events like these were obviously profoundly humiliating for the monks of St Augustine's and were passed over unmentioned in the later chronicles.[53] However, an earlier passage in these chronicles illustrates the growing tension between the two Canterbury communities. Lanfranc had apparently forbidden St Augustine's from ringing their bells at any canonical hour unless

---

48 The presence of Odo dates these events: Bates, 'Character and career of Odo', 18.
49 Clark, 'People and language', 27n.; Knowles, Monastic order, 116.
50 William Thorne's chronicle, 58.
51 M. Gibson, Lanfranc of Bec, Oxford 1978, 115.
52 Acta Lanfranci, in English historical documents, II: 1042–1189, 680.
53 Gibson, Lanfranc, 189.

previously rung in the episcopal church.[54] Events at Glastonbury in 1083 had already proved just how explosive such disputes over the introduction of new practices could be. At Glastonbury, the monks quarrelled with Abbot Turstin over the chant to be used in choir. This led to an ugly brawl, with eighteen wounded and three dead,[55] although it was admittedly the abbot's continental men-at-arms who committed the acts of violence. Naturally at Canterbury the citizens could not help but be very aware of so audible a conflict as one over the ringing of bells.[56] The clash was also clearly symbolic of Christ Church's endeavour to assert its authority over St Augustine's and a rejection of that house's claim to primacy.

Abbot Wido's behaviour, in the aftermath of this uproar, looks like an attempt to restore some dignity to an abbey which had been reformed and in many senses refounded. He oversaw the completion of Scotland's abbey church, the translation of the abbey's relics and the commissioning of Goscelin of St-Bertin's works.[57] Goscelin's Vita Mildrethae and his Libellus contra inanes S. virginis Mildrethae usurpatores were also written in the 1090s for St Augustine's with a very specific intention in mind. They were composed in response to the fierce and open competition from the priory of St Gregory, Canterbury, a house of secular canons. St Augustine's believed themselves to be the sole possessors of the relics of St Mildreth. St Gregory's, however, founded in 1084 or 1085 by Lanfranc, claimed to have possession of the relics of St Mildreth and St Edburg from 1087 or 1088 onwards.[58] They believed that the unidentified body that had been translated by Lanfranc to St Gregory's in 1085 was that of St Mildreth.[59] Lanfranc, at the request of the abbot of St Augustine's, had actually attempted to restrain the canons of St Gregory's from making this claim.[60]

The disruption caused by the uprising of 1088–9, coupled with Odo's rebellion in 1088, caused serious problems for Abbot Wido. Some time after his accession a certain Asketil, probably Asketil de Rots the abbey's tenant at Ashenfield, seized a parcel of abbey land.[61] The tithes granted by Odo of Bayeux and his men to the abbey were also supposedly stolen, a 'theft' possibly resulting from the regranting of Odo's forfeited lands by William Rufus. A writ of Rufus ordered that the abbot of St Augustine's should have the tithes

54 William Thorne's chronicle, 57. This dispute was still a sensitive issue after Lanfranc's death: Regesta, i, no. 459.
55 See ch. 8.
56 William Thorne's chronicle, 65. Abbot Hugh I secured the right from Pope Calixtus II to ring the abbey bells at any time.
57 For St Mildreth also see R. U. Potts, 'St Mildred's church, Canterbury: further notes on the site', Archaelogia Cantiana lvi (1943), 19–22; R. Sharpe, 'The date of St Mildreth's translation from Minster-in-Thanet to Canterbury', Mediaeval Studies liii (1991), 349–54.
58 Rollason, Mildreth legend, 21.
59 Ibid. 68.
60 Ibid.
61 Regesta, i, no. 351.

which he held on the day on which his father was alive and dead, 'no matter to whom the king has given the land from which the tithes come'.[62] The tithes granted by Herbert fitz Ivo were 'unjustly' taken by William Peverel, 'the lord of the aforesaid manors', William d'Aubigny was accused of stealing the tithes of Knowlton and Ringleton and Roger de Menires of taking the tithes of Buckland. Yet these men were all probably the new holders of these estates.[63] The dispute with the City of London over Stonar, in Sandwich, Kent, was settled to the abbey's advantage, but only after the case had come to trial.[64]

Although St Augustine's was the only vacant abbey not to be filled by Henry I in the first year of his reign, the king appeared to take an interest in it, granting an annual fair on the feast of the translation of St Augustine at Canterbury.[65] Hugh de Fleury (d. 1126), blessed by Archbishop Anselm in 1108, was apparently a competent abbot.[66] He is credited with having rebuilt the abbey's chapter house and dormitory from the funds which he had given the house at his entrance,[67] and he brought 'from across the sea' a great brass candlestick. According to a late source, he also procured privileges from Pope Calixtus II (1119–24) stating, amongst other things, that St Augustine's had the right to ring the church bells at any time,[68] while a number of *conventiones* survive from the abbacy, illustrating a return to healthy relations with local landholders. Hugh negotiated with Luuam, wife of Odo, a man-at-arms, over the return of land at Solton, in Kent, in exchange for 100s. and the grant of land at Higham, also in Kent.[69] Agreements were made with William of [?]idfield granting land in London and with Eadwin the overseer.[70] In addition Hugh arranged that commemoration should be made for the souls of the abbey's benefactors and the relatives of the house's brothers, both living and dead.[71] This was to take place on 11 July annually when thirty paupers were also to be fed in the hall. Furthermore, on the death of a monk, 5s. would be given from a special abbey fund. Hugh's deeds suggest that the lack of benefactors to the abbey was a matter of serious concern, calling for increased efforts on the part of the abbey to attract more. The recruitment of monks was also a problem as numbers had dropped to below sixty in the years before

---

62 Ibid. i, no. 351.
63 *William Thorne's chronicle*, 52.
64 This was a pre-Conquest dispute which had supposedly been settled by Harold Harefoot: S1467; *William Thorne's chronicle*, 59; *Regesta*, i, nos 371, 372. The dispute was still running in the latter part of the reign of Henry I: *Historia Cant.*, 360; *Regesta*, ii, no. 1644.
65 Ibid. ii, no. 652.
66 Eadmer, *Historia novorum*, 190.
67 *William Thorne's chronicle*, 63.
68 Ibid. 65.
69 BL, MS Cotton Julius D ii, fo. 106v.
70 Ibid. fo. 107r.
71 *William Thorne's chronicle*, 66.

1146.[72] The only grant Hugh received was a bequest of money from the abbey tenants of Selling, in Kent, Godeliva and her man Ælred.[73]

Hugh's successor, Hugh II of Trottiscliffe (1124/6–51), a monk of Rochester, was remembered at St Augustine's as an effective abbot, 'a man learned in monastic and secular learning [. . .] a most faithful administrator'.[74] Hugh reorganised the internal affairs of the abbey, granting income from specific mills, tithes and churches to the sacristy, almonry and infirmary.[75] His list of sources of income for the monks' clothing is very interesting as it mentions several estates that have not otherwise been identified in Domesday Book as belonging to, or subsequently having been given to, the abbey.[76] For example, the manor of Wheatley, in Essex, where Odo of Bayeux had held land in 1086 is referred to, but there is no mention of a grant or purchase in the sources.[77] Odo also held Offham, in Kent, and again its tithe appears in the possession of the abbey under Hugh II.[78] Gravesend was held by the abbey benefactor Herbert fitz Ivo, and the tithe of that manor is mentioned in Hugh II's grant, but there is no mention of any donation. Hugh's abbacy also saw a continuation of the litigation that had characterised the abbacies of his predecessors. Again, many of these cases were not new. The dispute over the tithe of Milton Regis had been fought before 1086 and was referred to in the *Excerpta*.[79] There was also a new dispute over tolls in Stonar, this time with the archbishop of Canterbury rather than the City of London.[80] Henry I made grants of warren on the Isle of Thanet, on the manor of Lenham, on his land in the hundred of Eyehorne, Stodmarsh and Littlebourne, all in Kent.[81] Grants of warren and similar rights to abbeys by Henry I were commonplace, but the grants he gave to St Augustine were relatively extensive. However,there is no evidence of any other benefactions having been made to the abbey in the time of Hugh II.

I began this chapter by remarking that the history of St Augustine's, Canterbury, exhibits many elements common to the history of many English

---

[72] Ibid. 80.

[73] BL, MS Cotton Julius D ii, fo. 107r.

[74] *William Thorne's chronicle*, 67–8.

[75] Ibid. 68.

[76] BL, MS Cotton Claudius D x, fo. 273r; *William Thorne's chronicle*, 69. Although the information contained in both texts is similar it is not identical. The manors granted in the Red Book version are Riple in Kent, Wheatley and Langdon in Essex, and *Wellinges*; the tithes granted are in Gravesend in Essex, Offham in Kent, the tithe of Lambert of *Sthoveldone*, the tithe of Ralph of Betteshanger, the tithe of Poynings in Sussex, the tithe of Haimo the chaplain of Finglesham in Kent and the tithe of the church of Fordwich. William Thorne's resumé adds the manors of Selling and Swalecliffe in Kent.

[77] *DB* ii, fo. 23a.

[78] Ibid. i, fo. 7b.

[79] *Excerpta*, 3; *Regesta*, ii, nos 1643, 1779.

[80] Ibid. ii, no. 1644; *Historia Cant.*, 360; *English lawsuits from William I to Richard*, ed. R. C. Van Caenegem (Selden Society cvi, cvii, 1990–1), i, no. 254.

[81] *Regesta*, ii, nos 1571, 1616, 1814.

abbeys after 1066. Yet closer analysis has also revealed those many elements that are missing. Unlike those of Abingdon or Thorney, the abbots of St Augustine's do not seem to have attempted to cultivate any sort of meaningful relationship with royal officials other than with Odo of Bayeux. During Odo's ascendancy this policy paid good dividends but after 1082 the abbey failed to replace him with another influential champion. For an institution which had struggled through the first generation of the Norman Conquest so well, St Augustine's never seemed to fulfil its early promise. The abbey had so much going for it; it was magnificently old, tremendously wealthy, it possessed the relics of England's arguably most famous saint, it was blessed by a number of able abbots and had territorially compact estates which should have been easy to look after. Yet the running battle with Christ Church, Canterbury, over its independence and the consequences of the 1088–9 riots seem to have left it inward-looking. Perhaps it was not the fact of the riot itself that put off potential benefactors, but rather the dispersal of the established community. The citizens of Canterbury had come, rather violently, to the monks' aid in 1089. They were hardly likely then to patronise the 'usurpers' installed in the abbey with Abbot Wido. The rebellion of the abbey's major benefactor, Odo of Bayeux, caused problems when his lands were regranted. It is little wonder then that the men of Kent had more long-lasting enthusiasm for endowing Rochester cathedral priory.

7

The Fenland Houses

The decision to consider the Fenland abbeys together has been influenced primarily by two factors.[1] The first is the unusual topography of this region. Its relative isolation and impenetrability, the result of the nature of the terrain, meant that the Normans remained distrustful of it and its inhabitants for a long time after the disturbances of the 1070s. The flourishing cult of the martyred Earl Waltheof and the fact that Ramsey, Peterborough and Crowland periodically had abbots of English origin well into the twelfth century served to perpetuate the sense of 'otherness' between the Normans and the leadership and personnel of these English monasteries.[2] The second element was the structure of tenurial landholding in the area. In the mid eleventh century the Fenland region was dominated by ecclesiastical landholders (see map 3). Consequently, the post-Conquest history of all five abbeys was closely intermeshed throughout the period. Certain aspects of their experiences, therefore, need to be considered in parallel in order to observe the various trends at play. This approach is particularly profitable in the light of the fact that Ely and Peterborough received relatively little in the way of religious patronage. Whilst therefore acknowledging their importance after the Conquest, in this examination of the patterns of religious patronage after 1066, these two wealthy monasteries will be largely on the periphery of the discussion.

Apart from St Benedict's, Ramsey, all the Fenland houses had originally been founded in the century or so following the arrival of St Augustine's mission in England. Each was established by, or with the help of, royalty: Ely by St Æthelreda, daughter of Anna, king of East Anglia; Crowland by King Æthelbald from the cell established by St Guthlac, a member of the Merican royal house; Peterborough by the monk Saxulf, with the help of Peada, king of Wessex; Thorney supposedly by Saxulf, founder of Peterborough.[3] Religious life at these houses perished in the face of the Viking invasions of the ninth century but they were refounded in the tenth by Bishops Æthelwold, Oswald and Thorketel with the help and generosity of King Edgar and local

---

[1]   Page, *Estates of Crowland abbey*; Miller, *Abbey and bishopric of Ely*; J. A. Raftis, *Estates of Ramsey abbey*, Toronto 1957; Raban, 'Thorney and Crowland abbeys', and *Estates of Thorney and Crowland*; King, *Peterborough abbey*.
[2]   These abbots of English origin were Waltheof at Crowland (1126–38), Godric at Peterborough (1101–2) and Aldwin at Ramsey (1091–1102, 1107–12).
[3]   Miller, *Abbey and bishopric of Ely*, 8–9; *Felix's life of St Guthlac*, ed. B. Colgrave, Cambridge 1956, 89, 95–9; Binns, *Dedications*, 69–70, 82, 87.

Map 3. The Fenland houses

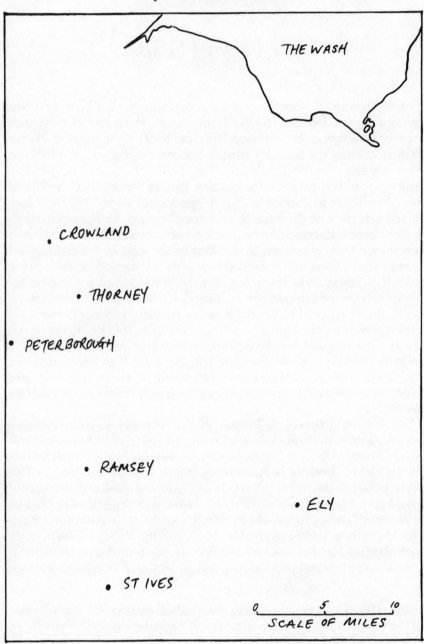

men like Ealdorman Æthelwine of East Anglia.[4] Ramsey, the only new foundation of the tenth century, was established in about 969 by Ealdorman Æthelwine and Bishop Oswald.[5]

Ely

All the Fenland monasteries were built on islands, or on land bordering water, in the midst of marshland,[6] sharing the strategic inaccessibility which was exploited by insurgents and refugees in the 1070s. In 1070/1 the isle of Ely became the centre of a rebellion by the English, while the revolt of the earls in 1075 reinforced uncertainties about the security of eastern England. The price the abbey of Ely paid for its entanglement in Hereward's revolt – aside from a payment of £1,000 – was the extensive spoliation of its lands.[7] In the course of the suppression of the rebellion numerous abbey lands were seized. For instance it is known that Eustace of Boulogne 'forcibly seized from the church' half a hide in Easton, Huntingdonshire, five years after the Conquest.[8] Furthermore, the lands of the rebels, confiscated during the course of Hereward's revolt, were rapidly granted out to the Conqueror's followers.[9] As some of this had been held from Ely, the abbey lost control, in many cases permanently.[10] At the best of times such lands were never easy to recover from Norman tenants and the troubles of the 1070s made it even more difficult. In the mid eleventh century Ely's lands had been worth approximately £900 in total; those still held in 1086 would have been worth something in the region of £795 in 1066, but by the time of the Domesday survey were worth only £816.[11] This fall in value of just over 11 per cent does not demonstrate the actual scale of the losses the abbey suffered after 1070/1 as a number of lands were recovered through litigation before Domesday.[12]

These extensive losses profoundly influenced the course of Ely's post-Conquest development particularly as abbots were involved in litigation well into the twelfth century. Two seven-year vacancies and the transformation of

---

4 Stafford, *East midlands*, 130.
5 For the tenth-century foundation and endowment of these houses see ch. 1.
6 *Chron. Hugh Candidus*, 4–7.
7 *Liber Eliensis*, 189–91; Knowles, *Monastic order*, 105.
8 In 1086 this land was still in Eustace's hands: DB i, fo. 208b.
9 Fleming, *Kings and lords*, 168.
10 For the different varieties of 'invasions' on Ely's lands see Miller, *Abbey and bishopric of Ely*, 66–7.
11 My own calculations. For other estimations see ibid. 16; Knowles, *Monastic order*, 702; W. J. Corbett, 'England 1087–1154', in J. R. Tanner and others (eds), *Cambridge medieval history*, Cambridge 1957, v. 521–53 at p. 509.
12 For the invasion of Ely's lands and subsequent litigation and recoveries see VCH, *Cambridgeshire*, i. 350–4; E. Miller, 'The Ely land pleas in the reign of William I', *English Historical Review* lxii (1947), 438–56; *Liber Eliensis*, 426–32; *English lawsuits*, i, no. 18.

the abbey into the seat of a bishopric in 1109 caused more disruption.[13] Religious patronage played a decidedly minor role in Ely's post-Conquest history, being limited to grants accompanying the entrance of individuals into the community none of whom, significantly, was of Norman origin. In the reign of Henry I three men, Bricstan of Chatteris, an Englishman, Ralph fitz Colswein, who judging by his name was presumably of English descent, and Hascoit Musard, who was a Breton, became monks at Ely.[14] The first two were local property-holders, whilst Hascoit's association with Ely was derived through the Breton bishop, Hervey, to whom he had previously granted land.[15] Although the clientele of St Æthelreda's shrine included 'persons of continental as well as native origins', none besides Hascoit chose to become its benefactors.[16]

Peterborough

At Peterborough in the mid twelfth century the Norman Conquest was viewed by the chronicler, Hugh Candidus, as nothing short of an unmitigated disaster for the abbey:

> For Abbot Thorold himself [. . .] evilly took away and gave the abbey's possessions to his relations and to the knights who had come with him, so that scarce a third of the abbey remained in demesne. When he came the abbey was valued at £1,050 but he so dispersed its estates that it was scarcely worth £500.[17]

It appears that Hugh exaggerated somewhat, as in 1086 the abbey's lands were valued at just over £303. Furthermore, although Domesday Book reveals that Peterborough's lands in Huntingdonshire, Bedfordshire, Lincolnshire and Nottinghamshire, had fallen in value since 1066 by 19 per cent, those estates closer to the abbey in Northamptonshire had almost tripled in value, from £69 to £189.[18] Hugh's assessment of the level of enfeoffment was also overstated as in fact only 46 per cent of Peterborough's estates were enfeoffed.[19] However, Hugh's 'stretching' of the figures should not diminish the fact that Peterborough was answerable for sixty knights, the heaviest quota of knights fees owed by any monastic community in the realm.[20] This

---

13 Miller, *Abbey and bishopric of Ely*, 75.
14 *Liber Eliensis*, 265–74, 277; *English lawsuits*, i, no. 204.
15 Bricstan was a money-lender and lived in Chatteris in Cambridgeshire, whilst Ralph was recorded as having possessed a house in *Saham*. Hascoit held lands as a tenant-in-chief in 1086 in Buckinghamshire, Gloucestershire, Oxfordshire and Warwickshire.
16 Ridyard, 'Condigna veneratio', 179–206 at p. 185; *Liber Eliensis*, 265, 270–4.
17 *Chron. Hugh Candidus*, 84–5.
18 My own calculations.
19 King, *Peterborough abbey*, 14–15.
20 Ibid. 14.

quota may have been high for an ecclesiastical house but not for a lay barony, and it essentially reflects the seriousness of the military crises of 1069–71, compounded by the earls' revolt of 1075.[21] Indeed, Abbot Thorold's first entrance into the abbey precinct, in the wake of the chaotic retreat of Hereward and the Danes, was allegedly in the company of 160 well-armed Norman soldiers.[22]

A catalogue of what can only be termed 'misfortunes' also befell Peterborough during this period. This included two fires, the first in 1070, the second in 1116 and the plundering of the abbey's treasures in 1070 and 1102 by thieves, and by Abbots Thorold and Henry.[23] The events of the Conquest also meant that at least one sizeable donation to Peterborough never took effect.[24] The monks' luck with their abbots was not much better. During the seventy years after the Conquest the abbey had a succession of abbots, the longest lived, Abbot Thorold (1070–98), was the most unpopular and four other of the eight held office for less than five years each.[25] The abbacy of Henry of Poitou (1127–31), kinsman of the king and a pluralist, was particularly distressing for the abbey as he cheerfully collected in all the abbey's dues and rents and sent them off to his other abbey of St-Jean d'Angély.[26]

It was not, however, all doom and gloom for the Peterborough monks in the reign of the Conqueror, for the king confirmed some of the grants made to the abbey in the pre-Conquest era, although at a price.[27] The abbey was also given three and a half hides in Orton Waterville, in Huntingdonshire, sometime before 1086,[28] and Henry I showed a significant degree of concern for the welfare of the house. The twelfth century also yielded some very significant benefits from the abbey's military tenants.[29] It seems likely that the building programme initiated by Abbot Ernulf (1107–14) led to negotiations with the abbey knights with the result that they agreed that 'each and every knight shall give two portions of his tithes to the sacrist of Peterborough. Moreover at the end of his life, a third part of his whole property, with his knightly accoutrements both in horses and armour, shall be carried with him to the burial of the dead man and offered to God and St Peter.'[30] Considering the exceptionally high level of enfeoffment on the abbey lands, this *conventio* was likely to bear much valuable fruit. The abbey's only other notable

21 Ibid. 16.
22 *Chron. Hugh Candidus*, 80.
23 Ibid. 82, 85, 87, 96–7, 99–104; ASC 'E', 1116.
24 *Anglo-Saxon wills*, no. xxxix, pp. 94–6.
25 These were Abbot Brand (1066–9), Abbot Godric (?1101–2), Abbot Matthew Ridel (1102–3) and Abbot Henry (1127–32).
26 For the abbacy of Henry of St-Jean d'Angély, son of Duke William of Aquitaine, see C. Clark, 'This ecclesiastical adventurer: Henry of Saint-Jean d'Angély', *English Historical Review* lxxxiv (1969), 548–60.
27 *Regesta*, i, no. 8; *Chron. Hugh Candidus*, 76–7.
28 DB i, fo. 205b.
29 *Regesta*, ii, nos 1244, 1750, 1858.
30 *Chron. Hugh Candidus*, 90–1.

benefactors were members of the knightly family living at Castor, in North-amptonshire. In the early twelfth century the ailing Robert of Castor gave the abbot and monks of Peterborough £50 of silver to have himself and his young son, William, enter the community as monks,[31] and in 1133 Richard of Castor, the eldest son of the family, also wanted to become a monk and bring his church and property to the abbey.[32] The benefactors that Peterborough, like Ely, succeeded in attracting were strictly local in their interests and drawn to the abbey by the promise of specific spiritual returns, invariably either entrance as a monk or burial in the abbey's cemetery.

Ramsey

Ramsey abbey, unlike Ely or Peterborough, was a place of relative peace and security during the disorders of 1069/70. In fact Prior Æthelwold of Peterborough chose Ramsey as a refuge for the precious arm of St Oswald when it was feared that the Danes might steal it.[33] In the light of the small *servitium debitum* of four knights owed by Ramsey, and the relatively small amount of land the abbey enfeoffed, the abbey would appear to have escaped lightly from the heavy measures that were levied upon Ely and Peterborough.[34] However, although Ramsey land values 'remained practically stable' in this period, this belies the fact that the abbey did actually lose a significant amount of land.[35] The Ramsey chronicler, in common with the Abingdon chronicler, complained that the Normans 'lawlessly' invaded several of the abbey's properties.[36] The list of allegedly violent dispossessions is much longer than Abingdon's. For example, Odo of Bayeux, Alan I Rufus, lord of Richmond, Walter Giffard, Eustace the sheriff and William de Warenne were all said to have seized abbey lands, or rights, 'by violence'.[37] Ramsey and Ely shared several of the same continental invaders, Eustace the sheriff of Huntingdonshire, Odo of Bayeux and William de Warenne.[38] The Ramsey chronicle and Domesday Book bear out these claims as they refer to losses in at least twenty locations.[39] In the twenty years after Hastings Ramsey lost control of lands

---

[31] Ibid. 91. For a discussion of this case see M. Chibnall, *Anglo-Norman England, 1066–1166*, Oxford 1986, 171–2.

[32] King, *Peterborough abbey*, 31.

[33] *Chron. Hugh Candidus*, 81.

[34] The enfeoffed land was worth only £24 9s. 4d.: Lennard, *Rural England*, 86–7; King, *Peterborough abbey*, 16. For a rosy view of Ramsey's post-Conquest fortunes see Raftis, *Ramsey abbey*, 23.

[35] Ibid.

[36] *Chron. Ramsey*, 172.

[37] Ibid. 144–5, 154, 174–6; *DB* i, fos 203a, 208a, 208c, 212a, 216a, 348b, 377b; ii, fos 159b, 419b.

[38] *Chron. Ramsey*, 175; *DB* i, fos 203a, 206a.

[39] After 1066 the abbey lost control of land at Bottisham and in Staploe hundred in Cambridgeshire; *Offerthun*, in Drayton, Morton and Isham in Northamptonshire; Tring,

which had been assessed in 1066 as just over £72.[40] If these lands are taken into account, Ramsey's possessions would have been worth something like £454 in 1066. By the time of the Domesday survey, however, its remaining possessions were worth £358 16s. 4d., a fall of about £96, or 21 per cent. Furthermore, because of the disruption that accompanied the Conquest, Ramsey did not gain possession of certain estates which were meant to be transferred to the abbey upon the deaths of the donors.[41] Such bequeathed lands amounted to some 36½ hides, and in 1086 were worth about £56. This substantial loss of revenue may have been used as part of the abbey's petition for a light military burden. It also explains why Ramsey's abbots were occupied in the law courts well into the reign of Henry I.

Ramsey's first Norman abbot, Herbert Losinga (1087–90/1), gave the cult of St Ives a massive boost by commissioning Goscelin of St-Bertin to rewrite the *vita* of the saint.[42] He also had the relics of St Ives's companions returned to a newly constructed church at their original place of burial in Slepe (later known as St Ives), in Huntingdonshire, which proved popular with pilgrims.[43] This subordinate shrine attracted grants in its own right. In fact the earliest benefactions centre around the church and shrine at Slepe, rather than Ramsey itself, but it appears that they were only made at the prompting of Abbot Bernard (1102–7).[44] Saewin the falconer, whose expertise had won him the high regard of the Conqueror and also the gift of two hides in Hemmingford from the abbot of Ramsey, 'because of his regard for the king',[45] gave to the abbey three virgates in Needingworth, in Holywell, Huntingdonshire; his wife, Aliman, gave another two acres and Alfwold of Stanton gave the meadow 'above that upon which the bridge is built and the land from the bridge to the end of the ford'.[46] Abbot Bernard himself gave ten acres of the abbey's demesne land in Slepe with twenty-six acres of land. Nigel Fossard promised Ramsey abbey his church of Bramham, in Yorkshire, with two

Therfield and Westmill in Hertfordshire; Langton by Horncastle, Wispington, Martin and Waddingworth in Lincolnshire; Cranfield in Bedfordshire; *Brunstanethorp*, Hemmingford Grey, Yelling and Sawtry in Huntingdonshire; *Manesfort* in Suffolk; Hilgay and sixty-seven socmen at Wimbotsham in Norfolk: *Chron. Ramsey*, 144–6, 152–4, 171–2, 174–5; *DB* i, fos 137b, 141c–d, 208a, 208c, 203a, 197d, 212a, 216a, 348b, 377b; ii, fos 159b, 419b.

[40] Not all locations can be identified so the total would have been much higher.

[41] These estates were Wood Walton in Huntingdonshire, Ugley and Helions Bumpstead in Essex, Abington in Cambridgeshire, Chalton in Bedfordshire and Waldingfield in Suffolk: *Chron. Ramsey*, 152–3, 146, 172.

[42] *Goscelini miracula Sancti Ivonis*, printed in *Chron. Ramsey*, pp. lix–lxxxiv. For St Ives see S. B. Edgington, *The life and miracles of St Ivo*, St Ives 1985.

[43] *Chron. Ramsey*, pp. lxxv–lxxvi; Edgington, *Life and miracles*, 25–6.

[44] *Chron. Ramsey*, 266. Grants are recorded as having been made in the time of Abbot Bernard (1102–5) and 'afterwards' during Abbot Aldwin's second period of government (1107–12).

[45] *DB* i, fo. 208a.

[46] Edgington, *Life and miracles*, 37–8.

carucates, the tithes of three of his manors and the tithe of his court, but this grant probably never took effect.[47]

On Bernard's death in 1107, the previous English abbot, Aldwin (1091–1102, 1107–12), who had been deposed in 1102, recovered the abbey, and himself added a considerable amount of property to the endowment.[48] However the bulk of the religious patronage received by both Ramsey and St Ives was small-scale and commonly integral to *conventiones* made with abbey tenants. Most of the grants made during the abbacy of Reginald (1113/14–31), a monk of Caen, were from neighbouring landholders and clerics, and were grants of property in places where Ramsey already held land. For example, on the feast of St Oswald, Everard, the priest of Burwell, in Cambridgeshire, gave eight acres which he had received from the abbot's chamber and also gave his own tithe along with the tithes of Richard fitz Spere, Alfwin of Shillington and Frebert of Barton.[49] Gilbert fitz Ingulf of Slepe made a grant of his land in Over, Cambridgeshire, to Abbot Reginald.[50] Siward, clerk of Wistow, in Huntingdonshire, gave the abbey his land and church, to hold whilst he lived, paying 20s. each year 'upon the altar of St Benedict'.[51]

The church at St Ives acted as a stronger focus for grants than Ramsey abbey itself until the middle years of Henry I's reign. This was to change with the construction of a new abbey church at Ramsey. From its inception in 1116, the building project acted as a stimulus to finding more money, and more efficient means of collecting dues from tenants.[52] In 1123, as the building was nearing completion, the pressure for cash intensified as the royal writ that year illustrates. Henry I ordered that the men of the abbey of Ramsey should 'render to the abbot quickly and justly, whatever they owe him in rent, farms, debts and pleas, according as he can show they are indebted'.[53] The construction of the new church also prompted a grant of ten acres of land in Martin, Lincolnshire, from a local Englishman, Wulfgeat. His donation was

47 *Chron. Ramsey*, 234; *EYC* ii. 330. Robert Fossard also granted the church of Bramham to Nostell c. 1126–9: ibid. ii. 337–9. A royal writ issued in the late 1120s ordered Nigel's heir, Robert Fossard, 'to do right to the abbot of Ramsey respecting the church of Bramham'. It therefore seems that the earlier grant to Ramsey was wholly or partially withdrawn: *Chron. Ramsey*, 231; *Regesta*, ii, no. 1630.

48 He granted a pasture farm, whatever land the monk Leofwin had cleared, one hide at Hurst, in Slepe, two acres, half a hide in Holywell, the fishery called *Flet*, and one acre in Houghton meadow: *Chron. Ramsey*, 266.

49 Ibid. 239; *Cartularium monasterii de Rameseia*, ed. W. H. Hart and P. A. Lyons (Rolls series lxxix, 1884–93), i. 132.

50 *Chron. Ramsey*, 242–3; *Cart. Ramsey*, i. 134–5.

51 *Chron. Ramsey*, 236–7; *Cart. Ramsey*, i. 130.

52 *Chron. Ramsey*, 229; *Cart. Ramsey*, ii. 102–3; *Regesta*, ii, no. 1410. Henry I ordered that the abbot of Ramsey should have stone for the building of his church.

53 *Chron. Ramsey*, 229; *Regesta*, ii, no. 1387.

apparently made in the unfinished church 'upon the new altar' dedicated to the Holy Trinity, with the carpenters and a mason acting as his witnesses.[54]

Collectively, St Benedict's abbots were active in securing royal charters and safeguarding and reorganising the abbey endowment.[55] Abbot Aldwin was particularly active in acquiring confirmation of a number of abbey rights and William Rufus restored Ramsey's *servitium debitum* to the 'remarkably light' quota of four knights from the temporary level of ten knights.[56] Aldwin also obtained the lucrative grant of a week's fair, from Wednesday in Easter week to the following Wednesday, at St Ives.[57] Nevertheless, despite evidence of royal favour and adept abbots, Ramsey did not receive religious patronage on anything like the scale of St Albans, Abingdon, Gloucester or even St Augustine's, Canterbury. The status of the abbey's benefactors was without exception modest, even if the status of its tenants was otherwise. The reason for Ramsey's failure to attract large-scale religious patronage would seem to lie in a combination of factors: the brevity of the rule of its abbots in the late eleventh century; the relatively late rebuilding of the abbey church at Ramsey; and, most important, the loss of lands after the troubles in the Fenlands which meant that the abbey's energies were absorbed by the expensive and time-consuming legal action needed to recover them.

In the reign of Henry I Ramsey abbey did establish a healthy tradition of attracting benefactions from local landholders. Although these were largely of a modest nature, they were becoming more substantial as the reign progressed. Indeed, two of the most substantial were made in the 1130s. Thus, in 1131, in the last year of Abbot Reginald's life, on the feast of the purification of the Virgin Mary, Hubert of Ste-Suzanne gave a hide of his demesne in Newnham, in Northamptonshire,[58] and in or before 1134, Albreda of Walton, daughter of Remelin and widow of Eustace of Sellea, granted Wood Walton, in Huntingdonshire, to Ramsey.[59] Wood Walton was a very attractive acquisition as it lay particularly close to the hundred of Hurstingstone and it was to have passed to the abbey on the death of its pre-Conquest tenant Saxi.[60]

---

[54] *Chron. Ramsey*, 245–6.

[55] *Regesta*, i, nos 330, 373.

[56] *Chron. Ramsey*, 209, 212; *Cart. Ramsey*, i. 235; *Regesta*, i, no. 462; Barlow, *William Rufus*, 292. Abbot Aldwin obtained from the king seven writs and a confirmation charter from 1100 to September 1102: *Chron. Ramsey*, 216–19; *Cart. Ramsey*, ii. 60, 82, 327; *Regesta*, ii, nos 528a, 574, 579, 580–3, 587; Raftis, *Ramsey abbey*, 28.

[57] *Chron. Ramsey*, 221–2, 265; *Cart. Ramsey*, i. 148, 240; ii. 101; *Regesta*, ii, no. 953.

[58] *Cart. Ramsey*, i. 256.

[59] *Chron. Ramsey*, 276–7, 318–19; *Cart. Ramsey*, i. 155–8; *Regesta*, ii, no. 1766.

[60] *Chron. Ramsey*, 146; Hart, *Charters of eastern England*, 352–6.

CASE STUDIES

Crowland

Although Thorney and Crowland were the two poorest Fenland houses in 1066, they made substantial gains in the century after Hastings, and were the only Fenland houses to possess dependent cells before 1135.[61] The Conquest had brought very different consequences for the richer Fenland houses, as their massive losses were compounded by the failure to acquire a significant amount of new property.[62] The study of Crowland in the post-Conquest era is complicated by the text known as the Historia Croylandensis, compiled in the fifteenth century, which purports to have been written by Abbot Ingulf (1085–1108).[63] Much in the text can be shown to be fanciful, such as the date of 1075/6 given for Abbot Wulfketel's deposition and Ingulf's accession, which is palpably incorrect, and such excesses of language as the assessment of Countess Judith as 'that most wicked Jezebel', clearly the reinterpretation of a later generation.[64] However, it is clear that the compiler of the Historia also drew on reliable twelfth-century sources and traditions.[65] For example it is very similar in content to the account of Crowland composed by Orderic Vitalis, who had visited the abbey himself sometime between 1109 and 1124, possibly in 1119.[66] Thus, the Historia duplicates Orderic's story of the divine retribution meted out by the late Earl Waltheof for the derogatory remarks made by Ouen, a Norman monk of St Albans (see below).[67] The generous grant by Guy de Craon of the church of Freiston, in Lincolnshire, with a sizeable endowment of land detailed in the Historia can also be verified from a number of other reliable sources.[68]

61 Raban, 'Thorney and Crowland abbeys', 61, 66.
62 Ibid. 60, 108.
63 Copies of the Historia Croylandensis survive in BL, MS Cotton Otho B xiii, and in BL, MS Arundel 178. These were published in Rerum Anglicarum scriptores veteres, ed. W. Fulman, Oxford 1684, and in The chronicles of Croyland by Ingulf, ed. W. de Gray Birch, Wisbech 1883. A third version, now lost, was published by Henry Savile in Rerum Anglicarum scriptores post Bedam, London 1596, and a fourth text is preserved in Rerum Anglicarum scriptores veteres. For a discussion of the reliability of the Historia Croylandensis see David Roffe, 'The Historia Croylandensis: a plea for reassessment', English Historical Review cx (1995), 93–108; Ingulf's chronicle of the abbey of Croyland with the continuation by Peter of Blois and anonymous writers, ed. H. T. Riley, London 1908, pp. ix–xv; Page, Crowland abbey, 4–5; W. G. Searle, Ingulf and the Historia Croylandensis, Cambridge 1894; E. A. Freeman, 'The false Ingulf and the miracles of Waltheof', in his The Norman Conquest, Oxford 1876, iv. 838–40. See also Chibnall's remarks in OV ii, p. xxv. (All subsequent references to Ingulf's chronicle are to the Riley edn.)
64 Ingulf's chronicle, 72–3, 75. For a discussion of these and others errors see Searle, Ingulf, 115–43.
65 These were John of Worcester, Orderic Vitalis, William of Malmesbury, John of Peterborough, Felix the monk and a Domesday satellite: Roffe, 'Historia Croylandensis', 94, 100–1.
66 Ibid. 105.
67 Ibid. 73, 98, 116–17; OV ii. 348–9.
68 Ingulf's chronicle, 126; Page, Crowland abbey, 10 and plate 1; F. M. Stenton, Documents

118

The real problem with using the *Historia*, however, lies in assessing the merit of those passages in the text which cannot be corroborated. The details of the terms on which abbey land was leased out after the fire of 1091 look very plausible but cannot be verified,[69] while other post-Conquest grants mentioned, in particular the numerous grants supposedly made at the laying of the new foundations of the abbey in 1114, cannot be authenticated from other sources.[70] People who were supposedly present then include Richard de Rullos, lord of Bourne, Robert, count of Meulan (d. 1118), Simon II, earl of Northampton (d. 1153), Robert, abbot of Thorney (1113/14–51), Geoffrey Ridel, who is known to have acted as justiciar in Northamptonshire, his wife Geva, Rayner of Bath, who was the sheriff of Lincolnshire from 1128 to 1130, and his wife Goda.[71] The presence of many of these dignitaries at the laying of the foundation stones is certainly feasible and even credible, yet without any other more reliable evidence to support the *Historia*, a large question mark remains over the donations supposedly given by them. Those benefactors of Crowland who can be identified from other, more reputable, sources generally gave to the abbey towards the end of, or after, the reign of Henry I. These included men such as Earl Gilbert, William de Roumare, earl of Lincoln, Leon d'Arceles, Geoffrey fitz Agge and Geolfus.[72] The gift of land in *Edrom*, in Scotland, was probably made in the time of Abbot Waltheof (c. 1124–38) by his brother, the earl of Dunbar.[73] Other, small-scale benefactors specifically requested spiritual services, for example Conan fitz Ellis, Walter of Lindsey and Gilbert of Folksworth, who wanted burial and to become monks of the community.[74]

It is not without significance that none of the three Crowland abbots whose actions occasioned the inception, and subsequently the promotion, of the cult of the English Earl Waltheof was of Norman origin. In fact Crowland did not have an abbot of Norman origin at any time during this period. Waltheof had been executed at Winchester in 1076 for his part in the earls' revolt of the previous year. Afterwards his body 'at the request of his wife Judith and with the permission of King William, was taken to Crowland by Abbot Wulfketel'.[75] Wulfketel (c. 1061/2–85/6), who had Waltheof buried in the

---

illustrative of the social and economic history of the Danelaw, London 1920, 376; Raban,'Thorney and Crowland abbey', 61; Spalding Gentlemen's Society, Wrest Park cartulary, fo. 28v; BL, MS Add. 32101, fos 9r, 32v, 89v.

69 *Ingulf's chronicle*, 99–101.

70 Ibid. 118–20.

71 Ibid. 245–50. The names of Geoffrey Ridel and his wife Geva were entered in the Thorney *liber vitae* in BL, MS Add. 40000, fo. 10v. For Rayner of Bath see remarks made by Green, *Government of England*, 233.

72 Raban, 'Thorney and Crowland abbeys', 72, 75–6. These grants were most likely made in the mid and later twelfth century.

73 Ibid. 87.

74 Ibid. 92.

75 OV ii. 344.

abbey chapter-house, was described rather enigmatically by Orderic Vitalis as 'an Englishman hated by the Normans'.[76] Abbot Ingulf (1085–1108) was of English birth and upbringing, but of Norman training.[77] Although the cult largely took off in the twelfth century as a result of the work of Crowland's French abbot, Geoffrey of Orleans (1109–c. 1124),[78] the fact that he was succeeded by an Englishman, Waltheof (c. 1124–38), son of Cospatric, earl of Dunbar, can only have served to maintain the distinctly non-Norman aura about Crowland and the cult of Waltheof.

Indeed, the cult that grew up around the tomb of Earl Waltheof was unique in post-Conquest England. Unlike the saints venerated at places such as Bury St Edmunds, St Albans, Canterbury, Evesham, Malmesbury and Durham, this cult was not an ancient one, the execution of Waltheof being still very much alive in people's memory. At first sight it seems that the contention over the cult was political rather than ethnic, being concerned with the question of the earl's guilt: Waltheof's downfall resulted from his supposed disloyalty to the Norman regime rather than his ethnic background. Yet politics and ethnicity were closely intertwined as this controversy divided English and Norman opinion along ethnic lines well into the twelfth century, the Normans believing him guilty, the English innocent. Orderic Vitalis relates an anecdote which illustrates that the split was still alive and well in the twelfth century. Ouen, a Norman monk, denigrated Earl Waltheof at Crowland 'saying he was a false traitor who had deserved execution as a punishment for his guilt'.[79] In retribution he was struck down with a severe sickness and died a few days later at his own monastery, St Albans. By the later years of Henry I's reign the opinion of others, amongst them Orderic and William of Malmesbury, was wavering in favour of Waltheof's sanctity and innocence, apparently compelled by evidence of the miracles at his tomb,[80] a shift in sentiment which explains the late date of the verifiable donations to the abbey made by Normans.

Waltheof was a member of the pre-Conquest aristocracy, and an opponent of the Norman regime; his death was therefore bound to be seen as a metaphor for the fate of the conquered English and his tomb as a focus for English feelings. When these factors were combined with Waltheof's extensive religious patronage and the perceived injustice of his death, it was only a matter of time before the pilgrims, evidently English, who flocked to his tomb were rewarded with a visible sign of his sanctity, i.e. by miracles. Orderic's description of the early years of the cult strongly suggests that popular, albeit

76 Ibid. ii. 344–5. Marjorie Chibnall explained this hostility on the grounds that 'Wulfketel probably came under suspicion for his friendship with Earl Waltheof'. For remarks on the cult of Waltheof see Southern, *Medieval humanism*, 137.

77 *Ingulf's chronicle*, 73; Searle, *Ingulf*, 195.

78 OV ii. 346. Geoffrey had been born at Orleans but had been monk and prior of St-Evroult.

79 Ibid. ii. 348; *Ingulf's chronicle*, 167.

80 OV ii. 350; William of Malmesbury, *De gestis pontificum*, 322.

unofficial, support germinated soon after earl's execution. He relates that the news of the occurrence of miracles c. 1112 at Waltheof's tomb 'gladdened the hearts of the English and the populace came flocking in great numbers to the tomb of their compatriot, knowing from many signs that he was already favoured by God'.[81] In the light of this comment, the assertion by the *Historia* that 'multitudes of the faithful flocked daily to his tomb' after the translation of Waltheof in 1091 looks credible.[82] How far these pilgrims 'offering up their vows [at Waltheof's tomb] tended, in great degree, to resuscitate' the monastery, however, cannot be substantiated.[83]

Thorney

Of all the Fenland abbeys discussed here Thorney, one of the poorest of the group in 1086, was perhaps the most successful of all in making 'considerable gains in both estates and spiritual interests in the century after 1066'.[84] Before the end of the eleventh century Thorney had secured grants from men of local importance and the abbacy of Robert de Prunelai (1113/14–51) witnessed an increase in the flow of grants from local baronial families. Despite, or rather because of, the paucity of its resources Thorney abbey came through the Norman Conquest somewhat more successfully than its larger and wealthier neighbours. The compact nature of its estates facilitated their defence:[85] out of the abbey's twelve Domesday estates, excluding Thorney itself, seven were close together in north Huntingdonshire with Whittlesey not far away in north Cambridgeshire.[86] In contrast with Crowland, its closest monastic neighbour, Thorney abbey was under the control of men of continental origin very soon after 1066. Furthermore, Abbot Gunter of Le Mans (1085–1112) brought the conventual life of Thorney into line with continental forms by introducing the customs of Marmoutier.[87]

The pattern of Thorney's landholding also influenced the pattern of patronage in this period. A glance at the typonymics of Thorney abbey's benefactors is enough to show that most of them were local men. Names like

---

81 OV ii. 348.

82 *Ingulf's chronicle*, 102.

83 Ibid.

84 Raban, 'Thorney and Crowland abbeys', 61.

85 Nevertheless, all of the abbey's more distant estates were at one time under threat of illegal encroachment in the post-Conquest period. Such events prompted royal writs to be obtained to protect the abbey's threatened rights in Charwelton, Twywell, Bolnhurst, Sawbridge, Sibston and Whittlesey: *Regesta*, i, nos 345, 476; ii, nos 586, 755, 975, 997, 1033, 1457.

86 The value of the abbey's remaining lands decreased between 1066 and 1086 by 5.8%.

87 OV vi. 150–2. Gunter was a monk of Battle abbey who had originally come from Marmoutier.

Roger of Stibbington (in Huntingdonshire), Tovi of Lowick (in Northamptonshire), Gilbert of Folksworth (in Huntingdonshire), Henry de Longueville (Orton Longueville, also in Huntingdonshire) and Robert of Huntingdon belong to men whose names are derived from holdings situated less than twenty-five miles from Thorney.

The grants of small parcels of land which Thorney was attracting during this period were no doubt also partly prompted by Gunter's complete rebuilding of 'a most beautiful abbey church'.[88] Donations were made by a certain Rainald, Odo Revel, Geoffrey de Trailly and Siward of Arden.[89] The Trailly family are an example of a family who rose in importance and influence in the county during this period.[90] Geoffrey de Trailly gave the church, some land and a tithe in Yelden, Bedfordshire, to Thorney before 1112. This grant was made with his wife Albreda and son Geoffrey who appear with him in the confraternity list. Siward of Arden's concerns were firmly located in Warwickshire where his father, Thorkell, had been tenant-in-chief in 1086, as well as an abbey tenant at Sawbridge.[91] Thorkell was one of a rare breed of English magnates who had done well during the Conquest years and whom the Abingdon chronicle had claimed was 'very much celebrated amongst the English'.[92] In the time of Abbot Gunter, Siward of Arden gave one virgate in Flecknoe, in Warwickshire, and in the time of Abbot Robert de Prunelai (1113/14–51) Siward gave the mill of *Rugenamie* with the service and land of Edric of Flecknoe.[93] The bond between the Arden family and Thorney abbey was embodied by Siward's brother, who was a monk there.[94] It is evident that Siward's pre-existing family ties with the abbey were enough to prompt gifts from Siward himself. It is also not impossible that these gifts were partly sales. Flecknoe is close enough to Thorney's holding of Sawbridge to make its acquisition a useful consolidation and it is not clear if anything other than spiritual favours were given for this gift.[95] In addition, during the abbacy of Gunter of Le Mans the abbey was held in some favour by William Rufus who granted Thorney two confirmation charters, a market to be held every

---

[88] Ibid. vi. 152.

[89] CUL, MSS Add. 3020–1, fos 414v–15r, 416r.

[90] Ibid. fo. 414v; Raban, 'Thorney and Crowland abbeys', 73. For Geoffrey's wife, Albreda, who was the daughter of the Domesday lord, Walter Espec, and co-heiress of William Espec, lord of Old Wardon barony, Bedfordshire, see Sanders, *English baronies*, 133.

[91] DB i, fo. 222c.

[92] *Chron. Abingdon*, ii. 8.

[93] CUL, MSS Add. 3020–1, fo. 416r. For the Arden family see A. Williams, 'A vicecomital family in pre-Conquest Warwickshire', *Anglo-Norman Studies* xi (1989), 279–95.

[94] The grant was witnessed by Siward's brother Peter who was described as a 'monk of the same house'.

[95] The Red Book makes several references to payments being made as part of quitclaims and to one sale. The transaction with Henry de Longueville for eight acres of meadow in Fen Stanton is openly called a sale: CUL, MSS Add. 3020–1, fo. 420r. The two other 'gifts' of land in Fen Stanton which include a sum of money given by the abbey *de caritate* appear to be part sale and part gift: ibid. fo. 418v.

Thursday at Yaxley, in Huntingdonshire, and the jurisdiction of Normancross hundred, all at a price.[96]

The abbacy of 'the vigorous and able' Robert of Prunelai was also of great benefit to Thorney. In the light of the substantial number of gifts that Robert acquired, Orderic Vitalis's high praise of him as a man who 'enjoyed a reputation for his scholarship among learned philosophers in the school of grammar and dialectic [. . . and] one of the most eminent of all the prelates of England' was clearly shared by others in England.[97] During his lengthy abbacy Robert saw the acquisition of more than eighteen donations. Many of these were from people with exclusively local interests such as Gilbert of Folksworth, Henry and Rorges de Longueville, Tovi and Agnes of Lowick, Roger of Stibbington and Robert of Huntingdon.[98] Others came from more well-known personages, several of them royal officials, such as Aubrey de Vere, William d'Aubigny *Brito* and his wife Cecilia, Hugh de Lisures, William Peverel of Dover, William Peverel of Bourn, as well as various members of the Clare family – Gilbert de Clare, Baldwin fitz Gilbert de Clare, Countess Rohaise and Countess Adeliza de Clermont, widow of Gilbert fitz Richard de Clare[99] – although it seems that Gilbert de Clare and his successors actually declined to fulfil his promise to the abbey of land worth 100s.[100]

William d'Aubigny *Brito*, the royal justiciar in Lincolnshire from 1128 to 1129, with his wife Cecilia gave land in Stoke Albany and Pipewell, in Northamptonshire.[101] It appears that this grant may also have failed to take effect as nothing further is ever heard of it in the Thorney sources.[102] William II Peverel of Bourn barony, in Cambridgeshire, became involved with the abbey by confirming the grant of seven acres in *Copthorn* (possibly Clopton), Cambridgeshire, and land in Botulph Bridge, in Huntingdonshire, which Hugh de Lisures had already made.[103] This confirmation was later supplemented by a gift of land in Weldon, in Northamptonshire.[104] There is another example of a confirmation of a tenant's gift leading to further involvement with the abbey at the end of this period. In 1137 Countess Adeliza de Clermont confirmed Tovi of Lowick's gift to the abbey.[105] Gilbert had earlier set a precedent for involvement by witnessing a charter of

96 *Regesta*, i, nos 345, 453, 475–7.
97 OV vi. 150.
98 CUL, MSS Add. 3020–1, fos 77r, 81v, 418r–19r, 420r.
99 Ibid. fos 82r, 205v–6v, 324v, 410v; Raban, 'Thorney and Crowland abbeys', 62, 71, 73, 75.
100 Ibid. 83. For the Lisures family see W. F. Carter and R. F. Wilkinson, 'The Fledborough family of Lisures', *Transactions of the Thoroton Society* xliv (1940), 14–34.
101 CUL, MSS Add. 3020–1, fo. 410v.
102 Raban, 'Thorney and Crowland abbeys', 83. 'William d'Aubigny' was witness to a quitclaim against the abbey of land in Huntingdonshire and 'William d'Aubigny *brito*' was witness to two royal charters concerning Thorney: CUL, MSS Add. 3020–1, fos 19v, 20v, 417v.
103 Ibid. fo. 82r.
104 *Mon.*, ii. 603.
105 Ibid. ii. 601.

Henry de Longueville.[106] Other members of the family followed suit. In 1139 Baldwin fitz Gilbert granted what would become the priory of St James Deeping and Countess Rohaise granted 20s. from a mill.[107]

The Thorney *liber vitae* offers another perspective on the abbey's relations with the laity.[108] This register of names, a necrology or a confraternity list, cannot show who the abbey's benefactors were as it does not mention donations.[109] What is evident, however, is that abbey benefactors were not the only personages entered in the list. A number of donation charters survive as copies in the Thorney Red Book and several of these do appear to have some correlation with the entries in the fraternity list. Geoffrey de Trailly, his wife Albreda, his sons Geoffrey and William, and 'all his offspring' received fraternity when he made his gift of the church of Yelden to Thorney.[110] Correspondingly, the *liber vitae* contains the names of 'Geoffrey de Trailly, his wife Albreda, Geoffrey his son and Robert, William, Gilbert' as well as another entry for 'Geoffrey de Trailly, his wife Albreda, and his sons and daughters'.[111] When Tovi of Lowick, Agnes his wife and his son Ralph gave land in Raunds, Northamptonshire, to Thorney, they were granted fraternity in return.[112] Accordingly, Tovi *de Lufico*, his wife Agnes and son Ralph are entered in the fraternity list.[113] The inclusion of a name into a fraternity list may well have been at the request of a kinsman, as was probably the case with Thorkell of Arden.[114] Yet, when Thorkell's son, Siward of Arden, had made a grant to Thorney it was 'for the salvation of my soul and my kin'.[115] The wording of this grant, then, does not imply that this was a request for fraternity for Siward or his father. Grants of fraternity were not only given to benefactors and litigants but also to local officials and were far more widespread than much of the surviving evidence would otherwise indicate. For example, Almodis the archdeacon and Robert of Yaxley both quitclaimed property to Thorney and appear in the fraternity list although the surviving documentation for the quitclaims does not specifically mention the grant of fraternity.[116]

Thorney abbey's post-Conquest experience was very different from that of its Fenland neighbours. For Ely, Peterborough, and to a lesser degree for Ramsey and Crowland, religious patronage was small-scale and almost exclusively restricted to the later years of Henry I's reign. At Thorney, grants were being

---

106 CUL, MSS Add. 3020–1, fo. 81v.

107 Ibid. fo. 410v.

108 Clark, 'British Library additional MS. 40,000', 50–68, 'A witness to post-Conquest English cultural patterns, 73–85, and 'The *liber vitae* of Thorney abbey, 53–72; J. S. Moore, 'The Anglo-Norman family', 170–4.

109 Clark, 'British Library additional MS. 40,000', 62.

110 CUL, MSS Add. 3020–1, fo. 414v.

111 BL, MS Add. 40000, fos 3r, 10v.

112 CUL, MSS Add. 3020–1, fo. 419r.

113 BL, MS Add. 40000, fo. 2r.

114 Ibid. fo. 3r.

115 CUL, MSS Add. 3020–1, fo. 416r.

116 Ibid. fos 417v–18r, 419r; BL, MS Add. 40000, fo. 10v.

made by local people before the eleventh century was out, the abbacy of Robert of Prunelai bringing a profusion of small grants. Furthermore, the stature of the abbey's benefactors was growing, if anything, not diminishing, throughout this period; elsewhere in England the social status of donors, in so far as there was a general pattern, broadly corresponded with the model of downward diffusion of cultural patterns through Anglo-Norman society.[117] Then, as far as the official promotion of saints' cults was concerned, it appears that Thorney abbey had a slight edge on its Fenland rivals. Folcard of St-Bertin's *vita* of St Botolph was composed sometime in the years between 1068 and 1085, whereas the *vitae* of the saints associated with Ramsey and Ely were not written until after 1087 and 1106 respectively.[118] The evidence that an unofficial cult was growing around the tomb of Waltheof at Crowland soon after 1076 is persuasive. The comparative development of respective building programmes is more difficult to ascertain, but the conclusion that these abbeys were in fierce competition with each other is inescapable. The writ of Henry I addressed to the abbot of Peterborough stating that the abbot of Ramsey was to be allowed to take stone from Barnack, in Lincolnshire, is evidence that there was some friction between the abbeys over access to building materials.[119] The defence of their rights in Barnack was a particularly sensitive issue for the abbey as it was claimed to have been granted by Earl Waltheof.[120]

It is not clear which was the first Fenland abbey church to begin its rebuilding programme. Peterborough was destroyed by fire in 1070 and must have been reconstructed thereafter, although explicit reference to rebuilding is not made until 1118, after a second fire in 1115.[121] Fire in 1091 necessitated the instigation of a fund-raising programme for the reconstruction of various monastic buildings at Crowland although the laying of the foundation stones of the new abbey church did not take place until 1114.[122] The construction of the massive abbey church, begun at Ely in the abbacy of Simeon (1082–93), was probably earlier than Gunter of Le Mans' (1085–1112) rebuilding of his church at Thorney. At Ramsey the construction of a new abbey church was a relatively late occurrence, beginning in 1116, but it was completed fairly rapidly in the 1120s. The building work begun at Peterborough in 1118 progressed slowly and with some difficulty. Abbot John of Sées (1114–25) 'worked hard at it but could not finish it' and it was left to his successor, Martin of Bec (1132–55), 'though there was

---

[117] For Duby's discussion of the nature of cultural diffusion see 'The diffusion of cultural patterns in feudal society', *Past and Present* xxxix (1968), 3–10 (repr. in his *The chivalrous society*, trans. C. Postan, London 1977, 171–7). See also Bouchard's observation on the status of benefactors in the eleventh and twelfth centuries in *Sword, miter and cloister*, 131–8.

[118] Ridyard, 'Condigna veneratio', 185.

[119] *Regesta*, ii. no. 1410.

[120] OV ii. 344; *Ingulf's chronicle*, 67.

[121] *Chron. Hugh Candidus*, 97, 105.

[122] OV ii. 346; *Ingulf's chronicle*, 98–101, 118–20.

great dearth in the monastery' to complete the church.[123] The monastic community and abbey relics did not enter the new church until the year 1140.[124]

The translation of saints' relics into new abbey churches can be used as an indication of how far and fast building work was completed. Although the earliest translation of 'relics' were those of Waltheof at Crowland in 1092, this was into the old abbey church and his cult was as yet unsanctioned by the Crowland monks.[125] The earliest translation of long-established saints' relics was at Thorney in 1098, into a substantially completed church, although it was not actually finished until 1108 and not dedicated until 1128.[126] Ramsey followed hot on the heels of the Thorney monks, when they translated St Ives's companions back to St Ives (Slepe) where a new church had been built, around the year 1100.[127] Abbot Richard de Clare (1100–2, ?1103–7) had the Ely saints translated into the new abbey church in 1106. There the saints' translation marked the beginning of a concerted effort to record and promote the *vitae* and miracles of the saints. New *vitae* of the saints were produced before 1135 and the hagiography of St Sexburga composed some time soon after about 1106.[128] The translation of 1140 at Peterborough was used as an occasion for the public display of the arm of St Oswald.[129] Building projects, translations of relics and dedications of new churches all acted as stimuli for attracting donations, as has been documented for Ramsey.[130]

The major landholders in the Fenland region, and in the surrounding counties in which the Fenland abbeys held large amounts of land, showed relatively little inclination to patronise the Fenland houses. In the early years after the Conquest there had been active hostility as well as indifference, as some of the largest holders of property in Cambridgeshire, Hardwin de Scalers, Picot of Cambridge and William de Warenne were accused by the Ely monks of being despoilers of abbey property.[131] Unless an English house possessed an abbot who was firmly in favour with the Normans, as at Bury St Edmunds, the lands of the wealthiest English monasteries were particularly vulnerable to despoliation, as the richest abbeys, Glastonbury, Ely and Ramsey, all discovered to their cost. Monks of Ely and Crowland were driven from their establishments at St Neots and Spalding by Richard de Clare and Ivo

123 *Chron. Hugh Candidus*, 98–9, 105.
124 Ibid. 108.
125 OV ii. 346; *Ingulf's chronicle*, 102.
126 *Mon.*, ii. 594. Abbot Gunter and Abbot Robert also took care to add to their collection of relics: Thomas, 'Cult of saints' relics', 233.
127 OV ii. 347; *Ingulf's chroncle*, 102; Edgington, *Life and miracles*, 25.
128 Ridyard, 'Condigna veneratio', 185.
129 *Chron. Hugh Candidus*, 105–8.
130 *Chron. Ramsey*, 229; *Cart. Ramsey*, ii. 102–3; *Regesta*, ii, no. 1410. Henry I ordered that the abbot of Ramsey was to have stone for the building of his church.
131 *Liber Eliensis*, 204, 210–11; *Regesta*, i, no. 276.

Taillebois respectively.[132] St Benet of Holme, in Norfolk, also suffered extensive losses at the hands of Roger Bigod and his followers.[133] Morevoer the major landholders in the Fenland region tended either to found their own religious houses in the locality or, because their interests were centred elsewhere, to found or patronise houses outside the region. Richard fitz Gilbert, whose lands centred on Tonbridge in Kent and Clare in Suffolk, founded a cell of Le Bec at St Neots before 1080 and another cell at Clare, in Suffolk, in 1090.[134] Alan I Rufus, lord of Richmond, who was the chief landowner in Norfolk and held considerable estates in Suffolk, founded St Mary's, York, and Swavesey as a cell of SS. Sergius and Bacchus, Angers.[135] Royal officials such as Picot, sheriff of Cambridge, Eustace, sheriff of Huntingdon, William Malet, one-time sheriff of Suffolk, and Roger Bigod, sheriff of Norfolk and Suffolk, founded new houses at Barnwell, Huntingdon, Eye and Thetford, respectively.[136]

It is evident that it was only the great Fenland houses that were ignored by the important landholders of this region, for a number of individuals who held significant quantities of land in the Fenland region patronised other English monasteries. For example, benefactors of Bury St Edmunds included Alan I Rufus, lord of Richmond, Countess Judith and Earl Waltheof, Haimo Pecche and Richard de Clare.[137] Earl Waltheof was, however, the conspicuous exception to the mixture of aggression and indifference displayed by the aristocracy towards the Fenland houses.[138] In his ten years after the Conquest he was an active benefactor of English abbeys such as Crowland, Bury St Edmunds, Tynemouth, Jarrow and the see of Lincoln and was also in confraternity with Ely and Thorney.[139]

It can be seen that the history of the Fenland abbeys after 1066 contrasts sharply with their pre-Conquest circumstances. As far as Ely and Peterbor-

---

[132] For Richard de Clare's grant of St Neots to Le Bec see Ward, 'Fashions in monastic endowment', 427–51 at p. 431.

[133] Stenton, 'St Benet of Holme', 225–35.

[134] For Richard de Clare's religious benefactions see Ward, 'Fashions in monastic endowment', 429–32.

[135] Binns, *Dedications*, 91, 106. For assessments of Alan's great wealth see Hollister, 'The greater Domesday tenants-in-chief', 219–48 at p. 242; Mason, 'The honour of Richmond', 703–4. For the earls of Richmond see Keats-Rohan, 'Bretons and Normans', 42–78 at pp. 46–8, 77–8, and 'William I and the Breton contingent', 156–72.

[136] Binns, *Dedications*, 72, 117, 119, 136; *Regesta*, i, nos 379a, 452, 682, 781, 834; ii. 410; *Mon.*, ii. 220; viii. 1272. For the history of Barnwell's foundation see *Liber memorandorum ecclesie de Bernewelle*, ed. J. W. Clark, Cambridge 1907, 38–43. For William Malet see Lewis, 'The king and Eye', 569–87. For Roger Bigod's other patronage see B. Dodwell, 'The foundation of Norwich cathedral', *Transactions of the Royal Historical Society* 5th ser. vii (1957), 1–18 at p. 15.

[137] *Memorials of St Edmund's*, i. 350; *DB* i, fo. 210c; *Feudal documents*, 159. For the descent of the Bourges lands in Suffolk see ibid. 152–3; Sanders, *English baronies*, 48.

[138] For Waltheof's career see Scott, 'Waltheof', 147–213.

[139] Ibid. 195; Cambridge, Trinity College, MS 0 2 1, fo. 5v.

ough were concerned some of their experiences closely resemble those of another abbey set in marshland, Glastonbury, for example in their extensive loss of land, prolonged litigation, the serious disruption of the daily life of the monastic communities and the large-scale enfeoffment of military tenants on abbey property. The other Fenland houses, Ramsey, Crowland and Thorney, while not escaping the negative effects of the Conquest, were more successful than Ely and Peterborough in attracting benefactors during the first half of the twelfth century. The post-Conquest confusion and the disturbances of the 1070s generated recurrent difficulties with troublesome tenants, while both great and small monasteries lost dependent cells through the aggression of the newcomers.[140]

None of the Fenland houses was singled out for favourable attention by the Anglo-Norman aristocracy in the way that St Albans, Abingdon or Gloucester were. Furthermore, although the despoilers of these monasteries were often men of national importance, their benefactors, at least until the last years of Henry I's reign, tended to be men of only local importance. There are clear signs at Ely, Peterborough and Ramsey of a preoccupation with agricultural organisation and with the internal administration of the communities.[141] Comparing the experiences of the five Fenland abbeys it appears that having an English abbot did matter to the Norman laity as far as religious patronage was concerned. That donations coincided with the abbacies of men of continental origin, particularly Normans, supports this notion. At Ramsey the escalation in numbers of donations coincided with the abbacies of Herbert Losinga and Reginald of Caen, at Peterborough with Ernulf and Martin of Bec and at Thorney with Gunter of Le Mans and Robert of Prunelai. Having an English abbot did not necessarily preclude donations, as proven by the fact that Abbot Aldwin at Ramsey acquired the promise of a generous grant from Nigel Fossard and Crowland attracted a number of grants during the abbacy of Waltheof. Yet benefactors must have felt more comfortable with continental abbots with whom they shared a common linguistic and cultural vocabulary. Furthermore, Peterborough, Ely, Ramsey and Thorney appear to have concentrated largely on cultivating *quid pro quo* relations with local landholders, offering specific spiritual returns, such as admission into fraternity with the house and entry in the *liber vitae*, or entrance as a monk, or burial in the house. Apart from Thorney abbey, the overwhelming bulk of the religious patronage received by these Fenland houses occurred in the reign of Henry I and was invariably an intensely local affair.

---

[140] Ely and Crowland monks were driven from their establishments at St Neots, which was granted to Le Bec by Richard of Clare, and Spalding, which was given to St-Nicholas, Angers, by Ivo Taillebois. For the history of St Neots see Chibnall, 'Priory of St Neot', 67–74.
[141] King, *Peterborough abbey*, 140; Miller, *Abbey and bishopric of Ely*, 70–1; Raftis, *Ramsey abbey*, 34–5.

8

The Old English Monasteries, Religious Patronage and the Anglo-Norman Aristocracy

How did the experiences of Abingdon, Gloucester, Bury St Edmunds, St Albans and St Augustine's, Canterbury, compare with those of the other Old English Benedictine monasteries? The difficulty with answering this question lies in the sheer diversity of the Old English monasteries in 1066. Generalisations about their fate as a group after that date will always be complicated by the variable status of the abbeys as well as by geographical differences: not only were they irregularly spread over the face of the country but wealth was also very unevenly divided, ranging from the very rich Glastonbury, assessed at £828 in Domesday, to the poorest, Horton, worth only £12 in 1086.[1] Furthermore, post-Conquest developments only served to accentuate and complicate the differences in wealth and status between the houses, while distribution amongst them for knight service was far from equitable. We are not dealing with a collection of comparable abbeys facing exactly the same problems.

I do not intend to attempt to construct a general survey of the history of the English monasteries after 1066. Two such surveys have already been undertaken: by Dom David Knowles and by Professor Frank Barlow.[2] My intention here is to explore the effect of the Norman conquest on the English monasteries through an analysis of religious patronage. With this purpose in mind, a designated cross-section of English houses will be scrutinised. The paucity of extant documentary evidence for many of the smaller monasteries makes this approach necessary. Inclusion in the cross-section discussed here, therefore, is strongly influenced by the volume of surviving source material. At the same time a conscious decision has been made to examine monasteries from all geographical regions of England i.e. from Wessex, Mercia and East Anglia, as well as both very rich and very modest abbeys. The Fenland houses, Ely, Ramsey, Peterborough, Thorney and Crowland, have already been considered as a group. Additional houses to be discussed include the very richest in 1086, Glastonbury, the most northerly, Burton, the most east-

---

1 Knowles, *Monastic order*, 101, 702–3. See also A. Ayton and V. Davies, 'Ecclesiastical wealth in England in 1086', in W. J. Sheils and D. Wood (eds), *The Church and wealth* (Studies in Church History xxiv, 1987), 47–60 at p. 56.
2 See Barlow, *English Church*, *1066–1154*; Knowles, *Monastic order*.

erly, St Benet of Holme, three houses from the south-west, Evesham, Malmesbury and Bath, the two crown-wearing locations of Westminster and Old Minster, Winchester, a second monastic cathedral priory, Rochester, and a nunnery, Shaftesbury.

That the Conquest increased consciousness of ethnic and cultural differences is incontrovertible.[3] The Conquest resulted in the English Church being brought into line with continental practices, which was partially achieved through the administration of men drawn from all over the continent.[4] It is very difficult to assess the extent of actual ethnic discrimination and bias against the English in the new order. Except for Abbot Godric of Winchcombe (1054–66) who lost his office almost immediately in 1066, there was initially a period of continuance with the organisation and personnel of the English Church. After the revolts of 1068–9, however, a number of bishops and abbots were deposed.[5] Thereafter, unless they had been directly involved in rebellion, like Abbot Ealdred of Abingdon, English abbots were allowed to live out the rest of their lives in office.[6] After their demise, however, they were invariably replaced by a continental. William the Conqueror was able to tempt a number of men of impressive ability across the Channel to take up service in the English Church. Of course not all were willing to make the journey. Lanfranc was certainly unwillingly to become archbishop of Canterbury in 1070, and Guitmund, monk of La-Croix-St-Leuffroi, refused point-blank the offer of an English bishopric.[7]

The Norman Conquest of England was a profound threat to the wealth and security of the English monasteries. Those monasteries that had been collectively involved in rebellion were punished; Abingdon was plundered and Ely suffered large-scale alienations for its part in Hereward the Wake's rebellion. They were not alone. Most monasteries experienced problems in maintaining their legal title to landed property and lordship over men. For many these problems occurred during the confusion of the first years after the

---

[3] For a discussion on the concept of race and peoples in the central Middle Ages see G. A. Loud, 'The 'Gens Normannorum' – myth or reality?', Anglo-Norman Studies iv (1982), 104–16, 204–9; Bartlett, Making of Europe, 197–242. For the legal distinction between French and English peoples see G. Garnett, 'Franci et Angli: the legal distinction between peoples after the Conquest', Anglo-Norman Studies viii (1986), 109–37. For a different perspective on the nature of relations between the Norman abbots and their monks see H. R. Loyn, 'Abbots of English monasteries in the period following the Norman Conquest', in D. Bates and A. Curry (eds), England and Normandy in the Middle Ages, London 1994, 95–103; P. Meyvaert, 'Rainaldus est malus scriptor Francigenus – voicing national antipathy in the Middle Ages', Speculum lxvi (1991), 743–63; J. Gillingham, 'The beginnings of English imperialism', Journal of Historical Sociology v (1992), 392–409.

[4] In the reign of Edward the Confessor men with French and Lotharingian connections held a number of ecclesiastical appointments in England but they only constituted a small percentage of the total number of prelates: Barlow, English Church, 16n.

[5] See D. Bates, William the Conqueror, London 1989, 143–4.

[6] See ch. 1.

[7] OV ii. 270–80.

Conquest, as at Abingdon, Burton, St Benet of Holme, Glastonbury, Ely and St Albans. Some abbeys had sustained extensive losses by 1086. The great wealth of the two richest houses, Ely and Glastonbury, must have attracted despoilers.

At Glastonbury in 1083 the new Norman abbot, Turstin (c. 1077–c. 1096), quarrelled with his English monks about what chant should be used in church.[8] Unfortunately this disagreement escalated into a bloody brawl when Turstin's household knights broke into the chapter, pursued a number of the monks into the church and fired arrows at them, killing three and wounding eighteen.[9] This infamous riot resulted in Abbot Turstin's expulsion and the dispersal of a number of the Glastonbury monks to other houses. Combined with almost total royal disinterest in the abbey, these events served to frighten off potential benefactors for many years, as insurrection and revolts did at Ely and St Augustine's, Canterbury.[10] By the time of the Domesday survey, Glastonbury had lost control over almost 100 hides of land, most of which were never regained.[11] These lands were worth approximately £95, representing 9 per cent of the total 1086 valuation of the Glastonbury estates. According to William of Malmesbury the twelfth-century abbots of Glastonbury devoted much of their energies to recovering these lost estates.[12] Abbot Herluin (1100–18) offered Henry I 1,000 marks 'pro terris a tempore Normannorum ereptis', and spent another 100 marks of silver and two marks of gold on recovering lands. Herluin's successor, Henry of Blois (1126–71), also went to much trouble to recover lost lands. The twelfth-century abbots of Glastonbury emerge from the sources as apparently effective and productive men, yet religious donations remained scarce.[13]

Whereas the sheer wealth and riches of the great abbeys of Ely and Glastonbury must have played a decisive role in attracting despoilers, para-

---

8   For Glastonbury in the twelfth century see M. Postan, 'Glastonbury estates in the twelfth century', *Economic History Review* 2nd ser. v (1952–3), 358–67; R. V. Lennard, 'The demesnes of Glastonbury abbey in the eleventh and twelfth centuries', *Economic History Review* 2nd ser. viii (1956), 106–18; Stacy, 'Estates of Glastonbury abbey'; A. Gransden, 'The growth of the Glastonbury traditions and legends in the twelfth century', *Journal of Ecclesiastical History* xxvii (1976), 337–58.

9   ASC 'E', 1083. William of Malmesbury, who was of the view that Turstin of Glastonbury 'sinned by accident rather than by design', believed the roots of the conflict lay in the fact that the church of Glastonbury had 'grown old in the Roman use' and the monks 'tolerated his practices less readily, perhaps because they were foreign, and they had not been instituted canonically from the bosom of the church': *Early history of Glastonbury*, 156–8.

10   Only a small handful of royal charters survive for Glastonbury: *Regesta*, i, no. 273; ii, nos 622, 895–6, 1525, 1590.

11   Stacy, 'Estates of Glastonbury abbey', 49–50.

12   Ibid. 50, 74.

13   For the post-Conquest abbots of Glastonbury see William of Malmesbury's description of their deeds: *Early history of Glastonbury*, 153–67. For the development of the buildings at Glastonbury see C. A. R. Radford, 'Glastonbury abbey before 1184: interim report on the excavations', in *Medieval art and architecture at Wells and Glastonbury* (British Architectural Association Conference Transactions viii, 1981), 110–34.

doxically the relative poverty of a house such as St Benet of Holme, worth £96 in 1086, also made it vulnerable to the invasions of Roger Bigod and his followers.[14] Although some lands were recovered in the course of William Rufus' reign, by the early years of the twelfth century, lost lands still amounted to some 78½ half acres, two houses, two tofts, pasture, a number of sokemen and the homage of numerous others.[15] The abbots of Holme were subsequently embroiled in sorting out and formalising tenurial relations with their tenants, other local landholders and royal officials.[16] Whether great or small, many Old English monasteries lost dependent cells through the aggression of the newcomers. For example, monks of Ely and Crowland were driven from their establishments at St Neots and Spalding, which were subsequently granted to alien houses.[17] The antithesis of this experience, however, was Bury St Edmunds which emerged in 1086 relatively unscathed. Many lands were never recovered at Ely and Glastonbury, but other houses such as St Albans, Thorney, Crowland and Abingdon also sustained losses but were later able to make good these misfortunes with new donations from the continental newcomers.

Despite the great disruption brought by the Conquest there was no wholesale replacement of the English monks. Where they were expelled in large numbers from their communities, as at Ely in 1072, Glastonbury in 1083 and St Augustine's in 1089, it was in consequence of suspected disloyalty and two particularly violent brawls, and in any case many of the banishments were only temporary.[18] The infamous riots at Canterbury and Glastonbury were the result of conflict over customs: the election of the abbot, timing of bell-ringing, the type of chant to be sung in mass.[19] The plantation of foreign monks in any significant number, such as the Le Bec monks who arrived at Ely with Abbot Simeon (1082–93), and those monks who had been at Christ Church, Canterbury and were moved to St Augustine's, Canterbury, in 1089, was exceptional.[20] When instances of what seem to be ethnic conflict are examined, more often than not the root causes are not ethnic, but cultural, focussed on linguistic and customary antipathies. It is evident that the English language was viewed with some distaste by the Normans. The twelfth-century chronicler, William of Malmesbury, refused to name the Thorney saints in his *Gesta pontificum* because of the 'barbarous sound' of their names.[21] The monks of St-Evroult changed Orderic's Anglo-Saxon name to

---

[14] Roger Bigod transferred some St Benet's estates to his new foundation at Thetford: Stenton, 'St Benet of Holme', 225–35.

[15] *Regesta*, i, no. 468.

[16] Ibid. ii, nos 987, 1094, 1306, 1408, 1714; BL, MS Cotton Galba E ii, fos 30v–1r, 33r–v, 54r–5v.

[17] See ch. 7.

[18] Knowles, *Monastic order*, 113.

[19] *Early history of Glastonbury*, 156–8; *William Thorne's chronicle*, 57.

[20] Knowles, *Monastic order*, 113.

[21] *Early history of Glastonbury*, 327; C. Clark, 'Notes on a life of three Thorney saints,

Vitalis because Norman ears found it 'inharmonious'.[22] Yet it was not just English given-names that were changed. Nest, Bernard de Neufmarché's wife who was named after her Welsh mother, had her named changed to Agnes.[23]

There are very few clear-cut cases of discrimination against English monks on the grounds of their ethnicity. William of Malmesbury, writing from a twelfth-century perspective, claimed that Bishop John of Tours thought the English monks at Bath 'stupid and barbarous', and gradually replaced them with foreign monks.[24] It is significant, however, that this cannot be taken as an example of Norman disdain for the English as the conquered race as John was French not Norman. On the contrary, English monks were valued for their maintenance of the oral traditions that surrounded saints' cults such as that of St Dunstan at Glastonbury.[25]

Whilst acknowledging the difficulties and distress brought by the advent of the Norman Conquest, there were also benefits, such as the multitude of new romanesque abbey churches built, the increase in size of monastic communities and, most important, the new benefactors who materialised. This is why Abingdon, Bury, Gloucester, St Albans and to a lesser extent St Augustine's, Canterbury, and Thorney were able to more than make good their losses.[26] Other houses also flourished under the Norman kings: Westminster, Evesham and the monastic community at Rochester. Many survived well enough, making some important gains, such as Malmesbury, Burton, Bath and Crowland, and in the early twelfth century even the beleaguered Glastonbury acquired two cells, at Basaleg in south Wales and Lamanna, in Cornwall.

The period when individual English monasteries began to receive patronage varied. For example, for Bath grants came in the reign of William Rufus but trickled away in the twelfth century. Evesham also received some grants in the late eleventh century, but more in the reign of Henry I. Burton and Malmesbury both received donations in the first twenty years after the Conquest and then little else. The five case studies contrast with this general picture by virtue of the sheer volume of grants they received, the size and type of grants made and the national and international status of many of their donors. Yet the chronology of the donations made to Gloucester, Bury St Edmunds, St Augustine's, Canterbury, St Albans and Abingdon was as varied as at the other English houses. The first three abbeys received patronage within the first twenty years of the Conquest, whereas Abingdon's fortunes

Thancred, Torntred and Tora', *Proceedings of the Cambridge Antiquarian Society* lxix (1980), 45–52.
[22] Idem, 'Women's names in post-Conquest England: observations and speculations', *Speculum* liii (1978), 223–51 at p. 224.
[23] Gerald of Wales, *The journey through Wales and the description of Wales*, ed. Lewis Thorpe, London 1978, 88–9.
[24] *Early history of Glastonbury*, 195.
[25] *Memorials of St Dunstan*, ed. William Stubbs (Rolls series lxiii, 1874), 421–2.
[26] Knowles, *Monastic order*, 425.

only took off in the reign of Henry I. St Albans and Gloucester flourished in the reign of William Rufus, whereas patronage at St Augustine's, Canterbury, came to an almost complete standstill after the chaos of 1089. Bury St Edmunds also experienced a drop in the number of grants made during the vacancies and upheavals that followed the death of Abbot Baldwin in 1098.

A sophisticated amalgam of factors influenced the pattern and timing of donations. Wealth and status, geographical location, the spread of landed possessions, the possession of saints' relics and the all-important personality of individual abbots, were all vital ingredients in this recipe. It needed the right combination of constituents, as well as the right timing, to produce patronage on the scale received by St Albans or Abingdon. The calibre of the abbot was especially vital. Thus it was no coincidence that explosions in the number of donations received by Gloucester, Abingdon, St Albans and Bury corresponded with the abbacies of exceptional men as abbots: Serlo, Paul, Richard d'Aubigny, Faritius and Baldwin. Virtuous Benedictine abbots were universally praised by their house chroniclers for increasing the prosperity of their abbeys.[27] Success was not only to be measured in the amount of donations received by an abbey, however; it was also seen in the efficacy of an abbot's administration, protection of a house's privileges, promotion of its saints and associated shrines, increases in the size of the community and building programmes. These all combined to generate and preserve the abbey's prestige and standing within the religious and lay community. Abbots were positioned at the heart of an intricate network of tenurial, social, spiritual and personal associations. These relationships encompassed abbey tenants, local landholders, royal officials, the abbot's kin, the abbey monks and even to a certain degree the royal court and the king himself. An astute abbot could manipulate these connections to his abbey's advantage to secure religious patronage and other useful benefits from the laity. Considerations such as locality and a family's past association with a house were always important motivating factors behind religious patronage, but it could take the personality of a particular abbot to translate such predispositions into concrete action and donations. The Norman Conquest not only made the need for such capable abbots, whether English or continental, more necessary than ever, but also stimulated the production of records to protect ecclesiastical possessions from the potentially rapacious Normans.

Determining lay attitudes towards the personnel of the English Church in the period immediately after the Conquest is no easy matter. This is why examining their actions as benefactors and petitioners for spiritual benefits is so important. It appears that having an English abbot did matter to the Norman laity, but there are also signs of positive ethnic discrimination. Susan Ridyard has skilfully argued that the attitude of post-Conquest continental churchmen towards English saints was 'characterised [. . .] by a businesslike

[27] J. Van Engen, 'The "crisis of cenobitism" reconsidered: Benedictine monasticism in the years 1050–1150', *Speculum* lxi (1986), 269–304.

readiness to make the heroes of the past serve the politics of the present'.[28] There was no Norman prejudice against Anglo-Saxon saints *per se*. Indeed, the continental newcomers seem to have been perfectly comfortable with the English personnel of an abbey, so long as a continental abbot was installed as its head. Within four years of the Conquest Bury St Edmund was perceived as a desirable place for Normans to spend their last years; although it had a French abbot it was still staffed by English monks.

Furthermore, in post-Conquest England it was still possible for English monks to make it through the ranks to the highest positions of authority, as they did at Bury St Edmunds, Burton, Crowland, Peterborough, Ramsey and Malmesbury. Benedict, Abbot Baldwin's prior at Bury St Edmunds was English, recruited from St John, Beverley.[29] Burton abbey had two Englishmen, Swein and later Edwin, as priors in the reign of Henry I.[30] A handful of Englishmen also became abbots in the reign of Henry I, men such as Waltheof (c. 1126–38), son of Gospatric, earl of Dunbar, who was abbot of Crowland and Eadwulf (1106–18), who was abbot of Malmesbury.[31] The wealthy houses of Peterborough and Ramsey also had Englishmen, Godric, the brother of Abbot Brand, and Aldwin, as abbots in the twelfth century.[32] There must have been many more men of English ancestry who held positions of authority in the monasteries, particularly in the reign of Henry I as the heads of the English abbeys were less frequently drawn from continental houses and often taken from the ranks of their own communities. However there is little chance of proving this, as in England after 1066 the parents of male children tended to favour continental names for their sons, regardless of whether they were French or English, and so given-names cannot be used as a guide to ethnic background.

Many English monasteries received continental abbots within ten years or so of the Conquest, and it is therefore not easy to decide whether the lack of patronage received by most English houses in the early years after 1066 was due to prejudice or to the confusion attending the settlement of England.[33] In a few cases it does appear that benefactors found English abbeys under the direction of continental abbots more acceptable recipients for their grants.

---

[28] Ridyard, '*Condigna veneratio*', 179–206 at p. 205.

[29] *Memorials of St Edmund's*, i. 351.

[30] C. G. O. Bridgeman, 'The Burton abbey twelfth century surveys', *Collections for a History of Staffordshire* (1916), 209–300 at p. 250. Swein was prior in the time of Abbot Nigel (1094–1114) and Abbot Geoffrey (1114–50), Edwin was prior in the time of Abbot Geoffrey.

[31] Knowles, Brooke and London, *Heads of religious houses*, 42, 55.

[32] Godric, brother of Abbot Brand (1066–69), was abbot of Peterborough from c. 1101 to 1102 and Aldwin was abbot of Ramsey from 1091 to 1102 and again from 1107 to 1112: ibid. 60, 62.

[33] Malmesbury received its first continental abbot in 1066/7, Peterborough in 1070, Abingdon in 1071, St Augustine's, Canterbury, in 1070, Ely sometime between 1066 and 1072, Winchester, New Minster, in 1072, Gloucester in 1072, Westminster c. 1072, Evesham in 1077, St Albans in 1077 and Glastonbury in 1077/8.

Despite the dynamic abbacy of Æthelwig (1058–77) Evesham abbey did not receive grants until the time of its first Norman abbot, Walter of Caen (1077–1104). Ramsey's last English abbot, Aldwin, ruled until c. 1112, and it was probably not entirely coincidental that it was only towards the end of the reign of Henry I that the abbey began to attract the local Anglo-Norman landholders as benefactors in any significant numbers.

Abbots could use a variety of devices for cultivating and capitalising on the nexus of relationships that encompassed them. These included direct requests for grants, for example leaning on relatives for donations, hospitality, the promotion of saints' cults, special privileges for pilgrims, appeals for funds for building new churches and cultivating connections with royal officials. There was always more than one way to exploit the whole range of different associations, from the king right down to the abbey's tenants. Strategies for exploiting these relationships ranged from efficient estate management, the professional services of physician-monks and abbots, to enhancing the spiritual reputation of the institution, offering social and spiritual support to laity and manipulating of hospitality and friendship. Obviously many of these elements were not just calculated ploys for patronage, but were goals in themselves. These strategies were commonly used by many abbots like Athelhelm (1071–83) and Rainald (1084–97) at Abingdon, Richer (1101–25) at St Benet of Holme, Reginald (1113/14–31) at Ramsey and Geoffrey (1109–c. 1124) at Crowland and were usually successful at attracting some level of patronage from landholders within the locality.

Proximity and familiarity with an abbey, as well as the spiritual and social functions performed by the inmates of that institution, often engendered donations from both abbey tenants and neighbouring landholders. These people, although not necessarily the most generous of benefactors, were usually the most consistent. At Abingdon, Gloucester and Westminster, local men and women were beginning to show their generosity in the reign of William Rufus, but at Thorney and Crowland such people only really acted as benefactors in any significant number in the reign of Henry I. Local support also proved to be the mainstay of Shaftesbury nunnery. From the first years of William Rufus' reign, if not earlier, the new Norman landowners who held estates close to the abbey sent their daughters there.[34] These were not the richest magnate families of post-Conquest England but rather royal officials such as Aiulf, sheriff of Dorset and Somerset, and Roger of Berkeley, the farmer of Berkeley.[35] Alvred *pincerna* of Robert, count of Mortain, Serlo de Burcy, Harding fitz Ednoth, Drogo of Montacute and Odo fitz Gamelin were all of moderate status within the locality. The nunnery attracted donations from only one man of national importance, Arnulf de Hesdin.[36]

[34] Cooke, 'Donors and daughters', 29–45 at p. 34.
[35] Ibid. 32–3, 35–6.
[36] Ibid. 32–5, 40.

Resourceful abbots could also use land tenure to cultivate potentially profitable relationships with royal officials. The rewards in prospect went much further than just religious patronage, for they might also afford a degree of political leverage on both a national and local level. In the early days of the Conquest Abingdon abbey had suffered particularly badly at the hands of royal officials and later abbots or their representatives all seem to have taken particular trouble to secure their favour by granting them land,[37] as, for example, when Prior Modbert assigned the manor of Leckhampstead to Herbert the chamberlain during the vacancy of 1097–1100.[38] Domesday Book testifies to the abbot of Ramsey making a grant of two hides in Hemmingford to Saewin the falconer, 'because of his regard for the king'.[39] Local sheriffs and justiciars were frequently the most important benefactors of the more modest Benedictine institutions. For example, Godric *dapifer*, sheriff of Norwich, and his wife Ingred, William of Mohun, the Domesday sheriff of Somerset, 'stung by fear of God', Geoffrey de Clinton, the royal justiciar and sheriff of Warwickshire, and the sheriff of Lincoln, Rayner of Bath, and wife Goda were benefactors of St Benet of Holme, Bath, Burton and Crowland abbeys, respectively.[40]

Endowment by influential men of this type was a double-edged sword which could have alarming consequences in times of crisis. During vacancies it was not unusual for such tenants to take the opportunity to attempt to disavow their obligations to the abbey. A handful of abbeys, in particular Bury St Edmunds and Ely, had command over local hundreds and therefore had relatively little to do with royal officials. Consequently no royal officials number amongst their benefactors. Æthelwig (1058–77), the English abbot of Evesham, acted for the king in both a judicial and military capacity in Mercia.[41] Although this did not directly translate into donations as such, Æthelwig used his position of power and influence to increase the potential income of his house by two-thirds by purchasing as many as thirty-one manors.[42] Æthelwig also managed to acquire possession of the lands of the

37 *Chron. Abingdon*, i. 494; ii. 2, 7.
38 Ibid. ii. 7, 43, 74, 128, 134–5, 166–7; *Regesta*, ii, no. 700; Douglas, 'Some early surveys', 618–25 at p. 625. See pp. 46–7 above
39 *DB* i, fo. 208a; Raftis, *Estates of Ramsey abbey*, 28. Eudo *dapifer*, William of Houghton, Henry I's chamberlain, William Nicholas, Henry's chaplain and William the royal butler were also tenants of the abbey.
40 *Mon.*, iii. 87; BL, MS Cotton Galba E ii, fo. 54r; *Two chartularies of the priory of St Peter at Bath*, ed. W. Hunt (Somerset Record Society vii, 1893), i. 38; *VCH, Staffordshire*, iii. 202; 'Ingulfi Croylandensis Historia', in *Rerum Anglicarum scriptores veterum*, i. 119.
41 Emma Mason, 'Change and continuity in eleventh century Mercia: the experience of Wulfstan of Worcester', *Anglo-Norman Studies* viii (1986), 154–76 at p. 167. For Æthelwig see R. R. Darlington, 'Æthelwig abbot of Evesham', *English Historical Review* xlviii (1933), 1–22, 177–98.
42 Clarke, 'Early surveys of Evesham abbey', 105, 107.

pre-Conquest landholders who had sought the abbot's protection, died in the conflicts of 1066 and forfeited their lands.[43]

The personal charisma or reputation for sanctity of an abbot could increase the stature of his community and attract new recruits.[44] Under Abbot Serlo Gloucester's reputation flourished sufficiently to entice monks away from other institutions.[45] The personal charisma of Abbot Faritius at Abingdon and his reputation for hospitality was an attractive force of a very different order from that of the sanctity of Anselm of Le Bec. Eadmer claimed that when Anselm made a visit to England, 'there was no earl or countess in England, or any other important person, who did not consider that he had lost a chance of gaining merit with God if he happened not to have shown any kindness to Abbot Anselm of Le Bec, at that time'.[46] This had practical benefits as Anslem returned to his monastery 'laden with many gifts, which are known to honour the needs of his church until the present day'.[47] Part of the reason for his popularity lay in Anselm's generosity as a host. He was 'vigilant and solicitous' in entertaining his guests, sparing 'neither himself nor his goods in this pious work'.[48]

The provision of food and shelter was a political performance and Anselm was not alone in using hospitality as a diplomatic tool. Faritius was evidently also a very popular host, entertaining many archbishops, bishops and nobles as his guests at Abingdon.[49] This socialising produced important results in the form of gifts from the likes of William de Courcy, the royal *dapifer*, in 1105, William, bishop of Winchester, in 1115 and Henry d'Aubigny, the Bedfordshire landholder, c. 1107.[50] Faritius was already favoured by Henry I and Queen Matilda as their physician and there were 'many who tried to reward his kindness with riches'.[51] Good relations could be extremely beneficial for an abbey. The monasteries that made the greatest gains after the Conquest were typically those such as Gloucester, Bury St Edmunds and Abingdon which the king and his entourage chose to promote by their generosity. Indeed, what distinguished the likes of Abbots Serlo, Paul, Richard d'Aubigny, Faritius and Baldwin from the less notable abbots was their

43 Ibid. 107. The lands of these men, who had commended themselves to Æthelwig, amounted to approximately £89 at Domesday values.
44 Knowles, *Monastic order*, 126, 160, 177, 181n., 679. Anselm of Le Bec was forever seeking to persuade people, especially his relatives, to become monks of Le Bec. See, for example, *Sancti Anselmi opera omnia*, iii. 120–2, 143–4, 156–7, 170–1, 211–12, 244–6, 249–55, 258–61, 276–8.
45 Lanfranc wrote concerning a monk who wanted to spend a year at Gloucester as, 'it is to his spiritual advantage to do so': *Letters of Lanfranc*, 168.
46 Eadmer, *The life of St Anselm, archbishop of Canterbury*, ed. R. W. Southern, Oxford 1972, 56.
47 Ibid. 57.
48 Ibid. 46; OV ii. 296.
49 *Chron. Abingdon*, ii. 44–6.
50 Ibid. ii. 49–52, 100, 111.
51 Ibid. ii. 45.

particularly fruitful relationships with friends in 'high places': the king, the royal court and Archbishop Lanfranc. Royal endorsement and backing was indispensable to Baldwin's successful abbacy at Bury St Edmunds. For Serlo and Faritius it was the combination of royal patronage and the accompanying access to the royal court that brought in large quantities of grants.

Westminster abbey and the monastic community that served Rochester cathedral should also be added to the list of royal-sponsored institutions. Compared with many of the other English monasteries Westminster was the recipient of an impressive quantity of patronage in the reign of the Conqueror. Most important, Westminster had the attention of both William the Conqueror and Henry I. The scale of royal documents granted by William to Westminster is simply unmatched at any of the other English monasteries.[52] There are forty-five writs and charters from the reign of William the Conqueror,[53] twenty-five of which have been identified as being genuine and another six probably based on authentic eleventh-century documents.[54] This level of involvement with the affairs of the Confessor's burial church shows a degree of care and concern rarely displayed by anyone other than the founder.

The Norman Conquest had produced very little change in the social make-up of Westmister's patrons; if anything their overall status rose. Besides the king, royal officials and their families, both English and French, made up the bulk of the benefactors. A major change, however, was the emergence as patron of one the realm's richest barons, Geoffrey I de Mandeville.[55] Geoffrey founded and endowed Hurley priory, Berkshire, in the reign of the Conqueror as a cell to Westminster and expressed the desire to be buried at Westminster where his first wife Athelaise was already buried.[56] A number of Geoffrey's tenants also made grants to Hurley.[57] Westminster was indeed granted significant portions of land by its benefactors. Some of these were local officials such as the Englishman Swein of Essex, an Essex tenant-in-chief of substantial means, who granted the abbey four hides in Tooting, Surrey.[58] Geoffrey, son of Count Eustace of Boulogne, made the grant, on behalf of his wife

---

[52] The Conqueror's writs and charters which survive for Bury St Edmunds, St Augustine's, Canterbury, and Ely barely reach double figures in each instance: Regesta, i, nos 12–13, 35, 40–4, 66, 98–100, 122, 129, 137–9, 151–7, 175, 188–91, 242, 258, 276. The extant documents for Gloucester, Ramsey, Malmesbury and Abingdon only reach double figures when added together: ibid. i, nos 36, 49, 128, 135, 177, 180, 200–1, 219, 225, 247, 288b.

[53] Ibid. i, nos 289–334.

[54] Ibid. i, nos 290–1, 294–6, 298–300, 303, 306, 308–16, 319–22, 325–6, 329–34. The two forged general confirmation documents were probably based on genuine eleventh-century information: ibid. i, nos 289, 328.

[55] Ibid. i, nos 209, 251, 402; Westminster abbey charters 1066–c. 1214, ed. Emma Mason (London Record Society xxv, 1988), nos 23, 43, 52, 436, 462; Acta, nos 308, 328.

[56] Binns, Dedications, 76.

[57] These included Eadric, Geoffrey's reeve, Thorold his dapifer, Geoffrey, son of Count Eustace, who made his grant with Geoffrey I de Mandeville's agreement: Regesta, i, no. 251; Mason, Westminster charters, no. 43; Acta, no. 328.

[58] Regesta, i, no. 181; Westminster charters, no. 24; Acta, no. 312.

Beatrice, of three hides at Balham and Walton, near Morden.[59] Robert fitz Wymarc, who supposedly had been present at the Confessor's deathbed and was at one time the sheriff of Essex, granted Westminster land at Cricklade, in Wiltshire.[60] The number of religious donations made to Westminster dropped in the reign of William Rufus despite continuing royal interest in the affairs of the monastery.[61] William fitz Nigel, constable of Chester, who was also a benefactor of Gloucester, gave Westminster land at Perton, in Staffordshire, 'in the time of earl Hugh of Chester'.[62] The twelfth century saw an increase in the number of grants being made, although their size did not match those given under the Conqueror. Henry I confirmed a number of restorations and grants to Westminster, as well as making a couple of grants himself.[63] The burial of his queen, Matilda, in 1118 in front of the high altar prompted grants from both Henry I and her brother David, who later became king of Scotland.[64] A few early twelfth-century donors with Anglo-Saxon names occur in the Westminster sources. These were the three daughters of Deorman the moneyer and Wulfric the moneyer of Henry I, who entered the house as a monk.[65]

A similar scene was being played out at Rochester.[66] In the last years of the Conqueror's reign a period of great acquisition began, which lasted throughout the reign of William Rufus. By the time of Bishop Gundulf's death in 1108, four major manors had been acquired.[67] It has been shown that the grants made by William Rufus to Rochester, 'were not as generous as they first appeared to be'.[68] Nevertheless, the fact that Rochester had previously held the lands which Rufus 'granted', by no means negates the value of the benefactions.[69] That William Rufus did take a particular interest in the welfare of Rochester, for whatever motive, is borne out by the number of royal writs and charters he issued in the community's favour.[70] Although Bishop Gundulf

---

59 *Regesta*, i, no. 202; *Westminster charters*, no. 21; *Acta*, no. 313.

60 *Regesta*, i, no. 417; *Westminster charters*, no. 32; *Acta*, no. 322.

61 *Regesta*, i, nos 306, 370, 381–2, 402, 420, 436, 454–5.

62 Ibid. ii, no. 1882; *Westminster charters*, no. 95.

63 *Regesta*, ii, nos 667, 903, 1123, 1178, 1377, 1878, 1880, 1882–4; *Westminster charters*, nos 66, 68, 72, 79, 86, 90, 92, 95, 350.

64 *Regesta*, ii, no. 1377; *Westminster charters*, nos 79, 99–101; *Regesta regum Scottorum*, I: *The acts of Malcolm IV king of Scots 1153–1165*, ed. G. W. S. Barrow, Edinburgh 1960, no. 6.

65 *Regesta*, ii, nos 1123, 1178; *Westminster charters*, nos 68, 72.

66 A. F. Brown, 'The lands and tenants of the bishopric and cathedral priory of St Andrew, Rochester, 600–1540', unpubl. Ph.D. diss. London 1974, 15, 39. For Rochester see also Oakley, 'St Andrew, Rochester', 47–60; M. Ruud, 'Monks in the world: the case of Gundulf of Rochester', *Anglo-Norman Studies* xi (1989), 245–60; *The life of Gundulf bishop of Rochester*, ed. R. Thomson, Toronto 1977.

67 Brown, 'St Andrew, Rochester', 41–4.

68 Ibid. 41, 43–4.

69 *Regesta*, i, nos 301–2, 355, 400, 450, 452; Brown, 'St Andrew, Rochester,' 43–4. Brown points out that Lambeth was meant to have been given to Rochester by Countess Goda, but was seized by Harold in 1066 and subsequently passed into the hands of Odo of Bayeux.

70 *Regesta*, i, nos 301–2, 355, 400, 450, 452. This compares well with the five William Rufus

was the prime mover behind the promotion of the house's fortunes, credit should also be given to Archbishop Lanfranc.[71] Freckenham, in Suffolk, had been restored to him by the Conqueror but he in turn restored it to Bishop Gundulf whom he considered the rightful owner. He also purchased Haddenham, in Buckinghamshire, to give to Rochester.[72] Royal interest in Rochester did not waver with the accession of Henry I, who was a generous benefactor himself, and confirmed a number of grants made by his barons.[73] He granted seven churches and the tithes of five of their parishes, tithes of the royal mill in Rochester, tithes in Strood and Chalk, in Kent, and various franchises, including the right to hold a two-day fair in Rochester.[74] The major grants received by Rochester were made 'by men who served on the king's council', such as Roger Bigod, Haimo the sheriff and Gilbert fitz Richard.[75] Other royal officials like Eudo *dapifer*, William d'Aubigny *pincerna* and Haimo *dapifer*, Robert fitz Haimo's brother, as well as King Henry I's son, Robert, were benefactors as well.[76] Men associated with members of the royal court were also induced to make donations such as Ralph, *pincerna* of Eudo *dapifer* and Wulfmar, man of Arnulf de Hesdin.[77] The relevance of the royal court here is given added significance by the fact that a number of benefactors, or their families, were also benefactors of Gloucester. These included Roger Bigod, Gilbert fitz Richard and Hugh and Henry de Port.[78] The *Vita Gundulfi* depicts Bishop Gundulf as a regular at Henry I's court and his part in the construction of the Tower of London may have developed earlier relations with the royal court.[79]

Of the three crown-wearing locations, Westminster, Gloucester and the monastic priory serving Winchester, Old Minster, it was the oldest foundation, Winchester, which received the least amount of support from members of the Norman royal court or the local aristocracy. Despite ambitious beginnings under William the Conqueror, Old Minster failed to capture the imagination of more than a handful of the Anglo-Normans. When Bishop Walchelin laid out the foundations of the new cathedral in the reign of the

---

writs and charters that survive for Gloucester, one for St Albans, four for Abingdon, five for Bury St Edmunds, seven for St Augustine's, Canterbury, two for Old Minster, Winchester, but does not top the ten granted to Westminster abbey.

[71] Brown, 'St Andrew, Rochester', 42. Brown suggests that Lanfranc was also responsible for influencing William Rufus' grant of the manor of Lambeth.

[72] Ibid. 42–3.

[73] *Regesta*, ii, nos 647, 901.

[74] Ibid. ii, nos 516, 517, 868, 882, 936, 943, 1728, 1867; Brown, 'St Andrew, Rochester', 56.

[75] Ibid. 53.

[76] *Textus Roffensis*, ed. T. Hearne, Oxford 1720, facsimile edn, ed. P. H. Sawyer (Early English Manuscripts in Facsimile vii, xi, 1957, 1962), fos 181v, 184v, 188v, 192r; *Regesta*, i, no. 451.

[77] *Textus Roff.*, fos 184v, 185v.

[78] Ibid. fos 182r–v, 185v, 198v; *Regesta*, i, no. 450.

[79] Ruud, 'Monks in the world', 249–53.

Conqueror, it was to be the second longest church in western Europe.[80] Beside confirming Winchester Old Minster's liberties, on his death-bed, the Conqueror made the grant of half a hide on the Isle of Wight.[81] William Rufus issued a number of writs confirming the grants of his father, and granted the abbey the lucrative right to hold a three-day fair at the church of St Giles, Winchester.[82] Aside from extending this fair, from three to eight days' duration, Henry I granted little that was new to Old Minster, but confirmed a number of gifts and disputed abbey lands.[83] Old Minster attracted only a smattering of grants from local men like Hugh the larderer in the reign of Rufus, and Hugh the potter, *serviens* of Henry I, and Bernard de St-Valéry, in the reign of Henry I.[84] A certain Gilbert of *Walmerfeld* also chose to become a monk at Old Minster before 1096.[85] Even if Old Minster's royal connection was in decline, the church 'remained a centre of pilgrimage to the shrine of St Swithun's'.[86] It is impossible, however, to establish whether sufficient money was brought in by visiting pilgrims to help pay for the completion of the massive new church.

The monastery of New Minster, Winchester, may have attracted grants, at the expense of the older and wealthier house, but this cannot be conclusively proved. Henry I certainly showed an interest in the physical state of New Minster, situated as it was on a cramped site in Winchester. The migration in about 1100 to Hyde, outside the north gate of the city, was undertaken under royal initiative and Henry I was in 'a real sense the founder of Hyde abbey'.[87] The only other indication that New Minster/Hyde won attention away from Old Minster survives in the abbey's *liber vitae*.[88] This manuscript includes the names of King Henry, Queen Matilda and their son William as well as the names of important men of the realm, some of whom were associated with the royal treasury at Winchester. Among these are Walter Giffard, Count Alan I Rufus (or Alan II Niger), lord of Richmond, and his brother Ribald and wife, Hugh de Port and his wife Orence, Herbert the chamberlain and Arnulf his son, Hugh the sheriff and his family and Geoffrey the royal *pincerna*.[89] Even if the inclusion of their names does not mean that these people were benefactors, it proves an association of some sort with the abbey. This relatively low level of religious patronage for the two Winchester monasteries

80 *Winchester in the early Middle Ages*, ed. M. Biddle, Oxford 1976, 308, 310.
81 BL, MS Add. 29436, fo. 12v.
82 *Regesta*, i, nos 287, 357, 377.
83 Ibid. ii, nos 490, 558, 597, 603, 625, 627–8, 745, 803–6, 884, 947–9, 1070, 1378–9, 1509, 1637.
84 *Chartulary of Winchester cathedral*, ed. A. W. Goodman, Winchester 1927, 7–8; *Regesta*, ii, nos 803–4, 1378–9.
85 BL, MS Add. 29436, fo. 12r; *Chart. Winchester*, 7–8.
86 *Winchester in the early Middle Ages*, 311.
87 Ibid. 318.
88 BL, MS Stowe 944. This is printed in both the de Gray Birch and the Keynes editions of the New Minster and Hyde *liber vitae*.
89 Ibid. 50–1, 65, 72–3.

is curious, especially in the light of the fact that there was little competition from new foundations in the locality until later in the reign of Henry I. The answer may well be that the high density of religious houses already established in the region left little room for local expansion without intruding onto another house's property.[90]

An abbot's initiative could play a pivotal role in the advancement of a saint's cult and the building programme inevitably associated with it. The translation of saints' relics was made necessary by the demolition of old churches and the construction of new ones. This in turn served to publicise the saints' cults and, it was hoped, to generate donations which would be used to finance construction. These objectives both depended on, and generated, endowments and offerings. The abbot's role in the promotion of a saint's cult was critical. Turstin at Glastonbury had attempted to promote the cult of St Benigius by translating the saint's relics from Meare in Somerset to Glastonbury.[91] At Bury St Edmunds the *De miraculis de Sancti Eadmundi* describes how on hearing of the miraculous cure of the pilgrim Wulfmar, Abbot Baldwin had the miracle publicly announced in the abbey church.[92] Pilgrims travelled from places throughout southern England and from the continent to visit the shrine of St Edmund.[93] It is evident that the promotion of a particular saint's cult could influence not only local people, but also cut through considerations of the locality and equally affect those further field and those high up in the social order. Robert fitz Haimo and his wife made a pilgrimage to the shrine of St Bernigius at Glastonbury.[94] St Aldhelm at Malmesbury was claimed to have affected a cure for Arnulf de Hesdin and attracted pilgrims from Wiltshire, Gloucestershire, Lincolnshire, the Isle of Wight and Cologne.[95]

Royal interest was also sometimes drawn by the presence of saints' relics. The Conquest quickly proved beneficial for the abbey at Burton-on-Trent as William the Conqueror became its most generous benefactor. The fact that the Conqueror showed a particular interest in this impoverished monastery was most likely due to his reverence for the shrine of St Modwenna which he personally visited.[96] On this occasion, William restored to Burton the land which he had taken in Coton-in-the-Elms, in Derbyshire.[97] He also granted

---

90 Sandra Raban noted that this was the state of affairs in the east midlands: 'Thorney and Crowland abbeys', 18.

91 *Early history of Glastonbury*, 156.

92 *Memorials of St Edmund's*, i. 83, 162.

93 See p. 73 above.

94 J. C. Holt, 'Feudal society and the family in early medieval England, III: patronage and politics', *Transactions of the Royal Historical Society* xxxiv (1984), 1–25 at p. 3.

95 *Early history of Glastonbury*, 422–3, 425–6, 434–41.

96 VCH, *Staffordshire*, iii. 200. For Burton see also J. H. Round, 'The Burton abbey surveys', *English Historical Review* xiv (1905), 275–89.

97 VCH, *Staffordshire*, iii. 201; *Regesta*, i, no. 223; *The Burton chartulary*, ed. G. Wrottesley (William Salt Archaeological Society v, pt i, 1884), 9, 14.

Cauldwell and Mickleover, in Derbyshire, and in the town of Derby, two mills, three houses, a meadow and the church of St Mary, and the church of Willington.[98] By the time of Domesday, of the thirty-two manors held by the monks of Burton, seven had been given by the Conqueror.[99] Unfortunately the Conqueror's sons did not take the same degree of interest in Burton as their father had done.[100] Henceforth almost all the benefactions the abbey received were inexorably linked to its position as local landlord and as provider of spiritual and social services.[101]

Malmesbury abbey, located in Wiltshire, worth £178 in 1086, also experienced a burst of religious benefactions in the reign of the Conqueror and appears to have been a pilgrimage centre of some importance. Charters and donations also indicate that Abbot Warin (1070–c. 1091) was in favour with the Conqueror and his wife in the 1080s.[102] Warin promoted the cult of St Aldhelm by having the saint's relics translated in 1078,[103] and was in attendance on the royal court in 1080 when he was sent news of the miraculous cure of Fulkwin, a deformed youth.[104] This caused much interest there and Bishop Osmund of Salisbury petitioned for, and received from Warin, part of the saint's body. In the following year, 1081, Queen Matilda made a grant of three hides in Garsdon, in Wiltshire, to 'the Virgin and St Adhelm of Malmesbury [. . .] at the prayer of Abbot Warin' and the Conqueror granted the abbey a five-day fair.[105] It is likely that Godwin and his wife Turgund who in 1084 granted Malmesbury the church of St Nicholas near London, were also pilgrims.[106] At least one 'pilgrim' had been brought to Malmesbury by the medical skills of the physician Gregory only to be cured by St Aldhelm.[107] Arnulf de Hesdin, the great magnate, came to Malmesbury seeking a cure for his hands which were afflicted with disease.[108] William of Malmesbury's *vita* of the saint gives the impression of Malmesbury as a flourishing pilgrimage centre in the 1120s, but there is little other evidence of religious patronage being given to the monastery. Apart from extending the grant of the fair at

---

98 VCH, *Staffordshire*, iii. 201–2.
99 *Chart. Burton*, 1.
100 *Regesta*, ii, no. 600. This refers to a lost writ of William Rufus for the abbey, otherwise no Burton writs survive for the reign: ibid. ii, nos 600, 766, 1063, 1073.
101 For example Roger de Fraeville and his wife, the daughter of Adeliza de Hesdin, confirmed Adeliza's grant of land in Wolston, Warwickshire, in return for the grant of fraternity and the promise of prayers: *Chart. Burton*, 32–3.
102 *Registrum Malmesburiense*, ed. J. S. Brewer (Rolls series lxxii, 1879), i. 326–8, 329, 330, 333; *Regesta*, i, nos 135–6, 247, 347, 434.
103 *The Oxford dictionary of saints*, ed. H. D. Farmer, 2nd edn, Oxford 1987, 11–12; *Early history of Glastonbury*, 423–5.
104 *Reg. Malmesburiense*, i. 246–8.
105 For Matilda's religious benefactions see BL, MS Add. 47847, fo. 20r. Matilda granted Warkton in Northamptonshire, 'of her own accord': *CDF*, nos 93, 196; *Regesta*, i, no. 247.
106 *Reg. Malmesburiense*, i. 328.
107 *Early history of Glastonbury*, 438.
108 Ibid. 437–8.

Malmesbury from three to five days, Henry I had very little to do with the abbey.[109]

Yet a royal sponsor was not always decisive in attracting high levels of patronage to a monastery. In the case of Evesham it was not the king's attention that brought prosperity but rather it was the monastery's own reputation and standing in both national and international Christian society. In the mid eleventh century the communities at Evesham and Worcester had 'achieved a reputation for austerity and holiness'.[110] Around 1070 Evesham attracted Rainfrid, a *miles* of the Conqueror, and a man of 'some social standing', as an adult entrant into the convent.[111] Rainfrid's admission into the community consequently inspired the expedition to Northumbria which culminated in the revival of monasticism north of the Humber.[112] Evesham also undertook a second colonising expedition to Odensee, in Denmark, in the reign of William Rufus.[113] Furthermore, during the abbacy of Æthelwig pilgrims from as far afield as Aquitaine and Ireland and 'many other lands' came to venerate the shrine of St Ecgwin at Evesham.[114] Abbot Walter later capitalised on this fame and sent the relics of St Ecgwin on a fund-raising tour to pay for the new abbey church, and planned other such tours.[115]

Despite the abbey's difficulties and preoccupation with their landed properties, having lost approximately 129 hides, worth £114 between 1076 and 1086, from the time of the Conqueror's reign, Evesham managed to attract a small number of wealthy and influential donors because of its reputation for spiritual dynamism.[116] Before 1086 Nigel, constable of Chester, gave the moiety of Thelwell, in Cheshire, a fishery and a hide in *Goldhore*.[117] In 1088 Robert of Stafford, nephew of Robert de Tosny of Belvoir, entered Evesham as a monk and granted the abbey two small manors.[118] Sometime between 1088

---

[109] *Regesta*, ii, nos 494, 971.
[110] L. G. D. Baker, 'The desert in the north', *Northern History* v (1970), 1–11 at p. 2.
[111] Ibid. 4.
[112] For this expedition and the revival of monasticism in the north see Knowles, *Monastic order*, 163–71; Baker, 'Desert in the north', 4–11; B. Meehan, 'Outsiders, insiders and property in Durham around 1100', in D. Baker (ed.), *Church, society and politics* (Studies in Church History xii, 1975), 45–58; D. Bethell, 'The foundation of Fountains abbey and the state of St Mary's, York in 1132', *Journal of Ecclesiastical History* xvii (1966), 11–27; Anne F. Dawtry, 'The Benedictine revival in the north: the last bulwark of Anglo-Saxon monasticism?', in Mews, *Religion and national identity*, 87–98.
[113] Knowles, *Monastic order*, 163–4; Clarke, 'Early surveys', 132. Clarke suggests that the departure of the twelve Evesham monks to Denmark was a sign that 'the reduced estates were incapable of supporting the number of recruits still seeking the Benedictine way of life nearer home'.
[114] *Chronicon abbatiae de Evesham ad annum 1418*, ed. W. D. Macray (Rolls series xxix, 1863), 91.
[115] Ibid. 55; Ridyard, 'Condigna veneratio', 205n.
[116] Clarke, 'Early surveys', 111, 117, 119–20.
[117] *Chron. Evesham*, 75. Nigel was succeeded by his son, William, who was a tenant before 1086 of Earl Hugh of Chester in several places in Cheshire.
[118] Ibid. 75; Clarke, 'Early surveys', 130.

and 1102 Roger the Poitevin granted Evesham Howick, in Lancashire, presumably a result of the abbey's northern connections.[119] Soon afterwards, in the first years of the twelfth century, Miles Crispin gave the abbey half a hide at Hillingdon, Middlesex.[120] Brian fitz Count was later to add the church of Hillingdon to this grant.[121]

Evesham also secured the backing of one particular royal official, a step which was to have practical results for the abbey. Before 1107 Ranulf the chancellor secured from Henry I, on behalf of the abbey, the grant of a port and a market every Thursday at Stow-on-the-Wold, in Gloucestershire.[122] Between 1104 and 1122 Warin Bussel granted the church of Penwortham, in Lancashire; in return the abbey was to have the church served by three monks and to receive Warin's son, should he decide to become a monk.[123] The Yorkshire tenant-in-chief, Robert Fossard, also granted Evesham the church of Huntingdon in the reign of Henry I.[124] Thus, despite the heavy loss of estates that the abbey sustained during the abbacy of Walter of Caen, overall Evesham was quite successful and, like many other English Benedictine communities, flourished; numbers of monks almost doubled in the period from 1078 to 1104, rising from thirty-six to sixty-seven.[125]

The governance of an abbey, especially a prosperous and expanding one, required sustained effort. Personality counted for a lot, and continuity was at a premium. The sheer longevity of many of the successful abbots ensured stability and provided continuity from reign to reign. Baldwin, the continental abbot of Bury St Edmunds from 1065 to 1098, is a excellent example of the benefits of continuity in a period of crisis. Henry of Blois governed Glastonbury abbey for over fifty years, Serlo and Baldwin for over thirty years each and Richard d'Aubigny for twenty-two years. These were all certainly abbacies of exceptional length. Most capable abbots ruled for about fifteen years, as in the case of Herluin of Glastonbury, Faritius, Scotland, Paul of Caen and Reginald. Yet longevity was not a prerequisite to a successful abbacy: Herbert of Losinga, who was abbot of Ramsey for only three years, achieved much in his time. Furthermore, sustaining momentum after the death of a particularly able abbot was not always easy. After Baldwin's death in 1098 Bury St Edmunds had plenty of problems. Prolonged vacancies also partially explain the failure of certain abbeys, such as Ely, to flourish.

After 1066 there were countless newly enriched donors in England, anxious to have their souls saved, who were looking for effective avenues for their generosity. This meant that, for a generation at least, the sheer scale and

119 *Chron. Evesham*, 75; Clarke, 'Early surveys', 131.
120 *Chron. Evesham*, 75; Clarke, 'Early surveys', 132.
121 BL, MS Cotton Vespian B xxiv, fo. 17r; *Chron. Evesham*, 75.
122 *Regesta*, ii, no. 831; *Chron. Evesham*, 98.
123 Ibid. 75; Binns, *Dedications*, 81.
124 EYC ii. 369.
125 Clarke, 'Early surveys', 133. For the post-Conquest growth in the numbers of monks in Benedictine houses see Knowles, *Monastic order*, 126, 160, 177, 182, 425–6, 679.

nature of religious patronage in post-Conquest England was different from anything likely to be found on the continent. Thus the Conquest itself created exceptional circumstances of which particularly adept abbots were able to take advantage. Gloucester's impoverished state in 1066 was a far cry from its standing in 1104. If it had not been for the particular situation created by the Conquest and Serlo's activities, it would most likely have remained an insignificant monastery. Baldwin was already in favour with the king before the Conquest, but his continental origins, combined with his medical skills, enabled him to secure a privileged place in the post-Conquest political world for Bury St Edmunds. Yet the fact that Baldwin's rise to authority pre-dated 1066 also suggests that the circumstances of the Conquest alone were not responsible for his success. The study of the abbacies of men like Serlo of Gloucester, Baldwin of Bury St Edmunds, Faritius of Abingdon, Paul and Richard d'Aubigny of St Albans, has already established that they were exceptional phases in the history of their abbeys.

However, in the twelfth century, increasing numbers of the Anglo-Normans chose to found and patronise the 'new' religious orders. Extensive religious patronage and the creation of new foundations were as much appropriate means of demonstrating new wealth and status, as cohesive components in honorial society. For the smaller Benedictine monasteries, as well as for Gloucester, Abingdon, Westminster, St Augustine's, Canterbury, and St Albans, the second and third decades of the twelfth century brought a drop in the number and size of the donations they received. Only Thorney stands as any sort of exception to this rule. The calibre of abbots had much to do with these fluctuations, for by the 1120s many of the remarkable abbots had died and it follows that prolonged or frequent vacancies had a profound impact on the flow of donations. But increased competition from the profusion of new small foundations that were springing up all over England in the early twelfth century was also beginning to take its toll on the level of donations being made to the established English houses.

PART TWO

ANALYSIS

9

The Motivation and Social Function
of Religious Patronage

When Odelerius of Orleans was trying to persuade Roger, earl of Shrewsbury, to found a monastery on his newly acquired lands in Shropshire he set out his case for religious patronage.[1] His argument, or rather Orderic Vitalis's argument, followed two main lines of reasoning. The first was designed to appeal to Roger's warrior mentality:[2] that, by establishing such a foundation, Roger would be supporting a very real Christian fight against the devil. He says of monasteries that 'countless benefits are obtained there every day, and Christ's garrison struggle[s] manfully against the devil'.[3] The virtues of monasticism are further expounded: 'who can tell all the vigils of the monks, their hymns and psalms, their prayers and alms, and their daily offerings of masses with copious tears?' This all led to Odelerius' second point, the fate of Roger's soul. The foundation of a monastery, he argued, would establish

> a citadel of God against Satan, where the cowled champions may engage in ceaseless combat against Behemond for your soul [. . .] The monks, in filial piety, will pray for you after your death [. . .] and I believe that their prayers, for whomsoever among the faithful they are offered, rise immediately to the throne of God, and that whatever they ask of the King of Hosts they surely receive.

This final point was the crux of the argument. Monks were perceived as serving God, in a very literal sense, and the intercessory role of Benedictine monasteries was one of vital importance to all benefactors, potential and otherwise.[4] Concern for the salvation of one's soul and the souls of one's ancestors was of fundamental importance to all men and women. It underpinned the medieval psyche.[5]

The aim of this chapter is to examine the personal impetus that inspired

[1] OV iii. 142–50.
[2] For the ritual aggression of the Cluniac liturgy see B. Rosenwein, 'Feudal war and monastic peace: Cluniac liturgy as ritual aggression', *Viator* ii (1971), 129–57.
[3] OV iii. 144. For a discussion of the mixing of the secular and spiritual in the concept of the soldier of Christ see I. S. Robinson, 'Gregory VII and the soldiers of Christ', *History* lviii (1973), 169–92.
[4] Orderic talks of Earl Hugh of Chester's foundation as 'a community of monks for God's service': OV iv. 142.
[5] For example, William the Conqueror founded Battle abbey 'for the salvation of all, and particularly of all those killed there': *Chron. Battle*, 148.

religious patronage given in post-Conquest England by both aristocratic and knightly society. This appraisal will be undertaken in the light of the recent work by Barbara Rosenwein, Constance Bouchard and Penelope Johnson on the social and symbolic role of religious patronage to continental houses.[6] It will be argued that, although the Norman Conquest created an exceptional set of circumstances, which influenced the mechanisms behind the choice of a particular religious house, personal motives for religious patronage resembled the continental model. In detail there were differences, but in general motivation included the desire for prayers, fraternity, burial in abbey grounds and the wish for the donor, or kinsman, to take up the monastic habit.[7] Many donors planned for their salvation well in advance, but some waited to be moved by personal crises, which could include illness, approaching death or even infertility. The role of women acting as conductors of religious enthusiasm also mirrored continental trends.[8] Analysis of the social status of donors in post-Conquest England would also suggest correspondence with the model of downward diffusion of cultural patterns through Anglo-Norman society.[9] However, in post-Conquest England diversification in the number of religious orders sponsored by individuals and families occurred a generation earlier than on the continent.

The English sources for the motivation driving religious patronage in post-Conquest England are generally less illuminating than their continental counterparts. Thus the personal considerations that moved donors to make gifts have to be teased out from unpromisingly brief and sporadic remarks in charters and registers. Sources also vary in nature and quality from house to house and from document to document. Charters that were copied and recopied into cartularies and registers would be edited and condensed by

6   For studies of the social and political significance of gift-giving in society see M. Mauss, *The gift: forms and functions of exchange in archaic societies*, trans. I. Cunnison, 2nd edn, London 1954; C. A. Gregory, *Gifts and commodities*, London 1982; G. Duby, *The early growth of the European economy: warriors and peasants from the seventh to the twelfth century*, trans. H. B. Clarke, Ithaca–New York 1974, 48–74; C. Lévi-Strauss, *The elementary structures of kinship*, trans. J. H. Bell, J. R. Von Sturmer and R. Needham, London 1969, 52–63; L. K. Little, *Religious poverty and the profit economy in medieval Europe*, London 1978, 3–18; P. Grierson, 'Commerce in the Dark Ages: a critique of the evidence', *Transactions of the Royal Historical Society*, 5th ser. ix (1959), 123–10.

7   For remarks on the Christian belief in the efficacy of prayer see J. Le Goff, *The birth of purgatory*, trans. Arthur Goldhammer, Chicago 1986, 11–12, 45–6, 102, 103; B. P. McGuire, 'Purgatory, the communion of saints, and medieval change', *Viator* xx (1989), 61–84. For spiritual benefits see Wardrop, *Fountains abbey*, 235–76; Wood, *English monasteries*, 122–35.

8   For remarks on women acting as transmitters of enthusiasm for a particular religious house see Johnson, *Prayer, patronage, and power*, 88; Bouchard, *Sword, miter and cloister*, 142–9. For more recent remarks on this phenomenon and crusading see J. Riley-Smith, 'Family tradition and participation in the Second Crusade', in M. Gervers (ed.), *The Second Crusade and the Cistercians*, New York 1992, 101–8.

9   For Duby's discussion of the nature of cultural diffusion see 'Diffusion of cultural patterns', 3–10. See also Bouchard's observation on the status of benefactors in the eleventh and twelfth centuries: *Sword, miter and cloister*, 131–8.

successive scribes. To later generations of monks certain details, such as witness lists and requests for prayers, were no longer seen as pertinent, unlike the 'when, what and by whom' aspects of a grant. In the late fourteenth-century cartulary of St Peter's, Gloucester, there is a copy of the donation by Harold of Ewyas of a number of his churches, chapels and tithes, just one of many possible examples which can illustrate this point briefly.[10] The charter states that the grant was made 'for the souls of my father and mother, for the soul of my wife and sons and my kin'. The grant was made in the chapter house at Gloucester, 'placed upon the altar of St Peter' and later confirmed 'by the hand of the venerable Bishop Bernard in the chapter of Ewyas'. There follows an extensive list of witnesses. Yet in the *Historia Sancti Petri Gloucestriae*, almost all of these details are omitted. All that is preserved is the date of the donation, by whom it was made, and what the grant entailed.[11] The editing of later scribes therefore acts against the preservation of information such as the motives expressed by donors. This must generate variations between religious houses which have little to do with differing motives, but rather with the nature of record keeping.

Gifts were made to religious houses for a very good reason: the salvation of the donor and sometimes of relatives, lords and friends as well.[12] Furthermore, there were many forms of compensation for the donor, such as merit in Heaven, the grant of 'society' or 'fraternity', and prayers.[13] In England the language used in donation documents is usually sparse and concise to the point of seeming entirely formulaic. However, specific assertions that a grant was given 'for the souls of my father and mother' or 'for the salvation of my soul' are commonplace.[14] Examination of the variations in the people featured in English evidence can be used to reach an understanding of the function of religious benefaction. I have compiled an inventory detailing the particulars of 185 non-royal donation charters which contain *pro anima* requests derived from the muniments of forty-eight religious houses, both great and small in scale and age.[15] Clearly, this catalogue is limited in its

---

[10] *Historia Sancti Petri Gloucestriae*, i. 285–6.

[11] Ibid. i. 76.

[12] Tabuteau, *Transfers of property*, 15.

[13] For spiritual privileges obtainable to continental benefactors see also White, *Custom, kinship and gifts to saints*, 28.

[14] For a discussion of the meaning of such statements see Tabuteau, *Transfers of property*, 15–16, and White, *Custom, kinship and gifts to saints*, 28–9. The words *pro salute* are commonplace in post-Conquest documents but do not always refer to religious patronage; they can also be applied in a broader sense to the performance of good works. For example, William the Conqueror's grant of the manor of Tewin in Hertfordshire to the thegn Haldane and his mother was made 'pro anima Ricardi filii sui': *DB* i, fos 141b–c. Bishop Seffrid of Chichester's management of the administration and spiritual life at Battle was purportedly undertaken 'for the salvation of himself and his sons': *Chron. Battle*, 138–9.

[15] These are Abergavenny, Abingdon, Barnwell, Basaleg, Bath, Bermondsey, Blyth, Boxgrove, Bridlington, Brinkburn, Burton on Trent, Bury St Edmunds, St Augustine's, Canterbury, Castle Acre, Exeter, Eye, Gloucester, Guisborough, Horkesely, Kenilworth, Kidwelly,

usefulness as it cannot claim to be comprehensive, but analysis of these petitions does reflect the interests and concerns of the donors for the spiritual fate of their kindred. They strongly suggest that the sentiments behind inclusion were by no means formulaic, or automatic, but were heavily influenced by the nature of the family.[16]

The most frequent element, as one might expect, was the formula 'for my own soul' (see table 1) which occurs in roughly three-quarters of the sample I have examined.[17] However, its absence from the remainder of the sample indicates that although it was the most popular type of request, its inclusion was certainly not automatic. Furthermore, the formula that a grant was made for the 'redemption of [the donor's . . .] sins' was actually relatively uncommon.[18] The numerous requests for the souls of the donors' fathers and mothers reveal a high level of concern for both parents, requests for the souls of fathers being slightly more common than for mothers. Marc Bloch argued that 'each generation had its circle of relatives which was not the same as that of the previous generation, the area of the kindred's responsibilities continually changed its contours'.[19] This is borne out by the fact that family beyond the first degree of affinity are usually relegated to inclusion in such groups as 'kin' or 'ancestors', and requests for the souls of grandparents are almost unknown. Where property had been inherited from kin other than the donor's parents, such as from uncles, they were accordingly remembered in their heir's acts of charity. Two instance of this occur in the charters of Ranulf I, earl of Chester, and Conan of Brittany.[20]

Requests for the souls of donors' wives were also popular, accounting for nearly a third of all requests made by men. Sometimes the information available is more detailed, such as in the case of William d'Aubigny *pincerna*, whose heart-felt concern for his recently deceased wife, Matilda, at her funeral is apparent.[21] The fact, on the other hand, that of the total of all male donors numerically only a quarter exhibited such concern for their wives's souls, may be a reflection of their greater concern with the souls of the dead,

Lenton, Lewes, Llanthony, St Aldgate, London, Malmesbury, Montacute, Nostell, St James, Northampton, Pontefract, Ramsey, Reading, Rievaulx, Rochester, Shrewsbury, St Albans, St Bees, Stoke by Clare, Thetford, Thorney, Totnes, Waltham, Westminster, Whitby, Worcester cathedral priory and Holy Trinity, York.

16 Emma Mason has done similar analysis, but on a smaller scale, using the Westminster charters: 'Donors of Westminster abbey charters', 23–39 at pp. 32, 34. See also J. T. Rosenthal, *The purchase of paradise: gift-giving and the aristocracy, 1207–1485*, London 1972, 11–30.
17 The figure for requests from joint donors has been doubled in the final figure to reflect the number of individuals involved.
18 For examples see *Blythburgh priory cartulary*, ed. C. Harper-Bill, Woodbridge 1980–1, i. 55–6; *The chartulary of Brinkburn priory*, ed. W. Page (Surtees Society xc, 1892), 1; *Mon.*, iii. 16.
19 M. Bloch, *Feudal society*, trans. L. A. Manyon, 2nd edn, London 1961, i. 138.
20 *The cartulary or register of the abbey of St Werburgh, Chester*, ed. J. Tait (Chetham Society, n.s. lxxix, lxxxii, Manchester, 1920–3), i. 47; *Mon.*, iii. 550.
21 *Mon.*, iii. 330–1.

Table 1
Groups and individuals for whom *pro anima* requests were made in a sample of 185 charters

Pro anima requests	Male donors	Female donors	Joint donors	Total
Self/selves	93	14	17 (x2)	141
Parents/kin	39	5	5	54
Grandparents	3	–	–	3
Father	61	5	1	67
Mother	50	4	–	54
Wife	45	–	1	46
Wife's parents	3	–	–	3
Brothers	20	2	–	22
Sisters	8	–	–	8
Husband	–	13	1	14
Ancestors/ predecessors	41	5	6	52
Nephews	1	–	–	1
Uncles	9	–	–	9
Sons	16	5	1	22
Sons/daughters-in-law	1	1	–	2
Daughters	5	–	1	6
Heirs/successors	19	1	2	22
Child/children	5	–	1	6
Lord	6	–	1	7
Friends	4	1	1	6
Men/vassals	3	–	–	3
Other named individuals	15	–	1	16
King and royal family	25	1	–	26
Total number of donors	143	21	21	185

than with the living, rather than their marital status or the status of wives within the kinship group.[22] Indeed, when Geoffrey de Mandeville gave Westminster abbey the manor of Ebury 'for the soul of his wife Athelaise who is buried in the cloister', his new wife, Lesceline, was present at the ceremony, but she was not included in his requests, although his sons and daughters were.[23] Concern for those already departed must also explain the high percentage of requests made for the souls of deceased brothers, amounting to just over one-tenth of petitions. Concern for the souls of deceased children, however, is relatively infrequent, and the living heir only merited a mention in one-tenth of all donations. The explanation for this must lie in the central position of the inheritance within the family. Claims to property were acquired through the donor's parents or wives and through the death of elder siblings, but not through his own children. In the wider scheme of things they therefore did not matter in quite the same way and were rarely mentioned.

Women's donations were much rarer than men's and were more often than not made jointly with a husband or adult son. Women's concerns, as reflected in the charters drawn up for them by the monks, broadly corresponded with men's, with two exceptions. The first is that almost all women acting as sole donor made requests for their spouse's souls, and secondly, just over a quarter of female donors also made requests for their sons' souls. For example, the wife of Azo Bigod made a grant to Shrewsbury abbey 'for the soul of her son Richard'.[24] However, only slightly over 10 per cent of men made requests for their sons. The explanation for the different degree of concern for spouses and sons probably lies in these women's marital status. Lone female donors were most likely to be widows, although only a few are actually known to have been widows at the time of their donations: Ermelina de Lacy made her grant to St Peter's, Gloucester, on the day of her husband's funeral; Countess Judith certainly made her grant to St Albans in the years after her husband's execution in 1076; Albreda of Walton was explicitly decribed in the Ramsey sources as the widow of Eustace of Sellea.[25] If the other lone female donors such as Aveline de Hasdin, Matilda de Hesdin and Gunnilda de Loges were also widows then their concern for their deceased husbands' souls needs little explanation. Futhermore, the relative freedom of action allowed to them as widows also enabled them to show maternal concern for the souls of their sons. In life these sons would have periodically acted with their widowed

---

22 For the position of the wife within the family see Bloch, *Feudal society*, i. 136; D. Barthélemy, 'Kinship', in P. Ariès and G. Duby (eds), *A history of private life*, trans. Arthur Goldhammer, London 1988, ii. 85–153 at pp. 115–22.

23 *Westminster abbey charters*, no. 436.

24 *Mon.*, iii. 519.

25 *Historia Sancti Petri Gloucestriae*, i. 33, 258; *Gesta abbatum*, i. 55; *Mon.*, ii. 220; *Chron. Ramsey*, 276–7, 318–19; *Cart. Ramsey*, i. 155–8; *Regesta*, ii, no. 1766.

mothers as donors, or in confirming their charters.[26] Conversely, the *pro anima* requests of husband-and-wife joint donations are characterised by the concern for the donors' own souls rather than for the deceased's.

Benefactors, if they made more than one gift or confirmation, did not always enter the same parties in their petitions. Changes in personal circumstance and in status must have influenced petitions, as did the death of spouses and close family. Bernard de Baillol gave at least three donation charters to Rievaulx: one petitions for salvation for his father, mother and brothers; another makes requests for the souls of King Henry and Bernard's uncle, Joscelin; a third appeals on behalf of the souls of King Henry, Bernard's kin, father, mother, Joscelin his uncle, his own soul and, finally, the soul of his wife, Agnes.[27] Elsewhere, confirming a grant to Whitby abbey, Bernard made his request for the souls of his father, mother, brother Guy, his sister Hawise, and all his kin.[28] Those outside the family group such as the royal family, overlords and friends, are also less frequently mentioned. The souls of kings, queens and their kin, were more frequently petitioned for in donations to 'new' foundations, rather than the established Benedictine houses. Presumably this was the consequence of seeking royal sanction for the establishment of new foundations. Thus people were evidently not chosen at random or solely because the donor felt he or she had a duty to do so. Not everyone included their parents, or even themselves, in requests. Such requests were the result of a mixture of family duty, personal feelings and feudal ties.

The diversity in the composition of requests indicates that religious patronage was a transaction to be negotiated like any other transfer of property. Gift-giving was, in essence, both a spiritual and a social contract, whose terms varied according to the status of the donor and the value of the donation. Founders of new monasteries were in a position to dictate, at length if they so wished, whomsoever they wanted to be included in their requests for 'the salvation' of souls. Walter Espec's foundation charter for Rievaulx, in Yorkshire, catalogues ten individuals, or groups of people, to whom the foundation is dedicated.[29] Hugh of Chester's foundation charter for St Werburgh, Chester, lists more than twelve people, or groups of people, whose souls the monastery was meant to benefit.[30] Even a non-founder could command an

---

[26] For an example of this see Susan Johns, 'The wives and widows of the earls of Chester, 1100–1252: the charter evidence', *Haskins Society Journal* vii (1997), 117–32 at p. 124.

[27] *Cartularium abbathiae de Rievalle*, ed. J. C. Atkinson (Surtees Society lxxxiii, 1889), i. 66, 67, 155.

[28] *Cartularium abbathiae de Whitby*, ed. J. C. Atkinson (Surtees Society lxix, lxxii, 1879–81), i. 55.

[29] *Cart. Rievalle*, 16–21. Walter's charter reads 'for the love of God, and the salvation of the soul of William, king of the English, and Henry, king of the English, and all his kin, and for the salvation of my father's soul, and of my mother's, and for the soul of Hugh *Wildecher* and for the soul of my wife's mother and father and all our kin and ancestors'.

[30] *Cart. Chester*, 16. Hugh's charter reads, 'for the advantage of the souls of King William, and William his father the most noble king, and his mother Matilda the queen, and his

impressive list such as the aforementioned Bernard de Baillol who made a request for seven people.[31] By confirming their predecessor's grants, heirs of donors were perpetuating the relationship with the house and sharing in the merit attained by the original donor.[32] In the last decade of the eleventh century William II de Warenne confirmed and augmented his father's endowment of St Pancras, Lewes. In his charter he declared that 'now I have received a share and association in the alms of my father and myself and all who have added, or shall have [. . .] that they might have, such reward from God as we hope to have'.[33] Desire for prayers in Hugh of Chester's charter of 1093 to St Werburgh's was central to his personal motivation. His charter affirmed that 'the authority and example of the holy fathers of the Church counselling us to commemorate the benefactions of contemporaries for the benefit of posterity, increase of prayers for the souls of the benefactors of the blessed church, and provision of models for men tending heavenward at the present day'.[34] For the author of the Battle chronicle, the 'fame of the virtue and holiness of God's servants at Battle' was closely linked with the activities of the monks of the abbey 'heaping up a great hoard of grace, freely for all'.[35] In other words, spiritual benefits were freely available to the abbey's friends and benefactors.

Pro anima requests for designated individuals meant that those people were to be prayed for in a non-specific way, as part of the collective crowd of 'benefactors'.[36] To secure personalised prayers one had to specifically request such spiritual privileges. Requests for masses or prayers for specified deceased people occur relatively infrequently in the sources. Hugh de Lacy was granted by the monks of Gloucester, 'the society and benefit of their house, with prayers to be made for him just as for themselves'.[37] Richard de Lestre restored certain property to the monks of Montacute on the understanding that his father's *obit* was to be observed at Cluny and Montacute and the monks were to 'sing twenty trentals of masses and one hundred psalters for the soul of his

---

brothers and sisters, and King Edward, that for the salvation of their souls, and for the souls of his father, mother, and ancestors, and heirs, and kin, and barons and all Christians alive and deceased'.

31 *Cart. Rievalle*, 155.

32 For the continuing relationship between a donor's family and continental houses see White, *Custom, kinship and gifts to saints*, 33; Rosenwein, *To be the neighbor*, 124, 132; Bouchard, *Sword, miter and cloister*, 150.

33 *Chartulary of the priory of St Pancras of Lewes*, ed. L. F. Salzman (Sussex Record Society xxxviii, xl, 1933–5), i. 19.

34 *Cart. Chester*, i. 15; *Mon.*, v. 111–13. William Peverel's foundation charter for the Cluniac priory of Lenton in Nottinghamshire states that he 'granted whatever his vassals should bestow on it for the benefit of their souls'. Roger the Poitevin's charter of 1094 refers to potential donors 'desir[ing] the prayers and benefits of the priory of Lancaster': CDF, no. 665.

35 *Chron. Battle*, 90.

36 Tabuteau, *Transfers of property*, 15.

37 *Historia Sancti Petri Gloucestriae*, i. 326.

father, Jordan'.[38] Others made provision for the future. Hawise, the wife of Ralph de Limésy, granted her husband's foundation of Hertford priory part of her dower lands 'on condition that upon her death an additional monk should be received into the priory to pray for her and her husband's souls, and his office was to be continued for ever'.[39] At St Pancras, Lewes, Alfred de Benedeville requested that two monks, one for himself and one for his wife, should pray for their souls.[40] Gregorius Ganet, chaplain of Huntingdon, made a donation to Thorney abbey which was 'for my anniversary to be celebrated each year'.[41] Geoffrey I de Trailly wanted a monk at Thorney to 'say a mass for his soul on the anniversary of his death'.[42] He also referred to the grant of 'fraternity or society' to himself and his family. The possibility of receiving the grant of 'fraternity', or 'society', was an important consideration for potential donors.[43] Charters periodically refer to the fact that benefactors were received into the 'fraternity' or 'fellowship' of a monastery.[44] An indispensable source of information for entrance into fraternity are *libri vitae*, or confraternity lists,[45] although the identification of the individuals entered in these lists is problematical as the majority of entries are simply single given names e.g. 'Roger, William, Robert, Nigel'. Fraternity lists survive for only a handful of monasteries – Durham, Hyde near Winchester, Lincoln cathedral, St Albans, Thorney abbey and Christ Church, Canterbury[46] – but this does not rule out the possibility that other houses also possessed them. Thus a charter of Hugh, earl of Chester, refers to a Book of Commemoration (in *Libro Commemorationum*) at Abingdon, wherein the names of his family were to be inscribed:[47] such a book has not survived to the present day. On the other hand, the fact that certain houses make no mention of a *liber vitae* of any sort does not mean one did not exist: the accounts of the donations made to St Albans make no reference to a fraternity list but one unquestionably existed, as a copy survives.[48]

For the ceremonial admission of lay people to confraternity, a gospel book

---

38 *Two cartularies of the Augustinian priory of Bruton and the Cluniac priory of Montacute*, ed. F. W. Weaver and C. H. Maxwell Lyte (Somerset Records Society viii, 1894), 168. H. E. J. Cowdrey has pointed out that Cluny 'carried a share in the prayers and alms not only of the mother-house but also of all its dependent houses': 'Unions and confraternities with Cluny', *Journal of Ecclesiastical History* xvi (1965), 152–62 at p. 160.

39 *Mon.*, iii. 300.

40 *Chart. Lewes*, i. 74.

41 CUL, MSS Add. 3020–1, fo. 41r.

42 Ibid. fo. 414v.

43 For counter-gifts in general see Tabuteau, *Transfers of property*, 115–19.

44 For fraternity at Rochester see Tsurushima, 'Fraternity of Rochester cathedral priory', 313–37. The scribe of the *Textus Roff.* uses the both the terms 'fraternity' and 'society'.

45 For English *libri vitae* see ch. 7.

46 See introduction.

47 *Chron. Abingdon*, ii. 20.

48 BL, MS Cotton Nero D vii, fos 118r–27v. The rubric reads 'the names of the laity received into fraternity'.

was 'instrumental'.[49] Lanfranc's *Monastic constitutions* set out the ritual by which a lay person was to be admitted to the 'society and benefit' of a house:

> If the applicant be a secular, and a distinguished person, he shall sit before or by the abbot, and when his request has been made known to the brethren he shall receive 'society' by taking into his hand a book of the gospels. Then he shall go round receiving the kiss of peace, which is not given when the applicant is a woman.[50]

References to the kiss of peace occur infrequently in the sources, but when Bernard fitz Aluin of Dunwich received the confraternity of Eye priory in the mid twelfth century, it is stated that 'he received the kiss of peace'.[51] When Ingelrann was received into the fraternity of Thorney abbey it was upon the *textum evangelii*.[52] As Ingelran was also granting land to Thorney his knife, as a token, was placed upon the altar in the church. It has been pointed out elsewhere that 'texts' and 'gospel-books' were also regularly used as tokens for secular transactions.[53] In the 1130s Haimo Peverel and his wife, Sibyl, confirmed the village of Kinnersley to Shrewsbury abbey 'in token thereof, [by] plac[ing] the gospels on the altar of the abbey'.[54] The public ceremonies which accompanied the donation of a gift were important occasions laden with symbolic meaning which acted to reaffirm the religious community's ties with neighbouring landholders.[55] Knives were 'the favourite symbols of conveyance in the Anglo-Norman period' and this was certainly true where religious houses were concerned.[56] In 1096 William Rufus had given a donation of land to Tavistock abbey by token of an ivory knife which was preserved in the shrine of St Rumon.[57] It may have been customary for the knives used in such ceremonies to be broken in order to detach them from their worldly function. When William fitz Baderon made his grant to Mon-

---

49 Clark, 'British Library additional MS. 40,000', 50–68, at p. 56. Cowdrey points out that at Cluny a layman received confraternity by ceremonially taking a copy of the Rule: 'Unions and confraternities with Cluny', 157. For symbolism used in formal ceremonies see J. Le Goff, *Time, work and culture in the Middle Ages*, trans. Arthur Goldhammer, Chicago 1980, 237–87.

50 *The monastic constitutions of Lanfranc*, ed. D. Knowles, London 1951, 114–15.

51 *Eye priory cartulary and charters*, ed. V. Brown (Suffolk Records Society xii, 1992), i. 251.

52 CUL, MSS Add. 3020–1, fos 414r–15r. For the use of symbolic objects in ceremonial transfers of property see Clanchy, *Memory to written record*, 254–60.

53 Clark, 'British Library additional MS. 40,000', 26n. For symbolism in general see Clanchy, *Memory to written record*, 20, 204–5, 229, 232.

54 *The cartulary of Shrewsbury abbey*, ed. U. Rees, Aberystwyth 1975, i. 28.

55 For the ceremony of land donation as a social event see Rosenwein, *To be the neighbor*, 48; Bouchard, *Sword, miter and cloister*, 150; White, *Custom, kinship and gifts to saints*, 37–9.

56 Clanchy, *Memory to written record*, 39. For examples of the use of symbolic objects see *Historia Sancti Petri Gloucestriae*, ii. 74; *Textus Roff.*, fos 185v, 194v; *Gesta abbatum*, i. 78–9; BL, MS Cotton Claudius D x, fo. 175r; *Chron. Ramsey*, 240–1; CUL, MSS Add. 3020–1, fos 415r, 416r.

57 *Mon.*, ii. 497.

mouth priory, Bernard, the king's chaplain, 'could not break the knife with his hands and so broke it beneath his foot instead'.[58] By renouncing, irrevocably, an object's normal use by breaking or 'killing' it, it was presumably dispatched from the physical to the spiritual world.[59] Thus, these broken knives were devoted to their intended supernatural purpose in much the same way that medieval pilgrims' badges were deliberately folded.[60] It is no coincidence, then, that the two surviving examples of English donation knives, given to Durham and Hatfield Regis, are both broken.[61]

Periodically, the ceremony of placing the gift on an altar in the church was referred to in the sources without identifying any token.[62] It was also common practice to offer charters at an altar.[63] The types of tokens employed in comparable transactions on the continent were more diverse in nature,[64] but in England there are relatively few references to any tokens other than knives being employed. Exceptions included Bernard fitz Aluin of Dunwich, who made his grant to Eye priory 'upon the altar by means of a staff',[65] and when William d'Aubigny *pincerna* gave his foundation of Wymondham, in Norfolk, the manor of Happisburgh, also in Norfolk, the donation 'was confirmed by the delivery of a silver cross, filled with relics which, with a gold ring and a silver cup for the eucharist, which he offered on the altar of the church'.[66] Sometimes the choice of token was made with the purpose of the gift in mind. When in 1090 Gilbert fitz Richard made a grant to Stoke priory, 'for the lighting of the church [and . . .] in token of this he placed a candlestick on the altar'.[67] Gifts were periodically assigned to a specific function such as funding the construction of a new abbey church, the illumination of the church, for the monks' provisions or even as endowment for the abbey *scriptorium*.[68]

---

[58] CDF, no. 1138. For discussion of this case see Clanchy, *Memory to written record*, 258–9.

[59] R. Merrifield, *The archaeology of ritual and magic*, London 1987, 112.

[60] Merrifield remarked that only a minority of objects ritually deposited seem to have been treated in this way, 'perhaps as a token of the intention of the rest': ibid.

[61] The Durham knife is discussed by Clanchy, *Memory to written record*, 38–40, 258, 311. The Hatfield Regis knife is referred to by Le Goff, *Time, work and culture*, 283.

[62] CUL, MSS Add. 3020–1, fos 418v, 419r, 420r; *Cart. Eye*, i. 123.

[63] Clanchy, *Memory to written record*, 156. Tabuteau points out that a symbolic object would also be placed 'in the hands of' the head or a member of the recipient community. In post-Conquest England this tended to occur when a religious community was granting property to a layman: *Transfers of property*, 121. For the placing of gifts on the saint's altar see Hudson, *Land, law and lordship*, 230.

[64] For the diversity of tokens used on the continent see Le Goff, *Time, work and culture*, 354–7.

[65] *Cart. Eye*, i. 251.

[66] *Mon.*, iii. 331.

[67] *Cart. Stoke by Clare*, i. 116.

[68] See, for example, *Chart. Burton.*, 50; *Historia Sancti Petri Gloucestriae*, ii. 22; i. 110–11. 50; *Cart. Bruton and Montacute*, 143; *Gesta abbatum*, i. 55; *Mon.*, ii. For the library at St Albans see R. W. Hunt, 'The library of the abbey of St Albans', in M. B. Parkes and A. G. Watson (eds), *Medieval scribes, manuscripts and libraries*, London 1978, 251–77.

The donation ceremony could take place on more than one occasion and in more than one location.[69] In 1100 Harold of Ewyas presented his donation upon the altar of St Peter in the chapter house at Gloucester, and again after 1105 'into the hand' of Bishop Bernard of St David's in the chapter house at Ewyas.[70] William de Tosny, son of the founder of Belvoir priory, confirmed his parents' donations to St Albans, first in the abbey chapter house and then on the altars of SS Alban and Mary when he made an additional grant.[71] Such action was a means of reiterating the relationship between the donor's family, the gift and the religious community.[72] The people who attended these events were not there by accident or by chance. Analysis of witness lists, where people can be identified, usually reveals a combination of abbey officials, the kin of the donor and landholders whose lands lay in the vicinity of the donated property.[73] Witnesses were a vital and indispensable means of validating rights to property, especially when any of the original participants died. Geoffrey of St-Calais, custodian of Battle abbey, had one eye on the future security of his abbey's possessions when he set in place the practice of 'during external business [. . . taking] care that not only the older brothers, but also the younger, should be present'.[74]

It has been pointed out by Stephen White that 'given the transcendent, as well as the practical import of gifts [. . .] the times for making them were not chosen randomly'.[75] He suggests that in south-western France 'the timing of some transactions may well have been linked to the liturgical calendar'.[76] In post-Conquest England the date when a donation was made was rarely noted, but at St Mary's, Abingdon, three donations took place on feasts associated with the Virgin.[77] Other donations were made at Easter, on St Leonard's day, and another was made on an unspecified but 'specially chosen day'.[78] Special occasions were seen as appropriate moments to make formal donations to religious houses. Such occasions could be the dedication of an abbey church, the entrance of the donor or kinsman to the abbey as a monk, and at funerals. Saer de Quincy made a grant of 10s. *per annum* to the priory of Little Dunmow when it was consecrated in 1104.[79] Henry I gave St Albans the manor of Biscot, in Bedfordshire, at the dedication of the church in 1115.[80] When William de Roville elected to make his donation, which secured his and his

69 For continental parallels see White, *Custom, kinship and gifts to saints*, 33.
70 *Historia Sancti Petri Gloucestriae*, i. 286.
71 Mon., iii. 288–9.
72 White, *Custom, kinship and gifts to saints*, 33.
73 English documents do not include the *laudatio parentum* clauses which were common in eleventh-century donation charters in western France.
74 *Chron. Battle*, 110.
75 White, *Custom, kinship and gifts to saints*, 31.
76 Ibid. 33.
77 *Chron. Abingdon*, ii. 141, 144–5.
78 Ibid. ii. 32, 100, 108.
79 Mon., vi. 145.
80 *Gesta abbatum*, i. 68; *Regesta*, ii, no. 1102.

wife's burial at Eye, he also gave his son, Rainald, to become a monk.[81] Entrance into a religious house as a monk was not so much a fitting occasion for a donation, as in practice as good as compulsory.[82] There are numerous examples of gifts being made to monasteries on the entrance of a relative or the donor himself. Walter de Lacy was given to Gloucester at the age of seven because of his parents' professed dedication to 'religion and the monastic way of life'.[83] In 1126 Richard fitz Nigel gave Gloucester his mill at Wotton under Edge, in Gloucestershire, when his two sons, William and Turstin, entered the abbey.[84] Godwin fitz Edith gave half a *mansum* to Rochester when his son became a monk.[85] Furthermore, entrance to an institution, *ad succurrendum*, also secured burial in the church cemetery for such people as Hugh de Port who entered Winchester abbey shortly before his death.[86] Death and burial provided another liminal moment deemed especially appropriate for donations. The occasion of the funeral of Matilda, wife of William d'Aubigny *pincerna*, prompted him to make some very generous gifts to Wymondham.[87] Robert of Bampton, son of Walter of Douai, made various grants to Bath abbey on the day of his father's burial there.[88] On 27 March 1085, after Walter de Lacy had been buried in the chapter house of Gloucester abbey, 'then, his wife Ermelina gave land to the same church, for the salvation of her husband's soul'.[89]

Many donors actually preferred to plan ahead and arrange for burial in the abbey cemetery well in advance.[90] At Cluny, confraternity brought with it to those who lived in a suitably accessible place the right to be buried in the lands of St Peter.[91] Durand of Butterwick granted land to Whitby 'for our bodies, and for our souls, and for the salvation of our friends'.[92] The burial choice of kin cemented links between a religious house and that family.[93] William de Roville and his wife Beatrix made a generous grant to Eye priory,

---

81 *Cart. Eye*, i. 123.
82 For discussion of monastic recruitment and entry-gifts see J. Lynch, *Simoniacal entry into religious life from 1100 to 1260: a social, economic and legal study*, Columbus 1976, 17–18, 27–36, 49–50. For entry-gifts see Tabuteau, *Transfers of property*, 16; Bouchard, *Sword, miter and cloister*, 52–3, 59, 64.
83 *Historia Sancti Petri Gloucestriae*, i. 15.
84 Ibid. i. 118; ii. 89.
85 *Textus Roff.*, fo. 192v.
86 *Historia Sancti Petri Gloucestriae*, i. 93. For conversions in later life see Bouchard, *Sword, miter and cloister*, 56–8.
87 *Mon.*, iii. 330–1.
88 *Two chartularies of the priory of St Peter at Bath*, ed. W. Hunt (Somerset Record Society vii, 1893), 39.
89 *Historia Sancti Petri Gloucestriae*, i. 73.
90 For a discussion of burial patterns and procedures see Golding, 'Anglo-Norman knightly burials', 35–48.
91 Cowdrey, 'Unions and confraternities with Cluny', 160.
92 *Cart. Whitby*, 176.
93 Golding, 'Anglo-Norman knightly burials', 37.

'so that they may be buried there with others of their relatives who already lie there'.[94] Burials also 'ensured that the family maintained an interest in the house and continued to make endowments'.[95] Matilda de St-Liz, daughter of Robert fitz Richard, gave land to the priory of St Neots 'for the salvation of my soul and my father's, whose body is buried there'.[96] Nigel d'Aubigny gave Eastwell, in Kent, to St Albans for his burial there, although he was eventually buried at Le Bec.[97] Several benefactors were clearly aware of the possibility that they might not die in England. Robert de Tosny, founder of Belvoir priory, arranged that 'if he should die in England' he was to be buried at St Albans or Belvoir.[98] Likewise, in the early years of the twelfth century a charter of Peter de Valognes, founder of Binham priory, settled that should his knights 'die in England, [they] are to be buried at Binham'.[99] It was all very well for wealthy magnates like Hugh de Grandmesnil and Eudo *dapifer* to have their bodies transported across the Channel, in either direction, but for many Normans the cost would have been prohibitive.[100]

Monastic writers did their best to warn laymen against postponing benefactions, as the potential donor 'knows not whether tomorrow will be propitious'.[101] Yet there were those who waited until a personal crisis such as approaching death, or fear of death, acted as a spur to their generosity.[102] Roger of Gloucester made a grant to Gloucester abbey while he lay dying at the seige of Falaise.[103] Wulfeva and Godfrey fitz Elinard both made donations on their deathbeds to Stoke by Clare priory.[104] Guy fitz Tezon had given a church to St Neots priory on 'the day that [he] ended his life'.[105] The anxiety caused by his approaching demise inspired Eudo *dapifer* to lavish additional gifts on his foundation of Colchester.[106] When in 1118 Nigel d'Aubigny lay dangerously ill, believing himself to be dying, he wrote to Henry I begging him to confirm the possessions he had restored to various religious houses.[107] On an earlier occasion when Nigel had been very ill he had written to the bishop of Durham, Ranulf Flambard, asking for intercession and pardon and

---

94   *Cart. Eye*, i. 123.
95   Golding, 'Anglo-Norman knightly burials', 37.
96   *Mon.*, iii. 473.
97   *Cha. Mowbray*, 6–7; *Regesta*, ii, no. 1161.
98   *Mon.*, iii. 289.
99   Ibid. iii. 345; *Regesta*, ii, no. 828.
100 OV iv. 336; *Mon.*, iv. 608–9.
101 *Chron. Battle*, 94.
102 For generosity inspired by personal crisis see White, *Custom, kinship and gifts to saints*, 33; Bouchard, *Sword, miter and cloister*, 190–2.
103 *Historia Sancti Petri Gloucestriae*, i. 69.
104 *Cart. Stoke by Clare*, i. 119.
105 *Mon.*, iii. 473.
106 Ibid. iv. 607–9. This additional gift was presumably also meant to compensate for burial costs.
107 Southern, *Medieval humanism*, 220–1; Greenway, *Cha. Mowbray*, 6–7. Nigel also wrote to his brother William, in more detail, requesting the same: ibid. 7–10.

he restored a manor to Durham.[108] Serious illness was also partly responsible for the transformation of Robert d'Oilly from Abingdon abbey's adversary to its stalwart supporter and benefactor.[109] His affliction was accompanied by a particularly vivid and foul nightmare which was sufficiently frightening to make Robert penitent.

The medical skills of some Benedictine monks were effective in securing donations from grateful patients and their families.[110] The fact that Baldwin, abbot of Bury St Edmunds, was in turn physician to Edward the Confessor, William the Conqueror and William Rufus, goes some way towards explaining the grants the kings bestowed on his abbey.[111] Likewise Faritius, abbot of Abingdon, who attended Queen Matilda at the birth of her first child, was held in royal favour and secured donations from other patients such as Robert fitz Haimo in 1107, Miles Crispin c. 1105 and Geoffrey de Vere, whom the abbot had personally nursed for three months.[112] It is reasonable to presume that in such cases fear and gratitude intermingled. Women, too, were not immune to the catalyst of illness and the fear of death, and what that might entail for their souls. Adeliza d'Ivry, widow of Roger d'Ivry, had been suffering from an incurable illness and gave Abingdon abbey a hide at Fencot, in Oxfordshire, 'for her eternal salvation'. Adeliza was probably another patient of Abbot Faritius.[113] Agnes, wife of Bernard de Neufmarché, made a benefaction to Brecon priory when she 'chanced to be taken ill'.[114] Hugolina, wife of Picot of Cambridge, whilst gravely ill made a vow that if she recovered she would found a house in honour of St Giles.[115] She miraculously recovered and, with her husband, in 1092 dedicated the church of St Giles, in Cambridge.

Vows to saints, or to God, made in moments of crisis were responsible for a range of spiritual acts such as pilgrimages, crusades, donations to saints' shrines and the foundation of religious houses.[116] It was traditionally held that William the Conqueror's post-Conquest grants to St-Valéry-sur-Somme and the foundation of Battle abbey resulted from vows made before and

---

[108] Ibid. 10.

[109] Chron. Abingdon, 12–15, 24–6.

[110] For the practice of medicine by Benedictine monks in post-Conquest England see Anne F. Dawtry, 'The modus medendi and the Benedictine order in Anglo-Norman England', in W. J. Sheils (ed.), The Church and healing (Studies in Church History xix, 1982), 25–38; C. H. Talbot and E. A. Hammond (eds), The medical practitioners in medieval England, London 1965.

[111] Dawtry, 'Modus medendi', 27–8; Talbot and Hammond, Medieval practitioners, 19–20, 29, 45–6, 66, 90.

[112] Chron. Abingdon, ii. 50, 57, 96, 97; Talbot, Medieval practitioners, 45–6.

[113] Chron. Abingdon, ii. 72.

[114] Chron. Battle, 88. According to Gerald of Wales she was the daughter of Richard fitz Osbern and his wife Nest, the daughter of Gruffydd ap Llywelyn: The journey through Wales and the description of Wales, ed. Lewis Thorpe, London 1978, 88–9.

[115] Liber memorandorum de Bernewelle, 38–9.

[116] For pilgrimages see Sumption, Pilgrimage.

during his 1066 campaign.[117] The foundation of Battle probably acted as penance for the bloodshed of 1066 and was bound up with the Penitential Ordinances of 1070.[118] The intervention of the saints was another motivating force for religious benefactions.[119] William the Conqueror, for example, is recorded as having shown appropriate respect for at least four English saints, St Cuthbert, St Æthelreda, St Edmund and St Modwenna.[120] He also made donations to the guardians of these saints at Bury St Edmunds and Burton.[121] Infertility drove Robert fitz Haimo and his wife to make a pilgrimage to the shrine of St Bernigius at Glastonbury.[122] There Robert promised the saint land worth 100s. if the saint gave them an heir. Although, Robert's wife quickly became pregnant they supposedly cheated the saint of the promised land and consequently his wife gave birth to a succession of daughters. On the day of the birth of Robert of Essex's son, Henry, Robert made a gift to Thetford priory.[123] Gunnora, his wife, also made a donation 'for the joy of the birth of her son Henry'.

Assessing the potency of saints' cults for attracting pilgrims and donations to their shrines is made difficult by the nebulous and uneven nature of the surviving evidence. The writing of saints' *vitae* and miracle collections may only denote a concern to preserve ancient traditions in writing. Such documents in reality probably only represent the tip of the iceberg as far as cults are concerned. For example, the *Liber Eliensis* contains numerous post-Conquest miracles performed by St Æthelreda and her companions at Ely, yet with only one exception there is no direct evidence of any donations having been made to the abbey. In contrast, at Bury St Edmunds the sources portray an energetic and widespread cult which appealed to Normans and English alike with attendant donations. Cults were also cultivated at Christ Church, Canterbury, for St Dunstan, for St Ives and St Botulph at Thorney,

---

117 Bates, *William the Conqueror*, 141, 150–1; The *'Carmen de Hastingae proelio' of Guy Bishop of Amiens*, ed. C. Morton and H. Muntz, Oxford 1972, 6; E. M. Hallam, 'Monasteries as "war memorials": Battle abbey and La Victoire', in W. J. Sheils (ed.), *The Church and war* (Studies in Church History xx, 1983), 47–57.

118 For these ordinances see H. E. J. Cowdrey, 'Bishop Ermenfrid of Sion and the penitential ordinance following the Battle of Hastings', *Journal of Ecclesiastical History* xx (1969), 225–42. Eustace fitz John was said to have founded Watton priory in Yorkshire in repentance for his part in the Battle of the Standard: Binns, *Dedications*, 175.

119 For saints' cults in general see P. Brown, *The cult of saints*, London 1981; P. Geary, *Furta sacra: theft of relics in the central Middle Ages*, Princeton 1978, and 'Sacred commodities: the circulation of medieval relics', in A. Appadurai (ed.), *The social life of things*, Cambridge 1986, 141–68; B. Ward, *Miracles and the medieval mind*, London 1982; R. C. Finucane, *Miracles and pilgrims: popular beliefs in medieval England*, London 1977; S. Wilson (ed.), *Saints and their cults*, Cambridge 1983.

120 For William's treatment of these saints and their communities see Ridyard, *'Condigna veneratio'*, 187–9; *Feudal documents*, 13; VCH, *Staffordshire*, iii. 200–1.

121 *Feudal Documents*, 13.

122 Holt, 'Feudal society and the family, 1–25 at p. 3.

123 *Mon.*, v. 142.

and rather less impressively for St Augustine and St Mildreth at Canterbury.[124] Saints' *vitae* and miracle collections were produced for these saints and also for the likes of St Odulf and St Wistan at Evesham and St Aldhelm at Malmesbury.[125] William of Malmesbury was also commissioned to translate a *vita* of St Wulfstan into Latin for the monks of Worcester, and to write the *vitae* of four early Glastonbury saints, while Osbert of Clare wrote a *vita* of St Eadburg for Pershore abbey.[126] Walter of Caen, abbot of Evesham, sent the relics of St Ecgwin on a fund-raising tour to finance the rebuilding of the abbey church.[127] It appears elsewhere that some members of religious communities acted as professional fund-raisers. For example, Arnold, monk of St-Evroult and brother of Robert of Rhuddlan, 'was entirely devoted to the needs of his church for whose sake he often crossed the Channel'.[128]

So far motivation for religious patronage has been discussed here only in terms of numerous individual cases. An attempt needs to be made to identify broader patterns of patronage in England and so make a comparison with continental trends. Georges Duby remarked that in the medieval west the flow of donations to religious institutions went through several phases of unequal flow, intensity and direction.[129] Constance Bouchard has reinforced this notion by commenting that Burgundian nobles did not always support local churches 'either uniformly or consistently'.[130] The height of their gift-giving came in the late tenth and early eleventh centuries, but 'the zeal of the donors waned in the second half of the eleventh century'.[131] Duby attributes this to two changes in attitudes towards religious patronage. The first was a new perspective on salvation which came to attach greater value to other 'good works' such as pilgrimages and helping travellers; as these were more difficult than simple donation, they were consequently more likely to earn salvation. The second was the movement of retrenchment by the aristocracy who were increasingly concerned to protect their landed inheritance. Their gifts subsequently became smaller and more infrequent. Bouchard also argues that in the twelfth century, in contrast to the eleventh, 'the great lords were largely replaced by members of the lesser nobility as the principal supporters of monasticism'.[132] Yet, Duby argues, 'the flow of gifts of lands had not entirely dried up, it had merely been diverted' to new orders like the

---

[124] For these cults see chs 6, 7 and also *Memorials of St Dunstan*; Ramsay and Sparks, 'The cult of St Dunstan', 311–23; *Felix's life of St Guthlac*, 11–12.

[125] *Chron. Evesham*, appendix; D. W. Rollason, *The search for St Wigstan*, Leicester 1981; William of Malmesbury, *De gestis pontificum*, 330–443.

[126] *Early history of Glastonbury*, 3.

[127] *Chron. Evesham*, 55.

[128] OV iv. 142.

[129] G. Duby, *Rural economy and country life in the medieval west*, trans. C. Postan, London 1968, 174.

[130] Bouchard, *Sword, miter and cloister*, 43.

[131] Duby, *Rural economy*, 174.

[132] Bouchard, *Sword, miter and cloister*, 132.

Cistercians, Carthusians and the military orders, the Knights Templar and the Hospitallars. Bouchard ties these two phenomenon together by maintaining that 'the Cistercian houses were patronised especially by knights, that is, new men'.[133] She also points out that 'though some families patronised the same houses generation after generation, it was possible for a family to change its allegiance in its support of monastic houses. The wealthier families might make gifts to a large number of houses, even though a less wealthy family might patronise only one or two houses.'[134] Towards the end of the twelfth century the support of multiple houses became increasingly common, but such families tended to choose foundations from the same order such as the Cluniac or Cistercian.

Elsewhere in discussing the vitality of the Benedictine order in the late eleventh and twelfth centuries it has been acknowledged that although donations to Benedictine houses from the laity continued to roll in, the truly sizeable gifts from kings and princes had 'probably peaked already in the eleventh-century'.[135] Penelope Johnson has traced the fluctuations in the flow of patronage received by La Trinité, Vendôme, and also noted changes in the status of donors.[136] The local supporters of the abbey in its early days, in the mid eleventh century, came from a wide range of social and economic groups. During the latter part of the eleventh century the abbey's supporting group shifted to become almost exclusively noble and by the twelfth century the abbey's benefactors 'came to be drawn almost entirely' from the area surrounding the abbey. At Le Bec, feudal ties also influenced patterns of patronage, as in 1077 the vassals of William de Vernon followed their overlord's generous example and made grants to the abbey.[137]

In England, for at least a generation, the Conquest created many social and political conditions that were not to be found on the continent. Yet very broadly speaking the shape and complexion of patronage corresponded with continental forms. The post-Conquest patronage received by the English monasteries was similarly neither uniform nor consistent. Furthermore, the earliest founders of religious houses in post-Conquest England were the richest men of the realm, whereas in the reign of William Rufus and especially in the reign of Henry I, founders and benefactors of religious houses were increasingly drawn from the knightly class. The *Textus Roffensis*, compiled in the early twelfth century, bears witness to the broad range of social status from which the benefactors of Rochester cathedral priory were drawn. Accompanying this shift in the status of donors came a change in the nature of gifts, as sizeable grants of land became rare, displaced by gifts of tithes,

133 Ibid. 133.
134 Ibid. 138.
135 Van Engen, ' "Crisis of cenobitism" reconsidered', 269–304 at p. 277.
136 Johnson, *Prayer, patronage and power*, 85–6.
137 V. Gazeau, 'L'aristocration autour du Bec au tournant de l'année 1077', *Anglo-Norman Studies* vii (1985), 89–103 at p. 92.

churches, mills and much smaller parcels of land. As on the continent, the late eleventh and early twelfth centuries in England saw the donation of churches and tithes to monasteries, inspired by changes in opinion fostered by the reform movement. The gifts which attended the foundation of new houses were almost exclusively of this modest type. Some English abbeys seem to have attracted particular types of gifts, for example St Albans specialised in receiving and nurturing priories and cells, while Gloucester received a number of Welsh churches, as well as churches in Buckinghamshire and Oxfordshire; yet other English abbeys, such as Bury St Edmunds and St Augustine's, Canterbury, are not recorded as having been given any churches at all.

The establishment of new foundations would also produce the phenomenon of local tenants 'rally[ing] round with grants' as Richard Mortimer noticed in the case of Stoke by Clare, Suffolk, with the Clare tenants.[138] For new honorial foundations, such as Eye, Chester, Bridlington and Lewes, patronage was drawn almost exclusively from the area surrounding the abbey. In contrast, particularly in the case of the richer English abbeys, another pattern of patronage overlaid this localised framework. The most apparent was the patronage that the king and the royal family granted. This transcended community patterns, in much the same way as did the donations received by the great continental houses such as Cluny and Le Bec. Another overlapping form of patronage was the granting of gifts by men of national importance who were often, but not always, closely involved with the royal government. Abbeys such as Abingdon appear to have actively sought reciprocal relationships with the royal officials they came in contact with. As far as considerations of the family were concerned, these influenced the profile of patronage in England as much as they did on the continent. This was something that could work within the local community or beyond, depending on the wealth and status of the family. Patterns of familial networks for gift-giving can be seen in England, for example the patronage of St Albans which spread throughout the branches of the d'Aubigny family tree. The role of women, acting as conductors of religious enthusiasm, also mirrored continental trends.

Towards the end of this period, however, the heir of a benefactor or founder was just as likely to found one or two of his own religious houses as to add to his predecessor's grants. The fashion for patronising several houses in England differs in essence from the continental practice in that it occurred much earlier and took a different form. Men like Eustace fitz John and Walter Espec, who began their careers in the reign of Henry I, between them founded Augustinian, Gilbertine, Premonstratensian and Cistercian houses

---

[138] R. Mortimer, 'Land and service: the tenants of the honour of Clare', ibid. (1986), 177–97 at p. 195. See also ch. 10.

as well as patronising Benedictine, Augustinian and Cistercian houses.[139] Before 1140 the Clare family endowed houses at St Neots and Stoke by Clare, established cells at Ceredigion, founded Tintern and Bourne and developed the priory of Little Dunmow; they were also patrons of Le Bec, Lewes and Gloucester.[140] The trend is one of diversification rather than straightforward diversion. Families such as the Clares were becoming increasingly interested in the new orders, but in the reign of Henry I, at least for the time being, Benedictine houses like Gloucester, Abingdon and St Albans were far from neglected, thereby giving weight to van Engen's assertion that 'a new vision of religious perfection need not require the decadence of the other; two or more may flourish in the same era [. . . and] the twelfth-century, especially the first half, marked the high point of Benedictine expansion'.[141]

Patronage of numerous religious orders was by no means unusual in the first third of the twelfth century, and was becoming increasingly common as the choice of orders grew.[142] Knightly families spread their interests as far and as wide as possible. Depending on the size of individual fortunes they founded or patronised as many different orders as they could.[143] Thus, although the

---

[139] Eustace founded Gilbertine convents at Watton and Malton, Alnwick for Premonstratensian canons and the Augustinian house of North Ferriby, as well as being a benefactor of Bridlington, Fountains, Gloucester, St Peter's hospital, York, St Mary, York, and Norton priory; Walter Espec founded the Augustinian house of Kirkham and the Cistercian house of Rievaulx. Brian Golding remarks upon the 'eclectic piety' of the earliest Norman founders and benefactors in England: 'The coming of the Cluniacs', Anglo-Norman Studies iii (1981), 65–77 at p. 67. Richard Mortimer has discussed the support of multiple foundations from different orders in late twelfth-century England: 'Religious and secular motives for some English monastic foundations', in D. Baker (ed.), Religious motivation (Studies in Church History xv, 1978), 77–85. For the Gilbertines see Brian Golding's new book which, unfortunately, came out too late for me to incorporate its findings fully in my book: Gilbert of Sempringham and the Gilbertine order: c. 1130–c. 1300, Oxford 1995.

[140] Ward, 'Fashions in monastic endowment', 427–51 at pp. 442, 430, 438.

[141] Ward points out that the Clares still supported Benedictine and Cluniac houses in the first half of the twelfth century: ibid. 438. See also remarks made by Van Engen, ' "Crisis of cenobitism" reconsidered', 274, 277.

[142] For remarks on the introduction and spread of new orders in twelfth-century England and Wales see Knowles, Monastic order, 171, 227–66; Dickinson, Austin canons; D. Postles, 'The Austin canons in English towns, c. 1100–1350', Historical Research lxvi (1993), 1–20; D. M. Robinson, The geography of Augustinian settlement in medieval England and Wales, Oxford 1980; J. Herbert, 'The transformation of hermitages into Augustinian priories in twelfth century England', in Sheils, Monks, hermits and the ascetic tradition, 131–45; R. A. Donkin, The Cistercians, Toronto, 1978, and 'The growth and distribution of the Cistercian order', Studia Monastica ix (1967), 275–86; D. H. Williams, An atlas of Cistercian lands in Wales, Cardiff 1990; C. J. Holdsworth, 'The Cistercians in Devon', in Harper-Bill and others, Studies presented to R. Allen Brown, 179–92; Bethell, 'Foundation of Fountains abbey', 11–27; S. F. Hockey, Quarr abbey and its lands, 1132–1631, Leicester 1970; Hill, English Cistercian monasteries.

[143] For a discussion of the connection between the emergence of new social groups and the development of new social institutions in Verona see Miller, 'Donors, their gifts and religious innovation', 27–42.

personal sentiments working behind religious patronage were seemingly universal, the timing and preferences of men and women in post-Conquest England did not exactly mirror trends on the continent. Perhaps the early support for multiple orders reflects the complexity of tenurial conditions in England, prompting benefactors to spread their generosity according to political dictates. It may also suggest that people in the first half of the twelfth century were hedging their 'spiritual' bets, eager to support new forms of the religious life, whilst still supporting the ancient established houses.

10

Structures of Lordship
and the Politics of Choice

In order to understand more completely the fate of the Old English monasteries after 1066 their collective experiences need to be set in the context of the new patterns of religious patronage that came into being in post-Conquest England. This chapter will investigate the structured context within which the individual decisions about patronage discussed in the previous chapter were made. It will be argued that the extent and nature of patronage given to new foundations was influenced by the structure of feudal lordship in post-Conquest England. The practical reasons that determined where a benefactor made a gift will be considered, in particular whether patterns of gift-giving can also tell us which lord benefactors identified their interests most closely with. Finally, the consequences of the emergence of this tenurial geography for the Old English houses will be examined.

The location of many of the monasteries founded by the Norman newcomers was, at least initially, determined by the methods of colonisation they employed. New religious houses were commonly established at the principal residence on a founder's estate, the *caput*, frequently accompanying castles.[1] Before the turn of the century Arundel, Belvoir, Dunster, Eye, Lewes, Montacute, Pontefact, Totnes and Tutbury had both castles and monasteries. John Le Patourel has observed that 'the combination of the castle, monastery and borough, or of two of these elements, formed one of the chief instruments of Norman colonisation in Britain'.[2] Religious patronage in post-Conquest England was never uniform in its character, but it was common for the generosity of the king and his tenants-in-chief to be copied by their tenants.[3] This has already been illustrated with the example of St Peter's, Gloucester, and to some extent with St Albans and Canterbury. This founder–tenant link can be detected amongst the benefactors of most new foundations in post-Conquest England. A cursory list of such instances could include Castle Acre, Chester, Huntingdon, Lenton, Lewes, Northampton, Pontefract, Shrewsbury, Stoke by Clare, Tewkesbury, Thetford and St Mary's, York.

[1] For the impact of castles on the structure of lordship in post-Conquest England see Richard Eales, 'Royal power and castles in Norman England', in Harper-Bill and Harvey, *Ideals and practice*, iii. 49–78.
[2] Le Patourel, *Norman empire*, 317.
[3] D. C. Douglas showed that the Norman barons followed the example of the duke during the monastic revival of the mid eleventh century: *William the Conqueror: the Norman impact on England*, London 1964, 105–18.

Until the turn of the eleventh century seigneurial foundations were comparatively few in number but impressive in their ability to attract grants from their founders' tenants. An examination of their geographical position reveals that their establishment was an integral part of the process of colonisation and consolidation in post-Conquest England, their location far from being random. In southern England these honorial-type foundations were situated on the peripheries of the kingdom. There were two main reasons for this. The first was that most other regions of southern England were already adequately served by English monasteries. The second was that by virtue of their position houses such as Lewes, founded in 1077 on the south coast, and Chester and Shrewsbury, founded in the reign of William Rufus near the Welsh border, were performing an important role in the process of control and settlement. The strategic position of St Peter's, Gloucester, also explains the Lacy family's involvement with that house in the late eleventh century.[4]

Not all lordships were conveniently provided with an honorial-type foundation. In northern England, which was more politically volatile than the south, the situation was very different. There were no English Benedictine foundations in operation in Yorkshire at the time of the Conquest,[5] and only a handful of new houses were established in the last decades of the eleventh century, which meant that the choice of recipient houses for patronage was limited. The Conqueror's reign saw the establishment of three foundations in the region: Selby, Whitby (founded by William de Percy before 1077), and St Mary's, York (founded by Alan I of Richmond before 1086). In the early years of Rufus' reign two further houses were established in York: the hospital of St Peter by William Rufus, and Holy Trinity by Ralph Paynel. Ilbert de Lacy founded the chapel of St Clement in Pontefract castle and around the year 1090 his son, Robert, founded the Cluniac priory of St John, Pontefract.[6] Count Alan of Richmond's foundation of St Mary's, York, not only received numerous grants from the men of the honor of Richmond but also from many of the other Yorkshire tenants-in-chief and their tenants. A list of such men includes Hugh fitz Baldric, Berengar de Tosny, Ilbert de Lacy, Gilbert de Gant, Osbert d'Arches, Geoffrey de la Guerche, Robert de Brus, Walter d'Aincourt, Gilbert Tison, Ralph Paynel, Stephen count of Aumâle, Robert de Stuteville, Bernard de Baillol, Nigel Fossard, Ivo Taillebois, Waltheof fitz Gospatric, Nigel d'Aubigny and Eustace fitz John.[7]

In the second decade of Henry I's reign the number of religious houses in

---

4 See ch. 3.
5 For monasticism in northern England in this period see J. E. Burton, 'Monasteries and parish churches in eleventh and twelfth century Yorkshire', *Northern History* xxiii (1987), 39–50; R. K. Rose, 'Cumbrian society and the Anglo-Norman Church', in Mews, *Religion and national identity*, 119–35.
6 Binns, *Dedications*, 85, 89, 91, 109; Mason, 'Pro statu et incolumiate regni mei', 99–117 at p. 107; Wightman, *Lacy family*, 61.
7 For example *Mon.*, iii. 548–54; *EYC* i. 266, 350, 354, 367, 395, 467, 473, 488; ii. 33, 37, 137, 379, 512; iii. 26, 29, 485. See also *Cha. Mowbray*.

Yorkshire slowly began to catch up with the rest of England with the foundation of a number of Augustinian priories: Bridlington, Nostell, Kirkham and Guisborough.[8] Later in the reign of Henry I other Augustinian priories were also established at Bolton and Woodkirk.[9] Alien priories were only established in the first two decades of the twelfth century – at Allerton Mauleverer and Burstall.[10] In the 1130s the Cistercian houses of Fountains, Rievaulx and the Savignac Byland were founded. The relatively sparse distribution of religious houses in Yorkshire meant that, at least until the mid twelfth century, those houses that were in existence received substantial support from the great lords of the region.[11]

Tenant patronage of lords' foundations points to a close relationship with the honorial community.[12] Lordship acted as a channel for lay piety and was associated with relatively small complexes of lands as well as with the great earldoms and honors. In the case of smaller lordships the number of potential tenant–benefactors for the lord's foundation was going to be fewer and the forces at work motivating donations weaker. Consequently the numbers of available tenant–benefactors for houses such as Belvoir, Wymondham and Binham were much smaller than those for Lewes, Chester and Stoke by Clare. Conversely, the relatively compact nature of the honors of Pontefract, Richmond, Chester and Shrewsbury explains the impressive extent to which the honorial barons supported their overlords' new foundations.[13] Indeed, the differing tenurial structures of the two honors of Shrewsbury and Chester explain the different patterns of patronage shown by their tenants. The honorial community which Hugh created found in the abbey of St Werburgh, Chester, a 'focal point for its loyalty to him and an expression of its cohesion as a group'.[14] Shrewsbury was tenurially less monolithic and the abbey tended to attract grants principally from those men whose interests were most closely associated with the earl and the honor, men such as Warin the sheriff, Rainald the sheriff, Robert fitz Tetbald and Roger Corbet.[15] Richard Mortimer has suggested that the foundation of Stoke by Clare served, perhaps deliberately,

---

8 Binns, *Dedications*, 123, 134, 138, 146. For the distribution of the new Augustinian foundations see Robinson, *Geography of Augustinian settlement*.

9 Binns, *Dedications*, 122, 157.

10 Ibid. 93, 95.

11 For the social status of the benefactors of Fountains in the mid twelfth century see Wardrop, *Fountains abbey*, 133 and chs iii, iv, v.

12 Many words were used in the eleventh and twelfth centuries for a complex of estates, including barony, honor and fee. 'Honor' is being used here as a convenient shorthand for these various alternatives and 'honorial community' refers to the tenants of a particular honor. See also D. Crouch, *The image of aristocracy in Britain, 1000–1300*, London 1992, 109.

13 For Chester see G. Barraclough, 'The earldom and county palatine of Chester', *Transactions of the History Society of Lancashire and Cheshire* ciii (1951–2), 23–57.

14 C. P. Lewis, *The Welsh Borders 1042–1087: a regional history of the Norman Conquest*, forthcoming.

15 *Cart. Shrewsbury abbey*, p. xiv, nos 34, 35; *Mon.*, iii. 513, 518.

to 'help concentrate [tenants' . . .] loyalty on their Clare connection'.[16] The dispersed nature of many honors and tenants with divided lordship meant that in many cases the patronage of a particular foundation demonstrated the association of a tenant's interest with the honor as well as being a mark of allegiance to the lord himself.

For Sir Frank Stenton post-Conquest society was one in which the honor was all-important, functioning as a 'feudal state in miniature'.[17] Stenton's depiction of the honor as an 'enclosed world' has been challenged and modified by scholars such as Marjorie Chibnall, David Crouch, Paul Dalton and Richard Mortimer,[18] whose work has emphasised the composite nature of the honorial baronage as a significant number of men held of several lords not one. Thus, 'honorial integrity was never absolute in England',[19] and dispersed honors and allegiances made for 'a maze of local interests and allegiances'.[20] The nature of the post-Conquest settlement ensured that the honorial baron with split allegiance was more common in England than in Normandy,[21] a situation of which contemporaries were well aware. The author of the *Leges Henrici primi* recognised the difficulties that arose when men were tenants of several lords or held lands remote from the administrative centre of the honor.[22] The text stated that 'if a man holds of several lords and honors, then however much he may hold of others, he owes more to him [. . .] of whose liege man he is'.[23] The *Cartae baronum* of 1166 shows that it was common for men such as Haimo Pecche, William Blund and Ralph Pirot to owe knight service to more than one lord.[24]

The fact that networks of religious affiliation did not coincide exactly with tenurial landholding patterns is also significant. Not all tenants patronised their lords' foundations. Men who held of more than one honor did not patronise all the religious foundations associated with those honors. The

---

16 Mortimer, 'Land and service', 195.

17 F. M. Stenton, *The first century of English feudalism 1066–1135*, Oxford 1932, 50.

18 Chibnall, *Anglo-Norman England*, 173; Mortimer, 'Land and service', 195, and 'Beginnings of the honour of Clare', 137; P. Dalton, *Conquest, anarchy and lordship, 1066–1154*, Cambridge 1994, 249–56. See also D. Carpenter, 'Debate: bastard feudalism revised: comment 2', *Past and Present* cxxxi (1991), 177–89 at p. 189; B. English, *The Lords of Holderness*, Oxford 1979, 156; J. Hudson, 'Milsom's legal structure: interpreting twelfth century law', *Tijdschrift Voor Rechtsgeschiedenis: The Legal History Review* lix (1991), 47–66 at p. 64, and *Land, law and lordship*, Oxford 1994; J. Boussard, *Le gouvernement d'Henri II Plantagenêt*, Paris 1956; C. P. Lewis, 'The formation of the honor of Chester 1066–1100', in *The earldom of Chester and its charters*, ed. A. T. Thacker (Journal of Chester Archaeological Society lxxi, 1991), 59–61.

19 David Crouch, 'Debate: bastard feudalism revised', *Past and Present* cxxvii (1991), 165–77 at p. 170.

20 Mortimer ,'Beginnings of the honor of Clare', 138.

21 Crouch, *Beaumont twins*, 131.

22 Carpenter, 'Debate: bastard feudalism revised', 185.

23 *Leges Henrici primi*, ed. L. J. Downer, Oxford 1972, 173.

24 Carpenter has also noted that this general situation provided many knights with 'a certain independence' from the honor: 'Debate: bastard feudalism revised', 189.

dispersed nature of many honors and the abundance of tenants with divided lordship meant that the threat of tenants patronising 'rival' honorial foundations was all too real. Richard Mortimer has shown how some Clare tenants in Suffolk also patronised Bury St Edmunds, whilst making donations to Dunmow priory in Essex and Merton and Waverley priories in Surrey.[25] When deciding which overlord's foundation to patronise many factors needed to be considered. Not simply the matter of from whom the most land was held, but where that land was in relation to the *caput* of the honor and the honorial foundation, and, in turn, where the money was coming from to finance donations.

Baronial officials were usually reliable patrons of their overlords' foundations, in Normandy as well as in England. Ralph, *pincerna* of Ilbert de Lacy, was a benefactor of Ilbert's foundation of St Clement's, Pontefract.[26] Robert fitz Tetbald was Roger of Montgomery's sheriff of Arundel and tenant in Sussex and Shropshire, holding lands worth just over £16 in 1086. He was a benefactor of Roger's foundation of Shrewsbury, but also of William de Warenne's foundation of Lewes in Sussex,[27] and did not become a benefactor of Sées, a house associated with the Montgomerys, until he was 'dreading the pains of hell' on his deathbed.[28] Other baronial officials too did not give exclusively to their lords' foundations. Alvred, *pincerna* of Count Robert and Count William of Mortain, was a benefactor of Robert's foundation of Grestain, William's foundation of Montacute in Somerset and St Albans, where Robert had been a benefactor with his wife Almodis, and where Robert's daughter Mabel was buried.[29] Alvred made a grant to Lewes priory with a number of other Mortain tenants,[30] but he was also a benefactor of Shaftesbury abbey when his daughter entered that house as a novice.[31] William fitz Nigel, constable of Chester, was a generous benefactor to St Werburgh's, Chester,[32] but he clearly had interests elsewhere as he was also a benefactor of Bridlington, which was founded by his brother-in-law, and Nostell, as well as of the monasteries of Westminster and Gloucester.[33] He also founded an Augustinian priory at Runcorn near his castle of Halton, in Cheshire, c. 1115 which he generously endowed with the help of two of his own tenants.[34]

---

25 Mortimer, 'Land and service', 195–6.
26 VCH, *Yorkshire*, ii. 165.
27 Robert fitz Tetbald was styled 'Robert of Arundel' in the confirmation charter granted to Lewes's mother house, Cluny: *CDF*, no. 1391.
28 Ibid. no. 655.
29 BL, MS Cotton Otho D iii, fo. 73r.
30 *Mon.*, v. 3; *Chart. Lewes*, i. 75.
31 Cooke, 'Donors and daughters', 29–45 at p. 36.
32 *Cart. Chester*, i. 40, 57, 233.
33 *EYC* xii. 143; *Mon.*, vi. 286; vi. 92; *Regesta*, ii, no. 1882; *Historia Sancti Petri Gloucestriae*, i. 105, 242.
34 *VCH, Cheshire*, iii. 165; Binns, *Dedications*, 145. For William's foundation see W. Beaumont, *A history of the castle of Halton and the priory or abbey of Norton*, Warrington 1873; J. P. Greene, *Norton priory: the archaeology of a medieval religious house*, Cambridge 1989.

The men who made up the bulk of the benefactors of the honorial foundations were of modest means and usually tenants solely of that overlord. For such barons there were strong forces at work which propelled potential patronage towards the religious foundation associated with the lordship or honor. In Sir Frank Stenton's list of the leading men of the honor of Peak four of his sole tenants of the honor, or their sons, were benefactors of William Peverel's foundation of Lenton.[35] The only baron with significant extrahonorial interests to patronise Lenton was Robert de Pavilly.[36] The tenants of the honor of Richmond who patronised their overlord's foundation of St Mary, York, held their lands almost exclusively of Count Alan.[37] Ensiant Musard, Ribald the count's brother, Robert de Mosters, Hervey, Ansketil, Odo the chamberlain and Wihomarc held lands both within and outside Yorkshire exclusively from Alan.[38] In the honor of Chester, where the leading barons' interests were divided between Cheshire and the rest of the honor, St Werburgh's was patronised by 'all the main honorial barons and one or two of the barons' own men'.[39] This was largely because of all the major barons of the honor, only Walter de Vernon held lands from another lord.[40] Honorial integrity was, therefore, instrumental in securing the scale of donations received by houses such as Lewes, Stoke by Clare and Chester. The scale and scope of such tenant donations has important implications for evaluating the existence and strength of any particular honorial community.

It is not clear how much actual 'choice' was available to many tenants. Persuasion and example are unknown quantities in deciding the criteria for giving gifts. Furthermore, from the language used in documentary sources, it is rarely obvious whence the initiative for the donations originally came – lord or tenant. In some foundation charters lords explicitly encouraged generosity from as many of their tenants as possible, whilst being careful to limit how much property they gave away.[41] According to the Stoke by Clare cartulary during a donation ceremony Gilbert fitz Richard, lord of Clare, candidly asked his tenants to give generously themselves: 'imploringly he ordered his barons to give to the church as much as they liked from their lands, churches

---

[35] Stenton, *English feudalism*, 98. These tenants were Robert de Heriz, Warner, Sasfrid and Payn. Benefactors of Lenton included Robert de Heriz, Geoffrey de Heriz, Robert fitz Warner, Sasfrid, Robert fitz Payn: Farrer, *Honors and knights' fees*, i. 148, 168, 171, 181.

[36] Ibid. i. 192.

[37] *EYC* v. 38, 124, 177, 181, 284–5, 306.

[38] *VCH, Yorkshire*, ii. 157–60.

[39] Lewis, 'Formation of the honor of Chester', 55, 59. For St Werburgh's and the earldom and honor of Chester see also R. V. H. Burne, *The monks of Chester: a history of St Werburgh's abbey*, London 1962; B. M. C. Husain, *Cheshire under the Norman earls, 1066–1237*, Chester 1973.

[40] Lewis, 'Formation of the honor of Chester', 60. Walter de Vernon was also a benefactor of St Werburgh's: *Cart. Chester*, i. 21.

[41] For this phenomenon in eleventh-century Normandy see Tabuteau, *Transfers of property*, 180–3.

or tithes without disinheriting their heirs'.[42] In 1094 Roger the Poitevin conceded that if anyone wished for the prayers and benefits of his foundation of the priory of Lancaster he might give as much as half his land and those without an heir who wished to give all their lands and enter the priory as monks had his blessing.[43] Similarly, Hugh, earl of Chester, and his wife encouraged their men to follow their example and give liberally to the new foundation at St Werburgh's.[44] Tenants were allowed to give lands not exceeding 100s. in annual value and enjoined to bequeath their bodies for burial in the abbey accompanied by *post obit* gifts of a third of their goods. At least eighteen of Hugh's tenants followed his advice.[45]

Lordship was, therefore, manipulated to procure 'donations' from tenants for chosen foundations. Robert Malet's foundation charter to Eye priory leaves little doubt as to the force of the lord's persuasion, addressing 'the other men, knights and sokemen of his jurisdiction he grants and commands that they shall make gifts to his monastery of Eye according to their resources'.[46] Lords could grant tenants' rights 'from under them' to their new foundations. It has been observed by John Blair in his work on Surrey that tenants-in-chief 'do not seem to have been barred from alienating the tithes of subinfeudated manors'.[47] John Blair has illustrated this phenomenon with the example of Gilbert de Clare who granted the demesne tithe of Salford, in Surrey, to Lewes priory. Gilbert's father, Richard de Clare, had enfeoffed Robert de Watteville with this manor sometime before 1086, yet the grant to Lewes was accredited to Gilbert de Clare, Robert's overlord.[48]

This was not an isolated instance of tenants having little 'choice' in the location or timing of their so-called generosity. Bartholomew de Glanvill gave to his father's foundation of Bromholm, in Norfolk, two parts of five of his men's tithes and the whole tithe of two others.[49] The Yorkshire tenants of the Lacy family conveniently switched their attention successively from St Clement's, Pontefract, to St John's, Pontefract, and then to Nostell, as and when the Lacys established each foundation. This would seem to suggest that either they were very supportive of their lord's new projects or that they did not have much actual choice in the matter. Wealthy undertenants also used this device to pad out their gifts. Herbert fitz Helgot granted to Shrewsbury abbey the vill of Norton and the church of Stanton 'with all his tithes, and [those] of all his knights and every thing that pertains to that church'.[50]

---

42 *Cart. Stoke by Clare*, i. 116.
43 CDF, no. 665.
44 *Cart. Chester*, i, p. lxxix, 17; VCH, *Cheshire*, iii. 133.
45 *Cart. Chester*, i. 18–21.
46 *Cart. Eye*, i. 16.
47 John Blair, *Early medieval Surrey*, Stroud 1991, 148.
48 Idem, 'Surrey endowments of Lewes priory before 1200', *Surrey Archaeological Collections* lxxii (1980), 97–126 at pp. 103–4.
49 *Mon.*, v. 63.
50 Ibid. iii. 519.

There are several examples of blocks of tenants entered in charters who gave similar quantities of tithes or other gifts to their lord's foundation. It is difficult to ascertain how much co-operation there was on the part of the tenants in these transactions. There are two considerable blocks of such grants given by Roger Bigod's tenants to Thetford.[51] A copy of William Peverel's charter confirms to his foundation, Lenton priory, 'all [that] my men contributed for the health of their souls, namely two parts of the whole of their demesne and of all the tithes they possess'. This grant was made by no less than twenty of William's men.[52] Likewise at Castle Acre William II de Warenne's confirmation charter lists the names of nine men who are described as the earl's 'men [who] gave their tithes'.[53] At the laying of the foundation stone of Norwich cathedral priory Hubert de Ria gave two-thirds of the tithes from his demesne in Norfolk and 'many other folk gave two thirds of their demesne and a few gave a third to the aforesaid monastery'.[54] Ralph de Limésy's grant of Hertford as a cell to St Albans was apparently made 'with the praise of his men'.[55] Later in the same document Ralph made the grant of the 'tithes of his men' suggesting that the impetus actually came from Ralph.

Rights associated with burial could also be granted by overlords in this way. Tenants received genuine spiritual and social benefits in return for their tithes, even if the initiative was not all their own. It seems likely that burial or some form of fraternity with the monks or canons of a house was granted in exchange for grants of tithes far more frequently than the records would otherwise suggest. The *Textus Roffensis* lists countless instances of 'society' granted in return for tithes given to Rochester cathedral priory.[56] At Peterborough the abbey knights negotiated with the monastery for burial rights in return for which

> each and every knight shall give two portions of his tithes to the sacrist of Peterborough. Moreover at the end of his life, a third part of his whole property, with his knightly accoutrements both in horses and armour, shall be carried with him to the burial of the dead man and offered to God and St Peter.[57]

In a dispute with Thetford over the location of Roger Bigod's burial the bishop of Norwich produced witnesses to testify that Roger had given his body 'with those of his barons' to Norwich cathedral.[58]

---

[51] Ibid. v. 149.

[52] Ibid. v. 111.

[53] Ibid. v. 50.

[54] *The first register of Norwich cathedral priory*, ed. H. W. Saunders (Norfolk Records Society xi, 1939), 50–1.

[55] *Mon.*, iii. 299.

[56] *Textus Roff.*, fos 183v–91r.

[57] *Chron. Hugh Candidus*, 91.

[58] *Mon.*, v. 152. For this dispute see Golding, 'Anglo-Norman knightly burials', i. 35–48 at pp. 35–6.

In 1107 Peter de Valognes granted to his foundation of Binham two-thirds of his knights who held from him in Norfolk, 'with their consent'.[59] Peter also promised that if these said knights died in England they were to be buried at Binham and that house would receive the manors of which it already received the tithes. Regardless of where these men were buried they were to pay one mark each year to St Albans, Binham's mother-house. When tenants supposedly asked their overlord to grant their lands, or asked for a confirmation charter, the driving force may well at times have been the lord rather than the tenants. Varying degrees of acquiescence appear to be at play in particular series of grants. When William de Braose made a grant to Battle abbey 'on behalf of a knight of his named Hanselin' he also made a grant of his own and assented to the two grants from Ralph fitz Theodore, another knight of his, and 'his man', Tetbert, who entered that house as a monk.[60]

The motivation and degree of compulsion behind donations to honorial-type foundations can, therefore, only be hazarded. Blocks of grants of tithes may actually have been systematically granted by overlords. Their occurrence, however, should not be over-emphasised; they were not uncommon but they were not the norm either. Grants of land and other property, on the other hand, would probably have been of a more genuinely 'voluntary' nature. It should be stressed that in general the physical proximity of these new houses would have prompted many tenants to give quite willingly, for they would receive very real spiritual, social and political benefits from patronising monasteries close to their holdings. It would otherwise be difficult to account for the sheer scale of gifts to houses like Chester and Lewes. Furthermore, a man with local landed interests needed only to be generous locally. To patronise a more distant foundation without greater means or influence would have been senseless. Clearly, since not all tenants did patronise their lords' foundations, the amount of 'force' the exercise of seigniorial rights or lordship could bring to bear was never absolute. The structure of lordship meant that those who did not give tended to have stronger claims on them elsewhere or else that they just did not give at all.

It remains to make some general observations on the influence of the family upon the character of religious patronage in post-Conquest England. What can be observed is that the shape of an aristocratic family tree often corresponded with patterns of patronage, that parents' foundations were almost always faithfully looked after by their heirs. For example, St Neots, in Huntingdonshire, which was refounded by Richard de Clare in the late eleventh century, was endowed by the descendants of Richard and his wife, Rohaise.[61] Successive generations, however, were rarely as generous as the original founders largely because although the older establishments were

59 Mon., iii. 346.
60 Chron. Battle, 88–90.
61 Ward, 'Fashions in monastic endowments', 427–51.

still maintained, newer family foundations usually soaked up fresh grants.[62] Looking at the grants of the Gant and Brus families it is clear that the heirs of the founders of Bardney, Bridlington and Whitby continued to patronise their foundations at least for a generation.[63] What is also interesting is that children other than the heirs, i.e. brothers, brothers-in-law and occasionally sisters, were patrons of each others' foundations. Walter Espec's sister, brother-in-law and nephews, who patronised Walter's foundation of Rievaulx, were all co-heirs to Walter's lands.[64]

When grants came from grantors distantly related to the founder by marriage, such as from Eustace fitz John to Bridlington, the influence of that connection was probably fairly weak. Many northern families married into others with which they had similar interests. William fitz Nigel, the constable of Chester who married Agnes de Gant, already held from the Gants at Bessingby in Yorkshire.[65] Patterns of patronage were therefore closely related to patrimony, inheritance and tenure but such associations rarely stretched further than one generation unless an inheritance was involved.[66] New landed interests, whether acquired or inherited, usually meant pious interests were reorientated. Ranulf Meschin only became involved with his uncle's foundation of Chester after he had inherited his earldom, following the death of his cousin Richard in 1120.

The motivation behind religious patronage was always mixed; primarily governed by locality, lordship and tenurial status, it could also be influenced by ties of family or friendship, by shifts in fashion and by personal preferences and personalities. Yet it is clear that overall it was determined by the structure of contemporary society. The king had the greatest degree of autonomy in deciding where to bestow his grants and privileges. His tenants-in-chief were to some extent tied to promoting and maintaining their honorial foundations but they were free to patronise elsewhere. For many of the honorial tenants a sense of duty and loyalty was mixed with what feudal bonds would allow. Tenants were expected to support the honorial foundation just as much as were the founder and his heirs. Split allegiance meant that many tenants were legitimately afforded a form of 'choice', which was nevertheless still heavily influenced by ties of family and neighbourhood. Thus, for tenants the strength of attraction of a foundation was closely connected with the structure of tenure in the honor. The large, compact honors exerted the strongest 'pull' on their generosity.

The 'looseness' of the honor could also redound to the benefit of the Old

---

62 For a survey of the changing relationship between barons and religious houses in England see Emma Mason, *'Timeo barones et donas ferentes'*, in Baker, *Religious motivation*, 61–75.
63 For monastic patronage over the generations see remarks made by Johnson, *Prayer, patronage, and power*, 86; Bouchard, *Sword, miter and cloister*, 150.
64 *Cart. Rievalle*, 21–2, 30–1.
65 EYC ii. 428.
66 This broadly corresponds with the structure of the kinship group as revealed by the analysis of *pro anima* requests, which has been discussed separately in ch. 9.

English monasteries. The patronage of the Old English houses, which were not directly associated with the Anglo-Norman aristocracy, or their honors, was largely piecemeal in nature and mostly given by local men and royal officials, who usually had interests in the region. The English monasteries did not, as a rule, act as seigneurial monasteries in the way that Chester, Lewes and Clare did. This was primarily because the English houses had not been founded by the families of the new lords of the Norman Conquest and were therefore not part of any predetermined feudal grouping. There are a few cases which appear to have been exceptions to this rule: St Peter's, Gloucester, Rochester, which served a bishopric, St Augustine's, Canterbury, and St Albans. Of these examples only the latter's consistent association with members of the d'Aubigny family and their tenants approaches that of a truly seigneurial monastery.

Although the Norman Conquest had effectively swept away long-standing ties with the members of the local aristocracy, the Old English houses still had the advantage of royal protection. Those to which the king showed special interest, such as Bury, Gloucester and Abingdon, stood to profit greatly. The example of the king and queen encouraged gifts from many of those associated with the royal court and the governance of the realm. Another advantage many of the Old English houses had over the new foundations was the possession of miracle-working saints' relics. Although some founders of new communities had realised the value of 'recycling' ancient religious foundations, such as at Whitby, Bardney, Hackness and Lastingham, few save Reading and the refounded St Frideswide's, in Oxford, could boast of important relics.[67] Several generations later the cult of the martyred archbishop of Canterbury, Thomas Becket, was to illustrate just how effective a popular cult could be in attracting benefactors from far and wide, and from amongst the ranks of the great as well as the humble. Much of the fame of Becket's cult was due to the skilful promotion of the 1170s as the monks of Canterbury sent abstracts of his miracles to numerous prelates and religious houses in England and France.[68]

Thus the tenurial structure of post-Conquest England permitted the Old English monasteries periodically to transcend ties of local lordship, but it would be wrong to suggest that they were entirely unique in this. A number of the new foundations were also able to achieve national importance, attracting patronage from beyond the assured circle of their founders' tenants. Sometimes this was the consequence of a dearth of viable alternatives, or of royal initiative, or because the house was celebrated for its spiritual character; exceptionally, it might be due to possession of an acclaimed relic. It has

[67] See Brian Kemp, 'The miracles of the hand of St James', *Berkshire Archaeological Journal* lxv (1970), 1–19; Henry Mayr-Harting, 'The functions of a twelfth-century shrine: the miracles of St Frideswide', in Mayr-Harting and Moore, *Studies presented to R. H. C. Davis*, 193–206.
[68] For the reaction of other pilgrimage centres to Canterbury see Sumption, *Pilgrimage*, 152.

already been pointed out that northern England was a region which was sparsely endowed with religious foundations until well into the reign of Henry I. As a consequence, St Mary's, York, attracted a legion of benefactors; many were tenants of St Mary's founder, but there were also many others who were not. They were Yorkshire tenants-in-chief and their tenants. Direct royal interest in the establishment and fostering of monasticism elsewhere in Yorkshire also stimulated collective support from the barons.[69]

The spiritual reputation of William de Warenne's foundation at Lewes, the first and greatest Cluniac house in England, drew numerous grants not only from the tenants of Warenne's Rape of Lewes, but also from the tenants of the other Sussex Rapes, Pevensey and Hastings.[70] That was not all; gifts also came from numerous men of national and international importance who gave properties in Surrey, East Anglia, Essex and Cambridgeshire and even further away in Wiltshire and Dorset. Outside Sussex the house attracted grants from the Clares and their tenants, Stephen of Blois, count of Mortain, Rotrou of Perche, Robert of Essex and Ranulf the chancellor.[71] The other notable Cluniac foundation at Bermondsey, near London, also drew grants from a wide range of donors not associated with one particular lord or honor including William Rufus and Henry I.[72] In the case of Reading, many of the factors already mentioned came into play: its royal founder, the possession of the hand of St James and its function as the burial church of (most of) the remains of Henry I.[73]

Thus the structures of lordship in large part worked against the Old English houses in many areas of the realm. However, lordship in England was by no means monolithic and the decision-making process that lay behind religious patronage was always multi-faceted. The Benedictines could use their privileged positions in society, as the guardians of saints' relics, as bestowers of spiritual benefits, as landlords and friends to charm the continental newcomers into giving them their hearts, souls and, of course, their donations.

---

[69] See remarks on royal involvement in Yorkshire made by Anne F. Dawtry, 'Monasticism in Cheshire 1092–1300: a tale of mediocrity', in Judith Loades (ed.), *Monastic studies: the continuity of tradition*, Bangor 1990, 64–74 at p. 68.
[70] *Cart. Lewes*, i. 12–20, 30, 32–6, 38–40, 65, 72, 75, 119, 131–2, 154, 157–9, 175; Farrer, *Honors and knights' fees*, iii. 308–13. See also Stephen's confirmation charter for some these grants: *CDF*, no. 1391. See also Golding, 'The coming of the Cluniacs', 65–77.
[71] Blair, 'Surrey endowments', 113.
[72] *Mon.*, v. 96, 100; *Regesta*, i, nos 340, 362, 383, 398, 640, 659, 664–5, 1021, 1350, 1743, 1990. Donors included William Rufus, Henry I, Countess Mary of Boulogne, sister of Queen Matilda, Geoffrey Martel, Hadwise de Gournay, Hamelin and Winebald de Ballon, Hugh de Beauchamp, Hugh Maminot, Ivo de Grandmesnil, Nigel de Monville, Odo Tiron, *miles* of Winebald de Ballon, Richard Guet, brother of the countess of Warenne, Bishop Robert of Lincoln (1093–1123), Robert, earl of Leicester, Robert the chancellor and William de Belmeis.
[73] Benefactors included the Empress Matilda, Robert, earl of Leicester, Adeliza d'Ivry, Queen Adelaide and Robert de Ferrers: *Mon.*, iv. 40–2; *Regesta*, ii, nos 1448, 1471, 1506, 1757, 1789, 1796–7, 1862–4.

Tenurial structures were never so restricting that houses such as Thorney, Crowland and Evesham could not cultivate a rewarding relationship with their neighbouring landholders. Consequently the Old English houses, as a group, were able to ride out many of the dangerous waves set in motion by the Conquest. After all not only had the Norman Conquest enriched many continental families, but the late eleventh and twelfth centuries witnessed increasing numbers of people of lower status who were choosing to give donations to religious houses, so that although the Old English houses were faced with stiff new competition the pool of benefactors grew substantially. The success of the largely urban Augustinian canons in the reign of Henry I and of the predominately rural Cistercians, in the mid twelfth century, shows that there were still significant areas of untapped generosity.

11

Religious Patronage
and the Anglo-Norman Realm

It remains to place the experience of the Old English houses in the wider context of cross-Channel religious patronage.[1] First the general trends and elements in post-Conquest religious patronage need to be identified. I will argue that very soon after the Norman Conquest the basic shape of religious patronage was in place. This consisted of three main groups: a solid core of benefactors who faithfully patronised continental houses throughout this period; those who consistently patronised houses on both sides of the Channel; and a growing body of benefactors who patronised and founded monasteries in England which had no connections with the continent. In the reign of the Conqueror the continental newcomers preferred to patronise continental houses rather than English-based foundations, and this was reinforced by more alien priories being founded than any other type of house. In the reign of William Rufus, however, there was a clear shift towards the founding and patronage of religious houses in England that had no obvious connection with the continent. Identifying fluctuations in trends is complicated by the fact that the status of founders and donors was rapidly broadening before the end of the eleventh century. Thus the extended pool of benefactors increasingly incorporated more men and women whose interests would only be served by the founding and patronising of religious houses in England. A hard core of families maintained, and even augmented, their support for continental houses and alien priories throughout the seventy-year period, but in the reign of Henry I there was a massive increase in the number of new foundations established and patronage given to houses in England, most of which had no connection with continental houses.

In order to gain a more precise understanding of the scale and nature of gift-giving to religious houses on both sides of the English Channel, the timing of new foundations and instances of individual donations have been tabulated and analysed. The figures for the incidence of founding new religious houses in England have been obtained from *Heads of religious houses*[2] where the information recorded has the advantage of defined limits, as almost all new foundations are included, and usually dated to within several years, to

---

[1] For a brief analysis of trends in aristocratic foundations and patronage in the late eleventh and twelfth centuries see Chandler, 'Politics and piety', 63–71.
[2] Knowles, Brooke and London, *Heads of religious houses*.

the reign of one monarch, or at worst to one century. The methodology used computes the number of new foundations established, but not the size of their endowment. The question of size can be approached by comparing the endowments of some selected foundations with grants to continental houses.

The fact of founding a religious house was of more lasting importance to a family than how much property was granted; the forces at work behind the decision to establish a new foundation, although broadly comparable, were not entirely identical with those involved in making a donation. All forms of patronage tended to act as bonds between donor and recipient house, but the commitment involved in establishing a new community was much more enduring and also involved considerably greater supervision on the part of the founder. Making a donation was usually less expensive than founding a house, and benefactors could afford to make overtly political gestures with their donations that a founder would think long and hard before doing. By looking at the pattern of patronage bestowed by the monastic benefactors of the Anglo-Norman realm degrees of 'preference' can be established. The benefactor who gave grants to Norman houses but founded an abbey on his English lands was making very different judgements from a donor who only made grants to houses in Normandy.

The analysis of new foundations is then compared with the results of computations based on a survey of gift-giving. Grants made by more than 800 individuals have been collated and analysed in a survey which includes well over 1,000 instances of religious patronage bestowed on hundreds of English, Norman and continental houses, and is as near to systematic as the availability of printed sources will allow. The majority of primary source material for continental houses has yet to be edited and published; consequently the data in John Horace Round's *Calendar of documents preserved in France*, serves here as the main body of evidence for the continental figures.[3] Any inadequacies of that volume will be compensated for by reference to a number of individual case studies of continental houses in order to corroborate trends in patronage.[4] It has to be accepted that the inadequacies of the data, particularly on the Norman and continental side, make the conclusions suggested

[3] E. King, 'John Horace Round and "The calendar of documents preserved in France" ', *Anglo-Norman Studies* iv (1982), 93–103, 202–4.

[4] For the amount of land given to continental houses by 1086 see Ayton and Davies, 'Ecclesiastical wealth', 47–60; Knowles, *Monastic order*, 703; V. Gazeau, 'The effects of the Conquest of 1066 on Norman monasticism in the valley of the Risle: continuity or break?', in Bates and Curry, *England and Normandy*, 131–42; H. Cam, 'The English lands of the abbey of Saint-Riquier', *English Historical Review* xxxi (1916), 443–7; Y. Poncelet, 'Les possessions anglaises de l'abbaye de Saint-Wandrille', *Annales de Normandie* xxxvii (1987), 149–71; L. Musset, 'Les origines et le patrimoine de l'abbaye de Saint-Sever', in *La Normandie Bénédictine*, Lille 1967, 366, and 'Actes inédits du onzième siècle: les plus anciennes chartes de prieuré de Saint-Gabriel', *Bulletin de la Société de Antiquiares de Normandie* xi (1952–4), 124–9.

provisional. None the less, the material which I have used constitutes a sufficient collection of data to produce a credible impression of trends and a sense of the proportions involved over the seventy-year period.

Table 2
The establishment of new foundations in post-Conquest England

Type of new foundation	Foundation 1066–87	Foundation 1087–1100	Foundation 1100–35	Total
Independent houses	9	5	5	19
Dependent houses*	6	7	32	45
Alien priories (including Cistercians/ Cluniacs)	18	14	39	71
Augustinian	–	3	49	52
Nunneries	1	1	12	14
TOTAL	34	30	137	201

* Dependent houses founded in England include houses founded from Cluniac houses in England such as Castle Acre, Lewes and Montacute, as well as from Cistercian houses in England such as Furness and Waverley. Those founded directly from Cîteaux and Cluny are included in the alien foundations category.

New foundations

Out of a total of 201 new houses founded during the period between 1066 and 1135 only one-third was established in the eleventh century and the remaining two-thirds were initiated in the reign of Henry I (see table 2). The rate at which new foundations of all types were established in England escalated from an average of 1.6 *per annum* in the reign of the Conqueror, to 2.3 *per annum* under Rufus, and then accelerated to the impressive average of 3.9 a year in the reign of Henry I. This last figure illustrates the explosion in the numbers of new foundations set up in the reign of Henry I. This development also attests to the different opportunities for religious patronage in England and Normandy. Not only had the fact of the Conquest created new wealth, power and status for many families but the country's sheer size presented greater prospects for personal advancement and expansion, particularly in the early twelfth century.

In the reign of the Conqueror, new alien priories outnumbered new independent priories, or those dependent on English houses, by eighteen to sixteen.[5] In the reign of William Rufus fourteen new alien priories were established, compared with the fifteen independent or English priories founded. The number of alien priories founded in the reign of Henry I was outstripped by new independent or English houses; in fact, they constituted less than one-third of the total. Thus, by the early twelfth century the bias towards founding houses unconnected with the continent is very evident. Paradoxically, throughout this seventy-year period links with continental institutions were still being renewed by founders of religious houses in England. Indeed, there were more new alien foundations in the last fifteen years of Henry I's reign than in the first twenty. Eighteen alien priories were established in the years between 1100 and 1120, an average of 0.9 *per annum*, and twenty-two between 1120 and 1135, 1.47 *per annum*.

The changing proportions of Norman cells established in comparison with the cells founded from houses in other parts of France sheds light on the effect of the political crises that resonated through the Anglo-Norman realm. In the reign of the Conqueror twelve of the eighteen alien priories in England were established from Norman houses, the remainder from Cluny, St-Nicholas, Angers, St-Florent de Saumur and La Charité-sur-Loire. As England and Normandy were ruled by two bellicose brothers in the years 1087–96 and 1100–6 it might be expected that cross-Channel links, including cross-Channel patronage, would be lessened, and indeed the political division of England and Normandy after the death of the Conqueror and before Robert Curthose left for the Holy Land in 1096 does seem to be reflected in the pattern of the new priories founded. Robert Curthose's rule in Normandy was a difficult time for the Norman abbeys anyway and it is significant that only two of the seven alien priories established in this period were daughter-houses of Norman monasteries. First, Blyth, in Nottinghamshire, was founded in 1088 as a cell of La Trinité-du-Mont, Rouen, by Roger de Builli and Muriel his wife.[6] As Roger was known to be in attendance on William Rufus in 1088–9, and also a benefactor of Gloucester, it can be assumed that the choice of La Trinité had tacit royal sanction.[7] Then, around 1094, Roger the Poitevin founded Lancaster as a cell of St-Martin of Sées in southern Normandy,[8] probably as a result of having come into personal contact with that community, which was just over fifteen miles from Argentan.[9] The mother-houses of the other new foundations were La Charité-sur-Loire,

---

[5] According to Matthew's calculations forty foreign monasteries and cathedral chapters were established in England before 1087: *Norman monasteries*, 13–14. Frank Barlow cites thirty priories or cells for Norman monasteries and fourteen for abbeys neighbouring the duchy during the years 1066–1100: *English Church, 1066–1154*, 185.

[6] Binns, *Dedications*, 94.

[7] Barlow, *William Rufus*, 95.

[8] Sées, Orne, arr. Alençon, chef-lieu du canton: *CDF*, no. 665; Binns, *Dedications*, 100. For Roger of Poitou see V. Chandler, 'The last of the Montgomerys: Roger the Poitevin and Arnulf', *Historical Research* lxii (1989), 1–14; Lewis, 'The king and Eye', 569–87 at pp. 573–4.

[9] Roger's younger brother, Arnulf de Montgomery, was also a benefactor of Sées sometime

Marmoutier, St-Vincent of Le Mans and SS. Sergius and Bacchus, Angers, all outside Normandy.[10]

In the remaining years from 1096 until Rufus' death only a tiny number of new foundations were established in England. These were Eudo *dapifer's* foundation at Colchester, the cathedral priory at Norwich and Arnulf de Montgomery's cell of Sées, Pembroke.[11] Thus, in the reign of William Rufus, the shift away from the establishing of Norman alien priories indicates that potential founders, who were of Norman origin, had virtually ceased their activities, whilst those founders from other regions of France, such as Anjou, Maine and Burgundy, were still very active. No doubt this phenomenon was precipitated by the political crises.

It was in the reign of William Rufus that St Albans founded three, and probably even four, cells; five other houses in England also founded cells at this time.[12] It is interesting that William Rufus' two wealthiest supporters in 1088, Earl Hugh of Chester and William I de Warenne, or rather his son William II, both founded religious houses in this period. These men were exhibiting their commitment to Rufus by founding religious houses that had no direct connections with Normandy, as well as binding their tenants' interests and loyalty to themselves. Earl Hugh founded St Werburgh's, Chester, and William II de Warenne founded Castle Acre as a cell to his father's Cluniac foundation of Lewes.[13] The other founders of religious houses in the period were typically royal officials such as Picot of Cambridge who founded Barnwell, Hugh of Leicester who founded Daventry, Eustace de Lovetot who founded Huntingdon and William de Mohun who founded Dunster as a cell of Bath abbey. The status of this group was comparable with that of those who had founded alien priories, men such as Roger de Builli and Ralph Paynel who founded Holy Trinity, York, as a cell of Marmoutier. Both had been loyal to William Rufus in 1088.[14]

In the reign of Henry I large numbers of founders of Norman origin were active again as the balance swung back in favour of establishing cells of Norman monasteries. Twenty-eight Norman mother-houses established priories in England in comparison with the eleven founded by houses outside

---

between 1098 and his exile in 1102 and founded Pembroke as a priory of Sées in 1098: EYC iii. 27–8; Binns, *Dedications*, 103.

[10] The cells were Abergavenny, Castle Acre, Daventry, Pontefract, Totnes, Tywardreath and York.

[11] Binns, *Dedications*, 103.

[12] These were St Albans's cells at Binham, Hertford, Tynemouth and Wallingford which were founded in the time of Abbot Paul (1077–93). Other cells established were at Castle Acre (by Lewes), Dunster (by Bath), Exeter (by Battle), Eynsham (from Stow) and Westbury-on-Trym (by Worcester).

[13] For Lewes see Golding, 'The coming of the Cluniacs', 65–77; Marvin Clarke, 'The early endowment of Lewes priory: with special reference to its spiritual possessions c. 1077–c. 1200', unpubl. M.Phil. diss. Reading 1995.

[14] Barlow, *William Rufus*, 72, 95.

Normandy.[15] There was little difference in the relative proportions between the first half of Henry's reign and the second. Before 1120 thirteen Norman cells were founded compared with five from other parts of France. Between 1120 and 1135 fifteen Norman cells were founded compared with six from other parts of France. In the second half of Henry I's reign the majority of the Norman foundations were cells of Savigny.

The political division of England and Normandy in the years 1100–6 does not appear to have affected the rate at which alien priories were being established.[16] Men of Norman origins were once again in evidence as founders, establishing six Norman priories. Only three French cells were founded from Marmoutier and Cluny before 1106. With the exception of Walter Giffard, the men who were founders of the alien priories like Richard de Redvers, Robert de la Haye, William de Falaise, Manasser Arsic and Fulk Paynel did not rebel against Henry, even though they had stronger interests in Normandy.[17] It is not easy to pinpoint the difference between the years 1087–96, 1100 and 1106 which explains the change in the patterns of new foundations established in England. By the early years of the twelfth century it is clear that we are seeing the fruits of a changing world, where personal advancement was marked by founding religious houses. What is particularly significant about this list of founders is that none qualify for inclusion in F. W. Corbett's class 'A' category of families, whose assets were valued at more than £750 in Domesday Book.[18] Furthermore, as, except for Walter Giffard, none was directly involved in rebellion against Henry, they could reasonably expect to maintain possession of their lands on both sides of the Channel. Thus the early years of the twelfth century witnessed a visible shift in the behaviour of one particular section of the Anglo-Norman aristocracy. In William Rufus' reign potential founders with Norman interests ceased to be

---

15 These were Andwell (Tiron), Appuldurcombe (Montebourg), Arundel (Sées), Barnstaple (St-Martin-des-Champs), Basingwerk (Savigny), Beckford (Augustinian) (Ste-Barbe-en-Auge), Boxgrove (Lessay), Buildwas (Savigny), Burwell (La Grande-Sauvre, Bourdeaux), Byland (Savigny), Cogges (Fécamp), Combermere (Savigny), Furness (Savigny), Goldcliffe (Le Bec), Hamble (Tiron), Hatfield Regis (St-Melaine, Rennes), Horsham St Faith (Conches), Lenton (Cluny), Llangennith (St-Taurin, Evreux), Loders (Montebourg), Minting (St-Benoît-sur-Loire), Monk Sherborne (Cérisy-la-Forêt), Neath (Savigny), Newton Longville (Longueville), Quarr (Savigny), Rievaulx (Clairvaux), Sele (St-Florent, Saumur), Sporle (St-Florent, Saumur), St Cross (Tiron), St Dogmael (Tiron), Stogursey (Lonlay), Stratford Langthorne (Savigny), Thetford (Cluny), Tickford (Marmoutier), Tintern (L'Aumône), Wareham (Lyre), Warmington (Préaux), Waverley (L'Aumône) and Weedon Lois (St-Lucien, Beauvais).

16 Approximately ten in six years, i.e. 1.67 *per annum*. These were Appuldurcombe (Montebourg), Arundel (Sées), Boxgrove (Lessay), Cogges (Fécamp), Horsham St Faith (Conches), Lenton (Cluny), Stogursey (Lonlay), Thetford (Cluny), Tickford (Marmoutier), and, sometime before 1102, Newton Longville (Longueville).

17 For the monastic foundations of the Redvers family see Hockey, 'House of Redvers', 146–52.

18 Corbett, 'England 1087–1154', 521–53.

active, presumably adopting a wait-and-see stance. Yet, during the years 1100 to 1106 it appears that some members of the aristocracy in England recognised the necessity of buttressing the bonds that existed between their holdings on either side of the Channel by establishing Norman cells on their English lands.

In the years before the battle of Tinchebrai in 1106 the number of those new foundations unassociated with continental houses was comparable to the number of new alien priories.[19] The men responsible for the non-continental foundations were either directly involved in Henry I's government, such as Aubrey I de Vere and William de Pont de l'Arche, or had been loyal supporters of William Rufus, like Robert fitz Haimo, who fought in Henry's *familia* in 1106, Hugh de Lacy and Ranulf Meschin, *vicomte* of Bayeux and lord of Cumberland.[20] Being the founder of a priory with no affiliation to a continental house by no means constituted an indicator of a family's future allegiance to the English king. William, son of Geoffrey Baynard, who had founded the Augustinian priory of Little Dunmow in 1104, lost his lands in 1110 when he rebelled against Henry I.[21]

In the context of burgeoning religious benefactions the continuing growth in numbers of new alien priories looks somewhat modest. The incidence of religious patronage documents the enduring popularity of the Benedictine order, and particularly of those houses affiliated to Cluny. Although the Benedictines had lost their monopoly, they were still remarkably popular: twenty-seven new cells were established before 1100 and a further eighty in the reign of Henry I. Establishing only a tiny handful of new priories in the early 1090s, the Augustinians went on to establish forty-nine communities in the reign of Henry I.[22] Correspondingly, the early 1130s saw the first trickles of what was to become a torrent of new Savingnac and Cistercian foundations, with strong continental links.[23] Yet, right up to the time of the death of

---

[19] There were approximately ten such foundations: Tewkesbury, Cardiff (Tewkesbury), Cranborne (Tewkesbury), Earls Colne (Abingdon), Hereford (Gloucester), King's Lynn (Norwich), Thetford (Lewes) and Wetheral (St Mary's, York) and two Augustinian houses, Little Dunmow and Southwark.

[20] Green, *Government of England*, 24; Barlow, *William Rufus*, 358. Hugh de Lacy had received the lands of his exiled elder brother in 1096 after remaining loyal to Rufus.

[21] Sanders, *English baronies*, 129.

[22] The early houses were established at Barnwell, Colchester and Huntingdon. The others were at Bodmin, Bolton, Breamore, Bridlington, Brinkburn, Bruton, Caldwell, St Gregory's, Canterbury, Carlisle, Cirencester, Dover, Dunstable, Great Bricett, Guisborough, Haughmond, Hempton, Hexham, Ipswich, Kenilworth, Kirkham, Launceston, Launde, Leeds, Little Dunmow, Llanthony, St Aldgate's, London, Merton, Missendon, Norton, Nostell, Oseney, Oxford, Pentney, Plympton, Repton, Southwark, Southwick, St Osyth, St Bartholomew's, Smithfield, St Denys Southampton, Stone, Studley, Taunton, Thurgarton, Ulverscroft, Warter, Warwick, Wellow and Woodkirk.

[23] Waverley and Furness were founded in the 1120s and thirteen other Cistercian houses were established in the five years between 1130 and Henry I's death. Amongst this number there were eight Savignac daughter houses founded before 1135. The Savignacs were later

Henry I the volume of donations received by Benedictine houses completely outstripped those received by the Augustinians and Cistercian houses.[24] The loss of their religious monopoly may have generated competition from an unfamiliar direction but the Benedictines were more than equal to the challenge.[25]

These shifts in the pattern of new foundations were not solely the result of changing fashions and tastes but were also a reflection of the broadening social pool from which the founders were drawn. Analysis of the social status of donors in post-Conquest England shows a correspondence with the model of downward diffusion of cultural patterns through Anglo-Norman society.[26] The first post-Conquest foundations in England were those of great barons like Hugh d'Avranches, Roger de Montgomery, William de Warenne, Geoffrey de Mandeville and Richard fitz Gilbert. All these men chose to be buried in their foundations in England, apart from Geoffrey de Mandeville who requested burial at Westminster, where his first wife was already buried.[27] By the early twelfth century the typical founder of a new Augustinian or Benedictine priory was a royal official like Roger Bigod, Aubrey I de Vere, Robert II d'Oilly, Hugh of Leicester, Payn fitz John, Roger de Mowbray or Geoffrey Ridel. As the status of the founders changed to include knightly landholders and royal officials, taken as a group, the priorities of founders and their motivations for the establishment of a new priory altered. Consequently, these men and women whose preoccupations were often dominated by things British, showed no interest in founding alien priories. Indeed, in such a context to do so would have been nonsensical. Furthermore, Augustinian and Cistercian houses were relatively cheap to establish and managed to fill a niche that the Benedictines had seemingly left open. Whilst Augustinian establishments tended to be small, urban and insular in their nature, Cistercian houses were physically isolated but politically and spiritually more closely associated with religious houses on the continent.[28] However, families that possessed continental lands, or who had already established links with continental houses, continued to maintain those ties. The pattern of new foundations thus mirrored both landholding patterns and the profile of feudal ties.

accepted into the order of Cîteau in 1147. For the relations between Savigny and its priories see Béatrice Poulle, 'Savigny and England', in Bates and Curry, *England and Normandy*, 159–68.

[24] For an assessment of the English Benedictine monks and the new foundations see remarks made by Bethell, 'English black monks', 673–98 at p. 687.

[25] These conclusions also support John Van Engen's observation that in the early twelfth century 'gifts continued to come in [. . . and] Benedictine abbeys were in general never so prosperous': ' "Crisis of cenobitism" reconsidered', 269–304 at p. 278.

[26] See Constance Bouchard's observation on the status of benefactors in the eleventh and twelfth centuries: *Cloister, sword and miter*, 131–8.

[27] *Westminster charters*, no. 436; Golding, 'Anglo-Norman knightly burials', 35–48.

[28] For the relative inexpense of establishing Augustinian canons see remarks made by Southern, *Western society*, 245–50.

Gift-giving

In the reign of William the Conqueror the continental newcomers clearly 'preferred' to patronise houses on the continent, and more alien priories were being founded than any other type of house (see tables 3 and 4).[29] Just under fifty grants were made to houses in England compared with just under eighty to continental houses by landholders with identifiable interests in England. The new alien priories founded in England in this period outnumbered new independent priories, or those dependent on English houses, by eighteen to sixteen. In the reign of William Rufus, however, there was a clear and severe shift towards the patronage of religious houses in England that had no obvious connection with the continent. Only around twenty-five grants were made to continental houses compared with more than 150 to houses in England.[30] Grants to houses located in England amounted to almost three times those made to continental houses. In the reign of Henry I the massive increase in the number of new foundations established in England was accompanied by an escalation in the scale of patronage given to houses that had no connection with continental houses. By the time of his death the English-based houses had received something in the region of 675 grants, whereas continental houses had received just over 100, averaging 3.3 donations *per annum*.[31] This was a significant recovery from the levels of patronage experienced under Rufus.

---

[29] *Antiquus cartularius ecclesiae Baiocensis*, ed. V. Bourienne, Rouen–Paris 1902–3, i, nos 1, 2, 5; *Chartes de l'abbaye de Jumièges*, ed. J.-J. Vernier, Rouen 1916, i, nos 31–3; C. Bréard, *L'abbaye de Notre-Dame de Grestain*, Rouen 1904, 28, 33–4; DB i, fos 20d, 24d, 25a; *Inventaire sommaire archives départmentales l'Eure*, ed. G. Bourbon, Evreux 1893, H, i. 13, 52, 77, 87, 262; CDF, nos 29, 77–9, 82, 88, 91–4, 115, 154, 165–6, 318–19, 421–2, 449–50, 463–6, 625, 655–7, 920, 967, 1016, 1110, 1112, 1116, 1130, 1133, 1135, 1174–6, 1194, 1201, 1203, 1206, 1211, 1375, 1386, 1409; *Regesta*, i, nos 6a, 20–1, 24, 26, 29, 46, 56, 69, 75–6, 96–7, 103, 105, 110, 116–17, 119, 126, 130, 133, 140, 142, 145–7, 150, 158, 161, 165, 168, 171–2, 183, 194, 199, 204, 227, 229, 255, 257, 285, 288a, 327, 342, 386, 1176; ii, nos 256, 645, 1290, 1575, 1721; *Mon.*, iii. 215–17; vii. 1101, 1108.
[30] CDF, nos 80, 94–5, 219, 312, 326, 423, 468, 622, 655–7, 659–66, 715–16, 1045, 1120, 1178, 1205, 1207, 1234, 1235–6, 1238, 1325–6, 1376, 1386; *Inventaire sommaire archives départmentales l'Eure*, H, i. 10–11, 47; *Mon.*, vii. 1074, 1109; *Regesta*, i, nos 285, 299, 321, 324, 325, 353, 360, 384, 397, 397, 410–11, 414, 483, 633; ii, nos 623, 1721.
[31] *Regesta*, ii, nos 72, 524, 593, 599, 601, 638, 646, 680, 715, 720, 735a, 949, 959, 1004, 1010, 1012–13, 1016, 1019–20, 1023–23a, 1083, 1086, 1088–9, 1098a, 1101, 1187, 1204a, 1212, 1214–15, 1223, 1236, 1240a, 1282, 1289–90, 1294, 1418, 1433, 1441–2, 1447, 1544–5, 1547, 1554, 1569, 1573, 1575, 1577–8, 1580–1, 1587–8, 1592, 1594–6, 1599a–1601, 1673, 1681, 1684, 1687–8, 1691–2, 1694, 1696–7, 1699–1701, 1706, 1708, 1711, 1713, 1720–1, 1764, 1820, 1874, 1892, 1903, 1909, 1910, 1912, 1918–19, 1921, 1924, 1926–8, 1932, 1942, 1959, 1963–4, 1967–8, 1973–4; CDF, nos 5, 8, 49, 96–7, 115, 118–19, 165, 167–8, 196–7, 199, 219–20, 232, 241, 282–4, 286–7, 289, 330, 335, 374, 392, 396, 425, 457, 459, 470, 472–8, 569, 609–10, 624, 627, 630–2, 635–6, 722–3, 792, 795–7, 798, 876–7, 921–4, 994–8, 1005, 1008–10, 1033, 1035, 1046–7, 1052–3, 1134, 1136, 1138, 1149–50, 1196–7, 1208–10, 1226, 1233, 1239, 1258–9, 1264, 1383, 1385, 1387, 1389, 1391–2,

Table 3
Timing of gifts made to religious houses in England, 1066–1135

Dates of donations**	Approx. number of grants
William I	47
William II	152
Henry I	675 (plus poss. 185)
1066x1100	83
1066x1135	196
Total	1,153 (1,338)

** Not all donations can be accurately dated to the reign of one king. Thus, those that can be dated to the late eleventh century are assigned to category 1066x1100, those that can only be dated to the Anglo-Norman period are assigned to category 1066x1135.

Table 4
Timing of gifts made by Anglo-Normans to religious houses on the continent, 1066–1135

Dates of donations	Approx. number of grants
William I	77
William II	25
Henry I	105 (plus poss. 11)
1066x1100	5
1066x1135	7
Total	219 (230)

Patterns in donations to monasteries and priories are thus broadly similar to the trends identified in the foundation of new religious houses. Both reveal a distinct shift away from the patronage of continental abbeys in the reign of William Rufus. It is clear that for some continental houses post-Conquest generosity was short-lived. For example, Lyre abbey acquired the bulk of its English possessions within the first ten years of the Conquest.[32] Furthermore, even in the reign of the Conqueror, 'even the richest, most powerful [. . .]

1411–12, 1417, 1455, 1459, 2009; Mon., vii. 1072; v. 198; *Inventaire sommaire archives départmentales l'Eure*, H, i. 4, 7, 11, 13, 77;
[32] For the endowment of Lyre see S. F. Hockey, 'William fitz Osbern and the endowment of his abbey of Lyre', *Anglo-Norman Studies* iii (1981), 96–105, 213–15.

alien monks had problems holding on to post-Conquest benefactions'.[33] The pattern of 'settlement and endowment of the alien monks was marked out before c. 1100', and the Normans, such as the Beaumont family, 'seem to have lost interest in some of their foundations'.[34] The big bonanza really began to run out of steam in the first decade of Henry I's reign, so that by the time of the death of Anselm of Le Bec in 1109 'all the major grants of property had been made. Those made subsequently were mostly smaller in size and value.'[35]

The figures for the early twelfth century force the inescapable conclusion that the majority of the continental newcomers preferred to give English lands to houses situated in England, the majority of which had no obvious connection with any 'homeland' across the Channel. Apart from the well-attested exploiters of England who were shipping the spoils of Conquest back to Normandy, there was another group of Normans who were more interested in their future in England.[36] These newcomers had already set about anchoring themselves in their various localities by patronising existing English houses such as Bury St Edmunds, St Albans and Gloucester. They also gave donations to their overlords' new foundations like Eye, Selby, Monks Kirby, Battle and St Clement's, Pontefract. Aside from the original endowment, benefaction to foundations like Lewes, Castle Acre, Nostell, Lenton and Stoke by Clare did not serve the same purpose as grants made directly to continental houses. The overwhelming majority of the donations made to these priories, usually by the founder's tenants, had everything to do with local, often honorial, considerations, and relatively little to do with that house's association with the mother-house on the continent. The families of many of such early benefactors, like the d'Aubignys of Cainhoe, the Fossards, the Glanvills, the sheriffs of Gloucester and both branches of the Lacy family, produced men who later established their own foundations in the reign of Henry I.

Yet there was continuing support for continental houses.[37] Right up to the time of the death of Henry I there still existed a sizeable hard core of benefactors who were continuing to support continental houses and their priories.[38] This group was numerically in the minority, but consisted of some of the wealthiest and most influential magnates of the realm – William II de

---

[33] Matthew, *Norman monasteries*, 41.

[34] Ibid.

[35] Gazeau, 'Effects of the Conquest', 132. This corresponds with general trends in religious patronage in England and elsewhere on the continent. For the decrease in the size of grants being made to religious houses in France see Van Engen, ' "Crisis of cenobitism" reconsidered', 277; Johnson, *Prayer, patronage and power*, 85–6.

[36] Bates, 'Normandy and England after 1066', 851–76 at p. 870. The same sentiment was previously expressed by Le Patourel, *Norman empire*, 334.

[37] For an assessment of this cross-Channel support see remarks made by Matthew, *Norman monasteries*, 28.

[38] Gazeau, 'Effects of the Conquest', 140–1.

Warenne, Stephen of Brittany, Walter II Giffard, Robert, count of Meulan, as well as lesser men like William de St-Clair and William Paynel. Of particular interest is the number of Henry I's 'new men' who were to be found patronising institutions on both sides of the Channel. These included Nigel d'Aubigny, Geoffrey de Clinton, Brian fitz Count, Robert, earl of Gloucester, and Stephen of Blois.[39] Others like Ranulf Meschin and Robert, earl of Leicester, had also been significantly advanced by royal favour.[40] The reason for this continuing 'loyalty' to continental houses can be only be understood if the pragmatic aspect of the outlook of potential religious benefactors is fully appreciated. These continental newcomers, wishing to establish priories in England, turned to institutions with which they were already associated to create and populate their foundations, simply because it was practical to do so.[41] Some continental institutions were better equipped and more prepared than others to take on such a task. Jane Martindale has shown how St-Florent de Saumur was probably chosen to establish new communities in England because of its 'long experience of living under the most disturbed political conditions' and because 'it was prepared to accept foundations of a relatively modest size'.[42] George Beech has also stressed the fact that founding a new monastery was 'no casual undertaking' and a founder 'could not take chances with the sponsoring mother abbey. It had to be a community with a proven reputation for its ability to manage new foundations.'[43] It was not only continental houses like Charroux, with more than 200 dependent priories, which specialised in establishing priories, but also English houses like St Albans which had six dependent priories by the early twelfth century. Not all the continental newcomers had ready-made ties with continental houses that they could call upon. As the twelfth century wore on other English abbeys such as Gloucester, Bath and Westminster and the new foundations like Nostell, Montacute, Lewes and St Mary's, York, established their reputations and were responsible for the establishment of numerous daughter-houses.

This group of Anglo-Norman benefactors continued to patronise continental houses for a number of other reasons too. Firstly because their family was already tied by earlier donations. Examples of this include the Clares and Le Bec, the earls of Chester and St-Evroult, the Montgomerys and Sées, the

---

[39] C. W. Hollister, 'Henry I and the Anglo-Norman magnates', *Anglo-Norman Studies* ii (1980), 93–107 at p. 105.

[40] Ibid. 99.

[41] See Jane Martindale's remarks on the advantages of establishing a 'foreign' priory in post-Conquest England: 'Monasteries and castles: the priories of Saint-Florent de Saumur in England after 1066', in C. Hicks (ed.), *England in the eleventh century*, Stamford 1992, 135–56 at p. 149.

[42] Ibid. 152.

[43] G. Beech, 'Aquitanians and Flemings in the refoundation of Bardney abbey (Lincolnshire) in the later eleventh century', *Haskins Society Journal* i (1989), 73–90 at p. 78.

Tosnys and Conches and the Lacys and La Trinité du Mont.[44] Secondly, because benefactors, or their families, still held land in the neighbourhood of a particular house, religious patronage continued to serve useful political and social functions. This has been skilfully illustrated by David Crouch's discussion of the foundation of Le Désert in Breteuil by Robert, earl of Leicester.[45] Grants of land in England made to continental houses were also a means of reaffirming association with continental lands. This was not purely from sentiment, or feelings of 'loyalty', as such, but was intricately bound up with the property that these donors still held on the continent. The Ballon family, for example, assiduously maintained their links with their region of origin, Le Mans and the abbey of St-Vincent.[46] There was also a clear correlation between changing patterns of religious patronage and landholding patterns with respect to the Clare family in the mid twelfth century.[47] J. H. Round decided that Henry de Port founded Monk Sherbourne as a cell to Cerisy 'for no better reason than his family came from that part of the Bessin, where Cerisy was situated'.[48] There was more to it than that as Henry de Port still held land in that region of Normandy.[49] It should be emphasised that it was not necessarily 'national or regional origin' which was decisive here, but the existence of a patrimony in the region of origin which affected political action.[50] Indeed, only when Waleran of Meulan was faced with the loss of his great Norman patrimony in 1141 did he 'swallow the bitter pill' and submit to the Empress Matilda.[51] Yet some members of the Anglo-Norman baronage who are known to have maintained their family estates in Normandy are curiously absent as benefactors on that side of the Channel. Such men as William Pont de l'Arche and Richard Basset were involved with their new Augustinian houses in England,[52] while the lack of interest in Norman monasteries shown by the wealthy Roger Bigod is understandable in the light of the fact that he 'may not have held more than half of a knight's fee in Normandy'.[53]

The pattern of religious patronage bestowed by Robert, count of Mortain, serves as a particularly good illustration of many of these phenomena in

---

44 For the role of land as a bond which united the lay and monastic world see Rosenwein, *To be the neighbor*; White, *Custom, kinship and gifts to saints*. For the earls of Chester see *Chester and its charters*. For the Lacys' connection with Rouen see Wightman, *Lacy family*, 60.

45 Crouch, *Beaumont twins*, 198.

46 L. C. Loyd, *The origins of some Anglo-Norman families*, Leeds 1951, 12.

47 J. C. Ward states that 'the acquisition of new territories and the endowment of monasteries went together': 'Fashions in monastic endowment', 427–51 at p. 427.

48 Cited by Matthew, *Norman monasteries*, 49.

49 Loyd, *Origins*, 79.

50 Compare with remarks made by Keats-Rohan, 'Bretons and Normans', 42–78 at pp. 43, 44.

51 Crouch, *Beaumont twins*, 51.

52 For these men see Le Patourel, *Norman empire*, 225–6. For the religious patronage of Henry I's royal officials see remarks made by Green, *Government of England*, 153–4.

53 R. H. C. Davis, *The Normans and their myth*, London 1976, 114.

action.[54] Robert founded the collegiate church of St-Evroult, Mortain, around the year 1082, and also patronised the abbeys of Grestain, Marmoutier, Caen, Préaux, Fécamp, Mont-St-Michel, St-Nicholas, Angers and St Albans.[55] Both before and after the Conquest of England it was Grestain that received the bulk of Robert's patronage. The reasons for this preferential treatment were two-fold.[56] The first was that Grestain had been founded by Robert's father, Herluin de Conteville, and Robert's patronage represented the continuing involvement of his family with the abbey. Secondly Robert's patrimony was located in the region south of the Seine estuary around Conteville and Grestain. Patronage of Grestain thus served valuable political and social functions within the heart of Robert's patrimony. Robert pursued a conscious policy of linking the two areas in which his Norman landholdings were concentrated by means of religious patronage. He accomplished this by granting lands in the Grestain region and in the area around his castle of Mortain to both Grestain and St-Evroult, Mortain. In contrast, the other continental houses that Robert patronised tended to be given lands in less strategically vital locations. In the 1060s Robert granted the abbey of Préaux part of his demesne in St-Clair, and before 1082 Marmoutier was given land at St-Evroult by Robert and his wife Matilda and in Herouville, near Caen by Robert.[57] Finally, Robert gave St-Etienne, Caen, land in Hauteville, in Manche.[58]

Robert's decisions concerning English lands and possessions were subject to similar considerations. Robert gave Grestain the lion's share of his English lands because it was the family foundation associated with his patrimony: it has been estimated that it received more lands in England than the total received by the other five continental abbeys patronised by Robert.[59] Préaux was granted Robert's sole holding in Berkshire in exchange for his earlier gift in St-Clair.[60] Between 1082 and 1084 Marmoutier at Tours was granted land in Dorset.[61] The abbeys of Fécamp and St-Nicholas, Angers, were granted solitary pieces of land in England.[62] Robert probably also founded the Cluniac priory of Montacute, in Somerset, in about 1078.[63] Examination of Robert of Mortain's religious patronage has indeed established that Normandy

54 For Robert count of Mortain see Soulsby, 'Fiefs of the counts of Mortain'; B. Golding, 'Robert of Mortain', Anglo-Norman Studies xiii (1991), 119–44.
55 For Robert's grants see Soulsby, 'Fiefs of the counts of Mortain', 10, 15, 22–6, 125–33, 137–41; Golding, 'Robert of Mortain', 141–4.
56 For the endowment of Grestain see D. Bates and V. Gazeau, 'L'abbaye de Grestain et la famille d'Herluin de Conteville', Annales de Normandie xl (1990), 5–30.
57 CDF, no. 1201; Soulsby 'Fiefs of the counts of Mortain', 22.
58 Ibid. 23.
59 For the English possessions of Grestain see ibid. 127–36. For the problems surrounding Robert's grant to Mont-St-Michel see Golding, 'Robert of Mortain', 143.
60 Soulsby, 'Fiefs of the counts of Mortain', 138.
61 Ibid. 137.
62 Ibid. 140–1.
63 Binns, Dedications, 115.

was the centre of Robert's world,[64] but considering the location of his patrimony, the broad geographical spread of his Norman lands and the exceptional authority he wielded in Normandy, his interests were always likely to focused on that side of the Channel.[65]

The pattern of religious patronage was always determined by a combination of landholding patterns and feudal bonds. The vast stretches of land held by men like Arnulf de Hesdin, the counts of Brittany, Earl Roger de Montgomery, or the smaller amounts of land concentrated in a number of regions like those held by Hugh de Port, help explain the geographically dispersed nature of their religious patronage.[66] Feudal bonds enduring from pre-Conquest tenure in Normandy could influence the character of religious patronage in England. It has been demonstrated that in Leicestershire and Warwickshire a periodic renewal of landholding ties did take place between England and Normandy in the sixty years after Hastings.[67] This happened at the level of both the magnates and the magnates' followers. David Crouch has judiciously observed that 'a religious act and a political statement could go hand in hand'.[68] Elsewhere, others have also drawn attention to the fact that religious patronage could act as an demonstration of social and political 'corporate solidarity with a feudal grouping'.[69]

The term 'loyalty' has been bandied about so far with little attempt at a definition or discussion of its implications. Some scholars have used the term 'sentiment' as a synonym for 'loyalty' or 'allegiance'.[70] Religious patronage

[64] For an assessment of Robert's significance in the Anglo-Norman realm see Golding, 'Robert of Mortain', 143.

[65] Golding has observed that the English manors granted by Robert to these houses 'were sometimes isolated and at a distance from the main areas of Robert's interest and control': ibid. 144.

[66] In 1086 Arnulf held land in ten Domesday counties; he was also a benefactor to Gloucester, Shrewsbury, St Albans, Préaux, Le Bec, Cluny and St-Georges, Hesdin. In 1086 Alan Niger of Brittany held lands in twelve Domesday counties largely concentrated in the north and east of the country; he founded St Mary's, York, and Swavesey as cells of SS Serguius and Bacchus, Angers, and was benefactor of Bury St Edmunds and Angers. Earl Roger de Montgomery held lands in fifteen Domesday counties and founded Shrewsbury and Arundel as cells of Sées, his Norman foundation; he also founded Troarn and Almenèches as well as being a benefactor of Cluny, Grestain, Holy Trinity, Rouen and St-Vincent, Le Mans. Hugh de Port held lands in nine Domesday counties, particularly in Hampshire and Kent, Hugh was a benefactor of Rochester, Winchester and Gloucester and his name is entered in the Hyde *liber vitae*.

[67] David Crouch, 'Normans and Anglo-Normans: a divided aristocracy?', in Bates and Curry, *England and Normandy*, 51–67 at p. 56.

[68] Crouch, *Beaumont twins*, 112.

[69] Martindale, 'Monasteries and castles', 138; Harper-Bill, 'Piety of the Anglo-Norman knightly class', 63–77 at p. 67. For more on this phenomenon see ch. 9.

[70] Katherine Keats-Rohan talks about a 'strong vein of sentiment in the formation of the parties before 1153, a sentiment that was rarely focused on the person of either Stephen or Matilda but was sharply focused on the patrimony and the kin-group of the individual': 'Bretons and Normans', 68.

has on a number of occasions been used as a means to gauge the nebulous feelings of 'tradition' and 'sentiment' which acted to bind the Normans 'tenaciously to their origins, even if their wealth and domicile lay elsewhere'.[71] My analysis, however, has shown that Normans retained a preference for giving lands to Norman houses for less than one generation after the Conquest. Only a hard core with landed interests in Normandy continued to maintain links with the continent in such a way beyond that point. The overwhelming majority of Normans in England preferred to patronise houses located in England. Yet all this does not necessarily negate any feelings of sentiment these people may have had for the 'old country'.

For the majority of people, most of the time, decisions about religious patronage were ruled by reason rather than sentiment. Patronage was a calculated act full of social, political and spiritual significance, involving grants of tithes, rents and land; it was something far too important to be left entirely to the whim of an individual.[72] Barbara Rosenwein's picture of Cluny's relations with the laity comfortably fits the pieces together as she argues that 'lay involvement with monks did not begin and end with a gift. Donations were only one part of the relationship [. . .] we find the same men and women not only witnessing donations but participating in sales, claiming and quitting their claims to land, and receiving grants from the monastery in turn'.[73] Normans who made donations to houses in England, rather than in Normandy, were acting according to the nature of their tenurial position and feudal loyalty rather than betraying any lack of empathy with Normandy.[74]

The perspective on the Normans taken by Orderic Vitalis, writing in the reign of Henry I, conflicts with this thesis. For him the Anglo-Norman realm was a world 'throughout which men whose origins were Norman were active, but of which Normandy was the centre'.[75] In reality, he was only partly right. The distribution of religious patronage has indeed shown that a class of Normans, whose interests were centred on Normandy, endured to the last days of Henry I's life, but Orderic's location in his monastery of St-Evroult in Normandy meant that his view of the Norman world was blinkered, both physically and intellectually.[76] It is hardly surprising, then, that he would have been oblivious to those other categories of men whose origins were in Normandy, but whose interests were Anglo-Norman or even exclusively British.

71 Green, *Government of England*, 153.
72 Constance Bouchard has argued that in Burgundy, in the eleventh and twelfth centuries, 'the decision to support certain monasteries [. . .] was usually made not even by an entire family but by one individual': *Sword, miter and cloister*, 248.
73 Rosenwein, *To be the neighbor*, 48.
74 For the importance of land in determining attitudes towards Normandy and England in the generations after Hastings see Crouch, 'Normans and Anglo-Normans', 61.
75 Bates, 'Normandy and England', 865.
76 For the travels of Orderic in England and on the continent see Chibnall, *World of Orderic Vitalis*, 36–7.

The structure of post-Conquest society was multi-layered and this was likely to create, in addition to the great cross-Channel aristocratic families, families with 'predominantly British interests'.[77]

Burial locations

The pluralist nature of Anglo-Norman society can also be illustrated through an examination of the location of the last resting-places of the Norman aristocracy. Golding's interesting study of 104 known burial locations has challenged some of the oft repeated assumptions made about the cultural and spiritual assimilation of the Normans in post-Conquest England. However, Golding's figure of over 80 per cent of his sample of 104 cases 'choosing' to be buried in England gives no indication of whether this inclination towards England was constant throughout the post-Conquest period or accelerated in the reign of Henry I. Using the eighty-four cases explicitly cited in Golding's article together with others discovered in the course of this research I have constructed my own sample of the known burial location of some 100 people (see appendix).[78] In addition to these there are another thirty-four or so individuals requesting burial in particular places in advance of their demise. Although my sample is not exactly the same as the one used by Golding it exhibits similar trends. That is, the overwhelming majority of the sample were buried in England and only thirty were buried on the continent, with a further three making provision to be buried abroad. What is interesting about the continental burials is that they were taking place at a fairly consistent rate throughout this period.[79] Thirteen dated burials of this sample occurred before 1100 and at least another ten took place after 1100 and before 1135.[80] However, this burial pattern makes perfect sense in the light of these particular families' continuing association with the continental houses, as has been discussed above.

The general profile of the distribution of burial sites between England and the continent appears to have been established fairly quickly after the Conquest. Around the time of the death of the Conqueror Walter de Lacy, Gundreda de Warenne, William I de Warenne, Athelaise, wife of Geoffrey I de

---

[77] Bates, 'Normandy and England', 860; Keats-Rohan, 'Bretons and Normans', 56.

[78] I have done this because Golding does not individually cite all 104 cases.

[79] *Recueil des historiens des Gaules et de la France*, ed. M. Martin and others, Paris 1738–1904, xxiii. 449, 452; *Monasticon diocesis Exoniensis*, ed. G. Oliver, Exeter–London 1846, 345; *Cha. Mowbray*, nos 2, 3; *CDF*, nos 235, 659, 1385; GEC v. 153, 155; vi. 641; vii. 521–6; xii, pt ii. 757–62; *Mon.*, ii. 608–9; OV ii. 282; iv. 72, 336–8; vi. 36, 146; Golding, 'Anglo-Norman knightly burials', 48. For the date of Robert of Mortain's death see J.-M. Bouvris, 'Aux origines du prieuré de Vains', *Revue de l'Avranchin et du pays de Granville* lxiv (1987), 74.

[80] Golding points out that only five Norman baronial families (Grandmesnil, Tosny, Pantolf, the counts of Eu and the Beaumonts) had regular burial in Normandy: 'Anglo-Norman knightly burials', 48.

201

Mandeville, Robert de Tosny, Robert of Stafford and Alan I Rufus, lord of Richmond, were all buried in England.[81] Of the nine richest lay men assessed in 1086 six chose to be buried in England.[82] The word 'chose' is used deliberately here. In the case of the richest Norman magnates an element of personal choice was available. For lesser magnates and barons, the idea of being able to choose burial location was seriously curtailed by practical and conceptual limitations. Golding argues that the 'place of death did not determine place of burial'.[83] In the case of the very wealthiest of the barons like Eudo *dapifer*, William I Giffard and Hugh de Grandmesnil, this can be proven,[84] for they had their bodies transported across the English Channel for burial in the other part of the Anglo-Norman realm. But while it was all very well for very wealthy magnates to do this, for many Normans the cost would have been prohibitive. Rohaise, wife of Eudo *dapifer*, wanted to be buried with her husband at his foundation of Colchester, but she died on the continent and her kin, 'wishing to save themselves the expense of such a burial', had her body taken to Le Bec and buried there.[85] The fact that so many Normans were buried in England may have little more significance than that they just happened to die in England. For many of the benefactors who arranged for burial at Rochester, Ramsey, Thetford, Gloucester, Eye and Bury St Edmunds burial anywhere other than in the vicinity of their landholdings was neither an option nor a likelihood. Except for the very wealthiest in society it is not possible, then, to reject the supposition that since most of these men 'spent much of their time in England, it is likely that a high proportion would die, and therefore be buried, in England'.[86]

Death abroad was always a possibility to be considered by those making provision for their burial.[87] Simon I de St-Liz's death on the way to the Holy Land apparently resulted in his burial at La Charité-sur-Loire rather than at his own foundation of St Andrew's, Northampton.[88] Nigel d'Aubigny had arranged for his burial at St Albans but on his death in 1129 was buried at Le

---

81 *Historia Sancti Petri Gloucestriae*, i. 73; *Chart. Lewes*, ii. 15–19; EYC iv. nos 3, 11; GEC x. 785–6; Mon., iii. 289; *Chron. Evesham*, 75; *Westminster charters*, no. 436.

82 Roger de Montgomery was buried at Shrewsbury, William I de Warenne was buried at Lewes, Alan Niger count of Brittany was buried at Bury St Edmunds, Hugh d'Avranches was buried at Chester and Geoffrey I de Mandeville was probably interred at Westminster where had asked to be buried: OV iii. 148; iv. 142, 302; GEC iii. 166–7; x. 785–6; EYC iv, nos 3, 11; *Chart. Lewes*, ii. 19; *Westminster charters*, no. 436.

83 Golding, 'Anglo-Norman knightly burials', 47.

84 OV iv. 336; vi. 36–8; Mon., iv. 608–9; Golding, 'Anglo-Norman knightly burials', 46. The brother of Robert of Rhuddlan, Arnold fitz Humphrey, who was buried at Chester, later had permission to have his body exhumed, and took his bones back to Normandy to be buried in the chapter house of St-Evroult: OV iv. 142–3.

85 Mon., iv. 608–9; Golding, 'Anglo-Norman knightly burials', 47.

86 Ibid. 46.

87 Ibid. 44.

88 GEC vi. 641. Golding, 'Anglo-Norman knightly burials', 43.

Bec.[89] Benefactors were well aware of the possibility that they might not die in England, but many made no provision for their bodies to be brought back to England. Robert de Tosny, founder of Belvoir priory, arranged that 'if he should die in England' he was to be buried at St Albans or Belvoir.[90] Likewise, in the early years of the twelfth century, a charter of Peter de Valognes, the founder of Binham priory, settled that his knights 'if they die in England, are to be buried at Binham'.[91] Conan IV of Brittany arranged to be buried at Jervaulx and, in 1128, Robert fitz Ercambald at Gloucester, each stipulating the proviso, 'if he should die in England'.[92] The implication behind these requests is that if these men died on the continent, then they would be buried there.

Factors determining burial location had more to do with where the patrimony lay, the location of the family foundations and the economics of transportation, than with such sentiments as regarding Normandy as the 'homeland' or 'feeling more at home in England than in Normandy'.[93] How else to explain the fact that the earls of Chester and Surrey were so quick to 'settle in' whereas the Grandmesnils and Beaumonts were still 'homesick' in 1136 and choosing to be buried on the continent? Many, whether buried in England or on the continent, were laid to rest in their own foundations: families never lost sight of the welfare of their own foundations, whose interests were inexorably and indefinitely bound up with their own.[94] For example, the fact that Hugh d'Avranches chose to be buried in his foundation at Chester (he had refounded St Werburgh's in 1091, possibly prompted by the rebellions of 1088) was a clear signal of his enduring personal and spiritual commitment to, and association with, the abbey and his honor.[95] However, had he died on the continent, it is not inconceivable that he would have been buried at St-Sever, Coutances, which he had refounded in 1085. Of the fifteen Normans who were buried in their own foundations in England only half of these establishments were actually daughter-houses of continental monasteries and three of these were Cluniac houses. There were not very many 'corners' of a 'foreign field that [were] for ever Normandy', here.[96]

In discussing the relationship between religious patronage, the Norman aristocracy and the English monasteries, many disparate strands have been examined in detail. Not all the threads can be tied neatly back together. On

---

[89] *Cha. Mowbray*, 6–7; Golding, 'Anglo-Norman knightly burials', 45.
[90] Robert was buried in Belvoir chapter house: *Mon.*, iii. 289.
[91] Ibid. iii. 345; *Regesta*, ii, no. 828.
[92] *EYC* iv. 64–5; *Historia Sancti Petri Gloucestriae*, i. 232–3.
[93] Golding, 'Anglo-Norman knightly burials', 41.
[94] Matthew remarked that 'it is improbable that the Beaumonts preferred to favour St-Evroult rather than their own foundations at Préaux, in Normandy, or Leicester, in England': *Norman monasteries*, 33. See also David Crouch, 'The foundation of Leicester abbey and other problems', *Midland History* xii (1987), 1–13.
[95] OV iv. 142.
[96] Golding, 'Anglo-Norman knightly burials', 47.

their arrival in England the Normans encountered an established network of Benedictine monasteries. When it came to religious patronage, considerations of national or international politics had to be measured against feudal, honorial or familial criteria. The continental newcomers were not a homogeneous cross-Channel elite with common political aspirations: they embraced several levels of wealth.[97] The super-rich magnates' interests straddled the Channel and many continental houses profited from their generosity, although 'perhaps the Norman Church gained less than might have been expected [. . . as in 1086] foreign houses only held about five per cent of the total wealth in the hands of religious houses'.[98] It should also be remembered that this was not a portion of Anglo-Norman society which had fossilised around the time of the death of the Conqueror, but one whose ranks were augmented in the twelfth century by a number of Henry I's 'new men' such as Nigel d'Aubigny, Geoffrey de Clinton, Brian fitz Count, Robert, earl of Gloucester, and Stephen of Blois. Thus at the time of the death of Henry I there existed a hard core of important benefactors whose territorial landholding patterns resulted in their continuing support for continental houses and their priories.

However, many of the continental newcomers did not have pre-existing ties with continental monasteries. Many who had made their fortunes through the Conquest of England had no patrimony to speak of on the continent. These people had not come to exploit England for 'Normans and Normandy', but for 'Normans' in England. As far as religious patronage was concerned there was no straightforward exploitation of English resources for the benefit of Normandy. The construction of some of the largest churches seen in western Christendom took place not in Normandy but in England. Indeed, far from aggrandising Norman churches, the Conquest had the effect of slowing down work on religious buildings in Normandy.[99] This was not the simple imposition of Norman tastes, either.[100] There was genuine cultural exchange taking place as Norman monks came to staff the newly-established alien priories in England, and English monks were sent to Normandy for instruction: some of them returned to England, while others did not.[101] The Normans had come to settle and in this context, their patronage of English houses alongside honorial-type foundations makes sense.

97 See Crouch, 'Normans and Anglo-Normans', 61.
98 Ayton and Davies, 'Ecclesiastical wealth', 59.
99 E. Fernie, 'The architectural evidence and the effects of the Norman Conquest of England', in Bates and Curry, *England and Normandy*, 105–16.
100 For the post-Conquest blending of Saxon and Norman architectural styles and methods see E. Fernie, 'The effects of the conquest on Norman architectural patronage', *Anglo-Norman Studies* ix (1987), 71–86. For the survival of Anglo-Saxon studies at Worcester, Exeter and Bury St Edmunds see remarks made by Loyn, 'Abbots of English monasteries', 95–103.
101 Gazeau, 'Effects of the Conquest', 133–4.

The most dedicated benefactors of almost all the English monasteries were drawn from their environs, reflecting the localised aspirations and concerns of the local elites of England.[102] Thorney, Ramsey, Gloucester, Abingdon, Rochester, St Albans and Westminster fulfilled similar spiritual and social functions to those of the honorial-type foundations such as Eye, Lewes, Clare, Lenton, Shrewsbury and Chester. With the exception of Gloucester, St Albans and Rochester, the English houses were outside any predetermined feudal grouping. Thus, within the framework of growing religious donations in favour of houses in England and for the establishment of new foundations, the established monasteries had to jockey for patronage, and the ability of the abbot to exploit the opportunities available was therefore crucial to the fortunes of his abbey. In these circumstances the patronage of certain English monasteries cut straight across local considerations. The most outstanding examples of this are Gloucester, Abingdon and St Albans which had cultivated special relationships with royal officials and the royal court. Politics determined the special interest of the king and his court in Gloucester and Bury St Edmunds as military and spiritual considerations had done at Battle abbey.[103] Ultimately, religious patronage cannot be used to disclose the depth of feeling about Normandy as the 'homeland', but it can reveal much about local conditions, honorial society and the structure of the kin group.

The existence of a genuinely cross-Channel aristocracy should not be denied or played down. There were aristocratic families whose connections with the continent remained strong throughout this seventy-year period. Connections with Normandy perceptibly faltered in the reign of William Rufus, but recovered before the end of the century, flourishing for the next thirty-five years. The capacity of cross-Channel landholders to survive the political division of the Anglo-Norman realm had in some ways already been proven in the years between 1100 and 1106. During this second separation of the two countries cultural and spiritual links had been maintained through the foundation of alien cells in England. By the time of the death of Henry I it is evident that the structure of the Anglo-Norman realm was subject to a number of seemingly contradictory forces. Henry I's 'restructured baronage' with their cross-Channel territories created a vested interest in maintaining the union of the two realms which had become Henry's priority.[104] Regional forces were certainly steadily growing but the Anglo-Norman realm was still structurally viable. The key to understanding such configurations is to be

---

[102] See Crouch, 'Normans and Anglo-Normans', 67.

[103] Eleanor Searle has illustrated how the enfeoffment of Battle abbey had both a military and spiritual purpose: 'The abbey of the conquerors: defensive enfeoffment and economic development in Anglo-Norman England', *Anglo-Norman Studies* ii (1980), 54–64, 197–81 at pp. 56–8.

[104] Hollister, 'Henry I and the Anglo-Norman magnates', 106; Bates, 'Normandy and England', 872.

found in the heterogeneous nature of post-Conquest society.[105] Anglo-Norman society was plural in its make-up and interests. There were sections of the aristocracy, both in England and Normandy, whose interests were either British or Norman, not Anglo-Norman.

---

[105] A number of scholars have rejected Le Patourel's model of 'one homogenous, aristocratic community', including Bates, ibid. 854, 860; J. A. Green, 'Lords of the Norman Vexin', in J. Gillingham and J. C. Holt (eds), *War and government in the Middle Ages*, Woodbridge 1984, 47–63, and 'Henry I and the aristocracy of Normandy', *La France anglaise au moyen age, actes de 111e congrès national des sociétés savantes*, Poitiers 1986, 162–73; Keats-Rohan, 'Bretons and Normans', 43, 44; Crouch, 'Normans and Anglo-Normans', 51–67.

Conclusion

In isolating and co-ordinating the experiences of the Anglo-Saxon monasteries this book has revealed just how varied their collective experience was. The English monasteries were not systematically discriminated against and there was no wholesale replacement of the English monks. It is true, however, that the possessions of the wealthier houses were particularly vulnerable in the first years after the Conquest. Wealthy houses such as Ely, Abingdon and Glastonbury suffered varying degrees of injury and support from the continental newcomers. The exception to this was Bury St Edmunds which sailed through the first twenty-five years after the Conquest with seemingly effortless ease. The abbacy of Baldwin at Bury demonstrates how monasteries in the hands of continental abbots, especially if they had friends in high places, had a distinct advantage over those with English abbots. The outstandingly successful abbacies of Serlo at Gloucester, Paul of Caen and Richard d'Aubigny at St Albans and Faritius at Abingdon can also be interpreted in this way. The personality and abilities of a particular abbot could be, and often were, decisive in ensuring that these houses flourished. Royal favour, or lack of it, could be equally critical for an abbey's prosperity. As a result, religious patronage was not only uneven in its distribution between monasteries but also between the abbacies of different abbots at the same institutions.

The experience of the English monasteries after 1066 must also be seen in the context of Lanfranc's efforts to bring the English Church into line with continental practice in government, in law and in liturgy. Although there was no systematic discrimination along ethnic lines by the new regime innovations in liturgical practice and the apparent denigration of the English language reinforced a sense of 'otherness' between the Normans and the personnel of the English monasteries. Cultural conflicts, such as those over liturgy at Glastonbury and over the timing of bell-ringing at Canterbury, although very rare, could rend communities apart, revealing the distance between the English and the newcomers. The flourishing cult of Earl Waltheof, with its political undertones, also served to reinforce the divide between Normans and local English. But by and large the Normans seem to have been perfectly comfortable with the English personnel of the abbeys, so long as a continental abbot was installed as head of the monastery. Furthermore, in post-Conquest England it was still possible for English monks to reach high office, as they did at Bury St Edmunds, Burton, Crowland, Peterborough, Ramsey and Malmesbury, well into the twelfth century.[1]

---

[1] *Memorials of St Edmund's*, i. 351; Bridgeman, 'Burton abbey surveys', 209–300 at p. 250.

This examination of patterns of gift-giving to religious houses in the Anglo-Norman realm is one of the few systematic studies of an aspect of the relationship between England and Normandy.[2] For Orderic Vitalis Normandy was the natural centre of the Anglo-Norman realm.[3] This book, however, has sought to look beyond the rhetoric of Orderic, to examine the concrete actions of the continental newcomers in England. The analysis of the distribution of grants given to monasteries has acted as an invaluable indicator of political and landed interests. The nature of the Anglo-Norman aristocracy was essentially plural: Le Patourel's model of 'one homogenous, aristocratic community' is only appropriate at the very highest level of the aristocracy. Other considerations such as locality, the needs of colonisation, kinship and social linkages, lordship and kingship cut across the unifying forces. There were sections of the aristocracy, both in England and Normandy, especially those on the peripheries of the realm, whose interests were not Anglo-Norman but essentially British or Norman. At the same time there were aristocratic families whose connections with the continent remained strong throughout the whole of this seventy-year period. Regardless of whether the 'sentiments' of the aristocracy still lay with Normandy, it did not affect their actions as religious benefactors; tenure of land and lordship did. The pluralist nature of Anglo-Norman society can be illustrated through the examination of the location of the last resting-places of the Norman aristocracy. Factors determining burial location had more to do with the place of death, where the patrimony lay, the location of the family foundations and the economics of transportation, than with regarding Normandy as the 'homeland' or 'feeling more at home in England than in Normandy'.[4]

In the late eleventh and early twelfth centuries gifts to religious houses most commonly took the form of grants of land, and rights over land. As medieval society was one in which the control of land was central to the exercise of power the giving of such gifts had profound implications for the standing of the monasteries in the world. The giving of gifts, in particular land, also had political significance in medieval society. Barbara Rosenwein's work on the 'social' significance of Cluny's property in the tenth and eleventh centuries has located that abbey at the centre of a network of personal and local relationships. The lands given to Cluny 'created and reinforced personal ties [. . . which] functioned to define groups and enforce social cohesion'.[5]

Swein was prior in the time of Abbot Nigel (1094–1114) and Abbot Geoffrey (1114–50) and Edwin was prior in the time of Abbot Geoffrey: Knowles, Brooke and London, *Heads of religious houses*, 42, 55.

2 For the other systematic study on the association between England and Normandy see David Bates's work on Anglo-Norman writs, 'The earliest Norman writs', *English Historical Review* c (1985), 266–84.

3 Idem, 'Normandy and England', 851–76 at p. 865.

4 Golding, 'Anglo-Norman knightly burials', 35–48 at p. 41.

5 Rosenwein, *To be the neighbor*, 48.

CONCLUSION

In England monasteries were likewise centred at the heart of local society, tied by tenurial, social, spiritual and personal bonds, although the social networks that surrounded some English houses, such as St Albans, Gloucester and Abingdon, were more extensive than others. The colonisation of England required that new networks of religious patronage be created. The location of certain new religious houses, for example Lewes, Chester and Shrewsbury, was determined by strategic considerations and performed an important role in the process of colonisation and consolidation. The post-Conquest settlement saw the gradual permeation of the socio-religious nexus by a structure which was quintessentially Norman. Many of the new foundations established by the magnates and barons of the realm acted as *foci* for the political loyalty of honorial communities. Lordship was also consciously employed as a channel for religious piety by the aristocracy. Decisions about religious patronage were heavily influenced by ties of family, tenure and neighbourhood. Yet, for the honorial tenant, a sense of duty and loyalty was mixed with what feudal bonds would allow. Tenants were expected to support the honorial foundation just as much as were the founder and his heirs. There were also practical reasons which recommended this course of action: spiritual ones as well as the desire to act in association with the peer-group within the locality. Yet the composite nature of honorial society in post-Conquest England meant that honorial loyalties diffused, as well as concentrated, the flow of patronage. Thus, the generosity of tenants was far from guaranteed. Tenants of more than one lord were often faced with a choice of honorial foundations to patronise, as well as the Old English houses. As the twelfth century wore on the alternatives became more numerous and more varied with the arrival on the scene of the Cistercians and Augustinians.

Judicious use of religious patronage could also infiltrate and establish authority within an acquired or confiscated honor.[6] Investigation of the distribution of religious patronage in England in conjunction with patterns of tenure and the structure of different lordships provides important clues to the nature of aristocratic power and the nature of the honor, as well as indicating which lord benefactors perceived as most important to their own interests. Analysis of religious patronage has therefore shed new light on the exercise of political power and the nature of tenurial conditions.

In no society is an individual a free agent. Donors were constrained and defined by the different groups in society to which they belonged as well as by contemporary beliefs on the best means by which to achieve salvation. Tension existed between the personal motivations behind making a donation and the practical reasons that determined where that gift went. Gift-giving is characteristic of all societies and remains an essential part of social behaviour in modern industrial society. Individual motivation behind gift-giving included the desire for prayers, fraternity, burial in abbey grounds and the

6   David Crouch, 'Strategies of lordship in Angevin England and the career of William Marshal', in Harper-Bill and Harvey, *Ideals and practice*, 8–9, 12–13.

wish for the donor, or kinsman, to take up the monastic habit. As a transaction that is based on 'obligation and self-interest', gift-giving also says much about the social context in which medieval religious patronage took place: the nature of kinship groups, family ties, the role of women, the role of saints' cults, the interaction of different groups in society, in particular between the clergy and laity, for example in the use of compromise in dispute settlement and the role of ritual and symbols in medieval society.[7]

It is clear that in eleventh- and twelfth-century England donors were obliged to work within the framework of the expectations of their kinship group.[8] Heirs were expected to maintain links with those religious houses their ancestors had founded or patronised. The memory of the grants of land made to monasteries remained strong in the minds of the donors' kin. Members of the aristocracy who made no grants or only inconsequential ones, such as the infamous Robert de Bellême, were atypical.[9] Even the supposedly irreligious William Rufus was a generous benefactor to a handful of chosen houses – Gloucester, Battle, Westminster, Rochester and Bermondsey.[10] To refrain from gift-giving would mean standing apart from many of the interlinked social and political structures of the realm.

The *pro anima* requests made in donation charters on behalf of kin reveal that, after their own souls, male benefactors were most concerned for their ancestors, specifically their fathers and mothers. This concern also manifested itself practically, as heirs invariably looked after their parents' foundations, consolidating and adding to their endowment. Brothers, uncles and children who had predeceased them were also remembered in their thoughts. Concern for siblings would sometimes find concrete expression as brothers, brothers-in-law and occasionally sisters patronised each others' foundations. Lone female donors also showed concern for their fathers, mothers and sons but principally for their husbands' souls. While men were concerned with the wider kinship group, women were more preoccupied with their immediate family: parents, husbands, sons, exceptionally brothers and daughters, but not sisters. The smaller number of grants women made, alone or with a male relative, illustrates that their ability to alienate land to the Church was very modest in comparison with their male kin. This is not to say that they had little

---

7 Mauss, *The gift*, 1. For a critique of Mauss's work on the gift economy see Rosenwein, *To be the neighbor*, 125–30. For dispute settlement see S. D. White, 'The settlement of disputes by compromise in eleventh century western France, 1050–1150', *Traditio* xliii (1987), 55–103; E. King, 'Dispute settlement in Anglo-Norman England', *Anglo-Norman Studies* xiv (1992), 115–30. For cases of compromise see pp. 45, 69, 75 above.

8 Joel Rosenthal, however, believes that in the fourteenth and fifteenth centuries 'people were always free – to give or not to give, and to give to whom they chose': *Purchase of paradise*, 124.

9 For Robert see Kathleen Thompson, 'Robert of Bellême reconsidered', *Anglo-Norman Studies* xiii (1991), 263–86.

10 Barlow, *William Rufus*, 113–15.

influence upon a family's decision about religious patronage as women could act as effective transmitters of enthusiasm for a particular religious house.

Throughout this period the English kingdom remained the land of opportunity for the Anglo-Norman baronage: its size meant that it was always going to offer greater potential for making donations to religious houses. Shifts in social conventions also meant that in the early twelfth century more and more of the lesser aristocracy and baronage were deciding to demonstrate their status by founding and endowing their own modest religious houses. Furthermore, in the five years before the death of Henry, the first of the new Cistercian foundations appeared in England. In the early twelfth century people were not always free to give or not to give, as social pressure, considerations of the locality and lordship meant that those who could afford to be generous usually were. Furthermore, the tension between what was expected, or demanded, of donors and their increasing enthusiasm for supporting new forms of religious life was resolved by the practice of patronising several houses. Depending upon the size of individual fortunes donors founded or patronised as many different orders as they could. Fashions in religious patronage had altered greatly in the seventy years that followed the battle of Hastings. The competition was certainly getting tougher but the Old English monasteries were still capable of attracting grants and were easily able to maintain their position as the richest group of religious houses in post-Conquest England.

APPENDIX

Burial Locations in the Anglo-Norman Realm, 1066–c. 1135

Known burial locations of individuals in England

Adeliza, wife of William d'Aubigny *brito* (Belvoir)
Agnes, wife of Aubrey II de Vere (Earls Colne)
Agnes de Ria, daughter of Robert de Tosny (Belvoir)
Alan I Niger, lord of Richmond (Bury St Edmunds 1089)
Alan II Rufus of Brittany (Bury St Edmunds c. 1093)
Athelaise, wife of Geoffrey de Mandeville (Westminster 1085x1110)
Aubrey I de Vere (Earls Colne c. 1112)
Aubrey II de Vere (Earls Colne 1141)
Bernard de Neufmarché (?Gloucester 1125)
Cecilia, wife of William d'Aubigny *brito* (Belvoir)
Edith Godwinson (Westminster 1075)
Edward the Confessor (Westminster 1066)
Eudo *dapifer* (Colchester 1120)
Geoffrey de Vere (Abingdon 1101x7)
Gilbert de Gant (Bardney c. 1095)
Godfrey, brother of Gilbert fitz Richard (Clare before 1090)
Godfrey, son of Richard fitz Gilbert (Stoke by Clare)
Gundreda de Warenne (Lewes 1085)
Hamelin de Ballon (Abergavenny t. Henry I)
Hawise, wife of Ilbert I de Lacy (Pontefract t. William Rufus)
Henry I (Reading 1135)
Henry de Ferrers (Tutbury 1093x1101)
Henry d'Oilly (Oseney)
Hugh Bigod, earl of Norfolk (Thetford)
Hugh d'Avranches (Chester 1101)
Hugh de Lacy (Weobley church before 1121)
Hugh de Montgomery (Shrewsbury 1089)
Hugh de Port (Winchester 1096)
Hugh de Tosny (St Aldgate, London, before 1126)
Ilbert I de Lacy (Pontefract t. William Rufus)
Jordan, nephew of Roger I de Builli (Blyth 1130)
Judith, Countess (probably buried at Elstow before 1090)
Mable of Mortain (St Albans before 1106)
Matilda, daughter of Earl Waltheof (Scone 1130)

Matilda, queen of England (Westminster 1118)
Matilda Bigod, wife of William d'Aubigny *pincerna* (?Wymondham)
Miles of Gloucester (Llanthony *Secunda* 1143)
Payn of Chadworth (Gloucester)
Ralph fitz Asketel (Hereford)
Ranulf Meschin, earl of Chester (Chester *c.* 1129)
Richard fitz Gilbert (St Neots *c.* 1090)
Roger Bigod (Norwich 1107)
Robert Curthose (Gloucester 1134)
Robert de Lacy (Pontefract 1120s)
Robert I d'Oilly (Abingdon *c.* 1096)
Robert II d'Oilly (Eynsham 1142)
Robert de Tosny (Belvoir 1088)
Robert of Rhuddlan (Shrewsbury but later moved to St-Evroult 1088)
Robert of Stafford (monk at Evesham late eleventh century)
Roger I de Builli (Blyth 1130)
Roger of Montgomery (Shrewsbury 1094)
Stephen of Brittany (St Mary's, York, 1136)
Swein, father of Robert of Essex (Westminster *c.* 1087)
Walter, nephew of Eudo *dapifer* (Colchester 1120)
Walter de Lacy (Gloucester 1085)
Walter of Gloucester (?Llanthony *Prima* 1129)
Waltheof, Earl (Crowland 1076)
William II, count of Eu (Hastings *c.* 1094)
William, count of Mortain (?Bermondsey 1140s)
William d'Aubigny *brito* (Belvoir 1133x46)
William de Lovetot and son Richard (Wirksop mid twelfth century)
William II de Percy (Fountains mid twelfth century)
William de Vere (Earls Colne)
William I de Warenne (Lewes 1088)
William II de Warenne (Lewes 1138)
William Rufus (Old Minster, Winchester 1100)

Requests for burial in England by individuals in advance of their demise

Æthgitha (Ramsey)
Athelhelm of Burgate (Earls Colne 1100x35)
Beatrix, wife of William de Roville (Eye)
Durand of Butterwick (Whitby)
Estimund (Ramsey)
Fulcard fitz Godric fitz Ringulf's father and mother (Ramsey)
Geoffrey I de Mandeville (Westminster)
Geoffrey de Trailly (Thorney)
Godyfe (Rochester)

Haimo Pecche (Bury St Edmunds)
Hugh, earl of Norfolk (Thetford)
Hugh fitz Goscelin (Dunstable)
knights of Peterborough abbey (Peterborough 1107x15)
Matilda, wife of Ralph fitz Walter (Thetford)
Rainald of Argentan (Ramsey)
Ralph fitz Walter (Thetford)
Ranulf, brother of Ilger, and wife (Ramsey)
Robert de Vaux (Thetford)
Robert fitz Ercambald (Gloucester)
Robert of Girton and wife (Ramsey)
Roger de Berkeley (Gloucester)
Rohaise, wife of Eudo (asked for burial at Colchester but buried at Le Bec)
Theo (Rochester)
three daughters of Deorman the moneyer (Westminster)
Wife of Ranulf, brother of Ilger (Ramsey)
Wife of Robert of Girton (Ramsey)
William de Roville (Eye)
William Pecche (Ramsey)

Known burial locations of individuals on the continent

Adeliza, wife of William fitz Osbern (Cormeilles)
Adeliza de Grandmesnil (St-Evroult 1091)
Beatrice, wife of Robert, count of Eu (Tréport 1085)
Emma, wife of Robert de Grandmesnil (St-Evroult)
Eustace count of Boulogne (Cluny c. 1125)
Helewise, wife of William of Evreux (Noyon)
Henry de Newburgh (Préaux 1118)
Hugh de Grandmesnil (St-Evroult 1098)
Hugh de Montfort (Préaux 1088)
Matilda, queen of England (La Trinité, Caen 1082)
Nigel d'Aubigny, Mowbray (Le Bec 1129)
Ralph I de Tosny (Conches 1102)
Ralph II de Tosny, youngest son of Ralph de Tosny (Conches 1126)
Roger de Tosny, eldest son of Ralph de Tosny (Conches c. 1091)
Richard de Redvers (Monteborg 1107)
Robert Bigod, son of Roger (Sées 1091)
Robert, count of Eu (Tréport 1089x94)
Robert, count of Mortain (Grestain 1095)
Robert I de Beaumont (Préaux 1118)
Robert de Grandmesnil (St-Evroult 1136)
Robert fitz Tetbald (Sées 1087)
Roger Beaumont (Préaux 1094)

Rohaise, wife of Eudo *dapifer* (Le Bec 1121)
Simon de St Liz (La-Charite-sur-Loire *c.* 1100)
Walter Giffard (Longueville 1084)
William the Conqueror (Ste Etienne, Caen 1087)
William fitz Osbern (Cormeilles 1071)
William of Evreux (St Wandrille 1118)
William Giffard (Longueville 1102)
William Pantulf (Norun, Normandy)

Requests for burial on the continent by individuals in advance of their demise

Adelina, wife of Hugh de Montfort (Préaux)
Humphrey de Vielles (Préaux)
Roger Baolt (Sées 1093)

Bibliography

Unpublished primary sources

London, British Library
MSS Add. 29436, 32101, 40000, 47847
MSS Arundel 68, 178
MSS Cotton Claudius C ix, B vi, D x
MSS Cotton Domitian A vii, A viii
MS Cotton Galba E ii
MS Cotton Julius D ii
MS Cotton Nero D vii
MSS Cotton Otho B xiii, D iii
MS Cotton Tiberius A ix
MS Cotton Vespian B xxiv
MS Harley 1005
MS Stowe 944

Cambridge, Trinity College
MS O 2 1

Cambridge University Library
MSS Add. 3020–1
MS Mm 4 19

Gloucester Cathedral Library
MS 34

Oxford, Queen's College
MS 367

Spalding, Gentlemen's Society
Wrest Park Cartulary

Published primary sources

Anglo-Saxon charters, ed. A. J. Robertson, 2nd edn, Cambridge 1956
Anglo-Saxon charters: an annotated list and bibliography, ed. P. H. Sawyer, London 1968. Rev. edn, ed. S. E. Kelly (first draft on disk July 1994)

Anglo-Saxon chronicle, ed. D. Whitelock, D. C. Douglas and S. I. Tucker, London 1961

Anglo-Saxon wills, ed. D. Whitelock, Cambridge 1930

Antiquus cartularius ecclesiae Baiocensis, ed. V. Bourienne, Rouen–Paris 1902–3

The Beauchamp cartulary: charters 1100–1268, ed. Emma Mason (Pipe Roll Society, n.s. xliii, 1980)

Bede, *Historia ecclesiastica gentis Anglorum*, ed. C. Plummer, Oxford 1896

Blythburgh priory cartulary, ed. C. Harper-Bill, Woodbridge 1980–1

The Burton chartulary, ed. G. Wrottesley (William Salt Archaeological Society v, pt i, 1884)

Calendar of documents preserved in France illustrative of the history of Great Britain and Ireland, ed. J. H. Round, London 1899

The 'Carmen de Hastingae proelio' of Guy Bishop of Amiens, ed. C. Morton and H. Muntz, Oxford 1972

Cartularium abbathiae de Rievalle, ed. J. C. Atkinson (Surtees Society lxxxiii, 1889)

Cartularium abbathiae de Whitby, ed. J. C. Atkinson (Surtees Society lxix, lxxii, 1879–81)

Cartulaire de l'abbaye de la Sainté-Trinité de Tiron, ed. M. L. Merlet, Chartres 1883

Cartularium monasterii de Rameseia, ed. W. H. Hart and P. A. Lyons (Rolls series lxxix, 1884–93)

Cartularium prioratus de Colne, ed. J. L. Fisher (Essex Archaeological Society Occasional Publications i, 1946)

Cartularium prioratus de Gyseburne, ed. W. Brown (Surtees Society lxxxvi, 1889)

The cartulary of Boxgrove priory, ed. L. Fleming (Sussex Records Society lix, 1960)

Cartulary of Oseney abbey, ed. H. E. Salter (Oxford Historical Society lxxxix, xc, xci, xcvii, xcviii, ci, 1929–36)

The cartulary of Shrewsbury abbey, ed. U. Rees, Aberystwyth 1975

The cartulary of Worcester cathedral priory, ed. R. R. Darlington (Pipe Roll Society, n.s. xxxviii, 1968)

The cartulary or register of the abbey of St Werburgh, Chester, ed. J. Tait (Chetham Society, n.s. lxxix, lxxxii, Manchester 1920–3)

The charters of Burton abbey, ed. P. H. Sawyer, Oxford 1979

Charters of the honour of Mowbray, 1107–1091, ed. D. E. Greenway, London 1972

The charters of Norwich cathedral priory, ed. B. Dodwell (Pipe Roll Society, n.s. xl, xlvi, 1974, 1985)

The charters of St Augustine's abbey, Canterbury, ed. S. E. Kelly (Anglo-Saxon Charters iv, 1994)

Chartes de l'abbaye de Jumièges, ed. J.-J. Vernier, Rouen 1916

The chartulary of Brinkburn priory, ed. W. Page (Surtees Society xc, 1892)

The chartulary of St John of Pontefract, ed. R. Holmes (Yorkshire Archeological Society Record Series xxv, xxx, 1899, 1902)

Chartulary of the priory of St Pancras of Lewes, ed. L. F. Salzman (Sussex Record Society xxxviii, xl, 1933–5)

Chartulary of Winchester cathedral, ed. A. W. Goodman, Winchester 1927

The chronicle of Battle abbey, ed. E. Searle, Oxford 1980

The chronicle of Glastonbury abbey: an edition, translation and study of John of Glastonbury's 'Cronica sive antiquitates', ed. James P. Carley, trans. David Townsend, Woodbridge 1985

The chronicle of Hugh Candidus, a monk of Peterborough, ed. W. T. Mellows, Oxford 1949

The chronicle of John of Worcester, II: The annals from 450 to 1066, ed. R. R. Darlington and Patrick McGurk, Oxford 1995

The chronicles of Croyland by Ingulf, ed. W. de Gray Birch, Wisbech 1883

Chronicon abbatiae de Evesham ad annum 1418, ed. W. D. Macray (Rolls series xxix, 1863)

Chronicon abbatiae Rameseiensis, ed. W. Dunn Macray (Rolls series lxxxiii, 1886)

Chronicon monasterii de Abingdon, ed. J. Stevenson (Rolls series ii, 1858)

The Domesday monachorum of Christ Church, Canterbury, ed. D. C. Douglas, London 1944

Eadmer, *Historia novorum in Anglia*, ed. M. Rule (Rolls series lxxxi, 1884)

────── *The life of St Anselm, archbishop of Canterbury*, ed. R. W. Southern, Oxford 1972

The early charters of the Augustinian canons of Waltham abbey, Essex, ed. R. Ransford, Woodbridge 1989

The early history of Glastonbury: an edition, translation and study of William of Malmesbury's 'De antiquitate Glastonie ecclesie', ed. John Scott, Woodbridge 1981

Early Yorkshire charters, ed. William Farrer, i–iii, Edinburgh 1914–16; *Early Yorkshire charters*, ed. C. T. Clay (Yorkshire Archaeological Society Record Series e.s. iv–xii, 1935–65) (e.s. iv, ed. C. T. Clay and E. M. Clay, publ. 1942, is the index to vols i–iii)

The ecclesiastical history of Orderic Vitalis, ed. M. Chibnall, Oxford 1969–80

An eleventh century inquisition of St Augustine's, Canterbury, ed. A. Ballard (British Academy Records of Social and Economic History of England and Wales iv, 1920)

English historical documents, I: c. 500–1042, ed. Dorothy Whitelock, 2nd edn, London 1979

English historical documents, II: 1042–1189, ed. D. C. Douglas and G. W. Greenaway, 2nd edn, London 1981

English lawsuits from William I to Richard, ed. R. C. Van Caenegem (Selden Society cvi, cvii, 1990–1)

Epistolae Herberti de Losinga, ed. R. Anstuther, New York 1846

Eye priory cartulary and charters, ed. V. Brown (Suffolk Records Society xii, 1992)

Eynsham cartulary, ed. H. E. Salter (Oxford Historical Society xlix, li, 1907–8)

Felix's life of Saint Guthlac, ed. B. Colgrave, Cambridge 1956

Feudal documents from the abbey of Bury St Edmunds, ed. D. C. Douglas, London 1932

The first register of Norwich cathedral priory, ed. H. W. Saunders (Norfolk Records Society xi, 1939)

Florentii Wigorniensis monachi chronicon ex chronici, ed. B. Thorpe, London 1848–9

Gerald of Wales, *The journey through Wales and the description of Wales*, ed. Lewis Thorpe, London 1978

Gervase of Canterbury, *Opera historica*, ed. W. Stubbs (Rolls series lxxiii, 1879–80)

Gesta abbatum monasterii Sancti Albani, ed. H. T. Riley (Rolls series xxviii, 1867–9)

Giraldi Cambriensi opera, ed. J. S. Brewer, J. F. Dimock and G. F. Warner (Rolls series xxi, 1861–91)

Goscelin of Saint-Bertin, *Historia translationis S. Augustini episcopi*, PL clv. 13–46

Hemmingi chartularium ecclesie Wigorniensis, ed. T. Hearne, Oxford 1723

Historia et chartularium monasterii Sancti Petri Gloucestriae, ed. W. H. Hart (Rolls series xxxiii, 1863–7)

Ingulf's chronicle of the abbey of Croyland with the continuation by Peter of Blois and anonymous writers, ed. H. T. Riley, London 1908

Inventaire sommaire archives départmentales l'Eure, ed. G. Bourbon, Evreux 1893

Jocelin of Brakelond, *Chronicle of the abbey of Bury St Edmunds*, ed. D. Greenway and J. Sayer, Oxford 1989

Leges Henrici primi, ed. L. J. Downer, Oxford 1972

The letters of Lanfranc archbishop of Canterbury, ed. H. Clover and M. Gibson, Oxford 1979

The letters of Saint Anselm of Canterbury, ed. W. Fröhlich, Kalamazoo 1990–4

Liber Eliensis, ed. E. O. Blake (Camden Society, 3rd ser. xcii, 1962)

Liber memorandorum ecclesie de Bernewelle, ed. J. W. Clark, Cambridge 1907

The liber vitae of the New Minster and Hyde abbey, Winchester, ed. Simon Keynes (Early English Manuscripts in Facsimile xxvi, 1996)

Liber vitae ecclesiae Dunelmensis, ed. J. Stevenson (Surtees Society xiii, 1841)

Liber vitae ecclesie Dunelmensis, ed. A. Hamilton Thompson (Surtees Society cxxxvi, 1923)

Liber vitae: register and martyrology of New Minster and Hyde abbey, Winchester, ed. W. de Gray Birch (Publications of the Hampshire Records Society v, 1892)

The life of Gundulf bishop of Rochester, ed. R. Thomson, Toronto 1977

The life of King Edward who rests at Westminster, ed. Frank Barlow, 2nd edn, Oxford 1992

Matthew Paris, *Chronica majora*, ed. H. Richards Luard (Rolls series lvii, 1872–82)

Memorials of St Dunstan, ed. William Stubbs (Rolls series lxiii, 1874)

The memorials of St Edmund's abbey, ed. T. Arnold (Rolls series lxxxxvi, 1890–6)

The monastic constitutions of Lanfranc, ed. D. Knowles, London 1951

Monasticon Anglicanum, ed. W. Dugdale, R. Dodsworth, B. Bandinel, J. Caley and H. Ellis, London 1817–30

Monasticon diocesis Exoniensis, ed. G. Oliver, Exeter–London 1846

Patrilogia latina, ed. J.-P. Migne, Paris 1844–64

The pipe roll of 31 Henry I, ed. J. Hunter, London 1929

Recueil des historiens des Gaules et de la France, ed. M. Martin and others, Paris 1738–1904

The red book of the exchequer, ed. H. Hall (Rolls series lxxxxix, London 1896)

Regesta regum Anglo-Normannorum, 1066–1154, ed. H. W. C. Davis and others, Oxford 1913–69

Regesta regum Anglo-Normannorum: the acta of William I, 1066–1087, ed. D. Bates, Oxford forthcoming

Regesta regum Scottorum, I: The acts of Malcolm IV king of Scots 1153–1165, ed. G. W. S. Barrow, Edinburgh 1960

The register of St Augustine's, Canterbury, ed. G. J. Turner and H. E. Salter, London 1915–24

Registrum Malmesburiense, ed. J. S. Brewer (Rolls series lxxii, 1879)

Regularis concordia, ed. T. Symons, London 1953

Rerum Anglicarum scriptores post Bedam, ed. Henry Savile, London 1596

Rerum Anglicarum scriptores veterum, ed. W. Fulman, i, Oxford 1684

Sancti Anselmi Cantuariensis archiepiscopi opera omnia, ed. F. S. Schmitt, Edinburgh 1946–51

Simeon of Durham, *Historia ecclesiae Dunelmensis*, in *Opera omnia*, ed. T. Arnold (Rolls series lxxv, 1882–5)

Stoke by Clare cartulary, ed. C. Harper-Bill and R. Mortimer (Suffolk Charters iv–vi, 1982–4)

Textus Roffensis, ed. T. Hearne, Oxford 1720, facsimile edn, ed. P. H. Sawyer (Early English Manuscripts in Facsimile vii, xi, 1957, 1962)

Thomas of Elmham, *Historia monasterii S. Augustini Cantuariensis*, ed. C. Hardwick (Rolls series viii, 1858)

Three lives of English saints, ed. W. Winterbottom, Toronto 1972

The treatise on the laws and customs of the realm of England commonly known as Glanville, ed. D. G. Hall, Edinburgh 1965

Two cartularies of the Augustinian priory of Bruton and the Cluniac priory of Montacute, ed. F. W. Weaver and C. H. Maxwell Lyte (Somerset Records Society viii, 1894)

Two chartularies of the priory of St Peter at Bath, ed. W. Hunt (Somerset Record Society vii, 1893)

Two of the Saxon chronicles parallel, ed. J. Earle and C. Plummer, Oxford 1892–8, i. 287–92

Vita Deo dilectae virginis Mildrethae, in D. W. Rollason, *The Mildreth legend*, Leicester 1982, 108–43

Vita Wulfstani, ed. R. R. Darlington (Camden Society, 3rd ser. xl, 1928)

Westminster abbey charters 1066–c. 1214, ed. Emma Mason (London Record Society xxv, 1988)

William of Malmesbury, *De gestis pontificum Anglorum libri quinque*, ed. N. E. S. A. Hamilton (Rolls series lxxxx, 1870)

William of Malmesbury, *De gestis regum Anglorum libri quinque*, ed. W. Stubbs (Rolls series lii, 1887–9)

William Thorne's chronicle of Saint Augustine's abbey, Canterbury, ed. A. H. Davis, Oxford 1934

Wulfstan of Worcester, *The life of St Æthelwold*, ed. Michael Lapidge and Michael Winterbottom, Oxford 1991

Secondary sources

Abou-El-Haj, B., 'Bury St Edmunds abbey between 1070 and 1124: a history of property, privilege, and monastic art production', *Art History* vi (1983), 1–29

Abrams, Lesley, 'The Anglo-Saxons and the christianization of Scandinavia', *Anglo-Saxon England* xxv (1995), 213–49

—— *Anglo-Saxon Glastonbury: church and endowment*, Woodbridge 1996

Ayton, A. and V. Davies, 'Ecclesiastical wealth in England in 1086', in W. J. Sheils and D. Wood (eds), *The Church and wealth* (Studies in Church History xxiv, 1987), 47–60

Baker, D., 'Religious motivation: biographical and sociological problems for the Church historian', in D. Baker (ed.), *Religious motivation* (Studies in Church History xv, 1978), 77–85

Baker, L. G. D., 'The desert in the north', *Northern History* v (1970), 1–11

Barkly, H., 'The earlier house of Berkeley', *Transactions of the Bristol and Gloucestershire Archeaological Society* viii (1882–4), 193–223

Barlow, Frank, *The English Church, 1000–1066*, London 1963

—— *Edward the Confessor*, London 1970

—— *The English Church, 1066–1154*, London 1979

—— *William Rufus*, London 1983

Barraclough, G., 'The earldom and county palatine of Chester', *Transactions of the History Society of Lancashire and Cheshire* ciii (1951–2), 23–57

Barrow, G. W. S., *The Anglo-Norman era in Scottish history*, Oxford 1980

Barthélemy, D., 'Kinship', in P. Ariès and G. Duby (eds), *A history of private life*, trans. Arthur Goldhammer, London 1988, ii. 85–153

Bartlett, Robert, *The making of medieval Europe: conquest, colonization and cultural change, 950–1350*, London 1993

Bates, D., 'The character and career of Odo bishop of Bayeux (1049/50–1097)', *Speculum* l (1975), 1–20

——— 'The land pleas of William I's reign: Penenden Heath revisited', *Bulletin of the Institute of Historical Research* li (1978), 1–19

——— *Normandy before 1066*, London 1982

——— 'The origins of the justiciarship', *Anglo-Norman Studies* iv (1982), 1–12, 167–71

——— 'The building of a great church: the abbey of St Peter's Gloucester, and its early Norman benefactors', *Transactions of the Bristol and Gloucestershire Archaeological Society* cii (1984), 129–32

——— 'The earliest Norman writs', *English Historical Review* c (1985), 266–84

——— 'Normandy and England after 1066', *English Historical Review* iv (1989), 851–76

——— *William the Conqueror*, London 1989

——— 'Two Ramsey writs and the Domesday survey', *Historical Research* lxiii (1990), 337–9

——— *Bishop Remigius of Lincoln 1067–1092*, Lincoln 1992

——— and V. Gazeau, 'L'abbaye de Grestain et la famille d'Herluin de Conteville', *Annales de Normandie* xl (1990), 5–30

Beaumont, W., *A history of the castle of Halton and the priory or abbey of Norton*, Warrington 1873

Beech, G., 'Aquitainians and Flemings in the refoundation of Bardney abbey (Lincolnshire) in the later eleventh century', *Haskins Society Journal* i (1989), 73–90

Bernhardt, John W., *Itinerant kingship and royal monasteries in early medieval Germany, c. 936–1076*, Cambridge 1993

Bethell, D. L., 'The foundation of Fountains abbey and the state of St Mary's York in 1132', *Journal of Ecclesiastical History* xvii (1966), 11–27

——— 'English black monks and episcopal elections in the 1120s', *English Historical Review* lxxxiv (1969), 673–98

Biddle, M. (ed.), *Winchester in the early Middle Ages*, Oxford 1976

——— 'Seasonal festivals and residences: Winchester, Westminster and Gloucester in the tenth to the twelfth centuries', *Anglo-Norman Studies* viii (1986), 51–72

Binns, A., *Dedications of monastic houses in England and Wales, 1066–1216*, Woodbridge 1989

Blair, John, 'Surrey endowments of Lewes priory before 1200', *Surrey Archaeological Collections* lxxii (1980), 97–126

——— 'Secular minster churches in Domesday Book', in P. H. Sawyer (ed.), *Domesday Book: a reassessment*, London 1985, 104–42

——— 'Minster churches in the landscape', in D. Hooke (ed.), *Anglo-Saxon settlements*, Oxford 1988, 35–58

———— 'St Frideswide's monastery: problems and possibilities', in John Blair (ed.), *Saint Frideswide's monastery at Oxford: archaeological and architectural studies*, Gloucester 1990, 221–58

———— *Early medieval Surrey*, Stroud 1991

———— *Anglo-Saxon Oxfordshire*, Stroud 1994

———— 'Debate: ecclesiastical organization and pastoral care in Anglo-Saxon England', *Early Medieval Europe* iv (1995), 193–212

———— (ed.), *Minsters and parish churches: the local church in transition, 950–1200*, Oxford 1988

———— and Richard Sharpe (eds), *Pastoral care before the parish*, Leicester 1992

Bloch, M., *Feudal society*, trans. L. A. Manyon, 2nd edn, London 1961

Blows, Matthew, 'A Glastonbury obit-list', in L. Abrams and J. P. Carley (eds), *The archaeology and history of Glastonbury abbey*, Woodbridge 1991, 257–69

Bond, C. J., 'The reconstruction of the medieval landscape: the estates of Abingdon abbey', *Landscape History* i (1979), 59–75

———— 'Church and parish in Norman Worcestershire', in Blair, *Minsters and parish churches*, 119–58

Bouchard, C. B., *Sword, miter and cloister: nobility and the Church in Burgundy, 980–1198*, Ithaca–New York 1987

Boussard, J., *Le gouvernement d'Henri II Plantagenêt*, Paris 1956

Bouvris, J.-M, 'Aux origines du prieuré de Vains', *Revue de l'Avranchin et du pays de Granville* lxiv (1987), 67–81

Bréard, C., *L'abbaye de Notre-Dame de Grestain*, Rouen 1904

Brett, M., *The English Church under Henry I*, Oxford 1975

Bridgeman, C. G. O., 'The Burton abbey twelfth century surveys', *Collections for a History of Staffordshire* (1916), 209–300

Brooke, C. N. L., 'St Peter of Gloucester and St Cadoc of Llancarfan', in N. K. Chadwick (ed.), *Celt and Saxon: studies in the early British border*, Cambridge 1963, 258–332 (repr. in C. N. L. Brooke, *The Church and the Welsh border*, Woodbridge 1986, 50–94)

———— 'Monk and canon: some patterns of religious life in the twelfth century', in W. J. Sheils (ed.), *Monks, hermits and the ascetic tradition* (Studies in Church History xxii, 1985), 109–29

Brooks, N. P. and H. E. Walker, 'The authority and interpretation of the Bayeux Tapestry', *Anglo-Norman Studies* i (1979), 1–34

———— *The early history of the church of Canterbury: Christ Church from 597 to 1066*, Leicester 1984

———— and C. Cubitt (eds), *St Oswald of Worcester: his life and influence*, Leicester 1996

Brown, P. *The cult of saints*, London 1981

Burne, R. V. H., *The monks of Chester: a history of St Werburgh's abbey*, London 1962

Burton, J. E., 'Monasteries and parish churches in eleventh and twelfth century Yorkshire', *Northern History* xxiii (1987), 39–50

—— *Monastic and religious orders in Britain, 1000–1300*, Cambridge 1994

Cam, H., 'The English lands of the abbey of Saint-Riquier', *English Historical Review* xxxi (1916), 443–7

Cambridge, Eric and David Rollason, 'Debate: the pastoral organization of the Anglo-Saxon Church: a review of the "minster hypothesis" ', *Early Medieval Europe* iv (1995), 87–104

Cantor, N. F., 'The crisis of western monasticism, 1050–1130', *American Historical Review* lxvi (1960), 47–67

Carey-Hill, E., 'Kenilworth abbey', *Transactions of the Birmingham Archaeological Society* lii (1977), 184–227

Carpenter, D., 'Debate: bastard feudalism revised: comment 2', *Past and Present* cxxxi (1991), 177–89

Carter, W. F. and R. F. Wilkinson, 'The Fledborough family of Lisures', *Transactions of the Thoroton Society* xliv (1940), 14–34

Chandler, V., 'Politics and piety: influences on charitable donations during the Anglo-Norman period', *Revue Bénédictine* xc (1980), 63–71

—— 'The last of the Montgomerys: Roger the Poitevin and Arnulf', *Historical Research* lxii (1989), 1–14

Cheney, C. R., 'Church-building in the Middle Ages', *Bulletin of the John Rylands Library* xxiv (1951–2), 20–36

Chibnall, M., 'Ecclesiastical patronage and the growth of feudal estates at the time of the Norman Conquest', *Annales de Normandie* viii (1958), 103–18

—— 'The history of the priory of St Neot', *Proceedings of the Cambridge Antiquarian Society* lix (1966), 67–74

—— *The world of Orderic Vitalis*, Oxford 1984

—— *Anglo-Norman England 1066–1166*, Oxford 1986

Clanchy, M. T., *From memory to written record: England, 1066–1307*, 2nd edn, Oxford 1993

Clark, C., 'This ecclesiastical adventurer: Henry of St-Jean d'Angèly', *English Historical Review* lxxxiv (1969), 548–60

—— 'People and language in post-Conquest Canterbury', *Journal of Medieval History* ii (1976), 1–33

—— 'Women's names in post-Conquest England: observations and speculations', *Speculum* liii (1978), 223–51

—— 'Notes on a life of three Thorney saints, Thancred, Torntred and Tora', *Proceedings of the Cambridge Antiquarian Society* lxix (1980), 45–52

—— 'British Library additional MS. 40,000 ff. 1v–12r', *Anglo-Norman Studies* vii (1985), 50–68

—— 'The *liber vitae* of Thorney abbey and its "catchment area" ' *Nomina* ix (1985), 53–72

—— 'A witness to post-Conquest English cultural patterns: the *Liber vitae* of Thorney abbey', in A. M. Simon-Vandenbergen (ed.), *Studies in honour of René Derolez*, Ghent 1987, 73–85

Clarke, Peter A., *The English nobility under Edward the Confessor*, Oxford 1994

Complete peerage (by G. E. Cockayne), rev. edn, ed. V. Gibbs, H. A. Doubleday and G. H. White, London 1910–59

Constable, Giles, *Monastic tithes: from their origins to the twelfth century*, Cambridge 1964

—— 'Review article: the *liber memorialis* of Remiremont', *Speculum* xlvii (1972), 260–77

—— 'The language of preaching in the twelfth century', *Viator* xxv (1994), 131–52

Cooke, K., 'Donors and daughters: Shaftesbury abbey's benefactors, endowments and nuns c. 1086–1130', *Anglo-Norman Studies* xii (1990), 29–45

Coplestone-Crow, B., 'The Baskervilles of Herefordshire, 1086–1300', *Transactions of the Woolhope Naturalists Field Club* xliii (1979), 18–38

Corbett, W. J., 'England 1087–1154', in J. R. Tanner and others (eds), *Cambridge medieval history*, Cambridge 1957, v. 521–53

Coulstock, Patricia H., *The collegiate church of Wimborne minster*, Woodbridge 1993

Cowdrey, H. E. J.,'Unions and confraternities with Cluny', *Journal of Ecclesiastical History* xvi (1965), 152–162

—— 'Bishop Ermenfrid of Sion and the penitential ordinance following the Battle of Hastings', *Journal of Ecclesiastical History* xx (1969), 225–42

—— *The Cluniacs and the Gregorian reform*, Oxford 1970

Cowley, F. G., 'The Church in medieval Glamorgan', *Glamorgan County History* iii (1971), 87–166

—— *The monastic order in south Wales, 1066–1349*, Cardiff 1977

Cownie, Emma, 'The unusual fate of St Peter's abbey, Gloucester: religious patronage in Anglo-Norman England', in D. Bates and A. Curry (eds), *England and Normandy in the Middle Ages*, London 1994, 143–57

—— 'The Normans as patrons of English religious houses, 1066–1135', *Anglo-Norman Studies* xviii (1996), 47–62

—— 'Religious patronage at post-Conquest Bury St Edmunds', *Haskins Society Journal* vii (1997), 1–9

Cox, J. C., *The sanctuaries and sanctuary seekers of medieval England*, London 1911

Craster, H. H. E., 'The parish of Tynemouth', in E. Bateson and others (eds), *History of Northumberland*, Newcastle-upon-Tyne 1893–40

Crouch, David, 'Geoffrey de Clinton and Roger earl of Warwick: new men and magnates in the reign of Henry I', *Bulletin of the Institute of Historical Research* lv (1982), 113–23

—— *The Beaumont twins: the roots and branches of power in the twelfth century*, Cambridge 1986

—— 'The foundation of Leicester abbey and other problems', *Midland History* xii (1987), 1–13

—— 'Strategies of lordship in Angevin England and the career of William

Marshal', in C. Harper-Bill and R. Harvey (eds), *Ideals and practice of medieval knighthood*, ii, Woodbridge 1988, 1–25

—— 'Debate: bastard feudalism revised', *Past and Present* cxxvii (1991), 165–77

—— *The image of aristocracy in Britain, 1000–1300*, London 1992

—— 'Normans and Anglo-Normans: a divided aristocracy?', in Bates and Curry, *England and Normandy*, 51–67

Dalton, P., *Conquest, anarchy and lordship, 1066–1154*, Cambridge 1994.

Darby, H. C., *The medieval Fenland*, Cambridge 1940

Darlington, R. R., 'Æthelwig abbot of Evesham', *English Historical Review* xlviii (1933), 1–22, 177–98

Davies, R. R., 'Henry I and Wales', in H. Mayr-Harting and I. R. Moore (eds), *Studies in medieval history presented to R. H. C. Davis*, London 1985, 132–47

Davis, H. W. C., 'The liberties of Bury St Edmunds', *English Historical Review* xxiv (1909), 417–31

Davis, R. H. C., 'The monks of St Edmund, 1021–1148', *History* xl (1955), 227–39

—— *The Normans and their myth*, London 1976

Dawtry, Anne F., 'The Benedictine revival in the north: the last bulwark of Anglo-Saxon monasticism?', in S. Mews (ed.), *Religion and national identity* (Studies in Church History xviii, 1982), 87–98

—— 'The *modus medendi* and the Benedictine order in Anglo-Norman England', in W. J. Sheils (ed.), *The Church and healing* (Studies in Church History xix, 1982), 25–38

—— 'Monasticism in Cheshire 1092–1300: a tale of mediocrity', in Judith Loades (ed.), *Monastic studies: the continuity of tradition*, Bangor 1990, 64–74

Denton, J. H., *English royal free chapels, 1000–1300*, Manchester 1970

Dickinson, J. C., 'The origins of the cathedral of Carlisle', *Transactions of the Cumberland and Westmorland Antiquarian and Archaeological Society* xlv (1946), 139–43

—— *The origins of the Austin canons and their introduction into England*, London 1950

Dodwell, B., 'The foundation of Norwich cathedral', *Transactions of the Royal Historical Society*, 5th ser. vii (1957), 1–18

Donkin, R. A., 'The growth and distribution of the Cistercian order', *Studia Monastica* ix (1967), 275–86

—— *The Cistercians*, Toronto 1978

Douglas, D. C., 'Some early surveys from the abbey of Abingdon', *English Historical Review* xliv (1929), 618–25

—— 'Odo, Lanfranc, and the Domesday survey', in J. G. Edwards, V. H. Galbraith and E. F. Jacob (eds), *Historical essays in honour of James Tait*, Manchester 1933, 47–57

—— *William the Conqueror: the Norman impact on England*, London 1964

Du Boulay, F. R. H., *The lordship of Canterbury: an essay on medieval society*, London 1966

Duby, G., 'The diffusion of cultural patterns in feudal society', *Past and Present* xxxix (1968), 1–10 (repr. in G. Duby, *The chivalrous society*, trans. C. Postan, London 1977, 171–7)

—— *Rural economy and country life in the medieval west*, trans. C. Postan, London 1968

—— *The early growth of the European economy: warriors and peasants from the seventh to the twelfth century*, trans. H. B. Clarke, Ithaca–New York 1974

—— *The three orders: feudal society imagined*, trans. Arthur Goldhammer, Chicago–London 1980

Eales, Richard, 'Royal power and castles in Norman England', in Harper-Bill and Harvey, *Ideals and practice of medieval knighthood*, iii. 49–78

Edgington, S. B., *The life and miracles of St Ivo*, St Ives 1985

—— 'Pagan Peverel: Anglo-Norman crusader', in P. W. Edbury (ed.), *Crusade and settlement*, Cardiff 1985, 90–3

Elkins, Sharon K., *Holy women of twelfth-century England*, Chapel Hill 1988

English, B., *The Lords of Holderness*, Oxford 1979

Farmer, D. H., 'The progress of the monastic revival', in David Parsons (ed.), *Tenth century studies*, London 1975, 10–19, 209

—— (ed.), *The Oxford dictionary of saints*, 2nd edn, Oxford 1987

Farmer, S., *Communities of Saint Martin: legends and ritual in medieval Tours*, Ithaca–New York 1991

Farrer, William, *Honors and knights' fees*, London–Manchester 1923–5

Fernie, E., 'The effects of the conquest on Norman architectural patronage', *Anglo-Norman Studies* ix (1987), 71–86

—— 'The architectural evidence and the effects of the Norman Conquest of England', in Bates and Curry, *England and Normandy*, 105–16

Finn, R. W., *The Norman Conquest and its effects on the economy: 1066–1086*, London 1971

Finucane, R. C., *Miracles and pilgrims: popular beliefs in medieval England*, London 1977

Fleming, R., *Kings and lords in conquest England*, Cambridge 1991

Foot, Sarah, 'Anglo-Saxon minsters: a review of terminology', in Blair and Sharpe, *Pastoral care before the parish*, 212–25

Franklin, M. J., 'The secular college as a focus for Anglo-Norman piety: St Augustine's, Daventry', in Blair, *Minsters and parish churches*, 97–104

Freeman, E. A., 'The false Ingulf and the miracles of Waltheof', in E. A. Freeman, *The Norman Conquest*, Oxford 1876, iv. 838–40

Galbraith, V. H., 'The East Anglian see and the abbey of Bury St Edmunds', *English Historical Review* xl (1925), 222–8

Garnett, G., 'Coronation and propaganda: some implications of the Norman claim to the throne of England in 1066', *Transactions of the Royal Historical Society* 6th ser. xxxvi (1986), 91–116

—— 'Franci et Angli: the legal distinction between peoples after the Conquest', Anglo-Norman Studies viii (1986), 109–37

Gazeau, Véronique, 'L'aristocration autour du Bec au tournant de l'annee 1077', Anglo-Norman Studies vii (1985), 89–103

—— 'The effects of the Norman Conquest of 1066 on Norman monasticism in the valley of the Risle: continuity or break?', in Bates and Curry, England and Normandy, 131–42

Geary, P., Furta sacra: theft of relics in the central Middle Ages, Princeton 1978

—— 'Sacred commodities: the circulation of medieval relics', in A. Appadriri (ed.), The social life of things, Cambridge 1986, 141–68

—— Phantoms of remembrance: memory and oblivion at the end of the first millennium, Princeton 1994

Gem, R., 'England and the resistance to romanesque architecture', in Harper-Bill, Studies presented to R. Allen Brown, 128–39

—— 'Reconstructions of St Augustine's abbey, Canterbury, in the Anglo-Saxon period', in Nigel Ramsay, Margaret Sparks and Tim Tatton-Brown (eds), St Dunstan, his life, times and cult, Woodbridge 1993, 57–73

—— and L. Keen, 'Late Anglo-Saxon finds from the site of St Edmund's abbey', Proceedings of the Suffolk Institute of Archaeology and History xxxv (1984), 1–27

Gerchow, J., Die gedenküberlieferung der Angelsachsen, Berlin 1988

—— 'Prayers for King Cnut: the liturgical commemoration of a conqueror', in C. Hicks (ed.), England in the eleventh century, Stamford 1992, 220–38

Gibson, M., Lanfranc of Bec, Oxford 1978

Gillingham, J., 'The introduction of knight service into England', Anglo-Norman Studies iv (1982), 53–64, 181–73

—— 'The beginnings of English imperialism', Journal of Historical Sociology v (1992), 392–409

Gilyard-Beer, R., 'The eastern arm of the abbey church at Bury St Edmunds', Proceedings of the Suffolk Institute of Archaeology xxxi (1970), 256–62

Golding, B., 'The coming of the Cluniacs', Anglo-Norman Studies iii (1981), 65–77

—— 'Anglo-Norman knightly burials', in Harper-Bill and Harvey, The ideals and practice of medieval knighthood, i. 35–48

—— 'Wealth and artistic patronage at twelfth-century St Albans', in S. Macready and F. H. Thompson (eds), Art and patronage in the English romanesque, London 1986, 107–17

—— 'Robert of Mortain', Anglo-Norman Studies xiii (1991), 119–44

—— Gilbert of Sempringham and the Gilbertine order: c. 1130–c. 1300, Oxford 1995.

Gransden, A., 'The growth of the Glastonbury traditions and legends in the twelfth century', Journal of Eccesiastical History xxvii (1976), 337–58

—— 'Baldwin abbot of Bury St Edmunds 1065–1097', Anglo-Norman Studies iv (1982), 65–76, 187–95

—— 'The legends and traditions concerning the abbey of Bury St Edmunds', *English Historical Review* c (1985), 1–24

—— 'The question of the consecration of St Edmunds church', in I. Wood and G. A. Loud (eds), *Church and chronicle in the Middle Ages*, London 1991, 59–86

—— 'The alleged incorruption of the body of St Edmund, king and martyr', *Antiquaries Journal* lxxiv (1994), 135–68

Green, J. A. 'Lords of the Norman Vexin', in J. Gillingham and J. C. Holt (eds), *War and government in the Middle Ages*, Woodbridge 1984, 47–63

—— *The government of England under Henry I*, Cambridge 1986

—— 'Henry I and the aristocracy of Normandy', in *La France Anglaise au moyen age: actes de 111e congrès national des sociétés savantes*, Poitiers 1986, 162–73

—— 'Unity and disunity in the Anglo-Norman state', *Historical Research* lxiii (1989), 115–34

—— 'Aristocratic loyalties on the northern frontier of England, c. 1100–1174', in D. Williams (ed.), *England in the twelfth century*, Woodbridge 1990, 83–100

—— *English sheriffs to 1154*, London 1990

Greene, J. P., *Norton priory: the archaeology of a medieval religious house*, Cambridge 1989

Gregory, C. A., *Gifts and commodities*, London 1982

Grierson, P., 'Commerce in the Dark Ages: a critique of the evidence', *Transactions of the Royal Historical Society* 5th ser. ix (1959), 123–40

Gurevich, A. J., *Categories of medieval culture*, trans. G. L. Campbell, London 1985.

—— *Medieval popular culture: problems of belief and perceptions*, trans. J. M. Bak and P. A. Hollingsworth, Cambridge 1988

Hallam, E. M., 'Henry II as a founder of monasteries', *Journal of Medieval History* xxviii (1977), 113–32

—— *Capetian France, 987–1328*, London 1980

—— 'Royal burial and the cult of kingship in France and England 1060–1330', *Journal of Medieval History* viii (1982), 359–80

—— 'Monasteries as "war memorials": Battle abbey and La Victoire', in W. J. Sheils (ed.), *The Church and war* (Studies in Church History xx, 1983), 47–57

Hare, M., *The two Anglo-Saxon minsters of Gloucester* (Deerhurst Lecture), Gloucester 1992

—— 'The chronicle of Gregory of Caerwent: a preliminary account', *Glevensis* xxvii (1993), 42–4

Harper-Bill, C., 'The piety of the Anglo-Norman knightly class', *Anglo-Norman Studies* ii (1980), 63–77

—— and others (eds), *Studies in medieval history presented to R. Allen Brown*, Woodbridge 1989

Hart, C., *The early charters of eastern England*, Leicester 1966

―――― 'Hereward the Wake', *Proceedings of the Cambridge Antiquarian Society* lxv (1974), 28–40

―――― *The Danelaw*, London 1992

Harvey, B., *Westminster abbey and its estates in the Middle Ages*, Oxford 1977

―――― *Living and dying in England 1100–1540: the monastic experience*, Oxford 1993

Harvey, S. P. J., 'Domesday Book and its predecessors', *English Historical Review* lxxxvi (1971), 753–73

―――― 'Domesday England', in J. Thirsk (ed.), *Agrarian history of England and Wales*, Cambridge 1988, ii. 45–138

Heighway, Carolyn and Richard Bryant, 'A reconstruction of the tenth-century church of St Oswald, Gloucester', in L. A. S. Butler and R. K. Morris (eds), *The Anglo-Saxon Church*, London 1986, 188–95

Herbert, J., 'The transformation of hermitages into Augustinian priories in twelfth century England', in Sheils, *Monks, hermits and the ascetic tradition*, 131–45

Heslop, T. A., 'The production of *de luxe* manuscripts and the patronage of King Cnut and Queen Emma', *Anglo-Saxon England* xix (1990), 151–95

Hill, B. D., *English Cistercian monasteries and their patrons in the twelfth century*, London 1968

Hill, David, *An atlas of Anglo-Saxon England*, Oxford 1981

Hillebrandt, Maria, 'Les cartulaires de l'abbaye de Cluny', *Mémoires de la société pour l'histoire du droit et des institutions des anciens pays bourguignons, comtois et romands* l (1993), 7–18

Hinton, D. A., *Archaeology, economy and society: England from the fifth to the fifteenth century*, London 1990

Hockey, S. F., *Quarr abbey and its lands, 1132–1631*, Leicester 1970

―――― 'William fitz Osbern and the endowment of his abbey of Lyre', *Anglo-Norman Studies* iii (1981), 96–105, 213–15

―――― 'The house of Redvers and its monastic foundations', *Anglo-Norman Studies* v (1983), 146–52

Holdsworth, C. J., 'The Cistercians in Devon', in Harper-Bill and others, *Studies presented to R. Allen Brown*, 179–92

―――― *The piper and the tune: medieval patrons and monks*, Reading 1991

Hollister, C. W., 'Henry I and the Anglo-Norman magnates', *Anglo-Norman Studies* ii (1980), 93–107

―――― 'The greater Domesday tenants-in-chiefs', in J. C. Holt (ed.), *Domesday Studies*, Woodbridge 1987, 219–48

Holt, J. C., 'Feudal society and the family in early medieval England, III: patronage and politics', *Transactions of the Royal Historical Society*, 5th ser. xxxiv (1984), 1–25

―――― 'The introduction of knight service into England', *Anglo-Norman Studies* vi (1984), 89–106

Hooke, Della, 'Wolverhampton: the foundation of the minster', in *Medieval art and architecture at Lichfield* (British Architectural Association Conference Transactions xiii, 1993), 11–16

Hudson, J., 'Life-grants and the development of inheritance in Anglo-Norman England', *Anglo-Norman Studies* xii (1990), 67–80

—— 'Milsom's legal structure: interpreting twelfth century law', *Tijschrift Voor Rechtsgeschiedenis: The Legal History Review* lix (1991), 47–66

—— *Land, law and lordship in Anglo-Norman England*, Oxford 1994

Hunt, John, 'Piety, prestige, or politics? The house of Leofric and the foundation and patronage of Coventry priory', in George Demidowicz (ed.), *Coventry's first cathedral*, Stamford 1994, 97–117

Hunt, R. W., 'The library of the abbey of St Albans', in M. B. Parkes and A. G. Watson (eds), *Medieval scribes, manuscripts and libraries*, London 1978, 251–77

Hunter, M., 'The facsimiles in Thomas of Elmham's *History of St Augustine's, Canterbury*', *The Library* 5th ser. xxviii (1973), 215–20

Hurry, J. B., *Reading abbey*, London 1901

Husain, B. M. C., *Cheshire under the Norman earls 1066–1237*, Chester 1973

James, M. R., 'The abbey of St Edmunds at Bury', *Cambridge Antiquarian Society* (Octavo Publications xxviii, 1895)

Jared, L. H., 'English ecclesiastical vacancies during the reigns of William II and Henry I', *Journal of Ecclesiastical History* xxxxii (1991), 362–93

John, Eric, 'The church of Worcester and the tenth-century reformation', *Bulletin of the John Rylands Library* xlvii (1965), 404–29

—— *Reassessing Anglo-Saxon England*, Manchester 1996

Johns, Susan, 'The wives and widows of the earls of Chester, 1100–1252: the charter evidence', *Haskins Society Journal* vii (1997), 117–32

Johnson, P. D., *Prayer, patronage, and power: the abbey of La Trinité, Vendôme 1032–1187*, New York 1981

Keats-Rohan, K. S. B., 'The devolution of the honor of Wallingford 1066–1148', *Oxoniesa* liv (1989), 311–18

—— 'The making of Henry of Oxford: Englishman in a Norman World', *Oxoniesa* liv (1989), 288–309

—— 'William I and the Breton contingent in the non-Norman Conquest 1066–1087', *Anglo-Norman Studies* xiii (1991), 156–72

—— 'The Bretons and Normans of England 1066–1154: the family, the fief and the feudal monarchy', *Nottingham Medieval Studies* xxxvi (1992), 42–78

Kelly, S. E., 'Some forgeries in the archive of St Augustine's Abbey, Canterbury', *Falschungen im Mittelalter*, Monumenta Germaniae Historica Schriften xxxiii (1988), 347–69

Kemp, B. R., 'The churches of Berkeley Hernesse', *Transactions of the Bristol and Gloucestershire Archaeological Society* lxxxvii (1968), 96–110.

—— 'The miracles of the hand of St James', *Berkshire Archaeological Journal* lxv (1970), 1–19

———— 'Monastic possession of parish churches in the twelfth century', *Journal of Ecclesiastical History* xxxi (1980), 133–60

Keynes, Simon, *The diplomas of King Æthelræd 'The Unready' (978–1016): a study in their use as historical evidence*, Cambridge 1980

———— 'A lost cartulary of St Albans', *Anglo-Saxon England* xxii (1993), 253–79

———— 'Cnut's earls', in Alexander R. Rumble (ed.), *The reign of Cnut: king of England, Denmark and Norway*, London 1994, 43–88

King, E., *Peterborough abbey, 1086–1310: a study in the land market*, Cambridge 1973

———— 'John Horace Round and *The calendar of documents preserved in France*', *Anglo-Norman Studies* iv (1982), 93–103

———— 'The foundation of Pipewell abbey', *Haskins Society Journal* ii (1990), 167–78

———— 'Dispute settlement in Anglo-Norman England', *Anglo-Norman Studies* xiv (1992), 115–30

Knowles, D., *The monastic order in England, 943–1216*, 2nd edn, Cambridge 1966

———— and R. N. Hadcock, *Medieval religious houses: England and Wales*, 2nd edn, London 1971

———— C. N. L. Brooke and V. C. M. London, *The heads of religious houses, England and Wales, 940–1216*, Cambridge 1972

Lambrick, G., 'Abingdon abbey administration', *Journal of Ecclesiastical History* xvii (1966), 159–83

Landon, L., 'The Bainard family in Norfolk', *Norfolk Archaeology* xxii (1926), 147–65

Lawrence, C. H., *Medieval monasticism*, 2nd edn, London 1989

Lawson, M. K., 'The collection of danegeld and heregeld in the reigns of Æthelred II and Cnut', *English Historical Review* cix (1984), 721–38

———— *Cnut: the Danes in England in the early eleventh century*, London 1993

Leclerq, J., 'The monastic crisis of the eleventh and twelfth centuries', in N. Hunt (ed.), *Cluniac monasticism in the central Middle Ages*, London 1971, 217–37

Le Goff, J., *Time, work and culture in the Middle Ages*, trans. Arthur Goldhammer, Chicago 1980

———— *The birth of purgatory*, trans. Arthur Goldhammer, Chicago 1986

Lemarignier, J. F., 'Aspects politiques des fondations des collegiales dans le royaume de France au XIme siècle, *Miscellanea del centro di studi medievali* iii (1962), 19–40

Lennard, R. V., 'The demesnes of Glastonbury abbey in the eleventh and twelfth centuries', *Economic History Review* 2nd ser. viii (1956), 106–18

———— *Rural England, 1086–1135: a study of social and agrarian conditions*, Oxford 1959

Le Patourel, J., 'The date of the trial on Penenden Heath', *English Historical Review* lxi (1946), 378–88

────── 'The reports of the trials on Penenden Heath', in R. W. Hunt, W. A. Pantin and R. W. Southern (eds), *Studies in medieval history presented to Frederick Maurice Powicke*, Oxford 1948, 15–26

────── *The Norman empire*, Oxford 1976

Levison, W., 'A report on the Penenden trial', *English Historical Review* xxvii (1912), 717–20

Lévi-Strauss, C., 'St Alban and St Albans', *Antiquity* xv (1941), 337–59

────── *The elementary structures of kinship*, trans. J. H. Bell, J. R. Von Sturmer and R. Needham, London 1969

Lewis, C. P., 'The Norman settlement of Herefordshire under William I', *Anglo-Norman Studies* vii (1985), 195–213

────── 'The king and Eye: a study in Anglo-Norman politics', *English Historical Review* civ (1989), 569–87

────── 'The earldom of Surrey and the date of Domesday Book', *Historical Research* lxiii (1990), 329–36

────── 'The formation of the honor of Chester 1066–1100', in A. T. Thacker (ed.), *The earldom of Chester and its charters*, *Journal of the Chester Archaeological Society* lxxi (1991), 37–68

────── *The Welsh Borders 1042–1087: a regional history of the Norman Conquest*, forthcoming

Leyser, K., 'The German aristocracy from the ninth century to the early twelfth century: a historical and cultural sketch', *Past and Present* xli (1968), 25–53

Little, L. K., *Religious poverty and the profit economy in medieval Europe*, London 1978

Lloyd, J. E., *A history of Wales from the earliest times to the Edwardian conquest*, London 1939

Loud, G. A., 'The *Gens Normannorum* – myth or reality?', *Anglo-Norman Studies* iv (1982), 104–16, 204–9

────── 'The abbey of Cava, its property and benefactors in the Norman era', *Anglo-Norman Studies* ix (1987), 143–78

Loyd, L. C., 'The origin of the family of Aubigny of Cainhoe', *Bedfordshire Record Society* xix (1937), 101–12

────── *The origins of some Anglo-Norman families*, Leeds 1951

Loyn, H. R., 'William's bishops: some further thoughts', *Anglo-Norman Studies* x (1988), 223–35

────── 'Abbots of English monasteries in the period following the Norman Conquest', in Bates and Curry, *England and Normandy*, 95–103

Lynch, J., *Simoniacal entry into religious life from 1100 to 1260: a social, economic and legal study*, Columbus 1976

McGuire, B. P. 'Purgatory, the communion of saints, and medieval change', *Viator* xx (1989), 61–84

McGurk, Patrick and Jane Rosenthal, 'The Anglo-Saxon gospelbooks of Judith, countess of Flanders: their text, make-up and function', *Anglo-Saxon England* xxiv (1995), 251–308

McKitterick, R. (ed.), *The uses of literacy in early medieval Europe*, Cambridge 1990

Martindale, Jane, 'Monasteries and castles: the priories of Saint-Florent de Saumur in England after 1066', in Hicks, *England in the eleventh century*, 135–56

Mason, Emma, 'English tithe income of Norman religious houses', *Bulletin of the Institute of Historical Research* xlviii (1975), 91–4

—— 'The Mauduits and their chamberlainship of the exchequer', *Bulletin of the Institute of Historical Research* xlix (1976), 1–23

—— 'Timeo barones et donas ferentes', in Baker, *Religious motivation*, 61–75

—— 'The king, the chamberlain and Southwick priory', *Bulletin of the Institute of Historical Research* liii (1980), 1–10

—— 'Pro statu et incolumiate regni mei: royal monastic patronage 1066–1154', in Mews, *Religion and national identity*, 99–117

—— 'Change and continuity in eleventh century Mercia: the experience of Wulfstan of Worcester', *Anglo-Norman Studies* viii (1986), 154–76

—— 'The donors of Westminster abbey charters: ca 1066–1240', *Medieval Prosopography* viii (1987), 23–39

—— 'Westminster abbey and the monarchy between the reigns of William I and John (1066–1216)', *Journal of Eccleasiastical History* xxxxi (1990), 199–216

—— ' "The site of king-making and consecration": Westminster abbey and the crown in the eleventh and twelfth centuries', in D. Wood (ed.), *The Church and sovereignty c. 590–1918: essays in honour of Michael Wilks*, Oxford 1991, 57–76

Mason, J. F. A., 'The honour of Richmond in 1086', *English Historical Review* lxxviii (1963), 703–4

Matthew, D. A., *The Norman monasteries and their English possessions*, Oxford 1962

Mauss, M., *The gift: forms and functions of exchange in archaic societies*, trans. I. Cunnison, 2nd edn, London 1954

Mayr-Harting, H., 'The functions of a twelfth-century shrine: the miracles of St Frideswide', in Mayr-Harting and Moore, *Studies presented to R. H. C. Davis*, 193–206

Meehan, B., 'Outsiders, insiders and property in Durham around 1100', in D. Baker (ed.), *Church, society and politics* (Studies in Church History xii, 1975), 45–58

Merrifield, R., *The archaeology of ritual and magic*, London 1987

Meyvaert, P., 'Rainaldus est malus scriptor Francigenus – voicing national antipathy in the Middle Ages', *Speculum* lxvi (1991), 743–63

Miller, E., 'The estates of the abbey of St Albans', *Transactions of the St Albans and Hertfordshire Architectural and Archaeological Society* v (1938), 285–300

—— 'The Ely land pleas in the reign of William I', *English Historical Review* lxii (1947), 438–56

—— *The abbey and bishopric of Ely*, Cambridge 1951

Miller, M. C., 'Donors, their gifts and religious innovation in medieval Verona', *Speculum* lxvi (1991), 27–42
—— *The formation of a medieval church: ecclesiastical change in Verona, 950–1150*, Ithaca–New York, 1993
Moore, J. S., 'The Gloucestershire section of Domesday Book: the geographical problems of the text, part 3', *Transactions of the Bristol and Gloucestershire Archaeological Society* cvii (1989), 123–48
—— 'The Anglo-Norman family: size and structure', *Anglo-Norman Studies* xiv (1991), 153–96
Morgan, M., *The English lands of the abbey of Bec*, London 1946
Morris, Richard, *Churches in the landscape*, London 1989
Morrison, Karl F., 'The Gregorian reform', in Bernard McGinn and John Meyendorff (eds), *Christian spirituality: origins to the twelfth century*, New York 1985
Mortimer, Richard, 'Religious and secular motives for some English monastic foundations', in Baker, *Religious motivation*, 77–85
—— 'The beginnings of the honour of Clare', *Anglo-Norman Studies* iii (1981), 119–41
—— 'Land and service: the tenants of the honour of Clare', *Anglo-Norman Studies* viii (1986), 177–97
—— 'The Baynards of Baynards Castle', in Harper-Bill and others, *Studies presented to R. Allen Brown*, 241–54
Musset, L., 'Actes inédits du onzième siècle: les plus anciennes chartes de prieuré de Saint-Gabriel', *Bulletin de la Société de Antiquiares de Normandie* xi (1952–4), 117–41
—— 'Les origines et le patrimoine de l'abbaye de Saint-Sever', in *La Normandie Bénédictine*, Lille 1967, 357–67
Nelson, L. H., *The Normans in south Wales, 1070–1171*, Austin, Texas 1966
Oakley, A. M., 'The cathedral priory of St Andrews, Rochester', *Archaeologia Cantiana* xci (1976), 47–60
Olson, Lynette, *Early monasteries in Cornwall*, Woodbridge 1988
Ortenberg, Veronica, 'Archbishop Sigeric's journey to Rome in 990', *Anglo-Saxon England* xix (1990), 197–246
Page, F. M., *The estates of Crowland abbey*, Cambridge 1934
Pallister, D. M., 'Review article: the "minster hypothesis" ', *Early Medieval Europe* v (1996), 204–14
Piper, A. J., 'The first generation of Durham monks and the cult of St Cuthbert', in G. Bonner, D. Rollason and C. Stancliffe (eds), *St Cuthbert, his cult and his community to AD 1200*, Woodbridge 1989, 237–46
Platt, C., *Medieval Britain from the air*, London 1984
Poeck, Dietrich, 'Laienbegräbnisse in Cluny', *Frühmittelalterliche Studien* xv (1981), 68–179
Poncelet, Y., 'Les possessions anglaises de l'abbaye de Saint-Wandrille', *Annales de Normandie* xxxvii (1987), 149–91

Pope, Janet M., 'Monks and nobles in the Anglo-Saxon monastic reform', *Anglo-Norman Studies* xvii (1995), 165–80

Postan, M., 'Glastonbury estates in the twelfth century', *Economic History Review* 2nd ser. v (1952–3), 358–67

Postles, D., '*Patronus et Advocatus Noster*: Oseney abbey and the Oilly Family', *Historical Research* lx (1987), 100–2

—— 'The Austin canons in English towns c. 1100–1350', *Historical Research* lxvi (1993), 1–20

Potts, R. U., 'St Mildred's church, Canterbury: further notes on the site', *Archaelogia Cantiana* lvi (1943), 19–22

Poulle, Béatrice, 'Savigny and England', in Bates and Curry, *England and Normandy*, 159–68

Pryce, H., 'Ecclesiastical wealth in early medieval Wales', in N. Edwards and A. Lane (eds), *The early Church in Wales and the west*, Oxford 1992, 22–32

Raban, S., *The estates of Thorney and Crowland: a study in medieval monastic land tenure*, Cambridge 1977

Radford, C. A. R., 'Glastonbury abbey before 1184: interim report on the excavations', in *Medieval art and architecture at Wells and Glastonbury* (British Architectural Association Conference Transactions viii, 1981), 110–34

Raftis, J. A., *The estates of Ramsey abbey: a study in economic growth and organization*, Toronto 1957

Ramsay, N. and M. Sparks, 'The cult of St Dunstan at Christ Church, Canterbury', in Ramsay, Sparks and Tatton-Brown, *St Dunstan*, 311–23

Raraty, David G. J., 'Earl Godwine of Wessex: the origins of his power and his political loyalties', *History* lxxiv (1989), 3–19

Reedy, W. T., 'The first two Bassets of Weldon: *novi barones* of the early and mid-twelfth century', *Northamptonshire Past and Present* iv (1966–72), 241–5, 295–8

Reuter, Timothy, *Germany in the early Middle Ages, c. 800–1056*, London 1991

Ridyard, S. J., '*Condigna veneratio*: post-Conquest attitudes to the saints of the Anglo-Saxons', *Anglo-Norman Studies* ix (1987), 179–206

—— *Royal saints of Anglo-Saxon England: a study of west Saxon and East Anglian cults*, Cambridge 1988

Riley-Smith, J., 'Family tradition and participation in the Second Crusade', in M. Gervers (ed.), *The Second Crusade and the Cistercians*, New York 1992, 101–8

Robinson, D. M., *The geography of Augustinian settlement in medieval England and Wales*, Oxford 1980

Robinson, I. S., 'Gregory VII and the soldiers of Christ', *History* lviii (1973), 169–92

Roderick, A. J., 'Marriage and politics in Wales 1066–1282', *Welsh History Review* iv (1968), 3–20

Roffe, David, 'The *Historia Croylandensis*: a plea for reassessment', *English Historical Review* cx (1995), 93–108

Rollason, D. W., 'Lists of saints' resting-places in Anglo-Saxon England', *Anglo-Saxon England* vii (1978), 61–93

———— *The search for St Wigstan*, Leicester 1981

———— *The Mildreth legend*, Leicester 1982

———— 'The shrines of saints in later Anglo-Saxon England: distribution and significance', in Butler and Morris, *Anglo-Saxon Church*, 32–50

———— *Saints and relics in Anglo-Saxon England*, Oxford 1989

Rose, R. K., 'Cumbrian society and the Anglo-Norman Church', in Mews, *Religion and national identity*, 119–35

Rosenthal, J. T., *The purchase of paradise: gift-giving and the aristocracy, 1207–1485*, London 1972

Rosenwein, B., 'Feudal war and monastic peace: Cluniac liturgy as ritual agression', *Viator* ii (1971), 129–57

———— *Rhinoceros bound: Cluny in the tenth century*, Philadelphia 1982

———— *To be the neighbor of Saint Peter: the social meaning of Cluny's property, 909–1049*, Ithaca–New York 1989

Round, J. H., 'The Burton abbey surveys', *English Historical Review* xiv (1905), 275–89

Rowlands, I. W., 'The making of the March: aspects of the Norman settlement in Dyfed', *Anglo-Norman Studies* iii (1981), 142–57

Ruud, M., 'Monks in the world: the case of Gundulf of Rochester', *Anglo-Norman Studies* xi (1989), 245–60

Sanders, I. J., *English baronies: a study of their origin and descent*, Oxford 1960

Schmid, Karl, *Kloster Hirsau und seine stifter*, Freiberg 1959

———— 'The structure of the nobility in the earlier Middle Ages', in Timothy Reuter (ed.), *The medieval nobility*, Oxford 1979, 37–59 (originally published as 'Über die stuktur des adels im früheren mittelalter', *Jahrbuch für Fränkische landesforschung* xix [1959], 1–23)

———— Euard Hlawitschka and Gerd Tellenbach (eds), *Liber memorialis von Remiremont*, Dublin–Zurich 1970

Scott, F. S., 'Earl Waltheof of Northumbria', *Archaeologia Aeliana* xxx (1952), 149–213

Searle, Eleanor, 'The abbey of the conquerors: defensive enfeoffment and economic development in Anglo-Norman England', *Anglo-Norman Studies* ii (1980), 154–64, 197–81

———— 'Women and the legitimisation of succession at the Norman Conquest', *Anglo-Norman Studies* iii (1981), 159–70, 226–9

———— '*Inter amicos*: the abbey, town and early charters of Battle', *Anglo-Norman Studies* xiii (1991), 1–14

Searle, W. G., *Ingulf and the Historia Croylandensis*, Cambridge 1894

Sharpe, R., 'Goscelin's St Augustine and St Midreth: hagiography and liturgy in context', *Journal of Theological Studies* xxxxi (1990), 502–16

—————— 'The date of St Mildreth's translation from Minster-in-Thanet to Canterbury', *Medieval Studies* liii (1991), 349–54

Sherlock, D. and H. Woods, *St Augustine's abbey: report on excavations*, Maidstone 1988

Smith, J. B., 'The kingdom of Morgannwg and the Norman Conquest of Glamorgan', *Glamorgan County History* iii (1971), 1–44

Smith, R. A. L., 'The place of Gundulf in the Anglo-Norman Church', *English Historical Review* lviii (1943), 257–72

Southern, R. W., 'The English origins of the miracles of the Virgin', *Medieval and Renaissance Studies* iv (1958), 176–216

—————— *Medieval humanism, and other studies*, Oxford 1970

—————— *Western society and the Church in the Middle Ages*, London 1970

Stafford, Pauline, 'The reign of Æthelred II, a study in the limitations on royal policy and action', in David Hill (ed.), *Ethelred the Unready: papers from the millenary conference* (British Archaeological Records lix, 1978), 15–46

—————— *The east midlands in the early Middle Ages*, Leicester 1985

—————— *Unification and conquest: a political and social history of England in the tenth and eleventh centuries*, London 1989

Stenton, F. M., *The early history of the abbey of Abingdon*, Reading 1913

—————— *Documents illustrative of the social and economic history of the Danelaw*, London 1920

—————— 'St Benet of Holme and the Norman Conquest', *English Historical Review* xxxvii (1922), 225–35

—————— *The first century of English feudalism 1066–1166*, Oxford 1932

—————— *Anglo-Saxon England*, 2nd edn, Cambridge 1956

—————— (ed.), *The Bayeux Tapestry: a comprehensive survey*, London 1957

Sumption, J., *Pilgrimage: an image of medieval religion*, London 1975

Tabuteau, E. Z., *Transfers of property in eleventh-century Norman law*, Chapel Hill 1988

Talbot, C. H. and E. A. Hammond (eds), *The medical practitioners in medieval England*, London 1965

Tatton-Brown, T., 'The churches of Canterbury diocese in the eleventh century', in Blair, *Minster and parish churches*, 105–18

Taylor, P., 'The early St Albans endowment and its chroniclers', *Historical Research* lxviii (1995), 112–42

Tellenbach, Gerd, 'Liturgische gedenbücher als historische quellen', *Mélanges Eugène Tisserant* v (Studi e Testi ccxxxv, 1964), 389–99

—————— *The Church in western Europe from the tenth to the early twelfth century*, Cambridge 1993

Thacker, Alan, 'Chester and Gloucester: early ecclesiastical organisation in two Mercian burhs', *Northern History* xviii (1982), 199–211

Thompson, Kathleen, 'Robert of Bellême reconsidered', *Anglo-Norman Studies* xiii (1991), 263–86

Thompson, S., *Women religious*, Oxford 1991

Thomson, R. M., 'Early romanesque book-illustration in England: the dates of the Pierpont Morgan 'vitae sancti Edmundi' and Bury bible', *Viator* ii (1971), 211–25

—— 'The library of Bury St Edmunds abbey in the eleventh and twelfth centuries', *Speculum* xlvii (1972), 617–45

—— 'Two versions of a saint's life from St Edmunds abbey: changing currents in a XIIth century monastic style', *Revue Bénédictine* lxxxiv (1974), 383–408

—— 'Twelfth-century documents from Bury St Edmunds abbey', *English Historical Review* lxxxxii (1977), 806–19

Tsurushima, H., 'The fraternity of Rochester cathedral priory about 1100', *Anglo-Norman Studies* xiv (1992), 312–37

Urry, W., 'The Normans in Canterbury', *Annales de Normandie* viii (1958), 119–38

Van Engen, J., 'The "crisis of cenobitism" reconsidered: Benedictine monasticism in the years 1050–1150', *Speculum* lxi (1986), 269–304

Vaughan, R., *Matthew Paris*, Cambridge 1958

Walker, David, 'Miles of Gloucester, earl of Hereford', *Transactions of the Bristol and Gloucestershire Archaeological Society* lxxvii (1958), 66–84

—— 'The "honours" of the earls of Hereford in the twelfth century', *Transactions of the Bristol and Gloucestershire Archaeological Society* lxxix (1960), 174–211

—— 'Gloucester and Gloucestershire in Domesday Book', *Transactions of the Bristol and Gloucestershire Archaeological Society* xciv (1976), 107–16

—— 'A register of the churches of the monastery of St Peter's, Gloucester', in *An ecclesiastical miscellany* (Publications of the Bristol and Gloucestershire Archaeological Society xi, 1976), 18–19

—— *The Norman conquerors*, Swansea 1977

—— 'The Norman settlement of Wales', *Anglo-Norman Studies* i (1979), 131–43

—— 'Gloucestershire castles', *Transactions of the Bristol and Gloucestershire Archaeological Society* cix (1991), 5–23

Ward, B., *Miracles and the medieval mind*, London 1982

Ward, G., 'The list of Saxon churches in the Domesday monachorum and the White Book of St Augustine's', *Archaeologia Cantiana* xxxxv (1933), 60–89

Ward, J. C., 'The lowry of Tonbridge and the lands of the Clare family in Kent, 1066–1217', *Archaeologia Cantiana* xcvi (1980), 119–31

—— 'Fashions in monastic endowment: the foundations of the Clare family, 1066–1314', *Journal of Ecclesiastical History* xxxii (1981), 427–51

—— 'The place of the honour in twelfth-century society: the honour of Clare, 1066–1217', *Proceedings of the Suffolk Institute of Archaeology and Natural History* xxxv (1983), 191–202

—— 'Royal service and reward: the Clare family and the crown, 1066–1154', *Anglo-Norman Studies* xi (1989), 261–78

Wardrop, J., *Fountains abbey and its benefactors, 1132–1300*, Kalamazoo 1987

White, L. T., *Latin monasticism in Norman Sicily*, Cambridge, Mass. 1938

White, S. D., 'The settlent of disputes by compromise in eleventh century western France, 1050–1150', *Traditio* xliii (1987), 55–103

—— *Custom, kinship and gifts to saints: the laudatio parentum in western France, 1050–1150*, Chapel Hill 1988

Whittingham, A. B., 'Bury St Edmunds abbey', *Archaeological Journal* cviii (1951), 168–89

Wightman, W. E., 'Henry I and the foundation of Nostell priory', *Yorkshire Archaeological Journal* xli (1964), 57–60

—— *The Lacy family in England and Normandy, 1066–1194*, Oxford 1966

Williams, A., '*Princeps Merciorum gentis*: the family, career and connections of Ælfhere, ealdorman of Mercia, 956–83', *Anglo-Saxon England* x (1982), 143–72

—— ' "Cockles amongst the wheat": Danes and English in the western midlands in the first half of the eleventh century', *Midland History* xi (1986), 1–22

—— 'A vice-comital family in pre-Conquest Warwickshire', *Anglo-Norman Studies* xi (1989), 279–95

Williams, D. H., *An atlas of Cistercian lands in Wales*, Cardiff 1990

Wilson, C., 'Abbot Serlo's church at Gloucester 1089–1100: its place in romanesque architecture', in *Medieval art and architecture at Gloucester and Tewkesbury* (British Architectural Association Conference Transactions vii, 1985), 52–83

Wilson, J., 'The foundation of the Austin priories of Nostell and Scone', *Scottish Historical Review* vii (1910), 141–59

Wilson, R. M., 'The French and English in England', *History* xxviii (1943), 37–60

—— *The lost literature of medieval England*, London 1970

Wilson, S. (ed.), *Saints and their cults*, Cambridge 1983

Wollasch, Joachim, 'Eine adlige familie des frühen mittlealters: ihr selbstverständnis und ihre wirklichkeit', *Archiv für Kulturgeschichte* xxxix (1957), 150–88

Wood, S., *English monasteries and their patrons in the thirteenth century*, Oxford 1955

Wormald, P., 'The uses of literacy in Anglo-Saxon England and its neighbours', *Transactions of the Royal Historical Society* 5th ser. xxvii (1977), 95–114

—— 'Charters and law and the settlent of disputes in Anglo-Saxon England', in W. Davies and P. Fouracre (eds), *The settlement of disputes in early medieval Europe*, Cambridge 1986, 149–68

—— 'Domesday lawsuits: a provisional list and preliminary comment', in Hicks, *England in the eleventh century*, 61–102

—— 'Æthelwold and his continental counterparts: contact, comparison, contrast', in B. Yorke (ed.), *Bishop Æthelwold: his career and influence*, Woodbridge 1988, 13–42

Unpublished theses

Abrams, Lesley, 'The pre-Conquest endowment of Glastonbury abbey: the growth of an Anglo-Saxon church', unpubl. Ph.D. diss. Toronto 1992

Allnatt, Richard, 'The history of New Minster, Winchester, and its estates, 900–1200', unpubl. M.Litt. diss. Oxford 1991

Blows, Matthew, 'Studies in the pre-Conquest history of Glastonbury abbey', unpubl. Ph.D. diss. London 1991

Brown, A. F., 'The lands and tenants of the bishopric and cathedral priory of St Andrew, Rochester, 600–1540', unpubl. Ph.D. diss. London 1974

Carley, D. F., 'Norman Conquest of Devon and Cornwall, 1067–1086', unpubl. M.Litt. diss. Oxford 1989

Clarke, H. B., 'The early surveys of Evesham abbey: an investigation into the problem of continuity in Anglo-Norman England', unpubl. Ph.D. diss. Birmingham 1975

Clarke, Marvin, 'The early endowment of Lewes priory: with special reference to its spritual possessions *c.* 1077–*c.* 1200', unpubl. M.Phil. diss. Reading 1995

Hemming, Eric Whiteside, 'Wills and inheritance in late Anglo-Saxon England, 871–1066', unpubl. Ph.D. diss. London 1991

James, D. D., 'A translation and study of the *Chronicon monasterii de Abingdon*', unpubl. Ph.D. diss. Rice 1986

Kelly, S. E., 'The pre-Conquest history and archive of St Augustine's abbey, Canterbury', unpubl. Ph.D. diss. Cambridge 1986

Raban, S., 'The property of Thorney and Crowland abbeys: a study in monastic patronage', unpubl. Ph.D. diss. Cambridge 1971

Soulsby, I. N., 'The fiefs in England of the counts of Mortain: 1066–1106', unpubl. M.A. diss. Cardiff 1974

Stacy, N. E., 'The estates of Glastonbury abbey *c.* 1050–1200', unpubl. D.Phil. diss. Oxford 1971

Taylor, P. J., 'The estates of the bishopric of London from the seventh century to the early sixteenth century', unpubl. Ph.D. diss. London 1976

Thomas, I. G., ' "The cult of saints" relics in medieval England', unpubl. Ph.D. diss. London 1974

Zeinelabdin, Amin Hamid, 'Eynsham abbey, 1005–1538: a study in medieval Benedictine monasticism', unpubl. Ph.D. diss. Newcastle 1983

Index

Grandborough (Bucks.), 82
Grandmesnil, Adeliza de, 214
Grandmesnil, Emma, wife of Robert de, 214
Grandmesnil, Hugh de, 164, 202, 214
Grandmesnil, Robert de, 214
Gravesend (Kent), 107
Great Gaddesdon (Herts.), 81
Great Livermere (Suffolk), 72
Great Malvern priory (Worcs.), cell of Westminster, 24–5
Great and Little Mongeham (Kent), 101
Greensted (Essex), 91
Gregorius Ganet, chaplain of Huntingdon, 159
Gregory, physician of Malmesbury, 144
Grestain abbey (Normandy), 176, 198, 214
Guerche, Geoffrey de la, 173
Guisborough priory (Yorks.), 174
Guiting Power (Glos.), 59
Guitmund, monk of La-Croix-St-Leuffroi, 130
Gundulf, bishop of Rochester (1077–1108), 104, 140–1
Gunnilda, daughter of Harold Godwin, 24
Gunter of Le Mans, abbot of Thorney (1085–1112), 121–2, 125, 128
Guy fitz Tezon, 164
Guzienboded, William, 49
Gytha, wife of Earl Godwin: flees the country, 40; religious patronage, 24

Hackness (Yorks.), 182
Haddenham (Bucks.), 141
Haimo *dapifer*, sheriff of Kent, brother of Robert fitz Haimo, 141
Halfdene, son of Brenting, 22
Halton castle (Ches.), 176
Hamelin, abbot of Gloucester (1148–79), 58
Hampton minster (Staffs.), 18
Hanney, Turold of, 49, 53
Hanney (Berks.), 38, 46, 49
Hanselin, knight of William I de Braose, 180
Harding fitz Ednoth, 136
Harehope (Northumb.), 91
Harold, Earl, son of Godwin; king of England (1066), 56; relationship with Abingdon abbey, 39–40; religious patronage, 24. *See also* Gunnilda
Harold Harefoot, king of England (1035/6–40), 21

Harpole (Northants.), 90
Harthacnut, king of England (1040–2), 21
Hartland minster (Devon), 24
Hartpury (Glos.), 61
Hatfield, Adam fitz William of, 93
Hatfield Peverel (Essex), cell of St Albans, 59, 90
Hatfield Regis priory (Essex), 161
Hauteville, Manche (Normandy), 198
Hawstead (Suffolk), 72
Helewisa, daughter of Walchelin son of Waard, 51
Hemmingford (Hunts.), 115, 137
Hendred (Berks.), 46, 85, 88, 91
Henry I, king of England (1100–35), 47, 50–1, 53, 60–1, 64, 76–7, 89–91, 94–5, 106–7, 113, 125, 131, 138–42, 145, 162, 169, 183, 190–1, 212
Henry of Blois, abbot of Glastonbury (1126–71), 131, 146
Herbert, chamberlain, 46, 137, 142
Herbert fitz Helgot, 178
Herbert fitz Ivo, 102, 106–7
Herbert Losinga, abbot of Ramsey (1087–90/1), 115, 128
Hereford, Gilbert, earl of, 75, 78
Hereford, St Æthelbert's, 18, 28
Hereford, St Guthlac's, 60–1
Hereford, St Peter's, 61, 213
Hereward the Wake, 130
Herluin, abbot of Glastonbury (1100–18), 131, 146
Herman, archdeacon, 72–5
Hermer, knight of Abingdon abbey, 42
Herouville, near Caen (Normandy), 198
Hertford priory (Herts.), cell of St Albans, 84, 159
Hertingfordbury (Herts.), 86
Hervey, benefactor of St Mary's, York, 177
Hesdin, Arnulf de, Domesday lord of Keevil (Wilts.), 54, 57, 64, 87, 136, 141, 143–4, 199
Hesdin, Aveline de, daughter of Arnulf, wife of Alan fitz Flaad and of Robert fitz Walter, 78
Hesdin, Ermelina de, probably a daughter of Arnulf, 64
Hesdin, Matilda de, daughter of Arnulf, wife of Patrick of Chadworth (*Caorches*), 93, 156
Higham (Glos.), 55
Higham (Kent), 106
Hill (Warks.), 42
Hillingdon (Middx.), 146

Hinton-on-the-Green (Glos.), 55

Hoche, Thorkell, 22

honors: officials of, 176; and religious patronage, 72, 76, 78, 91, 169, 172–84, 203, 205, 209

Hormer hundred (Berks.), 39, 49

Horton abbey (Dorset), 21, 129

Houdain, Hugh of, 76

Howick (Lancs.), 146

Hugh, son of William fitz Norman, 64

Hugh de Fleury, abbot of St Augustine's, Canterbury (d. 1126), 106

Hugh fitz Baldric, 173

Hugh fitz Fulbert, 102

Hugh fitz Goscelin, 214

Hugh fitz Norman, 61

Hugh fitz Osbern, 95

Hugh fitz Witgar, 53

Hugh II of Trottiscliffe, abbot of St Augustine's, Canterbury (1124/6–51), 107

Hugh the butler, 50

Hugh the larderer, 142

Hugh the potter, 142

Hugh the steward, 53

Huntingdon, Robert of, 122–3

Huntingdon, honor of, 72

Huntingdon priory (Hunts.), 127, 146, 172, 189

Hurley (Berks.), 87

Hurley priory (Berks.), cell of Westminster, 139

Hurstborne Tarrant (Hants.), 38

Hyde, near Winchester (Hants.). See Winchester, New Minster

Ilsley, Sewallus of, 46, 53

Ingelran, 160

Ingelric, priest, founder of St Martin-le-Grand, London, 25. See also Peverel, Ingelrica

Ingred, wife of Godric dapifer, 137

Ingulf, abbot of Abingdon (1130–59), 47, 51

Ingulf, abbot of Crowland (1085–1108), 116, 118, 120

invasions, Danish, 20–1

Isilia, daughter of Hervey de Bourges and Ievita, 75

Ivo, knight of William Rufus, 103

Ixworth priory (Suffolk), 76

Jervaulx priory (Yorks.), cell of Byland, 203

John, nephew of Waleran, 86, 92

John fitz Richard, father of Eustace and Payn fitz John, 59–60, 64

John of Sées, abbot of Peterborough (1114–25), 125

John of Tours, bishop of Bath (1088–1122), 133

Jordan, nephew of Roger I de Builli, 212

Joscelin 'the knight', benefactor of Abingdon, 51, 53

Judith, Countess, niece of William I, wife of Earl Waltheof, 71–2, 84–5, 88, 118, 127, 156, 212

Judith of Flanders, cousin of Edward the Confessor, wife of Earl Tostig, 25

Kilpec priory (Heref.), cell of Gloucester, 61

Kingsbury (St Albans, Herts.), 84

Kingsholm, Wibert of, 64

Kinnersley (Shrops.), 160

Kinwick (Beds.), 71

Kirkdale minster (Yorks.), see St Gregory's, Kirkdale

Kirkham priory (Yorks.), 173

Knebworth, Humphrey of, also called d'Anneville, 86, 88

knight service quotas, 37, 41, 43, 70, 88, 102, 112, 115, 117, 129

Knights Hospitallars, 168

Knights Templar, 168

Knowlton (Kent), 92, 102, 106

La Charité-sur-Loire abbey (France), 188, 202

la Haye, Robert de, justiciar of Normandy, 190

la Mare, Turstin de, 93

la Mare, William de, 93

la Val, Hubert de, 91

la Val, William de, 93

Lacy, Ermelina, wife of Walter I de, 54, 57, 59, 156, 163, 195

Lacy, Hawise, wife of Ilbert I de, 195, 212

Lacy, Hugh I de, son of Walter I de, 61–2, 64, 158, 191, 195, 212

Lacy, Ilbert I de, Domesday lord of Pontefract (Yorks.), 173, 195, 212

Lacy, Robert de, son of Ilbert I, de 195, 213

Lacy, Sybil de, niece and heiress of Hugh I de Lacy, 61, 195